Lillian Ross and Helen Ross

THE PLAYER

a Profile of an Art

WITH PHOTOGRAPHS BY LILLIAN ROSS

LIMELIGHT EDITIONS
NEW YORK

First Limelight Edition, October 1984

Twenty-one of these pieces originally appeared in *The New Yorker*. All of the photographs in "The Player" were taken by Lillian Ross, with the exception of those of Eileen Heckart and Lee Remick, which were taken by Eli Wallach. Michael Redgrave's photograph by courtesy of Michael Redgrave.

Library of Congress Cataloging in Publication Data

Ross, Lillian, 1927–
  The player: a profile of an art.

  Reprint. Originally published: New York: Simon and Schuster, c1962.
  Includes index.
  1. Actors—Biography—Addresses, essays, lectures.
I. Ross, Helen. II. Title.
PN2205.R58   1984   792'.028'0922   [B]   84–5706
ISBN 0–87910–020–6

CONTENTS

All the pieces in this book, while cast in autobiographical form, are based on interviews. The interviews, which took place between 1958 and 1962, were conducted informally and in the traditional manner; they were not tape-recorded. The authors talked with more than a hundred actors and actresses, and although, for various technical reasons, only fifty-five of them could be directly represented here, the others indirectly contributed a great deal of background, and the authors are grateful to them for their time and help. Among the fifty-five whose stories are told in this book—so assembled, it is hoped, as to make an aesthetic whole, and thus give a balanced and definitive picture of the art of acting—are some of the most eminent and most talented and most devoted people in the theatre, but the authors are very well aware that another fifty-five, equally eminent and talented and devoted, could be gathered together to the same purpose. If time and chance and the mechanics of book production had permitted, they would have been included, but since that was not possible, the authors wish to dedicate their book to all actors and actresses, outside as well as within these pages.

L. R. AND H. R.

KIM STANLEY

Unlike other artists, the actor has only his own body and his own self to work with. To exhibit oneself on the stage is quite a brave and wonderful thing to do.

I was born on February 11, 1925, in Tularosa, New Mexico. My parents were divorced when I was three. My father, J. T. Reid, is part Irish and part Cherokee Indian, and he married my mother, a German-English girl named Ann Miller, when she was sixteen. He's a retired professor of philosophy and education, and he now teaches a fishing class at the University of New Mexico, and writes about fishing and hunting. My mother paints as a hobby, and lives in Greenwich Village. I took my maternal grandmother's maiden name. My family were farm people on both sides. I had three older brothers: Howard, now

9

a psychiatrist in Milwaukee; Justin, a lawyer who recently gave up his practice to write, and who lives in New City, New York; and Kenneth, who was killed in the Second World War. My mother was an interior decorator, and moved us from one part of the Southwest to another. I felt lonely as a child; I dreaded the feeling of coming home to an empty apartment after school. I was a skinny kid. My mother likes to say that I inherited acting talent from my father, because he did some professional singing to work his way through college. Actually, nobody in the family was in acting. My first experience with it came when I was in the third grade, in Albuquerque, where my teacher, Violet C. Moore, took an interest in me. We still correspond occasionally. She took me home with her, gave me cookies and milk, and was very good to me. She is a lovely, warm, kind lady. She got me to act in a school play called "New Mown Hay." It was all about new-mown hay and a young man haying, and I was the ten-year-old ingénue in it. I can clearly remember the experience, doing something up there on the stage, and getting a feeling that was powerful and special, unlike anything else I had ever felt. I went to three high schools—first in San Antonio, then in Albuquerque, and, for my senior year, in Taos, where my father was working for his Ph.D. on a plan for adult education among underprivileged Indians. I spent that whole year with him, and I was one of three non-Mexican pupils in the school. I wrote a lot of poetry in my teens, and fluctuated between a desire to be an artist or a poet and a desire to be popular and be things like the May Queen. Ever since I was fifteen, I have painted and drawn— mostly charcoals and water colors, mostly of people. My husband, Alfred Ryder, an actor and director, is a wonderful sketcher.

I did my first real acting in 1942, when I was a sophomore at the University of New Mexico. I played the part of the young girl in "Thunder Rock." There was something about that character that I really responded to. I played a young, sort of selfish Viennese girl, who was, like all the other characters in the play, dead. At the time, I thought she was terribly poetic, because when you're seventeen it *is* poetic to be dead. I really felt I was not myself but this girl, and that hooked me. It meant escape from my own life then. Later on, of course, I learned that that isn't what the theatre is all about. Although I did really feel something about this girl I played, I wasn't thinking seriously about acting as a career. I had a Hard-Shell Baptist family background, for one thing. I went to a lot of movies in those days, and was a big fan of Bette Davis—which I still am—but I never considered myself pretty enough to be a movie actress. I saw Laurence Olivier and Merle Oberon in "Wuthering Heights" about twenty-five times. I just loved it. I went to see it again recently, and had exactly the same experience I had the first time. My father always thought acting was very silly, and I wanted his approval. To him, acting was not a serious occupation. I think he still regards fishing as more important. My mother was the only one who encouraged me to think about acting. I didn't see a professional play until I was in my teens, when "The Philadelphia Story," with Katharine Hepburn, came to San Antonio. I was overcome. I was transfixed. The impact of Katharine Hepburn's personality was fantastic. It was a comedy, but after the curtain came down I sat there and cried, because I wanted it to go on all night.

I got a B.A. in psychology at the University of Texas in 1945. I had intended at first to go on with my studies in psychology and to study medicine, but I had no enthusiasm for that. Besides, the director of the Pasadena Playhouse had seen me act in college, and offered me a scholarship. So I went to Pasadena, even though everyone in the family except my mother was against it. Pasadena turned out to be like a glorified junior college, and I quit after one year. I felt I was ready to take on life in a less diluted form. My experience in "Thunder Rock" had apparently released something in me, and I seemed to want to develop it. I had a friend working with a stock company in Louisville, Kentucky, who had also quit Pasadena. She wrote me that they needed a walk-on, so I went there and did a season of winter stock, at the Equity minimum of fifty-seven-fifty a week. I played mostly walk-on parts, although I had a couple of lines as a manicurist in "Boy Meets Girl." After four months there, I took a Greyhound bus to New York.

When I arrived in New York, in the spring of 1947, I had twenty-one dollars. It was raining. I got off at the Thirty-fourth Street station, and took the first room I saw—in a rooming house in the West Thirties. I didn't know one single person in the city. I still had a heavy Texas accent, although I had been working to get rid of it. Stanley Walker, who was a cousin of my mother's, had given me a list of names of theatre people to see about a job. I saw them, and they all told me to go back to Texas. But by then I had made up my mind that I was going to be an actress. I had no fear at all. I knew I was Duse. In a short period of time, everything had crystallized.

I stayed in that first rooming house, in a room with a bedbug-ridden bed, for a month and a half; I slept on the floor. Then I got a job in summer stock at Pompton Lakes. I played the ingénue in "Kiss and Tell" and leading roles in other plays, which were presented in the local high-school auditorium. But after playing the lead in "The Pursuit of Happiness" I got fired. It didn't make me feel that I couldn't act, but it came as a terrible blow. In those days, however, I was more sure of myself than I am now. It was the only time in my life that I was able to get myself to make the rounds of offices of producers and casting agents. Making the rounds is like trying to sell yourself, as if you were something on the hoof. I'd never be able to do that again. You couldn't get an agent unless you were known or were fantastically beautiful. I would get paralyzed, once in an office, and would be unable to remember the name of the play I was trying to get a job in. I hated the whole procedure. It was humiliating. They'd ask me what I had done on Broadway, and I couldn't speak. Emotionally, I couldn't take it. My hands would start sweating. I would feel like a cipher. Nothing was worth that. After about six months, I decided to get a job outside the theatre and save enough money to work in the Off Broadway theatre. I answered a newspaper ad for models to work in the dress house of Herbert Sondheim, whose son Stephen later wrote the lyrics for "West Side Story." I was hired as an outdoor-girl-type model—four showings a day for fifty-six dollars a week. It was deadly work. After about a year, I got married to the actor Bruce Hall. We lived in a cold-water flat at Third Avenue and Thirty-sixth Street, and we devoted all our spare time to readings at home with other actors. I read Juliet, Ophelia, and everything. Then I thought I'd save more money if I gave up modelling and got a job as a waitress, and I went to work in the cocktail lounge of the old Sheraton Hotel. In a good week, I'd make about ninety dollars in tips. I wore high-heeled shoes and a transparent skirt, and ads for the lounge would show a picture of me with the heading "I'm at the Sheraton Lounge. Where are you?" Bruce, in the meantime, got a job in Maxwell Anderson's "Joan of Lorraine," playing the part of one of Joan's brothers. I got to meet Ingrid Bergman, who played Joan. It was a very exciting time.

Then I read a want ad for models to tour Southern towns, modelling Balenciaga, Fath, and other designers, at a salary of eighty-five dollars a week, plus expenses. I did that for six months, and got home with two thousand dollars.

Back in New York, I knew I couldn't make the rounds any more, so I started going to the various Off Broadway groups to see if they would give me any little thing to do. I joined the Interplayers at the Provincetown Theatre, and they let me make and serve the lemonade at intermission but didn't let me act. My husband and I decided to separate, and I got an apartment in the Village. All the while, something was working in me, pushing me to be an actress, and it wouldn't let me alone. Michael Vincente Gazzo and Gene Saks were at the Provincetown, and the next year we formed our own company—Off Broadway, Inc.—and rented the Cherry Lane Theatre for our headquarters. Mike taught acting. It was my first brush with the so-called Method. The word "Method" has been so abused that it's lost its meaning. At the Actors' Studio itself, which is generally thought of as the home of the Method, it's referred to now as "the so-called Method." It was a real eye-opener to me. Mike was an exciting teacher. New things began happening to me as I attended the various classes in speech, dance, and acting. In the classroom exercises, I found myself doing things I hadn't known had anything to do with acting. I hadn't known that this was the way to get at those acting things, to use them in your work. There are times during your life when you suddenly have insight, and this was one of those times for me. I began to understand why I didn't like some of the acting I had seen, or why I missed something onstage even when I might like what I was seeing very much. In June, 1949, I appeared at the Cherry Lane in Gertrude Stein's "Yes Is for a Very Young Man," with Anthony Franciosa. We got very good reviews, and the agents began calling.

I was having a wonderful time doing plays that I didn't understand but that were very provocative. All kinds of new things were opening up for me. Like a new play by Robert Hivnor, called "Too Many Thumbs," which featured an ape turned man turned saint, who commits suicide. I played the ape's girl friend. Then I played the lead in "Saint Joan" at the Equity Library Theatre, and I really began to feel how much I had to study. There were so many problems in the play I couldn't solve. I didn't have the technique. In 1950, after making my Broadway début in "Montserrat" in November, 1949, replacing Julie Harris as Felisa, I went to the Actors' Studio for an audition and was accepted. After that, I was in the Broadway production of Lorca's "The House of Bernarda Alba," in which I had a beautiful part—the young daughter, Adela—and played with Katina Paxinou. It was a lovely play. Late in 1952, I was asked to read for "Picnic"—for the lead part of the older sister. I felt I couldn't play it. I had never been the prettiest girl in town. I wouldn't know how to play it. So I asked for the part of the kid sister, Millie Owens. I was told I was ten years too old, but I was determined to play the part. After I got it, I worked on it at the Actors' Studio with the Artistic Director of the Studio, Lee Strasberg. Strasberg is the greatest man in the theatre today—a completely dedicated man. He's an actor and director and an artist in his own right. He made it possible for the whole world to open up for me. I'd feel, That's what I want, that's what I've always felt. It was like coming home. It can't be understood by people who have never been to the Actors' Studio. The Studio is the place where you can learn under the most thoroughly trained eye. Wearing a leather jacket doesn't make you a Method actor, and Method actors do *not* mumble. The Method simply makes you as free as possible. I have a healthy respect for throwing oneself into a part, even with crudenesses, as against the polite, mechanized sort of thing. But I'm also a great admirer of Gielgud and Olivier, who are masters of their art, who know how to use the voice, who are experts at economy of movement.

I had a number of bad habits as an actress when I first met Strasberg. Like many actors, I mistook showing off for acting. He taught me the difference. Showing off mars a lot of good work. You shouldn't be busy showing how cute you are in front of the audience instead of exploring the person you're playing. You shouldn't let the audience control your performance, so that if they giggle, you do something else cute to get another giggle out of them. Being cute is not acting, and it's sad when a good actor falls into the being-cute trap. What I want to do on the stage is to express the playwright's meaning, to have an experience playing my part that expresses that meaning and illuminates it and lets the audience experience it, too. Whatever the actor *calls* it, that is, I think, what every good actor tries to do. It doesn't matter what kind of actor he says he is or whether he says he's Method or non-Method. I don't use the word "Method" if I can help it. The word doesn't matter. Whatever it is, it is there if you want to learn anything from it that might help you as an actor. It's a combination of things that help you do what you want to do in a part. Through his teaching, Strasberg gives you tools that make it possible for you to accomplish what *you* want to do. When you're playing a part and, say, the first scene begins to dry up, he may get you to think of something about the kind of day it is, the way the wind is blowing—just anything to reëxcite your imagination. You may do some little thing differently—without changing it so much, however, that it throws the other actors. Each person Strasberg works with comes out a much broader, fuller, deeper person, because Strasberg is interested not in exploiting talent but in nurturing it and making it grow. He insists that I work on comedy, for instance, which I haven't done on Broadway since "Bus Stop." I'm usually cast in tragic things. By doing comedy I can avoid some of the pitfalls—getting lost, copying myself. Talented people often try to copy themselves. One very famous actor, a leading star in movies who's been very success-ful in recent years, could have become the greatest actor of our time if he hadn't confined himself to making movies. They were superior movies but not enough for his talent to feed on. He acted superbly in the movies, but after a while he started imitating himself. He should have played "Hamlet" on the stage four years ago, instead of re-stricting himself to movies. No matter what you do in a film, it is, after all, bits and pieces for the director, and that's marvellous for the director but it doesn't allow the actor to learn to mold a part. In films, it's the director who is the artist. An actor has much more chance to create on the stage. I'm not an authority on movies. I've been in only one myself, "The Goddess," and it was a very bad one. It fell so short of what the real thing might have been. It more or less ex-ploited itself. And that always makes a potentially good movie much worse than simply a bad movie. I don't mean that actors shouldn't make movies or shouldn't make them in Hollywood, but I do think that Hollywood can't contain a really great talent, because even the best films are not enough to nurture that kind of talent. It's in the very nature of the medium—waiting for lights and technicalities, starting and stopping your part for a take of only a minute or two—that your sustained feeling gets cut off. Good film actors have to be fantastic magicians. A great actor must continue to act on the stage if he wants to keep his talent alive. That isn't to say that any great play is better than any great movie. We need both. All I mean is that when you stay *only* in movies—say, for ten years—your talent feeds on itself. But if you work on a part—even a little part, in a Chekhov play, for example, there is somewhere for you to go because you're the one who is molding your part.

When I first look at a script, my immediate responses and impulses are terribly helpful. I put down a lot of notes that make no sense to anybody but me. I don't study the script for character. I just read it. When I first read "A Far Country," the image of Freud's patient, Elizabeth, my part, came absolutely full-blown to me—a many-faceted, hard jewel that cracks open. Then, when you start to rehearse, with other people, something begins to happen. What it is exactly I don't know, and don't even want to know. I'm all for mystery there. Most of what happens as you develop your part is unconscious, most of it is underwater. Painting isn't the same kind of joy. Or cooking a good dinner, however marvellous that is. Or planting something in the ground and seeing it grow, which I love. No, in acting you get taken over by some force outside yourself. Something happens. And I do get affected in my real life by my parts. When I was playing Millie Owens in "Picnic," I always felt younger than my age. The only time I got really depressed by a part was when I played Blanche in "A Streetcar Named Desire," for eight weeks in Houston. By the end of that time, I was practically a basket case. At rehearsals, I wear the kind of clothes I wear in the part. It gives me a sensory feeling for the part. Wearing tight corsets and high heels while I was rehearsing Léa in "Chéri" actually affected my emotions in the role. And I find my own painting and looking at paintings helpful. Before we opened in "Chéri" in New York, I went to the Phillips Gallery, in Washington, and as I was standing there looking at the Renoir painting "Boating," I actually got feelings from it that I could use in my part—the way those women lean on their hands, the physicalization of it, that lovely roundness that they have. Paintings can be a help if you're working on a part that doesn't belong to your own immediate background. Each age has its own texture. You then have to make it somehow your own. I consider my portrayal of Léa in "Chéri" a failure, but I couldn't have gone on to play Elizabeth in "A Far Country" if it hadn't been for my experience in that part. Until I played Léa, most of my roles had been of the American genre. There had been nothing in my life to give me references to an aristocratic or upper-middle-class European style and milieu. I don't like to hear about actresses' doing extensive research for a part, but the fact is I did spend days and days in the New York Public Library working on the part of Elizabeth. I not only read Freud's writings about Elizabeth, I also looked at late-nineteenth-century Viennese prints that showed the physical constriction of women of the time, and studied the social context of the part. Also, because Elizabeth walks on crutches, I rehearsed on crutches. I was quite pleased when several Viennese members of the audience at "A Far Country" came backstage to congratulate me on what they said was my convincing portrayal of an upper-middle-class Viennese woman of that period.

I have two children, Lisa and Jamie, by my second husband, the director and actor Curt Conway, and a third, Laurie, by my present husband. I find I can't go straight from my kids to a part. I am with them, at our home in Suffern, until five, and I get to the theatre an hour and a half before the play starts. I can sleep on a picket fence, and on matinée days I take a long nap between performances. I get up every morning at seven to have breakfast with the kids, and then, if I'm working, I go back to bed. After a long run, I still find new satisfaction and new experiences in a part, but I begin to count the number of performances left to go, because I'm so anxious to be alone with my children. I try never to stay in a play longer than nine months—the length of time I played in both "Bus Stop" and "Picnic." After nine months, it begins to sound like a tape recorder—at least to me. By the time I reached my eighth month in "A Far Country," it was extremely hard work to keep it fresh and creative, and not sound as though I were calling in from Chicago. I don't see how some people can stay year after year in the same play. I'd go absolutely around the bend. To keep it fresh, I try to begin all over again in each performance, and I try to look at my character with new eyes. It's no fun to act the other way. I feel lousy afterward if it's just blah-blah-blah and I experience nothing. There are enough of those performances accidentally. Very long runs are good for producers but bad for actors. What originally drove me into acting, perhaps, was that I wanted to get away from home, and wanted to get into something my three brothers couldn't compete with me in. It's changed now. I would like to be able to spend more time with my husband and my children. And the pleasure of acting no longer has to do with the business of Just Look at Me. The pleasure now lies in the actual work. It's fascinating to show what the life of another person is like, when you have only yourself to draw on.

CEDRIC HARDWICKE

I do not regard the theatre as a place for literature; it is for the art of acting.

I was born on February 19, 1893, in Lye, Stourbridge, Worcestershire, which is ten miles from Birmingham. I'm the eldest of three children; the others, both girls, are married and lead conventional middle-class lives, one in Ireland and the other, a widow, in Canada. My father was a physician, and wanted me to study medicine. At the age of twelve months, I won first prize—a guinea—in a beauty contest sponsored by a paper called *The Baby*. At four, I was taken to a Wild West Show, and I immediately afterward set about putting on my own version of it, with one of my sisters as a bareback rider on a donkey. I wanted to be an actor from the time I was ten. I never wanted to do anything else. I was fascinated by acting. I'm the only actor I know who never wanted to do anything else. Acting is a wonderful profession, if it is properly pursued. It's far more enjoyable *pretending* to be a doctor than actually being one. I attended day school at Stourbridge, a couple of miles from home. I had a makeup box at home, and after school I'd constantly experiment with various kinds of disguises. I used to lead excursions of my classmates to the Prince of Wales's and the Theatre Royal in Birmingham and to the Alhambra in Stourbridge, the last wooden theatre in England, where I saw such classics as "East Lynne,"

"The Fatal Wedding," and "The Grip of Iron." To get me away from the Alhambra, my father sent me to a small boarding school, Bridgnorth School, in Shropshire. I was a strong student in English, history, and geography, and a shockingly weak one in mathematics. My parents liked the theatre and opera, and took me to see some of the great actors of the time, including Duse, Bernhardt, Coquelin, Ellen Terry, and Lucien Guitry, father of Sacha. I was seven or eight when I saw Coquelin as Cyrano, but I never forgot his impressive performance and his power of suggestion. Coquelin at that time used a long false nose in the first act of the play, a shorter nose in Act Two, and no false nose at all in Act Three, and nobody—including me—ever noticed it. The elder Guitry still seems to me in many ways the most magnificent actor I've ever seen. He was tremendously economical in his use of gesture, and when he raised his hand you would shudder. One barely perceptible gesture, and a thrill would go through the audience. All the great actors then had the same thing that great actors have today—the power to rivet your attention on them. However, many actors of the past were real spellbinders. John Barrymore was the last of them. They couldn't fit into the theatre today. Life was *thundering* away for them, not going off in little pops. If Henry Irving and Edmund Kean were alive today, they would probably be in business as executives or tycoons. The theatre wouldn't be big enough to hold them. Laurence Olivier and John Gielgud are the last of the great romantic actors. But even they are mild compared to the great actors of the past. You hear actors today being described as great actors, but they are not great actors until they are tested in a great part, like Macbeth or Hamlet—a part that challenges greatness, that demands a tremendous range and ability to express the great emotions. The misfortune of the theatre today is that it is denied its masterpieces. Producers don't find commercial success in "Hamlet." The great parts as they were played by the great actors called for a suspension of disbelief. They destroyed one's critical faculties. Of course, it's entirely possible that in the old days acting by candlelight permitted the actor to get away with more than when he acted by gaslight, when the audience could see more of what was going on on the stage. What is known as the ham actor was discouraged by gaslight. Long before my time, there was no way to dim the candles in the house, and the audience sat in a lighted auditorium during the play. These days, the theatre is dark and the light is fully on the actors. The audience does not have to work so hard to see the actors. The microphone has ruined the ears of the audience and made lazy listeners of them. All this has had its effect on acting. When I started acting, it was behind gas footlights. I remember the intense heat they gave off, and I remember how different acting in electric light felt at first. Fortunately, I was young enough to be plastic in the face of the change.

At twelve, I was organizing Shakespearean productions in the kitchen of our home, where I played Antonio in "The Merchant of Venice." At fourteen, I first played Hamlet, with a forty-three-year-old friend of my mother's playing Ophelia. My father regarded my theatrical ambitions with alarm. In England, actors were and still are classed as rogues and vagabonds. Bernard Shaw fought as nobody else did for recognition of the actor as an intelligent member of the community. Henry Irving was the first actor to be knighted—that was in 1895—and since then the actor has had to be given some recognition. Once I had definitely decided to become a professional actor, my father wanted me to have the best available training. So I went to the Academy of Dramatic Art, originally known as Tree's Academy, which had been founded by Herbert Beerbohm Tree. Roland Young and Carlotta Monterey, who later married Eugene O'Neill, were a couple of my classmates. I got very impatient with the Academy. It didn't take me long to learn that you can't really *learn* to act; you've got to get out and do it. Like most successful actors, I was atrocious as a young actor. Most good actors start by being very bad ones. I remember Olivier as a young actor. He was very noisy. He had no trace of subtlety. He shouted every part. Yet I knew instinctively he'd be a great actor. I was unorthodox, and had I been unorthodox in a manner that arrested attention, it might not have been so bad, but I could hardly be compared to any other living thing on earth. I fancied myself as an actor of character parts. All this sort of thing—the determination to be different—is good in a young actor. But what I liked in myself I did badly. One of the first lessons I learned was the tremendous sense of discipline one needs in acting in order to share one's experience with an audience. Today, so many young actors don't want to share anything with the audience, although sometimes I think that the inarticulate actor of today is perhaps the most merciful one. In the beginning, I never felt I had any personality of my own. I was happy only when I transformed myself with putty noses, moles, and all sorts of things I'd stick on. Then, as I began to work, the nonsense was beaten out of me. Development is something you're unaware of. Gradually, you discard the young rubbish, the overacting, the exaggeration—anything that diverts the attention of the audience from the important to the unimportant. Acting is a profession with no rules. But the actor must be creative, or else he's no good. It's an interpretive art, but only when it ceases to be simply interpretive and becomes creative is it any good.

I got on the stage in my first professional role in 1912, in London's West End; it was a walk-on part as a gentleman of the court in "The Monk and the Woman." My first speaking part was in "Find the Woman," doubling as a hotel lift operator and a butler, replacing my friend Roland Young, who was going to America. I had little to do in the play, but I was never bored. I'd stand in the wings, night after night, watching the other players—Arthur Bourchier, Violet Vanbrugh, A. E. Matthews, and James Carew, who had married Ellen Terry. Seventeen years later, I played with Carew again, in Shaw's "The Apple Cart." In 1913, I joined a touring company called the Benson North Company and toured South Africa and Rhodesia, and when I returned to London the next year, I played small parts in Shakespearean productions with the recently launched Old Vic Shakespeare Company, with Sybil Thorndike and William Stack and Estelle Stead. Then I enrolled for officers' training in the Army. I started with the infantry and was switched to the cavalry, and then to the Royal Army Service Corps Horse Transport. I landed in France in January, 1916. I saw front-line action, and about half a dozen times during the next few years I organized concert parties for the troops in France. I was discharged from the Army in the fall of 1921, and while I was spending some time at home, I joined the Birmingham Repertory Theatre, in nearby Birmingham. I returned to the stage to find the theatre changed. The cardboard theatre was gone. The play of ideas had come along to stay. Bernard Shaw, almost singlehanded, destroyed the old romantic theatre with his plays. Shaw taught me the social importance of the theatre. He dealt with the outstanding social and economic problems of the time. From him I learned that there is not much humor in truth but a hell of a lot of truth in humor. I came to know Shaw, and Shaw was a sort of godfather to me. After the war, the theatre was taken over by the playwrights, and away from the actors, and Shaw taught me the importance of the theatre critic, and the effect of the theatre on the times. It was the beginning of a long and marvellous friendship. While I was with the Birmingham Rep, I played many Shaw parts, including Captain Shotover in "Heartbreak House" and the He-Ancient in "Back to Methuselah," which was put on in London. It was my first leading role in London since I had started acting, twelve years earlier. Shaw directed the production—not officially, but he came around about a week before the opening and took over the direction. I not only learned about theatre from Shaw; he gave me significant and extremely helpful advice. One thing he always insisted on was that I not direct myself as an actor, because he believed you couldn't divide your attention. And early in 1950, when I was going to be in a charity performance of his "The Dark Lady of the Sonnets," Shaw wrote to me and said that I must positively not play the Beefeater—that I must play the part of Shakespeare or nothing. He wrote me that Burbage did not play Bernardo or Marcellus in "Hamlet." Anybody could play the Beefeater, he said, just as anybody could produce. He was against my taking on what he called "tuppenny-ha'penny jobs."

The year 1925 was for me the beginning of over a quarter century of playing leading parts in many great and good plays—"Caesar and Cleopatra," "Othello," "The Apple Cart," "The Barretts of Wimpole Street." In 1936, I came to Broadway, where I've appeared in over thirty plays, including "Antigone," "Candida," and "Don Juan in Hell." I've acted in about a hundred movies, some of which were "The Winslow Boy," "Becky Sharp," "On Borrowed Time," "I Remember Mama," "The Moon Is Down," "The Ten Commandments," and "Around the World in Eighty Days." I've been married twice, and I have a son by each marriage; Edward, the elder, is an actor in London, and Michael, the younger, is at Menlo School, in Menlo Park, California. While I was playing a Japanese businessman in the play "A Majority of One," I began writing my autobiography, which I wanted to call "Fifty Years Without Being Found Out." It was published as "A Victorian in Orbit." Lately, I've very much enjoyed acting in "The Gertrude Berg Show," on television. I'd say that the two big influences on me have been Bernard Shaw and Gertrude Berg.

I've reached an age where I feel I don't have to prove I can act. If I haven't proved it by now, I never will. Every actor goes through periods when he has to earn a living in a routine way. Your greatest reward comes when you do exactly what you enjoy most. *My* greatest reward came when I was able to do the role of the Statue in "Don Juan in Hell." There have been—and are—times when I have felt that what I would like most is to be a circus clown, a part in which I could rely entirely on my own sense of invention. I may do it still. Acting in the theatre requires that you sustain a performance, and I find it harder work than acting in movies. In a film, when all is said and done, good cutting can make a good actor out of a donkey. I never go to see myself in the movies—thanks to Bernard Shaw, really. I once said to him that it might be a good idea to go and see yourself, as a way of seeing what you do and learning to correct your faults. You're more likely, he told me, to destroy your virtues. If you watch yourself in the movies, you become terribly self-conscious and begin trying to make yourself like other people, when the one thing you have that counts as an actor is whatever you have that makes you different. You don't ever want to destroy that individuality. Theatre acting gives you a rehearsal period of three weeks. The movies don't allow time. During rehearsals for the stage, you adapt the character to yourself just as much as you adapt yourself to the character. You begin to feel it's right when you feel one little bit of it is right. The rest of it will then fall into place. You have an awareness of what you're doing, but it's instinctive. The best effects are the ones you are not conscious of. Actors began to decay when they began to *understand* what they were saying. All this playing around with psychoanalysis, all this looking deep within yourself, is ruining actors. It's ruining everybody, for that matter. The great Shakespearean actors didn't have the vaguest idea what the hell they were saying. Ellen Terry didn't know what it was all about, but she never made a mistake. I once saw her when she was quite old. She forgot her lines, stepped out of the play and said something to the audience, then stepped back into her part. I've always remembered one piece of advice Herbert Beerbohm Tree gave to an actor who was inclined to underact. He told him, "When an actor in my beautiful theatre carries onto the stage a candle, I tell the electrician to turn on two limelights, two whole battens of lights, and twenty lamps in the footlights, representing in all some six thousand candle power. In my beautiful theatre, one candle is represented by six thousand. Remember that when you act here." The theatre is for big dramatic effects.

Unless the audience gets it immediately, the audience doesn't get it at all. Acting is a physical thing. You're always part of the picture. You suggest physically as well as with your voice. Actually, the low point of acting is when you are using your voice. Ellen Terry, who had a most destructive charm, gave me her best advice when she told me, "My boy, act in your pauses."

The more I see of life, the more I prefer the world of the theatre to the real world. Strangely enough, the world has become more theatrical, while the theatre has become more drab. Good acting is good faking, really. You start to become the person you play only at the moment you start to play. When I wash my makeup off, I wash the part out of myself. For many people, a fake life is more interesting than a real one. The art of acting has always been the art of faking your own life and faking life for other people. You act for the audience. The amateur acts for his own pleasure; the professional acts for the pleasure of other people. Actors today have power. They go into every home by way of television. They give pleasure to millions. When I started out in the theatre, only a few people came to see actors act in the theatre. Today, because actors have power, a great many of them kid themselves into thinking that what they do is important. The attention they get and their publicity are way out of proportion to their real importance. I'm always embarrassed when I'm stopped on the street because I'm an actor. After all, what are we doing? We are the fakers of the world.

We live in an impatient age today. An actor wants to make a lot of money in a short time. When I started out, it took me twelve years to get an important part to play in London. But I was willing to wait. Acting was an obsession with me. It still is. Your only true guide is "I want to be an actor, and I cannot be anything else." If you ask "*Should* I be?" you should keep away from the theatre and not go into it at all.

MELVYN DOUGLAS

At times, I think that acting is no business for a self-respecting man. At other times, I feel that, in this ghastly, mechanical world we inhabit, anyone connected with any of the arts is very fortunate indeed.

I was born on April 5, 1901, in Macon, Georgia. My real name is Melvyn Hesselberg. My father, Edouard Hesselberg, was a musical prodigy, a concert pianist. He was a Russian Jew, from Riga, who came to America on tour as a young man and was persuaded to stay and teach at a college in Colorado, where he met my mother, Lena Shackleford. She was a Southern lady from Kentucky, and she died in 1960, at the age of ninety-three. My father died in 1936. I have one brother, George, two and a half years younger than I am, who lives in California and is in the real-estate business. I have a son, Gregory Hesselberg, born in 1925, by my first marriage, which lasted about a year. He is a painter, is married and has three children, and lives outside New Haven. I've been married to Helen Gahagan Douglas since 1931, and we have two children: Peter, twenty-eight, who is a Public Welfare Administration worker and is married, with two children; and Mary, twenty-three, who has a bent for both painting and acting. I live in New York, in an apartment on Riverside Drive, with one of the loveliest views of the Hudson

River in the whole city. When I was three years old, my father moved us to Nashville, Tennessee, where he got a job as head of the Music Department of Ward-Belmont School, a women's college. One of my horrible memories is of going to a grammar school that was set up in this women's college for the children of faculty members. Then, at the age of seven, I went to school for a year in Wiesbaden, Germany, where my father took the family for my mother's health. I learned to speak perfect children's German. My father tried to get me to study the piano and then the violin, but I resisted anything having to do with music; it was the old story of the musician's trying to force his art down his child's throat—unsuccessfully, to my sorrow in later years. When I was eleven, we moved to Toronto, where my father taught at a conservatory of music, and five years later we moved to Lincoln, Nebraska. My father was in charge of the Music School of the University of Nebraska for two years. I was a wild kid—tall, slender, and blond. At the age of fourteen, in Toronto, I lied about my age and tried to enlist in the Canadian Army, but my father stopped them from taking me. I had no interest in the theatre in those days—no appetite for it. I had seen one touring production of "Peter Pan" and a comedy based on "Buster Brown," a comic strip of the time. In Lincoln, a drama teacher at the university tried to get me to act in a school theatre he was running. I played a Hindu in a play called "The Little Princess," but I had no idea what it was all about or what I was doing. All it meant to me was a lark, a chance to get away from school for a day. In high school, I acted in one play, Barrie's "Quality Street." I played Valentine Brown, the lead. I became hopelessly confused in my lines, but my classmates presented me with a bouquet and I emerged feeling as important as a star athlete. I belonged to a high-school imitation of a college fraternity, a secret society of about twenty boys that was devoted to smoking, drinking beer, and staging violent initiations. Halfway through my junior year, the school authorities found out about us and we were all expelled. After that, I hung around the community stock company in the vague hope that it might lead me to adventure. We put on a play a week, and I had a few walk-ons, at a dollar a performance, in plays like "The Trail of the Lonesome Pine."

When I was seventeen, I ran away to Omaha and enlisted in the United States Army. I spent my service in Fort D. A. Russell, in

Cheyenne, Wyoming, and in Camp Lewis, Washington, as an orderly in a hospital ward and operating room. Just as I was about to work with a sanitary train—a sort of field-hospital unit—the war ended and I was discharged. In the Army, I met a young painter from Chicago, a well-read fellow, who gave me books to read. I read the works of Isaac Newton, Spinoza, and Schopenhauer, and I heard about artists and the arts. A whole new world was opened to me. In the meantime, my family had moved to Chicago, and after my discharge I joined them there. My father was giving piano lessons and working for a music-publishing firm. My parents wanted me to go back to school for a high-school diploma, and they wanted me to go to college. We had a lot of arguments about it. Around that time, I met a man named William Owen, who was well known in the Middle West as an actor, and who was a member of a group of artists, musicians, writers who got together regularly. Mr. Owen talked about the theatre in a way that was new to me. The stage, he said, was a place where you could do something creative. He lived in a rooming house, where he also gave acting lessons, and after a big row with my mother one day I left home and went to live in that rooming house. I studied with Mr. Owen for two years and supported myself by doing odd jobs— reading gas meters, and selling hats at Marshall Field's department store. Before I came into contact with Mr. Owen, being an actor to me was just an excuse for sleeping late. I more or less came of age in Chicago. Mr. Owen was an old duck with enormous enthusiasm and extraordinary idealism about the theatre, which he communicated to me, in terms of art. I'd tried to write poetry, and I had a feeling, no matter how undisciplined, for music, and I was doing a lot of exciting reading, and all this awakened nebulous, shapeless things in me—yearnings toward *some* sort of creative endeavor. It was 1919, and Chicago was a very lively place then. It was the time, in Chicago, of Maxwell Bodenheim and Floyd Dell, of Ben Hecht and Charles MacArthur, and our idols were Carl Sandburg and Clarence Darrow and Eugene Victor Debs. We were all sort of left of center. It was long before the days of commercial airlines, and most of the creative spirits of the Midwest came to Chicago and stayed. It was really a yeasty atmosphere. George Bellows had started teaching at the Chicago Art Institute and given it a shot in the arm, and it became an exciting place. And there were so many other things. Everywhere you went, you could hear good jazz.

I sometimes think I've never known anything since that was quite so heady and exciting. The bohemian gathering place of the day in Chicago was the Dill Pickle Club, on the Near North Side. The club, which was run by a wild-eyed man named Jack Jones, and which had its entrance in an alley, was a focal point for meetings, debates, plays, and weddings. You'd go there to hear about Charles MacArthur's latest newspaper exploits, which were renowned, or to talk about Ben Hecht's regular column in the Chicago *Daily News,* which was called "One Thousand and One Nights." You'd hear from or about Harriet Monroe, the editor of *Poetry,* or Jane Addams, of Hull House, or Alfred Kreymborg, an avant-garde poet who was then living in Chicago. Another of Mr. Owen's students was Ralph Bellamy. Mr. Owen taught me idealism and the importance of imagination in the theatre. He'd organize little dramatic presentations, which we'd do in schools or churches or meeting halls. We'd do "As You Like It," with me playing Orlando, for a flat fee of fifty dollars, split up evenly among the cast. Or I'd go out and do readings of Oscar Wilde's fairy tales, set to music, for five or ten dollars a night.

In 1920, Mr. Owen put together a Shakespearean repertory company, and I went with it on a short tour of Illinois, Iowa, Minnesota, and Wisconsin, playing second parts, like Mercutio in "Romeo and Juliet" and Claudius and the Ghost in "Hamlet." After that, I joined another small Shakespearean company, run by a man named John E. Kellerd, and toured with it throughout a good part of the country west of Chicago, and in Canada, playing such parts as Cassius in "Julius Caesar" and Banquo in "Macbeth." Those were the days before Actors Equity, and you went out on a tour at your own risk, hoping that it would get customers and you'd get paid. Nowadays, of course, a bond is posted, and if the tour is a flop you're brought back. In 1920, on a Kellerd tour, I found myself stranded in Toronto, with about twelve dollars. I couldn't get home, so I set myself up as a teacher of acting until I had enough money for my fare back to Chicago.

By the time I returned to Chicago, I was professional enough to acquire an agent, who got me into my first really commercial job— with the Dorothy LaVerne Players, a stock company in Sioux City, Iowa, where I did six months of stock. Like most of the stock companies in those days, we did all the current New York successes. I played Billy Benson in "East Is West," by Samuel Shipman and

John B. Hymer, which Forrest Winant had played in New York, and an underworld character in Bayard Veiller's "Within the Law." I was paid fifty dollars a week, out of which I had to buy my own wardrobe and pay my living expenses. I played seventy-five different parts in seventy-five weeks. A tour took the company to Evansville, Indiana, then to Madison, Wisconsin, where I met the girl, a student, who became my first wife. I started my own stock company, with which I made some money, and for the first time in my life I found myself with some money in the bank. After my marriage broke up, I took this money and went off to Europe for five months. I intended to go to Berlin and ask Max Reinhardt if I might work with him, but when I'd got as far as Paris I stayed there, because I became so fascinated with the city. Those were the Ernest Hemingway-Ezra Pound days in Paris. I went to the theatre constantly, and saw Molière performed at the Comédie-Française and Shakespeare at the Odéon. I saw Louis Jouvet play Faust, and found him startlingly interesting.

When my money ran out, I came home. I landed in New York with about fifty dollars in my pocket, and tried to get a job here, but nobody knew me. I lived in a residence club and went around to all the agencies. I'd been playing in stock companies for almost three years, and I'd played every kind of part imaginable, including all the big parts that had been played on Broadway by the stars of the day—Holbrook Blinn, Richard Bennett, Otis Skinner, Walker Whiteside, and, in farce, Ernest Truex. I thought I was pretty good. Actually, I hadn't begun to ripen in terms of searching the insides of a part. I had quite extraordinary facility; I spoke distinctly; I moved with assurance; I had developed an at-homeness onstage, which I have to this day, and which I think is terribly important for young actors. But I had not yet reached the point of inquiring deeply into the characters I was playing. It was all pretty superficial. If I had got a part on Broadway then, I would have fallen on my face. I had just agreed to take a job running an elevator in an apartment house on Park Avenue when I heard, via the grapevine, that Jessie Bonstelle, who ran two of the best stock companies of the time—one in Detroit and the other in Buffalo, the latter in a theatre owned and managed by Katharine Cornell's father—was in New York casting for her Detroit company. I barged into the Packard Agency office, where she was supposed to be, and was told she wasn't there. I saw her walk across the inner office, so I vaulted a railing and walked in there and began to talk. They tried to drag me out, but Miss Bonstelle said "Let him talk," and I wound up with a job in the Detroit company, at eighty-five dollars a week. Just before going to Detroit, I returned to Chicago. I played second parts, which was a bitter pill for me to swallow, but instinctively I knew that it was a sound thing for me to do. In my second season with the company, I played leading parts. It was good work. For the first time in my life, I was getting good direction, and I began to have some insight into what I was doing. Up to that point, I'd been learning the lines and putting on the makeup, and that was about all. Now I began to ask myself, "What does this particular man think about? What goes on in his heart to make him behave the way he does?" When I joined Miss Bonstelle, she was adamant about getting me to change my name. She said that Hesselberg was much too cumbersome to go up in lights. Douglas was the name of my maternal grandmother; by taking it, I felt that at least I was keeping a family name.

In 1926, I returned to New York. William A. Brady, who, along with David Belasco, Arthur Hopkins, and Brock Pemberton, was one of the big producers of the time, signed me to a three-year contract, at a salary of a hundred and fifty dollars a week, to do anything he wanted me to do. I tried out in a few farces in Great Neck and Atlantic City, and then I made my Broadway début, on January 12, 1928, in "A Free Soul," by Willard Mack. I played Ace Wilfong, a young San Francisco gangster-gambler—a Great Gatsby character but not nearly so good. It was a modest hit, and I went along with it for its run of a hundred performances. Two or three producers were asking to borrow me by then; I'd made enough of an impression for that. I was lent to A. H. Woods for a tour of "Jealousy," by Eugene Walter, with Fay Bainter, and then to John Tuerk, for a tour of "The Command to Love," by Rudolph Lothar and Fritz Gottwald, which Basil Rathbone had played in New York. The play had a big-shot cast—people like Mary Nash and Violet Kemble Cooper and Henry Stephenson, all top-flight exponents of what in those days was called drawing-room comedy. I'd never played with such accomplished actors before. I began to learn a great deal about poise and style, and I developed into a rather adept comedian—or at least they all told me so. In the summer of 1930, a writing team named Frederick and Fanny Hatton sent me to see David Belasco, because they thought I'd be right for a play he was planning to do called "Tonight or Never." I was ushered into his office, on top of the Belasco Theatre, on Forty-fourth Street. He sat behind his desk, with his white hair and his clerical collar, and as I went in I was picked up, as everybody was who went in there, by a spotlight. He asked me about my background, and what I told him seemed to impress him. When I said that I had one month left to go in my obligation to Brady, he sniffed a sniff of relish, and I could see that his interest was piqued. I wound up engaged for the lead in the play, at five hundred dollars a week—the best salary I'd ever had in my life. By this time, too, I had a New York agent, who did the talking about money for me. I played the part of a man-about-town, the Unknown Gentleman—an impresario who while scouting for talent meets the Prima Donna, played by Helen Gahagan. The play was a success, as almost anything Belasco did was bound to be. And Helen and I fell in love and were married during the run of the play. The wedding was held at her home, in Brooklyn. What days those were! Life hadn't become so mechanized. The theatre was far less commercialized. Conformity still hadn't taken hold.

It had never occurred to me up to this point that I would have anything to do with motion pictures, but now I suddenly got offers. In 1931, I went out to Hollywood under contract to Samuel Goldwyn, at a salary of nine hundred dollars a week. My first movie was the filmed version of "Tonight or Never," with Gloria Swanson playing the lead. She was at the height of her career, and the rumor was that she was going to make four pictures a year, at two hundred and fifty thousand dollars a picture. She'd arrive on the set with a retinue of servants, and at four o'clock she'd stop work. The servants would serve tea from a silver service, and we'd sit around and chat. Then we'd wrap up and go home. With that kind of beginning, I got an erroneous impression of how movies were made. Not many were made like that even in those halcyon days. I found the mechanics fascinating and exciting, and utterly different from anything I had known in the theatre. At first, I was impressed by the tricks—the miniatures used for sets, the staging of crowd scenes. Then I became aware of the difference in the acting. It seemed to me that acting in movies was personality exploitation. Acting was the most important part to me, and I found out after a while that it wasn't very interesting. I didn't think I was very good in movies. I didn't think I was photogenic. I didn't feel I belonged. I thought I was a run-of-the-mill leading man. I didn't like it. I was a body slave to the producers, like a ballplayer. I had neither the time nor the ability to enjoy what I was doing.

My second movie, "As You Desire Me," based on Pirandello's play, was with Greta Garbo. It was the first of three movies I made with her. She was a provocative girl. I found working with her an extraordinary experience. She wasn't a trained actress—and she was aware of that herself—but she had extraordinary intuitions, especially in the realm of erotic experience. I've never seen anything like her sensitive grasp of colors and shadings. Her acting made you feel that here was a woman who knew all there was to know about all aspects of love. I think her "Camille" is one of the greatest things of all time as a fantastic portrait of a woman in love. I was a little awestruck by Garbo at first, but I found her a very easy person to be with. We talked about everything, including her awareness of how she'd never really learned to be an actress. She was much more adept in the love scenes than in any other scenes. This impression was reinforced in my two other pictures with her—"Ninotchka" and "Two-Faced Woman." She produced an extraordinarily comic effect in "Ninotchka," not so much because of any comic sense she may have had as through the genius of the director, Ernst Lubitsch; he knew just how to make use of the stolid Scandinavian in her. But her love scenes left all of us astonished. She was utterly superb. In the scene in "Ninotchka" in which we come back to the hotel after drinking champagne and she behaves like a girl in love, she achieved a quality and a feeling that were literally breathtaking.

Movies give you a kind of buildup and national reputation that aren't always possible in the theatre. Altogether, I made fifty or sixty movies. Occasionally, now, I watch myself in them on television, and my feelings about what I see range from horror to some slight pleasure. I'm interested and amused to see what I did in those movies. By 1942, I was earning thirty-five hundred dollars a week, with a guarantee of at least forty weeks' work a year. I'd make over a hundred and eighty thousand dollars a year. But the money very soon ceased to be an attraction for me. Almost every part I played was a series of ghastly frustrations, especially when I had the kind of director I couldn't hold an intelligible conversation with, and I had a lot of that kind. If you work with an open-minded director, the part can become a voyage of exploration and discovery. Otherwise, it's just a matter of "Does the uniform fit properly?" and "Does he know his lines?" and "Let's shoot it." I rarely carried away the feeling of having lived through the experience of my part; I carried away only the memory of the plot and some of my own lines. Of all the movies I made, I liked just two or three, and that was chiefly because of the directors. The pleasure and satisfaction came from my relationship with the directors, rather than from the parts I played. Under the direction of Ernst Lubitsch, I had great pleasure making "Angel," with Marlene Dietrich and Herbert Marshall, and "That Uncertain Feeling," with Merle Oberon and Burgess Meredith. It was always a joy to work with Lubitsch. To begin with, he was an enormously engaging man, and brilliantly imaginative. Attempted imitations of his work are still going on in Hollywood, but the imitations don't come off. It's like trying to imitate a writer by using some of the same words he uses. Lubitsch loved actors. He loved seeing an actor's wit work. If the actor had anything to offer, Lubitsch had the ability to stimulate his imaginative processes, to help him find nuances of character and amusing ways of doing things. And you felt you could rely on his taste, which is a wonderful thing for an actor to be able to feel. One other man I was grateful to and happy to work with was Richard Boleslawski, who directed me in "Theodora Goes Wild," with Irene Dunne. He was a really creative guy, too—different from Lubitsch, but another one of the kind you always hope to find working in a supposedly creative field. Boleslawski was a person of substance, of taste and imagination, who was completely articulate and was able to make his own quality felt in his movies.

After nine or ten months in Hollywood, under contract to Goldwyn, I got so I hated it. My wife didn't make movies; while I worked in pictures, she worked in the theatre in Los Angeles. I had a seven-year contract, but in 1932 I was able to get out of it, and my wife and I took a trip around the world. We returned from Japan to California, where our son Peter was born. In January, 1934, I went back into the legitimate theatre, playing the lead in "No More Ladies," by A. E. Thomas. My wife went to Hollywood during that season to do "She," the only picture she ever made, and when my play closed, I went out there to spend the summer with her. While I was hanging around, I was put under a joint contract by Columbia Pictures and M-G-M. Columbia asked me to do a film called "She Married Her Boss," with Claudette Colbert. I agreed. They made it a condition that I do three pictures a year for seven years, with options. I did that, never thinking they'd pick my option up. But that first movie turned out to be one of the most successful pictures Columbia ever made, and the studio did pick up the option. So there I was, stuck again, and feeling that I was in the wrong place again—that it was the theatre that was natural to me. Then they began to give me the same kind of part over and over. My comedy role in that one successful movie was a salable commodity; they began exploiting what was supposed to be the comic Melvyn Douglas. Think of what M-G-M did to a fine actor like Frank Morgan. He just happened to do a few trick laughs in a picture, and from then on that was *all* that Frank Morgan did. I earned what became an international reputation for being one of the most debonair and witty farceurs in Hollywood. I was cut off from the world I knew.

In 1941, I went to Washington to work in the Office of Civilian Defense, and in 1942 I enlisted in the Army as a private. I'd been deeply involved with the Fight for Freedom Committee, headed by Wendell Willkie and Herbert Agar, and inasmuch as I'd been saying from the time England declared war that it was our war, I felt I had to take part. After basic training, I wanted to get overseas, which was impossible for an enlisted man of my age. I was offered a commission by the Officer Procurement Division and was sent to the Special Services School, and, finally, to the China-Burma-India theatre of war, where I had the job of organizing entertainment for troops in the area. My wife, meanwhile, had been elected to Congress from California. She served from 1945 to 1949. I was demobilized in November, 1945, and found myself still under contract to M-G-M and Columbia. I hung around New York for a while, and in 1946 I co-produced, with Herman Levin, the New York musical revue "Call Me Mister." Then I reported back to Hollywood, made a picture for M-G-M—"The Sea of Grass," with Spencer Tracy and Katharine Hepburn, directed by Elia Kazan—and made "The Guilt of Janet Ames," with Rosalind Russell, for Columbia. Fortunately, at that point my lawyer found a loophole in my contract and was able to get me out of it. I made a couple of pictures on a free-lance basis, and then, in March, 1949, to my delight and satisfaction, I returned to the Broadway stage, in

"Two Blind Mice," by Samuel Spewack. Being on the stage again was an exhilarating experience—the rehearsal period, developing in a part, playing to a live audience, the whole thing. The play lasted for a hundred and fifty-seven performances, and when it closed on Broadway, I went on a fairly long tour with it. I went right on with the stage, starring in "Glad Tidings," by Edward Mabley, in October, 1951, which I also staged, and which lasted for a hundred performances, and appearing in Edmund Wilson's unusual play "The Little Blue Light," which was produced by Peter Cookson, Hume Cronyn, and Martin Manulis, and the Brattle Theatre Company, at the ANTA Playhouse, in the spring of 1951. In November, 1952, I opened in "Time Out for Ginger," by Ronald Alexander, which had a season on Broadway and played about nine months in Chicago alone.

I did some television work, and then, in 1955, stepped in as Henry Drummond in "Inherit the Wind," by Jerome Lawrence and Robert E. Lee, for three months, in New York, when Paul Muni became ill, and continued playing the role on tour for a year. The years since then have been, except for my very early years, the most productive and most satisfying of my life. I took the leads in three other plays: "The Waltz of the Toreadors," by Jean Anouilh, on tour and then in New York; "The Gang's All Here," also by Lawrence and Lee; and "The Best Man," by Gore Vidal. And I've done acting in television and in movies as a free agent, doing what I wanted to do. In "Inherit the Wind," I toured all over the country. The play was about the Scopes trial. People who remembered Clarence Darrow would come by the dozen to see me after the play. Some people had loved him and others had hated him, but they all wanted to tell me what Darrow had meant to them. I was real to them in the part. I found it exciting to make the ideas in the play come to life. "The Gang's All Here" was based on the life of President Harding, but this time the authors didn't dig deeply enough into the hero's character. It was something of a challenge to take him, this very weak man, and make the audience sympathize with his ignominious defeat.

I don't know how good an actor I am. I have mixed feelings about doing the work. In acting, I draw on my own real experience or imaginative experience, and try to do it vividly and truthfully, so as to convince the audience. I begin by taking the text of the play as a guide. Step by step, I imagine what the character is—his personality, his thinking, his feeling. Sometimes a director can help you find these things. Then I call on the tools of the trade—my body movement, my voice, my physical relationship to the others in the play. I start slowly, in rehearsals, and then gradually speed up. I start loud and then gradually get softer. I never have an exact idea of what I'm going to do until I start rehearsals. Right in the middle of playing a scene, I sometimes think of something new to do, and do it.

An actor can't be a prude or a moralist. If he is, he shuts his eyes to the possibilities of feeling for or with another kind of human being, whatever he may be. In September, 1958, I played Joseph Stalin in a "Playhouse 90" television show, "The Plot to Kill Stalin." I was limited by time, but I did my best to understand what Stalin was and why he functioned as he did. Some young actors tend to use acting as a way of making a public show of their own attitudes toward life. An actor must put himself in the background. You must keep *yourself* out of the play. You must concentrate fully on the character in the play. The actor's self will come through automatically. His job is to portray his character with the greatest sympathy and understanding. No matter how well written the play is, it's the actor who brings it to life. At its best, acting is more creative than most people realize.

INGRID BERGMAN

What you bring to a part is what you have within you. It's your very first intuition about a part that comes out in the end.

I was born on August 29, 1917, in Stockholm, Sweden. I was an only child. My father, Justus Bergman, a painter and photographer who operated a camera shop on the ground floor of our apartment building, on the Strandvägen, the most beautiful street in the city, died when I was twelve. My mother, whose maiden name was Friedel Adler —she was a German, from Hamburg—died when I was two. My father was a handsome man—dark, tall, and heavy, but not fat. He took a lot of photographs of me, but I could never sit still for portraits. After my father died, I lived with his unmarried sister for six months, and then *she* died. Alone again, I went to live with my father's brother, who also lived in Stockholm. He had five children, the youngest of whom was a girl my age. I was a very lonely child. I didn't have many playmates. I grew up mostly with older people. I withdrew from younger people, making up my own stories, my own plays. My father took me to the opera, but I didn't like it. I asked him why they sang, why they didn't talk. My father was a good singer and had me take singing lessons. A year before he died, he took me to see a Swedish play, "Patrasket," by Hjalmar Bergman, which was about poor people. I loved it so much. My relatives had always called me silly for making up my own plays, living in a dream world. Now I saw grown-up people doing it on the stage, and nobody thought it was silly.

I went to the Lyceum School for Girls, in Stockholm, until I was seventeen. I didn't do any acting, but I read dramatic poems at school or in the evening for visitors to my uncle's house. I wanted to attend the state-supported Royal Dramatic Theatre School, but it was difficult to get into. My uncle was against my acting, but he said if I got into the school, it would be all right. I did get in. For my audition, I did three things: Strindberg's "The Dream Play," in which nothing happens but talk about the misery of life and death; a burlesque, from a German play, of a peasant girl teasing a boy; and Rostand's "L'Aiglon." Everybody else was doing "La Dame aux Camélias," and I wanted to be different. I was shy and scared, but I was also a show-off. If I was asked anything, I would blush. (I still blush today.) If I went into a room, I would knock a chair over. But although I was shy, I had a lion roaring inside me that wouldn't sit down and shut up. Everybody in the theatre, I think, is like that. People teased me, asking, "Why do you want to be an actress? You don't even know how to walk into a restaurant." To this day, I hate to make an entrance. It is difficult for me to get up on a dance floor, because I feel that everybody is watching. But if I played somebody else walking into a restaurant or getting up on a dance floor, I could do it. I couldn't be blamed. It wouldn't be *me*. After a year at the Royal Dramatic Theatre School, I was offered a contract with the Svensk Filmindustri. I was so young I had no patience with school. The school head has never forgiven me for leaving. He says I should have stayed and learned more about acting. But I was eighteen and confident. I thought the movies would be a short cut. I don't know much about acting, even today. I have never read anything about acting. Instinct is what I go on. The one year of school was wonderful training, and I'm sure I learned a lot about using the voice, using the body, listening to other people. Way down, whatever you learn stays with you.

I was married for the first time in 1937, to Peter Aron Lindstrom. My daughter Friedel Pia was born on September 20, 1938, and the Swedish version of the film "Intermezzo" was released late that year. I went to the United States the following year to make "Intermezzo" in Hollywood. In my first three movies in the United States—"Intermezzo," "Adam Had Four Sons," and "Rage in Heaven"—I played exactly the same kind of woman placed in three different stories. I started to get terribly worried. I felt I must change. For "Dr. Jekyll and Mr. Hyde" they wanted me to play the same kind of girl again, but I said no, I wanted to play the prostitute. So I did. I was against typecasting; I fought against it. The public already had me set in their minds as a type, but I fought it. I have always been called the great outdoor girl, but it is a big mistake.

It's true I love to live in the country. My home is now in Choisel, thirty miles from Paris, in an old French farmhouse with flowers and vegetable gardens. My son Roberto and my twin daughters Ingrid and Isabella are with me, and we have four dogs, six ducks, and some cats. My husband, Lars Schmidt, produces several plays in France and Scandinavia each year. We are in the heart of Europe, near the most enchanting town in the world. In the summer, we go to our place on Danholmen, an island off the Swedish west coast, where we don't have electricity and there is no telephone and we swim and read and eat only the fish we catch. We love to travel to New York, which is even bigger and noisier than Paris and is a very exciting place to work. I enjoy coming to New York. I find it very stimulating to work here in television. Television acting combines the best of the theatre and the best of movies. It is another new thing to do and to try. In making a movie, you say a line over and over, and by the time you've said it for the take, you don't remember what it is you're saying. Acting in the theatre, you have to shout, so that people up in the balcony can hear you. But when you do a television play, there are four cameras working at once, and you have both the wonderful intimacy of the screen and the live acting of the stage. In television, I know I have to be calm while everybody else is rushing around, and I love it.

When I first saw Roberto Rossellini's "Open City" and "Paisan," I thought they were so marvellous. I hated the monotony of making pictures in Hollywood. I had a very good life, but it had a certain boredom. With Rossellini I started all over again, and it was very good for me. When we made "Stromboli," we had the most difficult locations—never a comfortable dressing room—and we had to work with rank amateurs. Other people may not want that, but it was wonderful for *me*. But I *wanted* to change. When I gave birth to little Rob-

40

erto, the whole world started to throw stones at me. But I knew I had friends when I received a letter from Ernest Hemingway saying he wanted to be the baby's godfather. And when I came to New York to accept the New York Film Critics award for "Anastasia," Hemingway said, "I'll come with you and punch the first one in the nose who says anything bad to you." In Sweden, almost everybody hides inside himself. Everybody is afraid to be himself or herself. I have changed my life so many times. Each time, I started out with a suitcase and my clothes, and that was the way I wanted it. But whatever I do, I couldn't ever stop my career. My enthusiasm today is exactly the same as it was when I started going to dramatic school. I can't imagine what it must be like to get up every morning at the same time, go to a job, work for somebody you hate, doing typing. I remember in California, when I worked for Warner Brothers, driving to the studio early in the morning, coming over the mountains— the way the morning looked, the way the morning felt. And I was so grateful that I had got into work that I loved so much. You don't act for the money. You do it because you love it, because you must.

I never do a part that I don't like. I love working with actors. It is like being with one big group of children. The best actors have presence and personality, a gift that you have to be born with. You know what it is when you see it—an actor comes onstage, and if he has it, you wait for him to come back. Then, you need talent and discipline. To act with performers who have these qualities gives me great happiness. But I also feel that doing certain parts has significance for me. My playing Joan of Arc meant much more to me than just entertaining people. People had to know there were such people as Joan of Arc in the world. I think I have carried Joan of Arc with me all my life. She is like an old friend. I've always known her much better than anyone else. I've always loved the role of Joan, which I've played in a movie, a play, and an opera. I don't believe actors who say they become the part. You are, to some extent, carried away, and the part should become true to you, but *you* are always there. When you play a murderer, you don't go out and murder somebody. Creating a role is like making a painting—it is separate from you. Whenever I read a play or a story, I read leaning toward the part I feel I am going to play. It's the same as when I go into a projection room to see myself in a movie. I watch myself and nothing else. I sometimes don't even know what the rest of the movie is about. I always feel embarrassed when another actor asks me "How did you like me?" because I haven't even *seen* him. Many people say that actors can't grasp the quality of a part when they read a script for the first time. It's true that I may be somewhat off balance, but I feel I can read. I always try to figure out why a person behaves the way she does. I have to make my own foundation, my own little staircase. It's possible that the audience will never get it, but I always have to try my own way. When I played the part of Anastasia, I believed she was the Czar's daughter, so I played it that way. The director told me I played it so sincerely that everybody would believe she was the Czar's daughter. But my own idea was that she *was;* otherwise I couldn't have played it. How could I play it and lie? When I do a part, I always invent characteristics to bear out what I understand the part to be. If it is clear in your head, you can convey it. It's the little things that the audience sees. This we learn from films. I always want an explanation for everything in a part. What does this mean? *Why* open a window? I have to have it terribly clear in my mind. Then I try to behave as though I were another person. But I use my own ways. If you play twenty parts, you are certainly bound to repeat things, but I try within my limits to make each character a different person. There is a kind of acting in the United States, especially in the movies, where the personality remains the same in every part. I like changing as much as possible. The Swedish idea of acting is that you do change; you play another person each time. To me, doing that is natural.

BRANDON DE WILDE

Once, in a television play, the role called upon me to ask a girl to pass me the salt, and I wanted to give my line certain meaningful overtones, so I said to myself, "Salt is the most important thing in the world."

I was born on April 9, 1942, in Brooklyn. I'm an only child. My parents, Frederick and Eugenia Wilson de Wilde, are both former actors. My mother gave up acting when I was born. My father has been in the theatre since 1935, and is now a director and one of the most highly regarded stage managers in New York. I've been acting since I was seven. My father handles my professional affairs. We are free-lance and independent. There is nothing for us in life but the theatre. We love it, in a very realistic way. I spent the first three years of my life in Youngstown, New York, where, during the Second World War, my father was a first lieutenant and then a captain in the Army. After his discharge, we bought a house in Baldwin, Long Island, which we sold recently. We now live in a ten-room apartment in the West Eighties, in New York. As a very small child, I didn't have any special interest in acting. In the first grade at school, I was one of three silent little kittens in a class play. It embarrassed me. I kept trying to creep out of the room. I saw a lot of plays when I was a little kid, and the first show I loved was "Oklahoma!" When I was seven, a friend of ours named Theresa Fay, who was, and still is, casting director for the producer Robert Whitehead came to dinner at our house. She mentioned that they were looking all over New York for a boy to play an important role in a new play, "The Member of the Wedding," by Carson McCullers. I was in the second grade at the time, and was having trouble with my schoolwork, especially reading. When Terry suggested that I read for the role in the play, my father and mother said no; they wanted me to have an average, normal life. But Terry was persuasive. She told them that Harold Clurman was going to direct the play and that Ethel Waters and Julie Harris were cast for leading roles. So we decided to try it. I could read well enough to be able to memorize lines, and after I knew my lines, my father went over them with me. Then I was taken to Mr. Whitehead's office for a reading. He told us almost immediately that I could have the part, and we told him we would have to think it over. After I was cast, we had to drive down to Norfolk, Virginia, for my Aunt June's wedding. My father and mother taught me the lines of the play on the trip down. It was pretty much left up to me whether I wanted to become an actor. On the drive down, my father and mother asked me in many different ways whether I really wanted to do it. I still wasn't sure. On the trip back up, we worked on the lines carefully and seriously. My father would cue me, and I would say the lines, trying to understand them. When we got back to New York, Mr. Whitehead asked me whether I really wanted to do it, and I just said yes.

I was never nervous in "The Member of the Wedding," but I remember that the first time I got onstage, for a rehearsal, it looked like the biggest place in the world. Everyone and everything on it except me seemed big. When we opened in Philadelphia, an orchestra started playing, and I began to cry. I hadn't known there would be an orchestra, and the unexpectedness of it frightened me. But I quieted down before going onstage. The play itself didn't mean anything to me. It was about a twelve-year-old girl whose brother was going to get married, and who wanted to participate in the wedding. My part was that of her seven-year-old cousin, who wanted to be part of it all, too. But I didn't understand the play or the role. All it meant to me was acting— being on a stage with other actors. The excitement of it was what I liked. I loved the whole feeling of being in the theatre. I loved Julie Harris and everybody else in the play. I think we were a terribly close cast. All the others were always so nice to me. They were my friends. We would often have dinner together. We were in Philadelphia during the Christmas holidays—the first time in my life I'd been away from home at Christmas. My father and mother were with me, but it was still different from being home. On Christmas Eve, when I got to my dressing room I found a little tree, all trimmed, and presents from the cast. I had my eighth birthday during the run of the play, and the cast gave me a party. I received a Donaldson Award, for the best male début performance of the 1949–50 season. My father and mother casually mentioned the award to me, but I didn't see it until two or three years later. Even then, it didn't mean anything to me, though now I know it's a fine award. All my awards are hanging on the walls of our den. I was never allowed to read reviews. My parents didn't tell me about all the praise. I think they tried to keep me from getting conceited. My school life changed when I started to act professionally. In the morning, I would go to a private tutor's house a few blocks away from us in Baldwin, and the tutor would give me grammar-school lessons for two hours. In the afternoon, I went to regular classes in the regular school. I hated a lot of what happened at school. I think I became a bit of a wise guy; I know I got beaten up a lot. There was a big football field next to the school, and sometimes while I was walking across it a bunch of kids would come along and say, "Let's get that actor." There are bullies in every school. Lots of the other kids were my friends—and still are. In my last three high-school years, I studied in private tutoring schools for the most part, and today I go to a local tutoring school—Searing Schools—that gives advanced-placement courses. There just hasn't been time for me to go to college.

From the beginning, my father taught me that I had to believe in a character in order to have the audience believe in it. He showed me how I had to feel that I *was* the character. And he told me I must never try to imitate anyone else, even him. I got the idea, in my own way, from the start. I just always knew I was someone else on the stage. My father was stage manager of my first three plays, and made all the main decisions about what plays I did. It was natural for me to follow his advice. After I opened in my first play, I was offered roles in a lot of television dramas. We accepted two plays for "The Philco Television Playhouse," on N.B.C., and I had the experience of playing with all kinds of actors. I was in a play called "No Medals on Pop," with my father. It was about a kid in school who didn't worship his own father but did worship his gym teacher. My father had the part of my father in the play. Formerly, when I had watched my father on television, he had always been my father, not the character he was playing. But this wasn't the same as watching him, because in this one I was an actor with him. Then, at home, he was my father again, helping me with this part, too.

After appearing in "The Member of the Wedding" for about two years, I went out to Hollywood with my mother to make my first movie, "Shane," which was produced and directed by George Stevens, and which starred Alan Ladd, Jean Arthur, and Van Heflin. I was sort of bored by the long-drawn-out movie procedure, but the picture went over in a big way. In "Shane," I played a hero-worshipping boy who idolized a gunfighter. We made part of the movie on location in Jackson Hole, Wyoming. It was fun to be there, riding horses and wearing cowboy clothes. I'd been riding since I was five, but now instead of riding on bridle paths I could ride in the wide open spaces. On weekdays when I wasn't working, my parents, Jean Arthur, some wranglers I knew, and I went horseback riding, and I used to imagine that we were cowboys in the old West. By the time the movie was finished, I was nine. It was not long afterward that I made the movie version of "The Member of the Wedding." After "Shane," I rejoined "The Member of the Wedding" on the road, and then I went into my second Broadway play, "Mrs. McThing," by Mary Chase, with Helen Hayes. It opened in February, 1952, and I was with it for about six months. I never got bored while I was doing it, any more than I did while I was in my first play. I'm never bored onstage. When I first met Helen Hayes, I had no idea that she was a famous actress. I liked being in the play with her, but I never got to know her well. She was a good friend of my parents'. We often went to her house in the country for dinner, and while my parents talked to her I would try to play with her son, James MacArthur. He's about four years older than I am, and I guess he didn't like the idea too well. But sometimes he and I sneaked cigarettes together. By the time that play was finished, I was ten and a half, and in the fourth grade. My third play was "The Emperor's Clothes," which was written by George Tabori and directed by Harold Clurman. It was about the threat of Communism, and although it was a failure, lasting only sixteen performances, I thought it was a beautiful play. But the critics didn't dig it. Lee J. Cobb played my father and Maureen Stapleton my mother. The play had a feeling of mystery and heavy drama. It was the first time that I began to understand what I was doing as an actor. I was about eleven.

When I was eleven and twelve, I did a live-television series, called "Jamie," for a little over a year. It was specially written for me. I played an orphan who was shifted around from one family to another and finally found a home. My father was associate producer, together with David Susskind and Julian Claman. But it was all too much for me. The work was too hard. I had to go to school and learn things like geography and arithmetic, and learning lines for a new show every week was just too much. I began to hate rehearsing at home with my father. I liked rehearsing in the theatre, but when I was home I liked to go outside and play with the kids. I had terrible battles with my father. They would usually wind up with my calling him stupid and his calling me stupid—the way a lot of kids and their fathers yell at each other. We did that until I was about fifteen.

For four years, between the ages of eleven and fifteen, I did a lot of travelling back and forth between coasts for television and movies. One movie was "Good-Bye, My Lady," directed by William A. Wellman, which I made for Warner Brothers. It was really a beautiful movie, about a boy and his uncle—played by Walter Brennan—and a dog they found. The dog was a basenji, from Africa, which doesn't bark. After the movie was made, the studio gave the dog to me, and I named her Lady. I still have her. The movie is a real tear-jerker, but lovely. In some ways, that's the best part I've ever had. I like roles that are quietly emotional. Anybody can rant and rave. One picture I was in that my parents and I didn't like was "Night Passage," with James Stewart and Audie Murphy. It was the biggest cliché picture ever made. It had all the clichés from every other cliché picture in history. The only thing it left out was the Indians. About thirty-five people had a say in it. It was about two brothers, one good and the other bad, and when the Utica Kid, the bad brother, robbed a train, I carried the money in a shoe box. It was a mess. We call it "the money picture," because the only thing that we remember it for is that money in the shoe box.

We say no as often as we say yes to offers that come our way. We turned down twenty-five movie offers before we decided to do "Shane."

We've turned down at least a hundred and fifty movies since I started working. All three of us discuss every script that's sent to us. We each read it separately, then we talk about it—usually at dinner. We tear it apart and each of us gives his opinion. We turn down a script if it sounds too Hollywoody—a shallow, ha-ha, yippee thing. I'm always being offered parts as the good all-American boy. I suppose I have that kind of face. But I like to play parts with a little more depth. I'd prefer to play a kind of nut, with a kind of nastiness and meanness in him, rather than the boy next door who gets into a little trouble and then gets out of that little trouble. When we read the script for the recent movie "All Fall Down," which I made with Warren Beatty, we all came to the conclusion that the best part was the one offered to me—that of the younger brother—because he was not only the most sympathetic character but, in the end, the strongest and best. I got so wound up at one point in the movie—while I was telling my brother what a bum he was, because he'd made the girl who loved him, Eva Marie Saint, pregnant, and he'd disappointed his whole family—that I forgot that I was really just acting. I narrated the whole picture. Angela Lansbury played my mother, and Karl Malden played my father. I worked hard on that part. It's my favorite. I played a sixteen-year-old boy, but I felt bigger and older than I'd ever felt before. It may be because I felt I was really playing somebody apart from myself, for the very first time. I could *play* a sixteen-year-old boy rather than *be* a sixteen-year-old boy. I was older—nineteen— and still I could understand how a sixteen-year-old boy felt. I read the book the movie was based on four times, and felt I understood all the other characters as well as my own. It was the first time my father hadn't helped me with a role. When he saw the picture, he said my performance was great. That meant a lot to me. I was lucky in that movie. We had a good cast and a good director, John Franken- heimer, and we were given two weeks for rehearsal, so that it was almost like being in a play. Everyone came to the first day of re- hearsal knowing his lines and ready to rehearse, with the exception of one actor, who kept the script in his hands up until the last day and annoyed everyone else. It's difficult to act with someone who just sits and reads during rehearsal and is probably thinking he'll save the work until later. A selfish actor can throw a whole performance off. Once in a while, I'm selfish, too, but I try not to be. If the part calls for another actor to communicate with me, and he just sits with the script in front of his face, that's selfishness for its own sake. Some of our greatest actors are selfish actors, but they're not selfish in petty ways. They're not just upstagers. Lesser actors might get in front of other actors, which is strictly an amateurish thing, or they might step on somebody else's laugh or talk at the top of their lungs or make some gesture to take attention away from the actor who happens to be saying his lines. It's even possible to be selfish unknowingly. My father has taught me that many actors play for themselves only and don't listen to the other actors. I just don't ever want to be like that myself. No really great actor is selfish in that sense. Everything I've ever done with my father's guidance has turned out to be good. He can explain meanings in a character that are deeper than I'm capable of finding or understanding by myself. I've learned almost everything I know from my father, and when I understand as much about acting as he does, it will be all I need to know.

One of my favorite actors is Laurence Olivier. He never does anything in a part that's similar to something he's done in a previous part; he makes every role different. I don't think learning to act ever comes to an end. In addition to what I learn from my father, I learn technique by going to plays, listening to other actors, working with my directors, and asking a lot of questions. When I was in Hollywood making the movie of "Blue Denim," in which I played the part of the adolescent boy in love, I thought the way I played it was good but not good enough. I should have done better. I didn't make a good enough transition from being a boy to the realization that I was going to be the father of a baby. By then, I was seventeen. I work very hard when I'm learning a part. I spend three or four hours a night studying the script, alone, in bed. Along with memorizing my lines, I like to make a lot of notes about how I should move or look.

By the time I'm twenty-five, I want to be a director as well as act. My father and my lawyer and I have recently become a corporation, and we may do a television series soon, starring me. My true love is still the theatre, but the movies and television are also fine, as long as I can be acting. I haven't done a lot of things other kids get to do—I've gone to only three or four dances in my life—but I'm not sorry. I'd never want to give up acting.

SOPHIA LOREN

*Acting and living are quite close. You grow as an
actress when you grow as a person. The first essential
for an actress is to seem human.*

I was born on September 20, 1934, in Rome, Italy, as Sophia Scicolone.
I have one sister, Maria, four years younger than I am, and we are
very close. She is smaller than I am, and plumper, and has a good sense
of humor. As a child, she was always getting sick; she had every illness. I was always very healthy. My parents never married. My father
is a construction engineer. Before I was born, my mother won a contest
in Naples as a look-alike for Greta Garbo, and M-G-M asked her to
come to America, but my grandfather would not let her come. She
played the piano very well, but she never performed in public, because
she was afraid of going on the stage. She and my sister and I lived with
my grandparents in a small town, Pozzuoli, a few miles from Naples.
My mother dreamed of my someday becoming an actress, but she was
also afraid for me, because it is difficult for an actress to have a private
life, and the men are always around you. But the tendency of people in
a small town is to see everything small, and my mother, who had come
from Rome, felt confined, so I felt confined. Sometimes my mother tells
me now that she sees herself through me; everything I've done she
wanted to do. When she goes to see one of my pictures, she doesn't see
anything the first time. The second time, she recognizes me. The third
time, she begins to understand the picture.

I wouldn't change a thing I've done in my life. I was a very happy child. Not a thing troubled me. I enjoyed anything and everything. I had fun. I didn't worry. I am shier now than I was as a girl. Every Sunday after church, I went to the movies with my Aunt Dora, my mother's younger sister, who worked as a typist. She is totally, exclusively enthusiastic about my career and my work, without the slightest reserve. When she writes letters to me now, she writes on the envelope, "To the most distinguished and refined actress Sophia Loren." The first movie I saw, at the age of four, was an American film of "The Picture of Dorian Gray," with Hurd Hatfield, Angela Lansbury, and George Sanders. Next, I saw a film with Yvonne de-Carlo, whom I adored. After I saw Tyrone Power in "The Mark of Zorro," I went back to see it over and over again. I would go the first thing in the morning and stay through the last showing at night. There was always something magic to me about movies. I couldn't get over the way it was: on the wall, persons suddenly started to live. For years, I always used to look where the projector was, to see where the people came from. As a child, I was placid and optimistic and good-natured. I attended the Scuole Elementari for five years and the Scuole Magistrali for five years, and would have needed two more years to be a schoolteacher. By the time I was nine, I was quite grown-up. I started to have my own thoughts. I always wanted what I have now. I am quite satisfied. If I had stayed in Pozzuoli, I would have been a teacher or I would have been a housewife, with six children. I am not sorry I left. I wanted a career and also a husband. Money doesn't count very much now, but I have it. I have beautiful homes: a country house on the Bürgenstock, near Lucerne; an apartment in Rome, where my husband, Carlo Ponti, the movie producer, has his office; and a big house at Marino, in the country near Rome, where we are surrounded by olive trees. This house was built in the eighteenth century by a cardinal, and there are beautiful frescoes on the walls.

When I was fourteen, I entered a beauty contest for the selection of the "Queen of the Sea" of Naples and her twelve "Princesses of the Sea." There were three hundred and twenty contestants. I won second place and became one of the Princesses. The audience didn't like the girl who was chosen to be Queen, and when they don't like something in Naples, they get really excited; they threw things at her and shouted insults. After the contest, I went to a restaurant with my mother and ate pizza. I have always had a good appetite. Sometimes now I have days when I am nervous and don't eat at all, but most of the time I have a large breakfast—two eggs and bacon, bread and butter, orange juice, and coffee—and, for lunch, tuna salad with ham and bologna; and then a large Italian dinner. My prize for winning second place in the beauty contest was twenty-five thousand lire, and also some new wallpaper for my room. I still have that wallpaper in my room in my grandfather's house; it's white, with a pattern of big green leaves. I was also awarded two big enlargements of my photograph. I took these and the money and went with my mother to Rome. We had talked for years about doing it and now we did it.

In Rome, we stayed with relatives for the first three months, and went almost immediately to the big movie studio Cinecittà, where they were making "Quo Vadis," because we had heard that they were hiring many extras. A production manager accepted us, and later the director Mervyn LeRoy saw me and asked me if I spoke English. I said yes, of course. I had learned some English in school and also from the G.I.s when the Allies liberated Naples. So Mother and I both worked as extras in a crowd scene. We worked for one night, all night long, and went home at five o'clock in the morning with thirty-two dollars. We were so happy. It was the beginning of a dream coming true. Then my sister became ill in Naples, and Mother had to leave me and go back. I registered with an agency to do modelling and got some jobs posing for photographs for Italian comic-strip magazines. These Italian comics are called "fumetti," or "little smokes," and have novels illustrated by photographs, with the words coming out of the characters' mouths inside balloons. After two months, I entered the Miss Rome Beauty Contest of 1950. I did not win the contest, but I met Carlo Ponti, who was already a successful producer, and who is now my husband. He was a judge in the contest. He asked me to come to the judges' table, and invited me to come and see him in his office. I was very skinny and my hair was very, very short. I went to see him wearing a red dress with white dots that I had borrowed from a friend, because I did not have a good dress of my own. I made a screen test, and Carlo told me I did not photograph well and could never be an actress, so I left. But now I was known. My photographs were appearing in the fumetti. Photographers saw me on the street and stopped me. They are like that in Italy. Producers began to call me up and offer me little parts in movies. So I started.

In 1952, I took the name Loren, because it sounded melodious, and would be easier to remember and easier to pronounce than Scicolone. My first real part, in 1952, was as a swimmer in an Italian movie called "Africa Sotto i Mari," and my first leading role, in 1953, was as Aïda in "Aïda," for which Renata Tebaldi did the singing. After that, Carlo offered me a four-year contract with him, and I signed. We were married in Mexico in September, 1957. From the start, Carlo was different from all the other producers; he knew how to help me in everything. I was very fortunate to find a man like Carlo, who knows how to bring out what I have inside me. He has always made me understand. He never lectures. With him, I feel much more rational. When I first came to Rome, I was really an irrational Neapolitan kid. I was making mistakes in my life and my work, doing everything on instinct and doing everything wrong. I know now how wrong it all was. I learned so much from Carlo about acting and how to act. The only time I feel really tranquil and really complete is when I'm acting. I hide myself behind the character I play. It is very difficult when you are not cultivated and not educated enough to know what you are inside. At the age of eighteen, I did not know what I was inside. I went to a dramatic school for three months in 1952 and learned a little bit about walking and dancing, but after that I learned by myself. Most of all, I learned from Carlo.

I am scared to death of a live audience. When I appeared on "The Ed Sullivan Show" on television, I was terribly afraid. I don't feel prepared spiritually to face the public. But I am always happy when I am acting. Then I can do all the things I am afraid to do or cannot do in my real life. I had always wanted to be a nun, and some years ago I was offered the role of Mother Cabrini, the saint of immigrants in America, but the film was never made. Also, I had always wanted a daughter, and in "Two Women" I played the mother of a young girl and I really felt she was my daughter. I tried to understand how the character I played—the peasant mother—would feel. The movie was made on location in a part of the countryside between Rome and Naples that is called Ciociaria—a name that comes from "cioce," a special kind of peasant shoes. It is very beautiful country, picturesque and full of color. The most luxurious plantations alternate with stony areas. Its people seem harsh and uncommunicative, and they are of fiery character, but they are very frank, sincere, and reliable when you get close to them. I observed the peasant women of the region very carefully and tried to imitate their gestures and mannerisms. I hate to hear actors say things like "When I play a king, I *become* a king," because to me this is really phony talk. You feel what the character you play feels, but not completely. You never lose control. When you kiss on the screen, you don't really kiss.

I am good-natured when I work, and I do not mind working very hard. I do a lot of dubbing for my pictures. For example, I dubbed my own English for "Two Women," which was made in Italian. When you dub, you do not have as much feeling as you had when the movie was originally shot, and it is hard work. After I have been dubbing, I eat and then go to bed right away, because it is so tiring. I never rehearse a part in front of a mirror. It is phony, I think, to do that. I want to get it the way it should be when I am on the set, in front of the camera. Before I start to work on a part, I read the script, but when shooting starts, I like improvisation right on the set. Even when I'm not consciously thinking about a part, I'm really thinking about it all the time. When I get to the set, I sometimes know suddenly what I will do. I didn't rehearse at all for "Two Women." I get frightened when people watch me, but as soon as the camera starts to run, I feel protected, because I feel that everybody has his own work to do and is not looking at me. In public, when I am in a joking mood, I do not mind if people stare at me; I can enjoy it. I know they look because they are interested, and I try to imagine what they are thinking.

Everything about my work is very tiring, but also it is very fascinating. You always learn new things. I learned many things working with Cary Grant in the movie "Houseboat." He has such tremendous concentration. Many actors do not have the courage to stand still. They do not know how to look you in the eye. I often want to tell them— especially the new, young actors—"Please look at me." Cary Grant knows how to concentrate, how to look directly at you, but always with great relaxation. It is very important for an actor or an actress to look around at everything and everyone and never to forget about real life.

HUME CRONYN

*Perfectionism is a terrible burden. It's a drive I wish
I didn't have.*

I was born on July 18, 1911, in London, Ontario, the youngest of five
children—three boys and two girls. My great-grandfather was the first
Bishop of Huron. The house I was born in was the same house my
father was born in. One of my sisters lives there now. We were fairly
prosperous. I was thirteen years younger than the next-youngest child
in our family, and I was alone a lot as a child. My loneliness and the
whole business of pretending led me into acting, which I decided to do
at the age of six or seven. I was sent away to an Ottawa day school,
where I was the only boarder, when I was seven, and then I went to
Bishop Ridley College, a Canadian preparatory school, where I played
football, hockey, and cricket, and boxed. Nevertheless, I was miserable
at school. I was interested in poetry and drawing, and I was physically
the smallest boy in the school, and these things added to my feeling of
loneliness and isolation and homesickness. When I was ten, I put on an
impromptu production of "The Green Goddess." I played George
Arliss's part and loved it. I was my own audience in those days. It was
pure living in a dream world, which was much richer, much gayer, and
much more delightful than the world I really lived in. It pulled me out

of myself, and I didn't care much for myself anyway. My father had a wonderful voice and a wonderful build. If the Almighty had given me his gifts in addition to my own, I might have done more as an actor. My mother was a lovely woman. My father's sister once said about her—and I had it engraved on her tombstone—"Her entrance into a room was as though another candle had been lighted." Both my parents were great theatregoers and travellers. At fifteen, I was taken to London, England, for the first time, and saw plays there, all of which fed the fire in me.

In 1930, at McGill University, where I was studying law, I caught a kidney punch while boxing, and got a chill at the same time, with the result that I developed a cold in my kidneys. My doctor had a friend playing in the National Theatre Stock Company in Washington, and while I was convalescing, the doctor and I drove there. I wasn't going to pass my examinations anyway. The friend introduced me to the director, and I joined the company, at a salary of fifteen dollars a week. I played my first professional role, a newspaper boy in "Up Pops the Devil," at the age of nineteen. Six weeks and three bit parts later, I went home and told my family I wanted to give up law and go into the theatre and become an actor. I felt in my heart that acting would help me realize that wonderful line "Almighty God . . . So may we live . . . to catch the music to which this world is set by Thee." When my family realized that I was determined, they felt I ought to have the benefit of the best possible training, so I came to New York and enrolled in the American Academy of Dramatic Arts, where I stayed for two years—1932 and 1933. You may not learn how to act in a school, but you do learn a number of useful things, including vocal exercises such as "She left the web, she left the loom, she made three paces through the room," and "A wise old owl lived in an oak; the more he saw the less he spoke; the less he spoke the more he heard; why can't we all be like that bird?" When I left the Academy, I wrote to the administrative director, the late Charles Jehlinger, telling him how much the experience of studying there had meant to me. He wrote back and told me, "What you need is increased and never-ending experience in life." He was a great man. In 1934, I made my début on the New York stage, playing a janitor in "Hipper's Holiday." Then I worked in the Barter Theatre, and in 1935 I got a chance to audition for the job of assistant stage manager and understudy in the national

company of "Three Men on a Horse." In the worst tradition of Holly-
wood films about the theatre, I was given the leading role of Erwin,
which I played for nearly two seasons on tour. I worked with George
Abbott, a real, thoroughgoing professional, when I played in "Three
Men on a Horse" and "Boy Meets Girl" on tour, and then in "Room
Service," on Broadway.

My first marriage was made when I was terribly young, and it was a
failure from the start. I'm married now to the actress Jessica Tandy.
My wife and I have played together in several stage productions, including "The Fourposter," in which we played on Broadway for two
seasons and six hundred and thirty-two performances. We've been in
movies together, in one of which, "The Green Years," I played Jessie's
father. We had a television series for a while, called "The Marriage," and we've been in a number of television plays, including
"The Moon and Sixpence." If a husband and wife work together, it
can make life better for both of them.

After you've been in about fifteen movies, as I have—"Lifeboat,"
"Brute Force," "The Seventh Cross," and others—and directed six
Broadway productions, and written screen treatments for movies, which
I have also done, you develop too many ideas about acting. Most of us
are a little pathetic in our assumptions of artistry. Actors don't often
fulfill their obligations as artists, or transmit their experience in a form
that is clear to the audience. Acting can be an art, but it very rarely is.
An actor's instrument is himself. To have a responsive body and a
responsive voice requires a great deal of physical and emotional discipline. Your pores must constantly be open, to soak up what you later
give out. The best absorbers are the best emitters. There's a great
danger in trying to perfect detail. There are times when I feel I have
the soul of a filing clerk. Writers are the luckiest of all artists; they
have the greatest degree of independence. I used to write poetry. After
I made "The Seventh Cross," for M-G-M, in the early forties, I
went thirteen months without working; during that time I discovered some of the pleasures of writing. I wrote some short stories,
sold a story to R.K.O., and wrote a screen treatment of "Rope" for
Alfred Hitchcock, which he directed, and which his company produced. For a long time, I've been attracted to paintings, and I built
up quite a distinguished collection, which I later sold—an early Picasso, two Modiglianis, a Renoir still-life, two Vlamincks, and a Mary

Cassatt "Mother and Child." I think there is a strong relationship between painting and acting. When I'm building a role, I start with a series of mental pictures, and feel, This should have this shape, like a drawing.

There are two legitimate ways of approaching acting—Jessie's way, which is to start with what is inside yourself and go to the outside, and my way, which is working from the outside to the inside. I've learned that you need endless patience in working with actors, especially if you're directing them. Some of them seem to work so slowly. Then suddenly they begin to bloom. As an actor, you have to learn what kind of roles you can do. I took a bash at Hamlet in 1949. I found that I wasn't equipped to play him. I read Salvador de Madariaga's book about Hamlet as the poetic Hamlet, and that gave me an image to hold on to. What I learned is that to play Shakespeare well you should start as a young actor, doing small parts at first, giving yourself time to benefit from the growing process. The actor makes no profound contribution to society. He reveals a moment of truth, poetry, humor. God knows we're short on those things, but the actor's contribution isn't very much. And it isn't anything at all without the spark of talent. That's God-given and bloody rare, and even that doesn't amount to much without education, intelligence, and experience. A lot of acting is drudgery, and a lot of it is so dull: learning to put on makeup, learning to control your breath, learning not to let your face go to pieces. To act, you must have a sense of truth and some degree of dedication.

The first time I look over a play, I respond to the situations and to the characters as they're caught in the situations. Later on, I begin to see what may have to be erased. I always go through a process of collecting far more material than I can use. Then I try to retain what is essential. Intellection is important as a process of getting the best out of yourself. Once I get into a part, I find myself thinking about it all the time. It can become a kind of nightmare. Actors have no social life. We're constantly working. To go on being an actor, you need sheer animal energy. If you can't restock your energy, you have to hide your lack of it. Like getting above a cold. You can't have a cold onstage. When I'm working, I look forward all day long to that *one* drink before dinner. I don't want to talk then. Nor do I want to talk at all for fifteen minutes before going to sleep, or at breakfast. Jessie and I have a small island in the Bahamas, on which we've built a house. It's our retreat, cut off from everybody else. We get there by chartered sea-plane, and we have our own electric generator. We need that island. I come to life when I hit it and hit that water. After I've finished with a play or a television show, I'm desperate to hide out, to get away. Every actor has his own way of coming to life again. Going to the island is mine.

Some actors have a tendency to get absorbed in the details of what they do in a part, and that often makes the thing become mechanical. I try not to get trapped by the peripheral elements. I try to be guided by the questions, "What's basic here? Is it true? Can I make it simpler?" Olivier tells me there's no such thing as overacting. You can go as high as Everest, he says, if you can fill the space. Your own feelings are unimportant. You're not in a part to indulge in what *you* may feel. It simply doesn't matter how *you* feel. It's how the audience feels and how the author felt first that count. If you're acting a part, you've got to jump in and do it.

ZERO MOSTEL

The theatre is like a cathedral—I mean a shul. *At the end of it, there's a cup of hot tea.*

I was born on February 28, 1915, in the Brownsville section of Brooklyn. I am the next-to-the-youngest child of my father's second set of children; he had four children by his first wife, spaced three years apart, and four children by his second wife, also spaced three years apart. All but two of us are boys. One brother is in philanthropic work, and my other brothers are in various kinds of manufacturing or accounting. My father moved us from Brownsville to the lower East Side to Moodus, Connecticut, where he was in charge of a kosher slaughterhouse, and then to the Bronx, where he made sacramental wine. I went to P.S. 188, on the lower East Side, and I graduated from Seward Park High School, in Manhattan. My real name is Samuel Joel Mostel. The kids in school started calling me Zero, because I was always cutting up in class and appeared to be a hopeless student. I weigh two hundred and thirty-five pounds now; as a kid, I was terribly skinny. When I was seven, I played the part of a Red Cross nurse in a school pageant. I loved doing imitations and getting laughs from the other kids. My family always frowned on acting. My father, who died in 1945, was a very good-natured man, but he never came to see me on the stage, or when I worked in night clubs or in movies. Being an entertainer of that kind came under the heading of making fun of human beings, which is objectionable according to the orthodox Jewish religion. Both my parents had great humor. My mother was a wit, but never a sentimental one. Once, when somebody in our house stepped on our cat's paw, she turned to the cat and said sternly, "I *told* you not to go around barefoot!" For all the occupations I chose, my mother had one word: "Bum!" When I kept asking my father to give in and come to see me entertain, he would say, "I don't want the publicity."

In school, I found that I was very good at drawing and painting. I've never stopped painting. I've always had a studio to go to; even while I'm in a play, I try to go every day to my studio, which is now on West Twenty-eighth Street. I graduated with a B.A. from C.C.N.Y. in 1935 and went on to N.Y.U. to study art at night. During the day, I went to work, turning sleeves in an overcoat shop belonging to one of my brothers-in-law. I quit after four weeks. Then I got on the W.P.A., and moved into a ten-by-ten-foot room with another artist. The W.P.A. had classes in many branches of art—life drawing, painting, industrial arts. Most of the good artists were on the project, teaching and working. I taught life drawing and painting at the Ninety-second Street Y.M.H.A. We gave Artists' Balls, at which I would get up and joke and deliver chalk talks. Barney Josephson, who was running Café Society Downtown and Café Society Uptown at the time, heard me at one of the Artists' Balls and, in 1942, hired me to do an act at Café Society Downtown, at a salary of forty dollars a week. Then I moved to the Uptown, at a salary of a hundred dollars a week. Here I was a big night-club star, and yet when I had a date, all I knew to offer was "Let's go for a bite at Rudley's." A year later, I was booked into the Martinique at a salary of thirty-seven hundred and fifty dollars a week.

By this time, I knew that I wanted to be an actor. I was a comic. Most comics never bother to equip themselves as actors. Most of the young comics today have the misconception that if they do a series of gags in a certain pose, that's enough. But the best comics are also good actors. Chaplin is a wonderful actor. W. C. Fields and Willie Howard and Bobby Clark were real actors, and so are Bert Lahr and Joey

61

Adams and Shelley Berman. In France, the word *"comédien"* actually means both "comedian" and "actor." I wanted to play in the classic comic literature. I wanted to act in the plays of Molière, the daddy of all comic invention. I felt that I had to study everything if I wanted to act. I felt that an actor was better if he knew what was going on, if he was aware of the literary stage tradition. I wanted to know how to do Lear and Toby Belch and Falstaff. I had read all of Shaw and Molière by the time I was nineteen. In college, when my English professor was writing "You can't beat Thomas Wolfe" on the blackboard, I was reading "Ulysses" out loud in an alcove with other rebels. Years afterwards, when I was going to play Leopold Bloom in the Off Broadway production of "Ulysses in Nighttown," I found that I knew whole sections of it by heart. I was also fascinated by Molière in college, and when I read "The Miser" and "The Imaginary Invalid" and "The Bourgeois Gentleman," I automatically imagined what funny things you could do at this point or that point while playing the parts. I wasn't even thinking of acting then myself, though. In 1949, I went up to the Brattle Theatre, in Cambridge, Massachusetts, and played Argan in my own adaptation of "The Imaginary Invalid." A couple of years later, I went back there and played Sganarelle in "The Doctor in Spite of Himself." The part of Argan offers the finest of comic material. I'd never worked in a play until then, and I found it exciting, playing with an ensemble and in a part that offered the opportunity for me to do so much—acting, comedy, singing, and dancing, as well as creating a complete character. The part utilized what I felt I had. And I didn't have to work with a microphone or wear a blue suit and a tie. Bloom in "Ulysses in Nighttown" was another very rich part, and I enjoyed playing it. I wish I could play in "The Imaginary Invalid" on Broadway, but producers go wild when they hear the name Molière. They immediately start figuring out the cost of the costumes.

I was married in 1944 to the former Kathryn Harkins, who was a Rockette and a ballet dancer. We have two children—Joshua, who was born in 1946, and Tobias, born two years later. Both my sons are musical and are good chess players. I was in the Army for a while, serving in the infantry at Camp Croft and Fort Meade. Then I played all the big night clubs as a comic, was in the Duke Ellington musical "Beggar's Holiday," on Broadway, and played the London Palladium for three weeks. In the summer, I'd try to go where I could play

Molière. In 1950, I moved my family out to Hollywood to live while I made some movies. I played in "Panic in the Streets," directed by Elia Kazan, and in "The Enforcer," "Sirocco," and other pictures. I took a studio on Santa Monica Boulevard and spent a lot of time painting. But I hated Hollywood. Everything about it—the people, the climate, the business. Everything. My wife hated it. The kids hated it. We were all happy to get back to New York.

I've always been very choosy. I turned down the part of the peddler in "Oklahoma!," which the producers wanted to build up for me. The idea, they told me, was to get into a musical and make nineteen million dollars. I didn't want that. I wanted to be free to act and to paint. I'm constantly trying new things in painting. After I've done one thing, I go on to try something new. In the early forties, I painted socially satiric things, and later on I did more abstract painting. Lately, I've been working with a mixture of mediums—oils, crayon, pastels. Only a monomaniac does the same thing in all the arts. What I do in acting is something different. A guy's painting, if it's true, is of himself, always. Painting is a much more creative field than acting. You take up an empty canvas; you fill it. In acting, you've got something to start with. You're not always satisfied with what you put on the blank canvas, and here painting is like acting on the stage, you have a chance the next day or night to do it over. Painting comes from color, not from drawing. I'm a colorist. I never stop painting. You can't do it by fits and starts. If you paint, you've got to paint every day. Otherwise, the simple mixing of the colors becomes a terrific problem. I'm not unusual in wanting to act as well as paint. During the Renaissance, they worked at everything—jewelry, painting, dam-building, sculpture. There's no way of knowing which I need more, painting or acting. It's just that I have a need to do both.

I don't like to do a lot of things you have to do to become a success as an actor. I was the same way in painting. I never got into the social life of being a painter. When I finally succumbed and got myself an agent as a painter, only recently, he died. As an actor or anything else, I don't go to ladies' clubs. I'm not willing to make a business out of myself. If an actor gets that involved with himself, he's doing photographs in the morning, and then comes the meeting with the publicity man, then the session with his psychoanalyst, then the hot lunch at Sardi's. If you do a lot of that kind of thing as an actor, you get farther, but then you don't have time to paint if you want to go to your studio and paint. I'm particular about what I give my time to as an actor. I hate all plays with mothers and fathers in them. If I had to play the father of one of those terrible families, I'd flip my lid. I don't like acting when I have to do John loves Mary. I'm just as antagonistic to an Andy Wyeth painting or anything else I don't like: I like to do what I like, even if it's a commercial flop. I don't care what the theatre critics say. Critics don't know anything about acting. They slaughtered "Beggar's Holiday," and it didn't touch me.

I have an inclination to do wild things in plays. That's why I loved playing Bloom in "Ulysses in Nighttown." I started going to the Actors' Studio in 1950. The only part of it I like is where you get up and act. I like working from time to time at the Studio, but I haven't won any certificates for best attendance. I like to be with actors, to see what they do. I'm suspicious of ambitious people, though; I'm suspicious of too much conversation. I've worked with all kinds of directors. Some of the big-name directors destroy the most wonderful thing an actor has. Just because he has power and importance, the destructive director tries to bend you to what he calls his sense of production instead of letting you use your own configuration, your own way of merging your own personality with the character you're playing. A good director knows how to bring out your talent. One of the best directors I've ever worked with is Burgess Meredith, who directed me in "Ulysses in Nighttown." He's a wonderful actor himself—very inventive and very creative—so he can do a lot of the things he wants you to do on the stage. Sometimes he can make a single little gesture when he steps into a part, and it rubs off on you. He sees things a cut above realism. He has a conception of what a thing is, what it means. He knows how to make use of you as an actor, but always in good taste. It's very stimulating. And I don't feel the breath of ambition on him, which is always disturbing to an actor. I feel that his concern is for the play. Joseph Anthony, who directed me in "Rhinoceros," is one of the most wonderful directors, a guy with a world of patience, who knows exactly what you can do. He lets you do what you can do, and he's a marvel to work with. A bad director comes to a decision, and it's wrong, and what is primarily important to him is to prove that it is right. The best guide to acting is Bernard Shaw's phrase "the life force." When all the elements of art enter into it—the distortion, the reality, the naïveté—you have the life force. "Ulysses in Night-town" is larger than life, and my role in it was more than an adequate one. Working on a role like Bloom requires the exercise of your own taste in large measure. I playèd in "Ulysses in Nighttown" on and off for two years in New York, London, Paris, and Amsterdam, and never got bored; there was always something new to do, something interesting, something alive. I suppose that because I'm a painter I am automatically guided in acting by things that influence my painting. When I played in "Rhinoceros" and was supposed to turn into a rhinoceros, Joseph Anthony at first wanted me to run offstage, stick a horn on my forehead, and become a rhinoceros that way. I preferred to do it all in front of the audience. That's a painterly thing to do.

For me, the greatest actor in history was Raimu. There's never been an American playwright who conveyed a corner of American life the way Marcel Pagnol conveyed a corner of French life in his film trilogy "Marius," "Fanny," and "César," starring Raimu. Raimu captured life for me. He did everything full-scale, without an arid moment and with no tricks. The greatest actress was Laurette Taylor. I saw her eleven times in "The Glass Menagerie" on Broadway. The great ones just do it, and it's never vulgar.

JOAN CRAWFORD

I had the great advantage of growing up in front of a camera. I know just how to turn, just what to show on my face, and when to let the other actor have it. A movie actor or actress paints with the tiniest brush.

I was born on March 23, 1908, in San Antonio, Texas. My real name is Lucille Le Sueur. I did not meet my father, Thomas Le Sueur, until I was an established movie star. My mother had divorced him before I was born, and when I was a few weeks old she married Henry Cassin, who owned a small vaudeville theatre in Lawton, Oklahoma, so I spent my early years in Lawton. At six, I had an accident that kept me in bed for a year—I stepped on a broken bottle and cut my foot so badly that the doctors said I would never walk again—and when I was eight and a half, we moved to Kansas City, Missouri. My childhood is vague to me now. What I mostly remember is that it was exhausting. I went to school at St. Agnes Academy, in Kansas City, as a day student. When I was nine, my mother and my stepfather separated. My mother took over a laundry agency; my older brother, Hal Le Sueur, got a job as a soda jerk. I began waiting on tables and doing housework at the Academy to pay my tuition. After the sixth grade, I went to Rockingham, another private school, where I was the only working pupil. The school occupied a fourteen-room house, and I cleaned all fourteen rooms and also cooked meals, made beds, and washed dishes for thirty boys and girls. When I attended classes, I was too tired to absorb what I heard, too tired to learn very much, but I was always healthy, and I loved to dance. I learned every dance step I could, and I entered one amateur dance competition and won. I could do the Charleston and the Black Bottom better than anyone else in town. I knew I could beat the other kids, and I did. I knew I was born with talent, though I didn't know exactly what it was. After getting out of high school, I attended Stephens College, in Columbus, Missouri, as a working student, but I gave it up after three months. I wanted to take dancing lessons, but I didn't have the money. I got a job as a salesgirl in a Kansas City department store, for twelve dollars a week. After a quarrel with my mother, I went to Chicago and got a job doing one song and one dance at an out-of-the-way café, for twenty-five dollars a week. Two weeks later, I was dancing in the chorus line of the Oriole Terrace Club, in Detroit. From there, I went into the chorus of the J. J. Shubert revue "Innocent Eyes," in New York, and then into the chorus of the revue called "The Passing Show of 1924." After eight months in that, I was asked by an M-G-M talent scout to take a screen test.

On New Year's Day, 1925, I left for Hollywood to begin working for M-G-M, at seventy-five dollars a week. When I signed my contract, I thought that M-G-M wanted me because I could dance. Now I know that right from the start I was considered promising as an actress. I hardly had a chance to know what I was doing. My first role was as a chorus girl covered with imitation snow in "Pretty Ladies," in 1925. Dancing roles in movies were easy for me, even though I had never made the front line of the chorus on the stage. At that time, movies were still silents. We would work late at night, and on Sundays, if necessary, and it would take us all of four weeks to make a movie. I danced in almost every role. From the very first, it was important to me to become known as a movie star, to show the people back home in Kansas City what I really was. They had never believed in my talent. In "Sally, Irene, and Mary," which was made in 1925, I played the role of Irene, a dancer, and it was then that the studio changed my name to Joan Crawford. Among my other early films were "Old Clothes," with Jackie Coogan, and "The Only Thing," with Eleanor Boardman, and in 1926 I was Harry Langdon's leading lady in

"Tramp, Tramp, Tramp," and then played in "Paris," with Charles Ray. I was still a teen-ager, and even though I still wanted to be a star, I was really dancing to please my leading man and my director and my producer. I would do any kind of part they asked me to. I was working so hard I didn't have time for anything else. I played ingénue roles in "The Unknown," with Lon Chaney; "Twelve Miles Out," with John Gilbert; "West Point," with William Haines; and "Across to Singapore," with Ramon Novarro. It was work I thrived on and loved. In 1928, I was still thinking that dancing was my inborn talent. When I played in "Our Dancing Daughters" that year, and appeared dancing on a table, after coming out of a huge cake, I became known as a movie star, and my salary was raised to five hundred dollars a week.

The next year, 1929, I danced in "Our Modern Maidens," with Douglas Fairbanks, Jr., and I also danced in "Hollywood Revue of '29." It was between these assignments that I first had a chance to look around me and see what acting was. I admired Eleanor Boardman, and I watched Greta Garbo on her sets every chance I could get. I grew determined to become a dramatic actress. I started nagging Louis B. Mayer and Irving Thalberg to cast me in more and more dramatic roles. I would hang around the studio and get my hands on the new scripts, then take them home with me to read, and decide on the role I wanted. I relied on my instinct in choosing what was right for me, and my instinct rarely let me down. After deciding that I wanted a certain role, I got up and went after it. The written words weren't too important. I knew that if certain words or phrases stuck in my throat, I could call a little conference right on the set and have them changed to suit me better. I would go off in a corner with the director and the leading man, and together we would decide what we wanted the writer to change. I knew that the writer would be grateful to me. His words were dead words. They were brought to life by me.

I was at M-G-M for seventeen years. In the thirties, I was considered one of the ten biggest money-making stars for six straight years. Once I'd started on a role, it became like a horse race. I couldn't wait to go on. I worked hard on my preparations. If the script had been based on a book, I'd go back and read the book. I have almost total recall and a vivid imagination. I usually chose my own writers, producer, and director—I still do—and I'd enter them in the race. Once in a role,

I eliminated myself completely. I became the character I played. I portrayed so many girls and women who went from rags to riches that L. B. Mayer thought I represented Cinderella to the public. My audience was composed mostly of women. I began to beg to play bitches, so I got that kind of part, and liked it. I've known so many bitches, who never cared about the feelings of other people as long as they could get their own way. They just never gave a hoot how many people they rode over and hurt. Then I'd play another kind of role, and it was exciting to become the queen bee again. I've made about seventy-five pictures, and I remember every one of my important roles the way I remember a part of my life, because at the time I did them I *was* the role and it *was* my life, for twenty-four hours a day. When I was a teen-ager, comedy was the most difficult thing for me to do, and it still is. But dramatic roles are easy for me. In 1946, I won an Oscar for my role in "Mildred Pierce," and it was the easiest thing I've ever done. I've always drawn on myself only. That's one of the reasons nobody has ever been able to imitate me. And nobody can duplicate anything I've done. You always see impersonations of Katharine Hepburn and Marilyn Monroe, but no one can imitate me.

The pictures I loved more than any others I've ever made were the films with Clark Gable—"Possessed" and "Chained," among others—and "Mildred Pierce" and "Humoresque." The picture—and especially the opening—that I keep trying to forget is "Rain," in which I played Sadie Thompson. I did it in 1932, and I didn't understand that role then. If I were to do it now, I would understand it much better. Today, I would start my characterization from the inside. For the most part, though, the roles I've played have been right for me, even if not all my pictures have been successful. In the old days, we seldom had a single rehearsal. Our dream was to have two whole weeks just for a rehearsal period. Before going into a picture, I'd have a talk with Adrian, my costume designer, and then I'd have a talk with the director and the leading man. I'd work on getting the clothes fitted, and my wardrobe tested and just right, and the dialogue changed to suit me. When I make a picture today, it's still the same; there are so many people involved that I have to please—the co-star, the cameraman, the director. And I love to please them. Sometimes, in a difficult scene, when I have words I simply can't say, I call in the director or the dialogue director and I suggest just walking through the scene—not really doing anything, just indicating what I can do. That helps in getting the dialogue set.

When we actually start to shoot, I ask for one minute by myself. Then I go off into a corner and bring up the exact feeling I want to show. It can be tears, hysteria, laughter—anything. I need just one minute, and I can do it as high as the director wants it. If it feels true, and if techniques don't get in your way, it's right. Techniques grow with experience. Developing techniques is not like getting a whole new wardrobe; it's not planned. For me, a role isn't something you daub on and take off, like makeup. At the end of a day, I leave the part locked inside me. Only the makeup and the wardrobe are left at the studio. When I get home, I don't discuss my roles with my four adopted children. I have one son, Christopher, aged nineteen, and three daughters, Christina, aged twenty-two, and Cynthia and Cathy, fourteen-year-old twins. Around the age of ten, each of my children began to be proud of me. Before that, whenever we went to the movies to see me in an unhappy role, they would cry and wail, but I would say to them, "Look, darling, I'm right here." I'd hold their hands, and it would be all right.

A true actress is a woman who can portray a true character honestly and with pure emotion, and weave her way into the hearts of her audience and make them understand the character. The emotion must be honest and pure. I've learned about life from writers and directors, but mostly from myself. Writers give their words to paper. I give life to their words. I act more for myself than for others. But I never refer to a character I'm playing as "me." It's "her." Except for one picture I made in 1951, a cheap and corny one called "This Woman Is Dangerous," I've revelled in everything I've ever done. Acting is stimulating. It's exciting. It's competitive. It's challenging. It can be electrifying. It doesn't matter if the character is Mary Turner, in "Paid," or Mildred Pierce, I mold it, perfect it. A good actress can bring her audiences into her world and permit them to throw off their cares and fears temporarily.

My instinct in choosing the right part has failed me very seldom. In something called "Great Day," I was supposed to be a little Southern girl, digging her toe in the sand. Well, I'm a big gal. I'm only five feet four and a half, but I have very wide shoulders, and they give people the impression that I'm big. We had been shooting for ten or eleven

days, and each day I began to feel more wrong for the part. I sought
out L. B. Mayer and pleaded with him to look at the rushes with Thalberg and to take me out of the movie. I cried, and told him that I was
a big dame and I couldn't, for the life of me, dig my bare toe in the
sand. After ten or eleven days of rushes, they called the whole thing
off, with $280,000 still sitting on the shelf. They told me to stay home,
and I've never been sorry. I was just too big for the part. I'm so broad
I would look dumpy if I put on a little weight. My measurements have
changed very little since I started acting. I learned to stand tall right at
the start, and I've always exercised to look tall. Dancing did a lot for
me, giving me more freedom of body movement and more grace. If an
actress has no talent, she may just as well quit before she begins. Every
actress must have inborn talent.

In June of 1929, I was married to Douglas Fairbanks, Jr., and we
worked with each other to improve our acting. We were divorced in
1933, and two years later I married Franchot Tone, and began to
think seriously about going on the stage. I began to learn about things
like the Moscow Art Theatre. We built a theatre in back of our house,
in Brentwood, where we rehearsed and co-starred in radio performances of several adaptations of movies. We studied singing, too. I
started to study opera, and continued with it after our divorce, in
1939. In July, 1942, I was married to Phillip Terry while I was making
my last M-G-M picture under contract, "Above Suspicion," and we
were divorced after two years. I am a contralto, and for seven years I
thought I might become an opera singer. In opera, the whole body
moves and has a rhythm to it. It can contribute to acting a role. Every
actress should take some singing and dancing lessons. The opera lessons
gave me better control over my voice. Many beautiful actresses are
spoiled because they have no control over their voices. I've always
been terrified of the stage and of live audiences, and I still am. Sometimes when I go backstage to pick up Ethel Merman or Mary Martin
for supper and have to wait for her to dress, I go out on the stage
and, remembering her lines, I begin to imagine myself in her role and
start speaking her lines. Then, suddenly, I see all the empty seats
and imagine how it would be to see that many faces instead, and I
just get sick. When my fourth husband, the late Alfred N. Steele, who
was chairman of the board of the Pepsi-Cola Company, started taking
me with him on business trips for Pepsi-Cola to make promotional

appearances, I was terrified. Once, in Chicago, I was asked to appear before the food editors of every publication in the city and answer hundreds of questions. The only way I could answer in front of them all was to have the questions submitted on cards first. Acting in front of movie crews is different. You know they are friends, part of the family, and are watching out for your best interests. Now, after working for Pepsi-Cola for several years, making appearances on my own, it feels like a family, too. I prepare for each appearance the way I do for a movie role. It's all part of acting. Acting is the greatest of all the arts. I wish I had five hundred years to study it.

ALEXANDER DAVION

You must never lose your sense of fun, even if you're doing a very serious part.

I was born on March 13, 1929, in the heart of Paris. My father, Thomas Davion, a timber importer, is French, and my mother is English. I have one brother, Jack, a year and ten months younger than I am, who works as an engineer for Rolls-Royce in Montreal. My family moved to London when I was three. We lived in a lovely town house in St. John's Wood, near Lord's Cricket Ground, where actors go to watch the matches when they're out of work. I remember sounds and shapes in Paris from my first three years there, and I still have a tremendous nostalgic feeling for it. I always had a yen to act, as far back as I can remember, but I never used to say anything about it. Acting was something I just somehow felt that I could do. As a child, I could tell stories. I could make people laugh. I could romp about, pretending to be somebody else, pretending to be something else. It was always great fun. I was good at movement and dancing. At the age of two or three, I would dance for what seemed to me like hours at a

73

time. I have always loved music. I once started taking piano lessons, but I was too lazy to keep it up. My family hoped that I might become a lawyer or a doctor. I went to kindergarten in Hampstead, where I knitted a long pink scarf, and after that to a prep school, Hall School, where I had my first part in a play. It was all about spies and spying, and I played Nitro Glycerinsky, wearing a slouch hat and an overcoat with the collar turned up. When I was thirteen, I was sent away to boarding school—the Cheltenham School, in Gloucestershire. It was like any other public school, where your life is miserable, where the discipline is unbelievable, where everything around you does irreparable damage. The school was very tough, very hard. We worked long hours, and the prefects were allowed to beat the younger boys. The idea is that it supposedly stiffens your backbone. Boys who go there usually want to enter the Army. You must pass a stiff exam to get into the school. I chose Cheltenham myself, I suppose, because the war was on and I was very excited by it all. I discovered my mistake the first day I was there.

It was while I was at Cheltenham that I saw my first play, other than pantomimes I was taken to as a child. One of the masters took us to a local theatre to see a touring production of "Othello," with Frederick Valk, a famous German actor, as Othello, and with Bernard Miles as Iago and Hermione Hannen as Desdemona. I was terribly impressed. Valk could hardly speak English, but he had such a brilliant and imposing presence. And he had a magnificent voice. He could speak almost in a whisper, and one could hear him in the back of the theatre; his voice had fantastic resonance. He was a thick, big, ugly man but a marvellous, marvellous actor. I started going to movies when I was about ten. I grew up on American movies. The first one I saw, I believe, was "Modern Times." I was moved to laughter by "Modern Times," but I was also terrified by it. To me, Charles Chaplin is the finest artist there ever was. He's so moving and so beautiful to watch. In a personal way, I feel a certain part of London every time I see him—I feel Kensington, where he was born. I've read all the books on him there are. I understand his sort of comedy—the essence of his humor, his outlook on the whole thing. I had a sort of schoolboy crush on Clark Gable. To me, he was the epitome of masculinity, charm, and roguishness. I saw "Gone with the Wind" four or five times. I was also mad about Edward G. Robinson, Alan Ladd, and

James Cagney. I loved the gangster and Western films. I still think a good Western film is the best entertainment. At Cheltenham, I was very good at Rugby, and one year I broke both my ankles playing it. I never did any acting at public school, and I never talked about acting. It was considered sissy. I was in school during most of the war. I'd go home to London on vacations. One night when I was at home, we decided not to go to the shelter, and a bomb hit the house right next door to ours. I was in bed. I fell two floors down in my bed, and was pinned under debris. It took them three hours to dig me out, but I came off with only a broken wrist and a few bruises. My parents and my brother were cut by glass. I stayed at Cheltenham for two and a half years; then my father got into financial difficulties, because of the effect of the war on his business, and I was hauled out of school. I didn't want to go to one of the country schools. I'm not a snob, and wasn't then; it was just that I was becoming independent. I was sixteen, and I wanted to earn my own way. I decided I wanted to be a foreign correspondent, so I took a job as an office boy with Hulton Publications, Ltd., which published weekly periodicals. My main function was to run out for coffee. After six months of this sort of thing, I began to realize that one had to work one's way up. I decided to apply for admission to the Royal Academy of Dramatic Art. I never sat down and thought specifically, I'm going to become an actor. It was more that I was drawn to anything make-believe and theatrical. I wish now that I'd gone to a university, but at sixteen I just felt that I wanted to get out into the world. For my R.A.D.A. audition, I gave Shylock's "Hath not a Jew eyes?" speech from "The Merchant of Venice." I was superb as only a young person can be, I suppose. I gave it all the guns I had. I raved. I moved myself to tears. And I was accepted. I followed what is a more or less standard pattern for young actors. You start off with no knowledge—just raw talent and the consciousness of acting. Then you become terribly aware of all your thoughts—of what to do with yourself, and so on—at which point you're learning your technique the hard way. Then, after you've got a certain amount under your belt, you lose confidence, and you feel that you're being awful and that the talent isn't coming out. And then a day arrives when everything clicks into place, and you have the added element of experience behind you. Some actors never reach the fourth stage. Some never reach the third stage. And some never reach the second. I spent quite a bit of time in the third stage. My teachers told me things like "You never stand still when you're listening onstage." So I became conscious of being very bad. Eventually, I was able to assemble everything and work at it. The goal is quite simple: to get onstage and to create by visible and audible means a character that is not yourself and that will hold and move an audience.

A lot of actors have a pretty smile and are *simpatico* in a certain way. They have perhaps a five-year lease on life in acting. The great actors are quite another matter. Paul Scofield is the finest young English actor at this moment. Laurence Olivier has everything. He has enormous imagination and talent. He is so constructed, physically, that he is neither tall nor short, neither handsome nor unhandsome, neither fat nor thin, so he can be fat *or* thin, handsome *or* unhandsome, tall *or* short, or whatever the part calls for. He has a wonderful voice, which he has worked on. He has stamina. He can play a heroic character, and he's one of the few actors who can. He can portray a character with tremendous sweep and magnificence. He wants a theatre with life in it, and he cares about its modern as well as its classical aspects. He's always commissioning writers to write plays. He's willing to gamble by taking a part in a modern play. He's in the theatre because the theatre, in all its aspects, is to him the most important thing in life. Everything that has to do with the theatre—the lighting, the scenery, the makeup —is fascinating to him, just because it does have to do with theatre. He doesn't use the theatre as a means of making money. He is a completely dedicated man.

I was at R.A.D.A. for something less than a year and a half. The usual stay is about two years. At R.A.D.A., I was a bit of a rogue. I didn't really take life too seriously. I'd try to get away with all kinds of things by using charm. It was a cover-up, I suppose, for the way I felt about some of the people I encountered there. I've always been aware of the feelings of those around me, and I was then. I think every good actor must be aware. I can't stand people I call unaware, who are conscious of nothing and nobody but themselves, who don't respect other people's feelings. I'm no saint, but I believe there are two kinds of people, aware and unaware, and the same two kinds of actors. Awareness makes the difference between actors with a direction in life and actors who are interested only in material gain and have no feeling for the art of acting. With the second kind, it's all a selfish thing.

Those people usually have no humor, and I don't think an actor without humor can dig very deep. At the end of each term at R.A.D.A., there is a performance for the public, when promising students put on excerpts from plays. At the end of my third term, I played Harry, Lord Monchensey, in "The Family Reunion," by T. S. Eliot, a verse play that is very, very complicated. I didn't know what I was talking about, but I did it with my usual bravado. The next day, I heard from the Myron Selznick office, which was then an agency. They asked me to come in, and when I did, they promised me the world. I was full of high hopes. I felt, We're on our way. Then I went back to R.A.D.A. for my fourth term. It was right after the end of the war. Everybody, it seemed, wanted to become an actor, and there were too many people in every class. There were fewer good parts to play, and I had too many distractions. Again, I had that powerful feeling of wanting to get out into the world. I walked straight out at the beginning of the fourth term, right after prayers. There were frantic telephone calls from the school the next day. People got on the phone and said, "You should stay, at least until you do your public show." But I was too impatient. I said, "I'm leaving," and I left.

After that, the agent who had been interested in me sent me around to a lot of auditions, but nothing happened, except that I acted in a club theatre called the Q, playing the role of Paris in the pantomime-within-the-play in "The Rose Without a Thorn," with Francis L. Sullivan, for two weeks in December of 1947. Then I auditioned for the 1948 season at Stratford and was accepted, together with Edmund Purdom. I carried spears for nine months, and was bored stiff. But I learned a lot—things like how to find a yardstick for yourself, and what is good and what is not good. We also learned the plays of Shakespeare, and all that one can learn from watching actors like Godfrey Tearle, Ralph Richardson, and Paul Scofield, and Diana Wynyard and Margaret Leighton. Tearle was what I call one of the best actors in the grand manner. But you can watch only so much. That first season, I had two lines in "Othello;" I was the first officer in the first act, who says "A messenger from the galleys" and "Here is more news." The most terrifying parts are messengers. You come on in a rush, out of breath, and set the tone of what is to follow with your announcement that the soldiers are approaching. In a way, it's quite a responsibility. Or so I told myself when I had those two lines. Between seasons, in December, I played in "Toad of Toad Hall," in the parts of Fox, Chief Stoat, Turkey, and Chief Weasel. The second season, I played Young Siward in "Macbeth." I had about six lines, fought Macbeth at the end of them, and got killed. They asked me to roll down twenty steep steps after I got killed, and I did it, every step, just to show how coöperative I was. The third season, in 1952, I played Donalbain in "Macbeth"—one of Duncan's sons. The other son, Malcolm, was played by Laurence Harvey, who has since gone on to spectacular activities in films. John Gielgud directed, and he called us the wicked brothers. Gielgud is such a marvellous man. He'll change a whole scene in five seconds if he thinks of a better way of doing it, and you've got to keep right up with him. That production of "Macbeth" had Ralph Richardson in the title role and Margaret Leighton as Lady Macbeth. I was impressed by the cast, but after the King is murdered, Donalbain says goodbye to his brother and disappears forever. I felt I couldn't register in a small part. I was a bit frustrated, because I wasn't doing much at Stratford at all. My best work that season was as understudy at rehearsals to the actor playing Laertes in "Hamlet," with Paul Scofield and Claire Bloom. It was a lovely production. I played all the echoes offstage. Every time the Ghost spoke, I echoed.

I spent two very comfortable, closeted years at Stratford, though they did include a four-month Australian tour with the company's productions of "Much Ado About Nothing," in which I played a page and was used mostly to push scenery around, and "Macbeth," in which I again played the role of Young Siward. We toured four Australian cities—Melbourne, Adelaide, Brisbane, and Sydney. When I was asked to come back to Stratford for a third season, I said no, left for London, and wrote to a lot of repertory companies for a job. They were all full, and I couldn't get in. In 1950, I joined a small repertory company at Windsor, opposite Windsor Castle. It's a lovely theatre to work in. It's attended by local people, and the Queen usually makes an appearance once a year. It's her little baby. It's dead opposite the castle, and she can look out the window and see it. The theatre is very old, built of stone and wood, and it's a full professional theatre, with an orchestra pit and everything. At first, I was taken on for three weeks, at five pounds for the first week and ten pounds a week after that. In "The Lady's Not for Burning," I played the juvenile lead, Richard, the copying clerk in love—a spiritual love—with the daughter of the household, and when that was over, I was kept on for the rest of the season. I had six very happy months there. I played Albert Strachan, the lead, in "Pink String and Sealing Wax," a murder mystery, and a poor young violinist in "Pick-Up Girl," a sort of social play.

Next, I auditioned for Laurence Olivier for his own season at the St. James in 1951, and was signed by him. I replaced actors who were playing Bel Affris in Shaw's "Caesar and Cleopatra" and Dolabella in Shakespeare's "Antony and Cleopatra." It was a marvellous engagement, with Olivier and Vivien Leigh, who was his wife at the time— the King and Queen of the Theatre. Olivier would play Antony in "Antony and Cleopatra" at a matinée and Caesar in "Caesar and Cleopatra" that evening, with Vivien Leigh playing Cleopatra all the way through. As Bel Affris, I ran in and said, "Take heed, Persian. Caesar is by this time almost within earshot." I played it with bravado. Olivier said, "You're absolutely hopeless. Even if you do nothing but take your trousers down onstage, the feeling must be just as big. The gesture must have something behind it. When you make a gesture and there's no feeling behind it, that is ham acting." I was twenty-two. I've never forgotten it. Dolabella is a very good, well-rounded part. He's a young chap in Caesar's army who comes in to warn Cleopatra that Caesar is coming, and tries to stop her from killing herself. Anthony Quayle, who was running a season at Stratford, saw me and made me a very nice offer for a season there. Olivier had asked me to go to America with the tour of his season's plays, but I told him I wanted to go to Stratford, and he said, "Have my blessing." So there I was at Stratford again. I played Ferdinand in "The Tempest" and Silvius in "As You Like It," but it wasn't a very successful season, and I behaved rather badly, because I was bored. In 1953, I went back to Windsor for a season, and I did a lot of radio broadcasting, which in England is serious acting work. One day, the telephone rang at seven in the morning and a voice said, "Larry Olivier here." He was making the film "Richard III," producing and directing as well as acting, and his stand-in was ill. He said, "Would you come and play the scenes for me, so that I can look through the camera at how it will be?" I spent a marvellous ten days acting Richard III for him while he mapped the whole film out. Then I played a small part in the film—one of those awful messengers again, one of three who come in with bad news. After that, I went to Germany and toured British Army and R.A.F. and American Army camps there in "Seagulls over Sorrento," by Hugh Hastings, in which I played a Scots sailor. In January, 1954, I played Koch, the student who finds the woman dead, in "Crime and Punishment," in a production put on at the Arts Theatre. Later in 1954, I worked with the Ipswich Repertory Theatre, one of the best such theatres in England, for a few weeks. In 1955, I replaced another actor as Ambrose Kemper, the artist, in "The Matchmaker" for nine months in London, where it was a steady commercial success. Tyrone Guthrie, who directed the play, said that my part was one of the dullest, dreariest parts any actor could ever hope to play. After London, I opened with it in December, 1955, on Broadway and then played it for six months on the road. I went along with it all the way. We were with it in Hollywood for three weeks. Then I came back to New York. I was torn between wanting to make a big success on Broadway and wanting to return to London, where I was better known. I stayed in New York, as an understudy in "Look Back in Anger," and then played Romanoff in "Romanoff and Juliet" for six months on tour. We ended the tour in Hollywood.

Being keen on movies, I decided to stay on in Hollywood. I stayed for two years—until late 1961. I appeared in one movie, "Song Without End," in which I played Chopin—a supporting role. I hated it. Hollywood is fine for some people, but for me making that movie was very dull, very boring. The movie had shots of some of Europe's beautiful concert halls, but it was a complete distortion of Liszt's life. I'm glad I stayed as long as I did, because I got rid of a lot of notions about the desirability of becoming a rich, glamorous Hollywood actor. I'm keen on movies, but I got disillusioned very quickly with the kind of work you have to do there as an actor, and with the whole feeling of the place—the slavery to the dollar, and the tremendous effort that is put into sheer rubbish. I won't ever try to do what I did in those two years—not ever again. It just isn't worth the price you have to pay. Deep down, you know whether or not you've got the talent, and if you feel you've got it, you just have to handle yourself with integrity. It would be easy, in a way, to travel the road of some English actors who have become big stars in Hollywood. To me, however, they are a big joke. I'm glad that no serious offer came my way while I was in Hollywood, because I might not have had the strength to turn it down. You're really at a low ebb there. In Hollywood, actors rely completely on their agents. Actors sit there basking in the sun and waiting for calls from their agents, and getting more and more demoralized. In my two years there, I worked mostly in television movies—the worst of all. I got hired for about seventy-five per cent of the jobs that my agent sent me to be interviewed for. I had been looking forward to making Western movies, but the television ones I was hired for were entirely different. I was in a couple of Westerns, each of which was made in about two and a half days, and was all very hit and miss. I was in one "Have Gun, Will Travel," with Richard Boone, and I was in one "Zane Grey Theatre," with Mel Ferrer. I was in a "Perry Mason" as a rich young man who was suspected of murder but hadn't done it. In "Hong Kong," another series, I played a captain of the Hong Kong police—got out my gun and shot a few people, and tracked down a few people. I was in "Thriller," playing a young man in love with somebody very dreary, and I was in "Roaring '20's," playing a king on a visit to New York who falls in love with a gangster's moll.

In the fall of 1961, I returned to New York, to see what I might find in the way of a job in the theatre, and I saw a billboard outside the Lyceum Theatre announcing that Robert Shaw, Donald Pleasence, and Alan Bates were rehearsing in "The Caretaker." The play was one I had read and loved. Bates was going to leave the cast after the pre-Broadway tour plus four weeks, and I auditioned for his part and got it. It's the best contemporary play I've ever been in. There are so many bad plays one must be in just to keep working, but this was a play I had no doubts about. I started out pushing things a bit too much. In one scene in particular, in which I shared a sandwich with the old tramp, I was missing points; I wasn't getting the reaction I knew I should be getting from the audience. After a while, I relaxed a bit in the part, and the reaction came back from the audience. I found that by doing it naturally, playing it as simply as I could, without bravado, I created the effect I wanted. The lines of the play are so good, so right; there isn't a line that is redundant. I compare this play to a musical score. The play is all in the text. There wasn't much for the director to do. He had only to be a referee; there was nothing for him to mold. In a good play, the director's main function is to cast the parts. In a bad play, the director comes into his own. "The Caretaker" was a tremendous exercise in concentration. You could never let go for a moment. If one of the three of us in the cast was off key, the whole play went down the drain. It is said that actors give two or three performances a week and do the rest of the eight on technique. In "The Caretaker," I think we did five or six performances a week. I learned an incredible amount simply by working with Donald Pleasence in this single play. Things like how to hold a pause—just pure know-how. The audience dictates the sort of performance you give. If the audience has a sense of humor, you know it and are affected by it. Audiences do, strangely enough, take on a personality in the actor's mind. You know whether you have a tremendously sympathetic and intelligent audience that enjoys what you do, or whether it's just a lump of pudding. Donald is particularly good at sensing what the audience will take. I don't mean he ever panders to an audience. But if he feels that it's getting the fine points, he'll dwell on them a little longer. American audiences sometimes seem to want things cut and dried. There's a kind of desperation you sense in some American audiences. In America, the ticket prices are so high that audiences become frantic. They want their money's worth; they want to be sure of getting something culturally important. In England, there's a greater interest in the actors. Audiences go to see the actors and talk about *them:* He was good in "King Lear" and not so good in "Hamlet."

The theatre *is* terribly important today. People are so self-concerned now, so wrapped up in how much money they're making, and the theatre gets them all together and takes them out of themselves and makes them think. There's an enormous sense of satisfaction onstage when you achieve a moment you've worked very hard for—when you have a welding of the audience and the actor, and the actor lets the audience in on what he's doing. It's important to keep your enjoyment of acting. If acting becomes too intense and too lacking in fun, it can turn into a terrible chore. If you go on with the feeling that *success must happen,* everything is bound to become boring and pompous. Acting for yourself is a bit of a bore. You act for the audience. It's a marvellous, marvellous profession.

HENRY FONDA

Acting is putting on a mask. The worst torture that can happen to me is not having a mask to get in back of.

I was born on May 16, 1905, in Grand Island, Nebraska, just west of Omaha. I'm the oldest of three. My sisters, Harriet and Jayne, are married to businessmen and live in Omaha and in Pasadena, California, respectively. My father, William Brace Fonda, owned a printing company in Omaha, where I was raised. He died in 1935. My mother, an angelic woman, died the year before. I look like my father. To this day, when I walk past a mirror and see my reflection in it, my first impression is: That's my father. There is a strong Fonda look. It's in my sisters, in their children, in my children. The name Fonda is Italian in origin. There were Fondas in the Apennine Valley, near Genoa, who migrated to Holland around 1400 during a religious revolution. Around 1628, Fondas were among the Dutch settlers who settled in upper New York State, where, in a town called Fonda, both my father's mother and his father were born. Omaha has never ceased being my home. I always stop in Omaha when I'm going from one coast to the

83

other. As a child, I lived in four different houses in and around Omaha, and went to three different grade schools. Then, when I was thirteen or fourteen, we settled down in a big wooden clapboard house in Omaha, and I attended Omaha Central High School. I got my full growth when I was a senior in high school. My son Pete grew in the same way. He stands six feet two—an inch taller than I am. I had what I regard as a normal youth. My close friends today are the friends I grew up with: Bill Reed, an insurance man in Omaha; Charles Dox, a banker in Chicago; Bill Johnson, a California businessman. We swam naked in sand pits and built shacks out of lumber we stole off construction jobs. As a kid, I'd go downtown on the streetcar to my father's office, and he'd give me a nickel to go to the nickelodeon, where I saw the early Charlie Chaplin and William S. Hart pictures. Starting when I was twelve, I worked in my father's printshop in the summers, at two dollars a week. When I was going to high school, I always worked in the summers. It never occurred to me to question it; I just assumed I'd have to work. My mother was a Christian Scientist. My grandmother was a Second Reader in the church. Dorothy Brando, Marlon's mother, who was an amateur actress, was a close friend of Mother's in and out of the church.

I started out wanting to be a writer. At ten, I wrote a story called "The Mouse," which was told from a mouse's point of view. We were living in a suburb of Omaha called Dundee, and the story was published in the Dundee newspaper. I took up journalism at college, at the University of Minnesota, and I worked at two jobs while studying —trouble-shooter for the Northwestern Bell Telephone Company, and director of various sports and other activities at a settlement house. I'd take the streetcar from the campus to the settlement house, on the other side of town, in temperatures that went as low as thirty below zero, and in the basketball season I'd play on the team as well as coach it. For all that I got thirty dollars a month, plus room and board. Dad sent me ten bucks a week. It was exhausting. I did it for a year, and then I went home for a rest. While I was home, I got a message from Do Brando to call Gregory Foley, the director of the Omaha Community Playhouse. She knew that I was at loose ends, and that I was the right age and type to play a juvenile lead they were looking for. I called Foley, and was told to come over to his headquarters—a studio with a skylight, which was kind of bohemian for Omaha. Foley, a short,

red-headed Irishman, handed me the published version of "You and I,"
by Philip Barry, and asked me to read the part of Ricky, the juvenile
lead. First thing I knew, I was cast in the play. I was sure I didn't want
to do it. At rehearsals, I found myself in another world. It was a nightmare. I didn't dare look up. I was the kind of guy who thinks everybody is looking at *him*. I was very reluctant. I had no ambition to be
an actor. But it was summer, and I had nothing else to do, so I joined
the company. I stayed on at the Playhouse as an actor for two nine-
month seasons and did four principal roles. I practically lived at the
theatre. I painted scenery, soaked up the sight of the lines of rope that
go up to the grid, smelled greasepaint, smelled smells I had never
smelled before. My parents weren't particularly for it, but they accepted it. After the first season, in the summer of 1926, I answered an
ad for the job of office boy with the Retail Credit Company. I got the
job—filing and cross-filing. I was just learning the system when Foley
called me to ask if I would play the lead in George Kaufman's and
Marc Connelly's "Merton of the Movies"—the part Glenn Hunter had
played on Broadway. I said yes, but when I came home with the news,
I was greeted by ice. Dad said it wasn't a good idea to quit my Retail
Credit job. However, I was twenty-one and stubborn, and I said I was
going to leave home, if necessary. My mother tried to straighten things
out diplomatically, but Dad wouldn't speak to me for a month. The
upshot was I did both; I went to work at Retail Credit at seven in the
morning and rehearsed for the play at night and on Sundays. On opening night, I got my first feeling of what acting was all about. I liked the
whole idea of getting up there and being Merton. I was given an ova-
tion. When I got home, Dad was sitting in the living room behind his
newspaper, and one of my sisters was starting to criticize my performance when, from behind the newspaper, Dad said, "Shut up. He was
perfect." One of the reviews of the play said, "Who needs Glenn
Hunter? We have Henry." I played Merton for one wonderful week.

I might easily have become a credit manager in Omaha and done
community theatre for kicks, but then, in the spring of 1927, I suddenly had an offer to spend a week in New York seeing all the shows,
as a present from the mother of a local Princeton boy. I was supposed
to pick him up and drive him home for Easter. When I told the
manager of the credit office, he was shocked. He had big plans to send
me to the home office in Atlanta for managerial training. But I made

the trip to New York, and saw nine plays in six days, including "The Constant Wife," with Ethel Barrymore. I loved every minute. When I got back from New York, Foley offered me a job at the Playhouse as assistant director, at a salary of five hundred dollars, for the next season. It seemed fine to me. I did a lot of things, including acting and designing scenery. Ever since kindergarten, I'd been able to draw. My main acting assignment was to play opposite Do Brando in Eugene O'Neill's "Beyond the Horizon." I was living at home, and I was beginning to think there was such a thing as making a living in the theatre. By the end of the season, I knew I wanted to go to New York.

For three months in the summer of 1927, I did some one-night stands throughout Iowa and Illinois promoting a new movie about Abraham Lincoln; I had written a sketch for an actor named George Billings, who hired me to assist him in his act, which consisted of his doing an impersonation of Lincoln while the orchestra played "Hearts and Flowers." Then I went back to the Playhouse. In June, 1928, a friend of the family drove me to Cape Cod, where I wanted to get a job with the Provincetown Players. I was apple-cheeked, and I looked like a farm boy. I had about a hundred dollars saved up. I walked into the theatre, was told they had nothing, and walked out. I took the train over to Dennis and, in the middle of the afternoon, walked into the Cape Playhouse, where the company was rehearsing. I stood around, too scared to ask anybody anything, and then I went to a nearby boarding house to arrange to spend the night. It turned out that all the company were staying there—Laura Hope Crews, Peggy Wood, Minor Watson, Romney Brent. I told them my name, and they were all very kind, all terribly nice people. It didn't occur to me to ask if I could join the company, but there must have been something in my face, because they asked me if I'd like to stick around, as third assistant stage manager, at no salary. I stayed. They gave me a bit part in Kenyon Nicholson's "The Barker," and I was as unprofessional as possible— stood in a corner learning my lines while the others were rehearsing. The mark of an amateur. I was a really naïve guy. Then the actor who was going to play the juvenile lead dropped out, and the part was given to me. A friend of mine came to see me in the play, and he invited me to drive with him to Falmouth, where a group he knew called the University Players Guild had just founded a summer theatre, with John Swope, Bretaigne Windust, Joshua Logan, Charles Leatherbee, and Kent Smith. All of us loved each other at first blush. Margaret Sullavan came to Falmouth in the second year, and Jimmy Stewart in the third. I moved to Falmouth, and in the next four summers I was in about twenty plays. Everybody did everything—box-office work, ushering, painting scenery. The first summer, I had my first lead, in "Is Zat So?" I felt I was now in the world of the theatre. I was committed to it.

At the end of that summer, everybody else went back to college, and I went to New York. I was excited. I was nothing but optimistic. I hardly had anything to eat for weeks. It never occurred to me to be discouraged. I wasn't terribly smart. If I'd been smart, I would have given up and gone home. Bretaigne Windust had told me, "Let's face it, Hank. You're a scenic designer." But I wanted to be an actor. I was making myself a little dizzy. I was damn sure I was a good actor, and sure that eventually I was going to prove it. My first season in New York, I became the best-known unknown actor in town. All the offices knew me. All the agents knew me. I lived on 114th Street in a ten-dollar-a-week room. I joined Equity. I learned that Equity listed all plays in production on its bulletin board. I didn't present myself well to producers, but I knew I was good. I had learned I was good when I played Merton in Omaha. Thirty-five years later, I can still remember the way I felt as Merton. There was a kind of breathless feeling I couldn't ever recapture. It was like being ten years old and playing cops and robbers.

Practically everything that has ever happened to me has been the result of coincidence. It's been a matter of getting the lucky break, of being in the right place at the right time. For the next few years, I took odd jobs, such as doing plays for children, including plays of Shakespeare's that I not only hadn't ever acted in before but hadn't even read. I had a walk-on part in "The Game of Love and Death," a Theatre Guild production about the French Revolution. On Christmas Day, 1931, during a winter season I spent with the University Players Guild in Baltimore, I was married to Margaret Sullavan. It was a first marriage for both of us, and it didn't last long. She was established, and I had to find a job. I went back to Omaha in the spring of 1932 and played at the Community Playhouse in "A Kiss for Cinderella," in which Dorothy McGuire, then fourteen, played Cinderella. I worked as a backstage helper with the Surrey Theatre, in

Maine, in the summer of 1932. I moved actors' trunks, and so on, until the scenic designer quit halfway through the season. Then I became the scenic designer. In the summer of 1933, I designed scenery for the Westchester Players, in Mount Kisco, and played some parts. Any summer theatre would have hired me as a scenic designer. In the spring of 1934, I was in Leonard Sillman's "New Faces," on Broadway, in which I did comedy skits with Imogene Coca. Leland Hayward, an old friend, saw me in that show, and he became my manager-agent. That summer, I went back to the Westchester Players as the star, in leading parts. I knew then that the door was going to open. I could smell it coming. The graph had been in that direction. Leland Hayward wired me to come to Hollywood, but I wasn't interested. The theatre was my first love. It was. It is. But I went out anyway, and when Leland asked me to sign up with Walter Wanger, I asked for what I thought was the impossible amount of a thousand dollars a week. But Wanger said yes, so I signed a contract to do two pictures a year, with provisions for my going back to the legitimate theatre, and the next day went right back to Mount Kisco. June Walker, who had seen me as the tutor in Molnar's "The Swan," at Mount Kisco, told Marc Connelly to get hold of me for a new play he had written with Frank B. Elser, "The Farmer Takes a Wife." Connelly borrowed me for it from Wanger. I did it first as a play and then as a movie.

It was easy to make the transition to movies. I started to act in the film version of "The Farmer Takes a Wife" the way I always did for a play, and Victor Fleming, the director, told me I was mugging. And that's all it took. I just pulled it down to reality. You don't project anything for movies. You do it as you would in your own home. Because of all the experience back of me in the same part, it didn't bother me to work out of continuity, the way you do in making a movie. Of course, there's very little personal satisfaction in doing those bits and pieces for a movie. You don't really have any recollection of having created a role. But in the beginning the money made it pretty attractive. After doing "The Farmer Takes a Wife," I made two movies for Wanger—"The Trail of the Lonesome Pine," with Sylvia Sidney, and "The Moon's Our Home," with Margaret Sullavan. I wanted to get my feet back on the boards, but I wasn't getting any plays submitted to me, and I kept making more movies, including "Jezebel," with Bette Davis, "Jesse James," with Tyrone Power, and "Young

Mr. Lincoln," in which I played the title role. One movie I was eager to do was "The Grapes of Wrath"—the part of Tom Joad—and I had to sign a seven-year contract with Fox to get the part. I regretted it, but signed. Then I couldn't get out of the contract. I made all kinds of movies I hated. My gorge rises when I remember them. I did make a few I liked, though, including "The Lady Eve" and "The Male Animal," on loan-out. After "The Grapes of Wrath," I made "The Ox-Bow Incident," but it took long sessions of violent argument with Darryl Zanuck to get him to allow me to do it. In 1956, I acted in "12 Angry Men," which I co-produced with Reginald Rose, and which won many awards. I'm prouder of that than of almost anything else I've done in my career.

In 1942, I was thirty-seven. I enlisted in the Navy and served as quartermaster third class on a destroyer in the Pacific. Later, the executive officer on the destroyer recommended me for a commission; I was flown to 90 Church Street and discharged, was then immediately commissioned as a lieutenant (j.g.), and joined Air Combat Intelligence. At that time, I wasn't eager to go back to movies, but after the war I did go back. I made a John Ford picture, "My Darling Clementine," and other pictures, and then I went into Thomas Heggen's and Joshua Logan's "Mister Roberts" on Broadway. I'd never been in a long run before, except for a hundred and four performances in "The Farmer Takes a Wife." "Mister Roberts" was a love story backstage. We were all just crazy about the play. If anybody let down, he had thirty other guys on him. It really was like being in love. You had this good feeling in the guts practically all the time. I love to act, and in this play I always knew everything I was going to do but could make it look like not acting at all. It was so wonderful acting with a guy like Robert Keith, who played Doc. Being on the stage with this man was the most fun I've ever had. I'd still be in my dressing room waiting to go onstage and I could feel the hackles rising in anticipation, the skin tingling. One of my joys was for Josh Logan, who had directed the play, to come to a performance and say, "Fonda, you son of a bitch!" To have him recognize the way the part got better all the time. It never got static. The pitfall you get into in most long runs is you stop listening. It's a subtle thing. It never happened in "Mister Roberts." The thing I try to do onstage is to create the illusion that it's happening for the first time. In two years, not a performance got by of all the performances we did that the audience didn't get what it came for; for them it was happening for the first time. I never got tired of it.

I'm suspicious of anything that happens too fast or too soon. When you have the part you are playing under control, it seems to be effortless, but it's not. I baby up on a part. I get the feeling gradually. I learn the lines gradually. You feel your way in every instance. You find your way onstage. You get closer to your lines, then begin to find ways of doing them. I always know when it feels real to me. My daughter Jane and my son Pete both have stage presence. You're not aware that you've got it. It's just the magic thing the audience can see when the actor walks out on the stage. There are a lot of actors who have *only* presence. If you've got it, you thank your lucky stars, because you don't have to work so hard. It's wonderful to know you can get your audience just by walking out on the stage, because of your good voice, other physical things, and a lot more that are absolutely intangible. But in addition to having stage presence you have to know what you are doing. I was surprised and delighted when I found that my children knew. In fact, I was absolutely floored. Recently, Jane told me that something had happened to her in a play she was in. She said, "Dad, I felt that my real emotion had taken over." When my emotions take over in a part, it's like a seaplane taking off on the water. I feel as if I were soaring. If five times out of eight a week the emotions take over, you've got the magic. But you hold it back just enough. It's just like holding a horse back. It's got to be thought out, and you've got to listen to the others, or you start blubbering all over the place. Normally, when I start working on a play, by the second week I don't have the script in my hand any more and I can feel the character coming to life. I get frantic when it's not happening, because it means to me that the words, the scenes are not right. When it's difficult, it's awful. When it begins to be less difficult, I begin to find the blood, the breath of the part and I'm less myself.

The theatre is where I really get my kicks. When you make a movie, and people say you're great, you like to hear them say it, but you don't have the feeling you've lived your character or built your emotions one on top of another. In movies, you hit emotion maybe once in a scene. Live television is like the theatre. You're on and you're committed to it, the way you are on the stage. Film television is like movies. You do television movies to make a buck and save a buck. I was damn lucky I became an actor. Theatre is the only thing I understand. I can't really talk about anything else. In company, I don't have small talk. It's pretty silly to begin with, and I don't know how to do it at all. When you've exhausted the weather, and where you've been, and where they've been, you're stuck. When I get stuck, I feel everybody is looking at me and I want to hide. I like to be the observer.

I've had practical problems to face as an actor. On the practical side, I recently appeared in a television series called "The Deputy," which is now bringing me an income from reruns. My first reaction was to resist it, because I still feel I have a future and I didn't want to be identified with one character. But we found a way for me to limit my appearances in the weekly films; in some of them I appeared in just one scene. I did the series because the show is something I produced and partly own. If I didn't do things like that, I wouldn't be able to live the way I do—raise a family, put the children through college, dress well, have a town house in New York, have a villa on the Riviera, go to Cape Cod, travel when I feel like it, and do a play once a year. This is what being an actor has given me, and I say, Thank God that's what I am. But what I get out of acting is worth more than any money. I'm happiest and most relaxed when I'm on-stage. I look forward to it. It's terribly important to me to be good. When strangers come up to me, wherever I am, and say, "Mr. Fonda, I hope you don't mind, but thank you," I am very pleased. They're not just fans who want to say they've seen a movie star. They have had pleasure, and you've given it to them.

JANE FONDA

What I like even more than the acting itself is just being in the theatre, especially during rehearsals, as a member of a group working together, in the same place, for the same goal, under one spotlight surrounded by darkness, like a family in the living room.

I was born on December 21, 1937, in New York City, and was taken at the age of a few weeks to Hollywood, where my father, Henry Fonda, had been persuaded by Twentieth Century-Fox, his movie studio, to make his home for a while. I have a brother, Peter, two years younger than I am, who left the University of Omaha in 1960, his junior year, to act in a comedy on Broadway, then got married and went out to Hollywood on a movie contract. I have a half sister, Frances, six years older than I am, who is a painter and lives in Rome, and an adopted sister, Amy, sixteen years younger than I am. Amy was adopted by my father and Susan Blanchard, his third wife. My mother, Frances Seymour Fonda, who was my father's second wife, died when I was twelve. She was the eldest of seven children, and was a great beauty, and had a great head for finance. Before marrying my father, she was married to George Tuttle Brokaw, a lawyer and sportsman who came of a famous New York family. Even though I was never close to her, I know how loving and generous she was. If you lose your mother before you're old enough to get close to her, you almost never understand her as an individual in her own right, and that's what happened with me. As children, Peter and I lived on a twenty-four-acre farm in Brentwood. It was quite isolated around there, and Pete was my main companion. We had three dogs and a cat, and a lot of chickens, and some rabbits—who were my best friends for a while—and we had flower and vegetable gardens. I loved my job, which was to collect the newly laid eggs. Our house was unusual around there; it was a sort of New England setup transplanted to California. My father did everything possible to make it look like a genuine old New England house; it had shingles made to look weather-beaten, and a lot of Early American furnishings—cobblers' benches, braided rugs, lamps made from butter churns. We had a large dinner bell on our roof that could be heard for a mile around. We had a swimming pool, but my father disguised it to look like a pond. My father loved the farm and often plowed the fields himself. We had two mules, and Pete and I would go out in the hills on them and explore. There were bobcats, coyotes, and rattlesnakes in the hills; one of the things I learned at school—the Brentwood Town and Country School—was how to treat rattlesnake bites. In the hills, Peter and I played big roles in our own kind of Westerns, living the way we thought our father lived in the movies we'd see him in. I was scared to death when I saw my father in John Ford's "Drums Along the Mohawk." For two days, in the movie, my father ran from one fort to another as a settler, and then there was a big life-and-death battle, with the Indians massacring the whites, but the whites finally winning. It was the longest movie of my life, as I waited for my father and the whites to win. Peter and I saw "Fort Apache" when we were in our teens; in that one my father was the bad man and got killed. Recently, in a Hollywood theatre, I saw two of my father's old movies— "Jezebel," with Bette Davis, and "The Lady Eve," with Barbara Stanwyck—both of which he made shortly after I was born. At home, my father always wore levis and work clothes that made him look like a cowboy, and Pete and I would try to copy him in every respect. My father would bring his Hollywood friends in—John Wayne, Ward Bond, and John Ford—who dressed the same way, and they would sit around the house playing cards and talking like cowboys.

I don't remember owning a dress until I was about eight. I was always in blue jeans, day in and day out, and my hair was cut short. I'd sit on the roof of our house with Pete and I'd say, "Tell me the truth, Pete. Which one of us could lasso a buffalo better?" I didn't

have much to do with my half sister Frances. I didn't understand her.
I'd sometimes watch her through a window when she gave what I
thought were wild parties. She got married very young—she has
since been divorced—and after that I hardly saw her. Every once in a
while, I'd be taken to a birthday party given for one of Joan Crawford's children. I was abashed to learn how different their life was
from ours. Joan Crawford's little girl and her friends wore pretty,
frilly dresses and knew what to do with their hands and how to be
polite and how to stand and how to walk and how to talk. At those
parties, I usually ended up by crying, and our nurse would have to
take me home early. What I liked best as a child was horses. I
started riding when I was five. I used to spend a lot of time hanging
around riding stables near our house. When I was ten, my father left
for New York to appear on Broadway in "Mister Roberts." Six months
later, the whole family moved to Greenwich, Connecticut. I went to
Greenwich Academy for three and a half years. At first, I lived with my
maternal grandmother in a house in Greenwich my mother had rented
before she died, and later the same year I lived with my mother's
sister and her husband, who also had a house in Greenwich. They had
no children of their own. When I was fourteen, my father was staying
at Oscar Hammerstein's town house in New York, so I stayed there, too.
If you have glamorous parents, you just have to live a special way. I
loved New York, but I didn't have any friends here. I felt sort of special
living my way, but I rather envied girls with what looked like normal
family lives, and I often pretended to my classmates that my life was
like theirs. Four months after my father married Susan Blanchard, Mr.
Hammerstein's stepdaughter, in December, 1950, I went to live with
them. I was very fond of Susan, and it felt almost like having a whole
family again. The following summer, my father was making the
movie version of "Mister Roberts" in California and Hawaii, and I
went along; part of the time we stayed in a hotel at Waikiki Beach.

Between the ages of thirteen and seventeen, I attended the Emma
Willard School, in Troy, New York—a boarding school. I was potentially a good student, but I was always getting into trouble of some
kind. In my first year, my best friends were the white mice we used
in biology class, and on my first vacation home—my father was making
a movie in Hollywood, and since he had sold the farm, we stayed in
the old Marion Davies mansion, which had been turned into a hotel

—I brought the white mice with me and let them escape in the back yard. I got into all kinds of scrapes at school, and depended on the Fonda name to get me out of them. Once, I poured lighter fluid down the hall from my room to the room of a girl I didn't like, and set fire to it, knowing it would burn itself out before it did any real damage, but at the same time would leave no doubt that I didn't like that girl. In my second year at school, I joined the drama class. I acted in a few school plays and gave some readings during the next three years. I loved doing it. I wasn't self-conscious yet, and I didn't know what it meant to develop a character. I liked my costumes, and putting on the makeup, and getting all that attention. I would always go up in my lines. It was a bit of a romp. It had nothing to do with acting. My very first part at Emma Willard was the male lead in the Christopher Fry play "Boy with a Cart," put on as a Thanksgiving Day special in chapel. All I remember about it was wearing green tights, a green burlap-sack blouse, and a green hat with a feather in it. I also played Lydia Languish in "The Rivals." Acting was better than studying math, and that was all it really meant to me. I was supposed to be learning the feminine graces—how to walk, what to do with my hands, and so on—but it was all puzzling to me. People always said I was a fine, healthy girl, and called me a mature child. So helpful, they said, and so understanding. I wasn't a mature child at all. At home, I never showed anything I felt. I kept a poker face, and that made people conclude that I was mature. We were not a demonstrative family. I grew up not knowing how to show hatred, anger, or grudges. I just stored it all up. It was a great disadvantage to me as an actress, I discovered later on. There was an exception, though. Around the stables, I'd get into fights with the stable boys. I'd usually start the fights with the boys. I'd kick them and hit them. My arm was broken once in a fight with a boy. I also broke an arm in a fall from a horse. Another time, I broke my wrist while I was roller-skating in a hall at home. I was always banging myself up. I'd seen so many of my father's movies where he was a hero and beat people up that I got the idea that I had to do it, too. Physical prowess was what counted. When I was nine, I had my first crush on a boy. At first, he didn't notice me, and that was fine, because I could just melt into the background and watch him. But one day he asked me to go to a dance with him. My answer was to hit him as hard as I could. I just never got the idea of how people were supposed to behave with each other.

The summer after I graduated from Emma Willard, I lived with my father in Rome while he made "War and Peace." We lived on an estate outside the city, and I had nothing to do except eat figs and get fat and watch Gina Lollobrigida, a neighbor, through binoculars. Then I went to Vassar College. I stayed two years, trying to study French and the history of music, among other liberal-arts subjects, and just got by. I didn't like it. I kept thinking how expensive it was and how someone else ought to be in my place, getting some benefit out of the school. I had a few friends at Vassar—not very close, except for Leland Hayward's and Margaret Sullavan's daughter, Brooke, who was considered very beautiful and very talented and was expected to become an actress. She had been a lifelong friend. I never went to dances, because I considered it square to go to school dances. And I never had dates. I considered myself ugly. The college put on the Lorca play "Amor de Don Perlimplin con Belisa en su Jardin," and I played the lead, a young Spanish girl who stood in a window and sang songs, and cuckolded her husband. I knew almost nothing about the motivations of the character I played. By then, I was self-conscious enough to look for things in the character, but I didn't know how. There was nothing behind the emotions I showed. I didn't know how to show that the emotions came from something and that the words had meaning. I really hadn't decided to become an actress at that point. I even thought that I didn't *want* to be an actress. What I wanted was to get out of Vassar. When I was in my second year, I told my father that I wanted to get out of the United States, that I wanted to go to Paris and study painting. Ever since my finger-painting days in kindergarten, I'd been rather good at it. I'd done quite a bit of it—always still-lifes. After my second year at Vassar, I went to Paris, and lived with a French family. I enrolled in two schools—the Académie Grande Chaumière et Colorassi and the Académie Julian. I went in with my canvases and paints, and then began to feel very lost. I didn't know anyone at either school and couldn't understand French and thought everyone was watching my clumsy efforts to paint. I still go in for some of that nonsense; when I go to ballet school, for instance, I feel that everyone is watching me. In Paris, I gradually spent less and less time in art class and more and more time on the Left Bank, hanging around little bars and antique shops and the Flea Market. I was supposed to stay a year. After a month, I was sleeping more and studying less. That Christmas, I came home to spend the holidays with my father, and he persuaded me to stay home. He wasn't fooled. He knew pretty much how it was for me in Paris.

Back in New York, I began to study French and Italian at the Berlitz School. I lived with my father and his fourth wife, Afdera Franchetti, in their town house, on East Seventy-fourth Street. Next door was the Mannes College of Music. From my bedroom I could hear the students practicing. I decided to study piano there, and took lessons for a few months. But it was too frustrating. I wanted to jump in and start playing concertos, instead of studying scales. I kept on with painting lessons, at the Art Students League, but painting became steadily less enjoyable and more difficult to do. I thought people who looked at what I painted expected something of me that I couldn't live up to. As soon as I finished a canvas, I'd be hyper-critical of it. I thought about becoming an actress. That was what I wanted to do more than anything else, so I spent a lot of time figuring out reasons I *didn't* want to act—it was selfish and egotistical, it gave no enjoyment, I wasn't pretty enough, and so on. Once, when Brooke Hayward and I were riding in a car with David Selznick, he told Brooke that she had star quality, that she was beautiful, glamorous—everything I thought I wasn't. All I felt was awkward. But I longed to act. I would think about it and tremble. I knew I'd have to please so many people—fellow-actors, authors, directors, producers, and critics—whereas in painting I was my own master. When, years later, I finally committed myself to acting, I never again picked up a paint brush or felt the need to.

My father had nothing to do directly with my wanting to act. Something must have rubbed off, though—a temperament, a need for the theatre. I really admired my father's acting. He's never bad, no matter what he's playing in. My favorite movie of his is "The Grapes of Wrath," which he made when I was two years old. It was beautifully written and directed, and deals with a subject that was important to my father. He believed in it socially and politically. He was Tom Joad, and he loved that character, and it shows, and that's why I like it the best of all his movies. When I was sixteen, I appeared with him in "The Country Girl" in a summer benefit in Omaha. I had about five small scenes, in the part of the ingénue and my real father's granddaughter, in the play within the play. I was supposed to act very tremulous. For preparation, I asked a stage-hand to shake me up and push me out onstage. At another point, I was onstage with Dorothy McGuire, who was playing my father's wife in the play, and I was supposed to be upset, so I tried to pretend to myself that my father was dead. I didn't really know what I was doing. I had no awareness of the other players, and I didn't like the experience. After my first year at Vassar, my father played in "The Male Animal" at the Cape Playhouse, in Dennis, and I played a small part with him—the young sister of the English professor's wife. I did it because I had nothing else to do. And I kept wondering what people would think of me. I wasn't able to forget that the only reason I was in the play was that Henry Fonda was my father.

In the late summer of 1958 came the turning point in my life. That's when I met Lee Strasberg. I'd gone out to Hollywood to be with my father while he made a movie. I was feeling sort of desperate. I was almost twenty-one. I knew that at the end of the summer I'd have to come back to New York with my father. I still didn't have anything definite to do. None of the things I'd tried to do really satisfied me. I had become friendly with Susan Strasberg, and one day she introduced me to her father. He was out there with his wife, Paula, who was coaching Marilyn Monroe in "Some Like It Hot." I told Lee I was interested in acting, and after talking with me he agreed to accept me as a student in his acting classes. For the first time in my life, I felt I was talking with someone who didn't feel he *had* to be nice to me because of my father. He was the only person I'd ever known who was interested in me without having to be. I told him I had exhausted all the things I'd *thought* I wanted to be. He didn't ask me to read for him. He just asked me questions. Why was I interested in the theatre? What did I expect from the theatre? Who was my favorite actress? And so on. At the time, my favorite actress happened to be Geraldine Page, because I couldn't forget her performance in "Mid-Summer." As soon as I came back to New York, three weeks later, I set about becoming independent. With a roommate, Susan Stein, I moved into a small apartment a block from my father's house, and I started modelling. I'd done one fashion layout for *Town &*

Country earlier that year, so I was able to register with an agency and start getting modelling assignments. I was a success as a model, which surprised me, because I'd always thought that I had a bad figure, that I was too fat, that my hair was wrong, that I was clumsy. I would compare myself with other models, who seemed so willowy and graceful, and not at all like me. But there must have been something about the way I photographed that caught on. I was paid fifty dollars an hour, only ten dollars short of the top fee. I kept thinking that anyone who didn't look like Suzy Parker might as well give up, but apparently I came along at a time when they were beginning to use more natural-looking models. In July, 1959, my photograph, by Irving Penn, appeared on the cover of *Vogue;* I was wearing a gold linen sheath. I used to hang around the newsstands watching the faces of the people who bought the magazine. I thought I looked pretty but not really beautiful. In January, 1960, in my second *Vogue* cover, also by Penn, I was shown wearing a blue silk dress. I have had pictures on six magazine covers since I began modelling.

In October, 1958, I started classes with Lee Strasberg. Before that, everything I'd done had seemed wrong. Now I knew I'd never be satisfied doing anything but acting. Lee's classes, which are separate from the Actors' Studio, are held above the Capitol Theatre. He takes students who are of interest to him, and he doesn't care what anybody else says or thinks about it. Once he's picked people who are of interest to him, he tries to find out who they are. He brings out what is in you. He shows you how to use yourself, and not something borrowed from someone else. The classes are a groundwork for acting, like grammar for English. He told me I had too much of a façade and that it would greatly limit me in acting if I held on to it. The first time he met me, he said, he couldn't tell anything about me except that I had a certain look in my eyes. Lee somehow imparts dignity and gives you confidence in yourself. With Lee, I learned that every need has a counter-need. I also learned that somewhere inside you is an experience similar to the one you are playing. For example, if you play a murderer, you don't have to have had the experience of actually murdering someone, because somewhere inside yourself you will find some relevant experience. In one of my recent movies, "The Chapman Report," I play a frigid woman, a widow. To do it, I don't have to be like that woman. Instead, I call on what every woman has

99

felt at some time in her life—doubts about herself. This feeling is enough to give me insight into the way that woman feels. In January, 1961, I did my first audition for the Actors' Studio. After my final audition, I plan to work there as much as I can.

When I'd been studying with Lee for six months, I went out to Hollywood to make my first movie, "Tall Story," with Anthony Perkins, which was produced and directed by Joshua Logan. Just before I left New York, I got a chance to play the ingénue in "The Moon Is Blue," with Harold Lang, for two weeks at the Fort Lee Playhouse, in New Jersey. I jumped at it. This time I was on my own, and it felt pretty good. After that taste, I knew I'd be out looking for parts. "Tall Story" is about a tall girl who goes to college to find a husband and chooses a school with a championship basketball team. A subplot has to do with the bribing of team members. I found it all very strange. I felt alone, surrounded by lights. I didn't question Josh. I'd known him all my life, and I thought that if he believed I could do it, I could. But the role itself didn't mean very much to me. I just came to the set whenever I was called. Three years later, I was walking along Forty-second Street and saw the words "Tall Story" in lights, with my name, on a movie marquee, and I felt proud. When the movie was finished, Josh told me he was going to direct the Broadway production of Daniel Taradash's "There Was a Little Girl," and asked me if I wanted to play the lead in it. I was enthusiastic, and said yes. My father thought the play and the part weren't right for me; it was about rape, and I was to play the girl who was raped. I think he wanted to protect me from what he thought might be a disaster. But I thought, Who am I to turn down such a part—the leading role in a Broadway play? I knew that practically every young actress in New York had auditioned for the part, and after I had read for it ten or fifteen times, the director and the producers wanted me. Three days before I accepted the part, my father called me up and begged me to turn it down. But I didn't. I went into the play with a complete lack of fear. I loved the rehearsals. I loved working with Josh Logan. I loved working with a group, and I began to see for the first time that when a group work together with real love, art happens. I savored every morsel. It was like belonging to a family. I was doing exactly what I wanted to be doing. I enjoyed making myself fit the part, making myself frail as a woman, and vulnerable, and weak. I had always thought of myself as strong and independent, a self-sufficient type, in blue jeans, and I enjoyed playing a dependent-girl role. Before that, in my real life, I used to sit and wonder just what it was that other people did and what there was to do. Now I began to have some idea of what there was to do, and what I had been missing. I loved the routine of acting in a play every night. I had had so little responsibility in my life that I loved having demands made on me—to be someplace at a definite hour, with something definite to do. I began to feel a connection with myself. I felt accepted. Everything I do now leads up to and goes into my acting. For my second Broadway play, "Invitation to a March," in October, 1960, I'd get to the theatre a good two and a half hours before the other members of the cast.

Everything is best for me when I'm onstage. That's when I come alive. Everything seems so much fuller when I can discover something I can add to a part I play. I do it all for myself. I care about the audience, but I don't act for it. I used to think how nice it would be if I could do all my acting as readings, on a bare stage, alone, under a hard light. But I act for myself first in order to act for others. I started out acting for myself in "Invitation to a March." The part of Norma Brown was the story of me—of a conventional girl, a sleeping beauty who is awakened to love by the kiss of a boy. I knew just what I wanted to do with the role, but other people had other ideas, and I think we lost the human reality of the girl. When the play opened, I was acting for others. I was doing what they thought the audience wanted me to do, rather than what I wanted to do, so I came out like a thin, slick, Ginger Rogers ingénue. I wanted the humor to come from the conflict in the girl, her struggle with herself, but instead I had to do a funny painted poster of a girl. Anyway, I went on doing what others wanted me to do. Finally, what I came to like about the play was going to the theatre and just knowing what I would be doing day after day. I had a sense of belonging. It didn't matter to me in the least how many people came to see the play. Often it felt better when we had a small house. I had so little experience and knew so little about the technique of how to sustain a performance, and after the play opened, I lost what little I had had when I believed in the part. I might have sustained my performance if I had been able to hold to what I originally felt about the part. My father, however, thought all along that the play was marvellous. One thing I did like about the play was not having to carry the main responsibility of it. I enjoyed the opportunity of working with two fine actresses, Eileen Heckart and Madeleine Sherwood. I learned that they were able to sustain their performances whether the audience was or wasn't responding, and laughing at the expected times. They could play to a full house or to a small house. At first, I used to wonder at the way they did it, and then I found that I was able to do it myself. In the beginning, when I first went out onstage I always felt like apologizing to the audience. I suppose I felt unworthy to appear before it. If I sensed resentment on the part of anybody in the audience, I'd start to fade out. For a long time, I felt I had to know who was in the audience. Sometimes I'd go up to the balcony to look at the faces and guess how they were going to respond to me. If I saw mean faces, I'd feel terrible.

I'd like someday to be as good an actress as Geraldine Page or Kim Stanley. The better I get as an actress, the freer I feel. Actresses have to exhibit themselves, to hang themselves up on a clothesline. Onstage, you often find that you're free to do what you can't do in real life. When I first read a script, I wonder about the kind of person my character is. I don't think very much about the others in the cast. I get the smell of the character I'm going to play. I try to establish rapport with her. The first time I read "Invitation to a March," I was so moved that I laughed and cried. I knew just what I wanted to do with the role. The girl was like me, in that she tried to reconcile her strong emotions and what she knew was possible in the world with what she'd been told she could expect in life. I loved the idea of doing that. In my own life, I was brought up to be well-mannered, no matter where I was or what I was doing. At parties, even today, I work at being charming, though I may not feel in the least like being charming. I show an interest in people I'm not the least bit interested in. Onstage, I found, I didn't have to do anything of that kind. Playing a role, I was free to reveal exactly what I felt.

SIDNEY POITIER

*When I experience a moment of total communication
between me and the audience, I feel, Well, maybe
they do accept me as an actor.*

I was born on February 20, 1924, in Miami, Florida. I was the
youngest of eight children, but now there are only six of us; my sister
Teddy died several years ago, and my brother Cedric, who was a
waiter in Nassau, died in 1961, leaving six children of his own. My
father also died in 1961, in a little house in Nassau that I'd got for
him and my mother a few years before. To my parents, what started
happening to me after I left home was all very strange. I was still
their baby—so much so, I'm afraid, that it was sickening. They'd see
me in movies, and they'd wonder what on earth I was doing there.
Most of the time, I've felt exactly the way they did. My eldest brother,
Cyril, is forty-six and does odd jobs in Miami. He has twelve children.
The other children are Ruby, a housewife in Miami; Redis, a waiter
in Nassau; Reginald, a maître d' at the British Colonial Hotel, in
Nassau; and Carl, a waiter in Nassau. When I was three months old,
my family moved to Cat Island, in the Bahamas, where my father
worked as a tomato farmer. We stayed on Cat Island until I was eleven,

and then we moved to Nassau. I could swim when I was three. I could climb trees as well as Tarzan himself. There were no automobiles on Cat Island, which is about fifty miles long and averages ten miles wide, and there was nothing to get in my way. I had freedom. I was never watched. From the time I could walk, I had complete freedom to learn by trial and error. When I was three, I would go out and be alone on the island all day. I had my own imagination as a companion. I'd imagine I was a big fisherman going after big fish, or I was a farmer working in the fields. When I was five, I once walked across the island, all by myself, which would be like walking from Brooklyn to the Bronx. I got to the middle of the island, and there wasn't a human sound—only birds and little insects. Finally, I came to the other side of the island, and I played out there for half a day, all alone, hunting turtle eggs. My mother used to cook the turtle eggs I brought her. Our kitchen was outside, with an open grill. Our house was stone and had a thatched palm-leaf roof—very primitive. When I got home after being out on the island all day, nobody ever noticed. My mother just said, "Sit down and eat your dinner."

In Nassau, I went to school for a year and a half, then quit to work at odd jobs, to help support the family. My father was unable to work, because of arthritis and rheumatism. I was always hungry as a kid. To this day, between huge meals, I'm hungry, and I fill in with Mars bars, Snickers, Oh Henrys, and Life Savers. So far, I've never been to a dentist. When I was fifteen, I was sent to Miami to live with my brother Cyril. I felt I wasn't wanted there, so before very long I set off for New York City. It took me three and a half months to get here. I rode a freight train, then walked, and then worked in the kitchen of a summer-resort hotel in the mountains in Georgia, where I saved up thirty-nine dollars—enough to take a bus the rest of the way. I arrived early one morning, with a dollar and a half and no clothes except what I had on—a shirt and blue jeans—and one extra shirt. I took the subway to Harlem, and then came downtown that same afternoon, walked down Broadway from Fiftieth to Forty-second Street, and spent all the rest of my money on hot dogs and malted milks. That night, I got a job at the Turf Restaurant, as a dishwasher, for four dollars and eleven cents a night. For the next few months, until I had saved enough money to buy myself a coat and a suit, I slept either in Penn Station or in the Greyhound Bus Terminal that opens off it or on the roof of a building on Fifty-first Street, across from the Capitol Theatre. Soon after Pearl Harbor, I enlisted in the Army. I was trained to be a physiotherapist, and I served with the 1267th Medical Detachment, stationed at the Northport, Long Island, Veterans Hospital, which was a mental institution. I was discharged in December of 1944. In the Army, I was very rebellious. I was always restless, and the restlessness manifested itself in a violent thrashing about—something I still have as a carry-over today. The minute I have to do something and I don't want to do something, I become rebellious. It was a strange period for me. I couldn't read as well as I wanted to. To me, words were terrible. I was unable to learn them from the dictionary; I had to hear new words, or read them in a cluster of old words, so that I could figure out their meanings in relation to the words I did understand. I used to read anything I could get my hands on—newspapers, magazines, Army manuals. The other guys used to make fun of my West Indian accent, but I could always take that kind of ribbing. I had the qualities of a regular guy, even though I was never admitted into the inner circle.

After getting out of the Army, I continued to read the newspapers, not only to help myself learn words but to follow the want ads. The New York *Journal-American* had the best ads for manual laborers, and I learned a lot of new words about industry and the trades from those ads. One day, I read in the *Amsterdam News* that the American Negro Theatre was looking for actors. I was not satisfied with the idea of working with my hands, so I went over to the American Negro Theatre, which was in the basement of the 135th Street branch of the Public Library. It was a small place, with a small, low stage, and it had a capacity of about a hundred. The ad said that they were holding auditions. There were a lot of wooden chairs, unoccupied, in the auditorium, and onstage were the people holding auditions. A giant of a man—Frederick O'Neal, co-manager of the A.N.T., who is now a good friend of mine—was in charge. He told me they were looking for actors for a play called "Walk Hard," adapted by Abram Hill from Lew Zinberg's novel "Walk Hard—Talk Low." He handed me the script, pointed to a place somewhere in the middle, and said "Read." So I started to read. I read it terribly. I was a lean, lanky kid. I had just about my full growth then—six feet two and a half—but I had a baby face, and my voice was sort of high; it has deepened considerably over the years. And in reading I sounded like a West Indian. O'Neal was bugged with me. He said "Forget it." If he had said "Thank you very much. Sorry, but not right now," or something like that, I would have walked out of there and never come back or tried to do anything like that again. But the way he said "Forget it" made me feel as if I had been attacked. I felt chopped down a peg. Don't chop me down a peg, or, if you do, do it for good reasons that you tell me about. I was extremely sensitive then about not being able to rise above working with my hands, so I walked out of there determined to go back and show that man I was not destined to be a laborer all my life. I had to vindicate myself.

I bought a radio and embarked on listening to voices, night after night, for the next six months. It was a cheap little box radio, but it had good reception. Every night, I'd start at the top of the dial and go all the way to the bottom. I was living in a five-dollar-a-week room rented out in someone else's apartment—the way they still do in Harlem—on 118th Street near Morningside Avenue. I'd take my supper, usually a loaf of raisin bread and a bottle of Pepsi-Cola—I never drank milk; I hadn't tasted fresh milk since I was twelve years old—up to my room. I'd lie on my bed and listen to the news, to plays, to commentators—to everything. The point was that I was going to rectify what was wrong with my speech and go back and say "Aha!" and thumb my nose at that man and then walk out and go on and pursue my life. In addition to listening to the radio, I read whatever I could get my hands on—mostly magazines. I went to see my first play, "Anna Lucasta," and was completely taken with how the stage looked—so bright, so pretty, with all those lights. Late in 1945, I went back to the American Negro Theatre. This time, the A.N.T. school auditions were being held from seven to eleven at night, and there were three judges —O'Neal, the director Abram Hill, and the acting teacher Osceola Archer. I wore my only suit—a handsome brown suit—and a yellow shirt and a great big flowery yellow-and-brown tie and brown shoes. I was decked out to beat the band. I sat there listening to other people audition. They knew what plays were, and they read scenes from them. I had come prepared to read a paragraph from a story in *True Confessions*—a girl was talking to her boy friend about her ideas of life and marriage, or something like that. Then they called my name, and my throat went dry. My legs began to buckle. I got up onstage and read, in a shaking voice, my paragraph from *True Confessions*. The judges weren't indulgent. They were cold—cold and exacting. They said, "O.K., now we'll give you an improvisation. You're in a jungle. A sniper shoots at you, and your buddy is killed, and you can't see the sniper, and you crawl along the ground and then get up and say, 'Come and get me.' " So I did my improvisation. I got down on the floor and got my famous brown suit all dusty. Then they said "All right, thank you," and I went home. I didn't know whether I had shown them anything or not. All I knew was that I was on pins and needles. About a week later, I got a postcard from the A.N.T. saying to come in. I hadn't expected it, and I hadn't not expected it. I went in, and they said they'd take me into the school for three months, on a trial basis.

I didn't have much money, but I was able to pay the A.N.T. a few dollars a week, and for the rest of the tuition I did odd jobs and janitor work backstage. During the day, I worked with my hands, washing dishes in a restaurant or pushing a handcart in the garment center, but my mind was always on the A.N.T. At night, I went to A.N.T. drama classes—diction, body movement, and so on. Soon I was hooked. At the end of the three months, they wanted to let me go, because they didn't think I was very good. I begged them to give me an extension, and they did. I was still very inhibited, because of my accent. The more people snickered at the way I talked, the more I withdrew, until a friend of mine in the class helped me to come out of myself. In the fall of 1946, I was hired by the director James Light to play Polydorus in an all-Negro production of "Lysistrata" at the Belasco Theatre. It closed after four performances, but I was a sensation, because I was scared to death, and that was exactly what the part of Polydorus called for. When I got out onstage on opening night and looked into the sea of faces in the audience, I went panicsville. My one thought was, If only I can get out of this. I had twelve lines to say, and I think I managed to get six of them out. I couldn't talk above a whisper. I was shaking all over. Finally, I ran off the stage before I was supposed to. I stopped the show cold. The next morning, while I was trying to get lost, I learned that the notices killed the show but some of them mentioned me, and people were asking about that young actor who played Polydorus. I was offered a job right away, at sixty-five dollars a week, as understudy to all the young actors in a Broadway revival of "Anna Lucasta." I was with the play from 1947 until

1949, and sooner or later I played all kinds of parts in the play, including the male lead for a while on tour.

At that point, I knew that I really liked to act. I was green, I was pretty bad at it, but I knew I was bad, and I knew how much better I could be. I began to have a feeling for what I was doing. My experience was restricted. Whatever natural ability I had was getting me by. But now I had a feeling for acting, and knew that what I needed next was experience. In 1949, I played in my first movie, an Army Signal Corps documentary called "From Whom Cometh My Help." The next year, I made my first Hollywood movie, "No Way Out." Then I was in "Cry, the Beloved Country," "Red Ball Express," "Go, Man, Go," "The Blackboard Jungle," "Edge of the City," "Something of Value," "The Mark of the Hawk," "The Defiant Ones," and "Porgy and Bess." I returned to Broadway in March, 1959, to take the lead in Lorraine Hansberry's play "A Raisin in the Sun." I was married in 1950 to Juanita Hardy, a dancer, whose sister is married to the fighter Archie Moore. We now have four small daughters and own an old house up on a hill, with seven acres of woods, in Pleasantville. There's a lot of room for the kids, and it's quite beautiful. I like the summers there, but I've never been able to negotiate winters around New York. I was born in the sun, and I always feel the cold and the dreariness of winter. But I want to stay near New York, and I tell myself that it's the winters that make the summers so wonderful. When I have to go to Hollywood to make a movie, I'm all right. Actors, like other artists, can live anywhere. Wherever I am, I gather and store up impressions, whether I just stay home and cook and go to bed or visit friends or explore new territory and sample local tastes. An actor can be anywhere.

If I had stayed in the Bahamas, I would probably have become a waiter, like my brothers. I became an actor not for self-expression but for success. To have money. To be recognized on the street. When I thought of what I *wanted* to do, I wanted to rest for three months on a boat, fishing in the Bahamas, just kind of lallygaggin' around, never coming into port except for food and supplies. Without success, that would be impossible. I got no satisfaction from working in a kitchen. I never settled; I was always moving. I wanted to make a better-living. I knew from reading the gossip columns that actors made money. Fortunately, I became an actor early enough to apply what the actor mostly applies—his body. Acting is the only area in which you don't have to have a high-school education or a degree or a special skill. When you are creative, you have to work with the life you are familiar with. The reality I carry into the theatre is the only reality I know. I've always had imagination, but my imagination is part of my reality. When people talk about my talent, I really don't know what they mean. Even if you are gifted with genius, you are only the sum total of your environment. To me, my wherewithal, in addition to my body, is what I simply feel as my freedom. After I got to Nassau, at the age of eleven, I discovered the movies. I used to go all the time. They were mostly Westerns. I used to relive all the movies for the other kids. I played the good guys and the bad guys, all at the same time, and I used to have a spellbound audience. I could do that because I had freedom. I act now with the same freedom.

We can try to intellectualize about the satisfactions of acting. We search the intellect, but that is one of the most dangerous areas to look for anything in. When I listen to people trying to talk about their ideas, I see the intellect straining at its own limits. For the most part, my work in movies, especially over the last few years, has brought me diminishing creative satisfaction. To get pleasure out of being in a movie, I have to work with a director who is able to inspire me. If the director knows more than you know and can find a way to bring out what is in you to be brought out, then you come alive. But if you know in your heart that the director is making a mistake, or maybe that a whole movie is a mistake, it's like going up a dead-end street. You keep looking and hoping for a little opening in the fence where you can slip through, but you never find it. That's what happens when you try to make a film with people who are not essentially film-makers. I have tried to do the best I could with every picture I've been in. But all my experience has taught me that films, to be any good, should be made by film-makers. By Ingmar Bergman, Federico Fellini, Michelangelo Antonioni, Roberto Rossellini, John Huston, Stanley Kramer, Billy Wilder, William Wyler—not all necessarily in the same class but all film-makers. A film-maker is somebody who is able to exercise complete authority over the film he is making.

I went back to Hollywood in the summer of 1959 and made an innocuous, pointless film for Columbia Pictures called "All the Young Men." It had no rhyme or reason. It was a waste of time. I played a Marine sergeant who took command of his unit in a perilous situation

109

in Korea. Why spend a million dollars producing a picture about war that makes no salient point about war, pro or con, and is hardly a work of art? That movie was a menagerie of violent exercises in human destruction. You saw an awful lot of people blown up, you saw an awful lot of places bombed, and by the last reel you were asking "Why?" Just to kill some time. I was unable to work in that movie, even on an elementary level, with any degree of imagination. The producers seemed willing to settle for what would have been the first step in a stage rehearsal, and print it. I signed for it while I was in New Haven with "Raisin in the Sun." I was committed to do it. The original script said an awful lot about people and war, but then we didn't do what was in the script. On the other hand, I enjoyed making "A Raisin in the Sun" as a film. I knew every facet of the character and of the play, and I felt I had control and was able to take care of myself. However, the next year, "Paris Blues," in which I played a jazz musician, was all wrong from beginning to end. The novel on which the movie was ostensibly based really went into the lives of jazz musicians in Paris, but what we did was not that. Also, the original script I read, by a wonderful screenwriter named Irene Kamp, was not the script we wound up with. By the time we were finished, five other writers had been called in, one after another, to change the script according to some idea that one or another of a dozen people connected with the movie had for making it a success. It was a shambles. I found out once and for all that a bunch of people can't do it. One person has to do it. A group of people engaged in a collaborative creative effort must respond to one person. Mistakes are probably going to be made, but they will be the mistakes of one person, and so they won't be so bad. A halfhearted mistake is a devastating mistake.

When I act on the stage, it's a total experience. With me—as with other actors, I believe—it's quite a job to prevent the work from becoming mechanical. You have to find ways to keep refuelling the impulse. You can't hang an impulse up on a peg and then take it down the next night. It's instantaneous. It cannot be repeated. If you try to harness it, you take away the nowness of it. But it has to be manufactured synthetically when things aren't going right—when your energy is low, when you've eaten too much, when you haven't cleansed your mind of your own thoughts and worries so you can flood it with the part you're playing. You cannot will a response. When I feel good and right, I experience complete communication with the audience. But each performance is different, and if I expected to feel that good every night, I'd be disappointed. There's no one way of acting, but my way is to try to feel the experience of the moment and to have each moment flow out of the last and into the next.

There is a sense of self that is important to me when I try to work creatively. I find it in what I think of as the gears of the mind. So far, I've discovered only three speeds, but maybe there are more. At the most common speed, the mind is open to all distractions and sensations. It is giving constant attention to one or another of a thousand different things. At the second speed, the mind is working between two opposites, feverishly, because it wants something and is evaluating things in order to put them to use. The third gear is the idle gear. That's the gear we live in all too little, the gear we shift into after a hard day's work, when we couldn't care less whether anything happens or not. That's when all your thoughts are held momentarily in abeyance. You have just enough of a buzz on to encourage the opposite of good sense. I get myself into a part by shifting my gears in that order. When I go from second to third, I'm shifting from the battle of the opposites to a state of timelessness. All I know about it is that that's what happens when I act. It feels good. For me, acting is a refuge and a respite from the battle of the opposites: to be successful or not to be successful, to go home or not to go home, to smoke or not to smoke, to eat lobster or not to eat lobster—to be or not to be. The only way I can transcend the battle is to act. When I play someone else, I am no longer caught in the battle; the person I'm playing is caught. I accept someone else's circumstances and I cease to function as Sidney Poitier. I have peace. I feel it. It's now. It's great. It's encompassing. It's got you. You're secure. Everything you do is absolutely meant to be done. It leads you, every now and then, to transcend the battle so completely that you give a performance that is absolutely shattering, even to yourself.

People call me an artist. Even though I don't deserve it most of the time, it's nice to hear. Only, I always ask myself, "Now, *what* have I created?" And that immediately pushes me back into the battle. I'm always asking myself whether or not I'm an actor. The essence of the actor is a composite of his physical construction, his voice, his disposition, and the intangibles of his own character. I'm always asking myself

111

what makes the difference when *he* walks onstage, instead of somebody else. What is it that creates the illusion for the audience? Acting is not only an interpretive art, it's a creative art. A play stands as still as death itself unless the actor brings it to life. People aren't going to get up off the paper and walk around. The actors do that for them.

JULIET MILLS

I know that someday I'm going to play Shakespeare's Juliet.

I was born on November 21, 1941, in London, during the blitz. My father is the actor John Mills, and my mother is Mary Hayley Bell Mills, the playwright and novelist. My godmother is Vivien Leigh, and my godfather is Noël Coward. My little sister, Hayley, has played in "Tiger Bay," with my father, and in "Pollyanna" and other movies. I also have a little brother, Jonathan, born in 1949, who wants to be an actor. I never had any doubt that I would be an actress. When I was a very small child, my mother would pack a lunch and take me to the motion-picture studio where my father was making a movie, and the three of us would have lunch together. My mother is like a little mother hen, always running around the world trying to keep us all together. Since Hayley became a movie star, Mother has had to stay with her in Hollywood when she makes a film there, and she doesn't like it there, so she leaves whenever she can bring us all together again. I love my godparents. Whenever Vivien Leigh needs me to talk to, I'll be there.

113

I've always wanted to be an actress, and really wanted to *act*. I never wanted my appearance to be the main thing. I do worry about my weight, because I have a tendency to be on the plump side. But just think of Charles Laughton. Right from the start, he was on the plump side, but look at the wonderful actor he turned out to be. Or Shelley Winters, who gets heavy once in a while, yet is such a good actress. So your appearance can't really stand in your way. When I was nine, my father sent me to ballet school. He told me that learning to dance would help me learn to act. Dancing gave me control of my body, and grace in my movements onstage. By the time I was sixteen, I was dancing five hours a day. I stopped when I got my first stage role, in "Five Finger Exercise," which I played in the West End and on Broadway. I had gone to a toddlers' school in Kensington and then to the Old Vicarage School, in Richmond, Surrey, and after that, at the age of nine, to Elmhurst, a private boarding school just outside London. There was no question of my going to college. In England, the only girls who go to college are the type who expect to become doctors. I've never thought about getting married, but then you never know, do you? A lot of girls I've known kept saying they were never going to get married, and then suddenly I would be getting invitations to their weddings. I believe that every girl should go to boarding school. At boarding school, I found out how lucky I was to have such a happy home. At school, every person is an individual, and you have to cope with her. I wanted to be head girl, and our headmistress did pick me. My last year at school, we did a play about the French Revolution. I played a very old, filthy, grotesque revolutionist. I loved it. At Elmhurst, I worked in dramatics. When Hayley started to act, I wrote a play about an orphanage, with a special part for Hayley called Angel—one of the orphans, who is deaf and dumb, and a boy. Hayley's got a face all her own. I've already been in three films with my father, and I'd like someday to be in a play with both Hayley *and* my father.

I love to go to movies, and I especially love the movies starring my father. I've seen "Great Expectations" thousands of times. That's my favorite. When I was four and used to watch him making the movie at the studio, I could never see any similarity between watching him in front of the camera and actually watching the movie. When I see "Great Expectations," I get thoroughly involved in the film. There's a scene in the beginning where a little boy is suddenly confronted in a graveyard by a convict. It used to frighten me. For years, I had nightmares about that scene. Even now, I can watch my father making a movie and then, when I see the film, get all involved in it. I haven't learned anything at all from watching movies being made. Everything I've learned has been from watching people. I watch people on the street when I'm walking. I watch them in shops when I'm doing my marketing. I watch them in Central Park, at the Wollman Memorial, where I go skating when I'm in New York. I'm aware of how people behave when they think no one is looking at them. A good actor also watches the good or bad points in other actors' performances. I'm always thinking of how I could do a part that someone else is playing. In New York, after the theatre, I go to old movies and watch the way the actors do their parts.

More than anything else, I want to play Juliet at Stratford. I know I can do it better than anyone else. Nearly always, actresses who play Juliet are women in their thirties or forties. Producers seem to think that older women can understand Juliet's feelings better than a girl who is actually Juliet's age. I think I know how Juliet felt, and understand what she did. I think I understand a lot more about Juliet than women in their thirties do. I think women in their thirties have forgotten how a girl feels when she's in her teens and in love.

Everyone I admire leads a disciplined life. Personally, I hate getting up late. I never drink. I don't smoke. When I'm in a play, I am usually in bed by 1 A.M. and up by 10 A.M. I like to do things and see things. In New York, I have gone for rides on the Staten Island ferry a dozen times, and I love taking the boat that circles the island of Manhattan. I've seen through the glamour and excitement of the theatre since I was ten. I knew by then that all was not bright lights and greasepaint. All the marvellous applause can be exciting and inspiring, but it can also be nerve-racking and disappointing if you aren't succeeding at what you are doing. I can still be impressed by an actor, though. When I first met Montgomery Clift, I could hardly speak.

When I'd played in "Five Finger Exercise" for two years, I got a little bored in my part. I'd explored every corner of it, it seemed. The thought of getting stale simply terrified me. It's very important to me to feel my own individuality in acting. I want to be me. When

115

I started working on my part for "Five Finger Exercise," I didn't learn the role line by line. At rehearsals, when I was asked whether I could do this or that, I'd say yes to everything. Then I'd try it out on the quiet by myself. For example, I had to fall down some stairs in the play. I didn't know how to do it at first. I would come to the theatre very early and try it out by myself, and that way I learned how to do it. The best way is not to think about it, just to do it.

I have no ambition to have a flat of my own in London. We live in the country, and unless I get a good part I just want to stay home. I don't see enough of Hayley. Whenever I talk to her on the telephone and she's far away someplace, she cries. Daddy says that to be a good actor you have to have something in you. You can let it go or you can do something with it. A great deal can be learned, but not unless you have the talent to begin with. Acting is a gamble. You are paid only when you are working. It is also an adventure. From month to month, you have no idea what is around the corner. Acting is definitely an art, but, as in all art, there are good artists and bad artists. Some actors get into a rut and then don't seem to make any effort to get out of it. They seem to enjoy their own misery in staying in the rut. They never ask themselves what it is they are doing. I think it is in your own hands whether or not your acting makes you happy—makes you feel good about what you are doing. England has lots of repertory companies. I'll join one of them and look for new and different roles. I think I'm going to be a good actress.

WILLIAM HOLDEN

Once you make up your mind about what you're
going to do in acting, you can pretty well slot it. I
like to think of emotions as being a series of cloaks
hung on pegs; I take them down as I find I need them.

I was born on April 17, 1918, in O'Fallon, Illinois. My real name is
William Franklin Beedle, Jr. When I was three, my father, a chemist,
moved the family to Pasadena, California, where he went into the
chemical-analysis business. My brother Bob was a Navy pilot who
died at the age of twenty-one; he was shot down in the South Pacific
on January 1, 1944. My brother Dick is in business with my father in
Los Angeles. My mother taught English in the Pasadena and Monrovia
school systems for many years, then retired, and now is active in
various church groups. My father, an amateur gymnast, gave me special lessons in tumbling and physical training. My mother encouraged
me to sing in church choirs and to mind my manners. I played my
first dramatic part at the age of ten—Rip Van Winkle in my school's
annual sixth-grade play. I kind of liked it. At Pasadena Junior College, I studied chemistry, which I hated. Everybody in the family but
me took it for granted that I would go into my father's chemical
business. In 1938, I got my first big acting opportunity, in the Pas-

adena Workshop Theatre's production of "Manya," a play about Marie Curie. I played the part of her father-in-law, eighty-year-old Eugène Curie. I was seen on opening night by Milton Lewis, a talent scout from Paramount Pictures. A couple of years earlier, I had taken a seven-month auto trip with a friend. We had visited New York, and I had decided then to go to New York after graduation from college and study acting. Instead, two weeks after I was seen by the scout I signed a contract with Paramount at a salary of fifty dollars a week, and had a part in "Million Dollar Legs" in which I said two words—"Thank you." I was one of a group of promising youngsters known at Paramount as the Golden Circle, which also included Betty Field and Robert Preston. I wanted to be the best motion-picture actor in the world. My heroes were Fredric March and Spencer Tracy. They were my ideals. I used them as a kind of goal for myself. I had enough of the extrovert in me to want that kind of recognition. Paramount took stock of my hobbies: in addition to doing gymnastics, I liked to ride my motorcycle at very high speeds; I was an expert horseman and rifle shot; I played the piano, clarinet, and drums. The studio executives decided that I needed a new name. "Beedle," they said, sounded too much like an insect. So I was named Holden, after a West Coast newspaperman.

Rouben Mamoulian, at Columbia Pictures, saw my screen test and hired me for the title role in "Golden Boy," with Barbara Stanwyck and Adolphe Menjou. It was my starting point. I don't think anybody had as much determination and ambition as I had the day I started making this movie. Then, one day in 1939, I went to the opening of "Golden Boy" and saw my name up on the marquee. There was my name in lights. And I suddenly knew that it didn't mean a damn thing to me. It's been that way ever since. I don't enjoy seeing myself on the screen. You might say I'm not my type. I'm ugly. I'm too fat and would like to be thinner. I'm *simpático* with people who are not gross. For twenty-two years, I've put up with a lot of asinine suggestions made by various studio experts about how to change myself —to fix the shape of my eyebrows, and stuff like that—but I've always refused to do it. I may not like the way I look, but I take myself the way I am and do the best I can with it. Being a movie star and seeing myself on the screen don't make me feel good. In fact, they make me feel kind of sad. But I do the best I can with all that, too.

I'm not like Garbo or Gregory Peck. I can walk down Fifth Avenue and I won't have any trouble with people staring at me. They don't recognize me. I just look like one of them. I think of myself as a fair contemporary actor-reporter of scenes in which people pretty much like me figure. I never think of myself as an actor the way Alec Guinness is an actor. He can do anything. He's completely devoted to acting. He can act anywhere. I can act only in films, and even there I'm limited. I'm best at playing someone relevant to our lives today. Rarely have I stepped into a period film. I've just never felt qualified to do it. When I work, I work hard, and I always try to satisfy my own taste. I'm not a great believer in audience appeal or in fans. I don't believe the fans establish the criterion in films. I think we establish the criterion for the fans. The motion picture is not a pure art form. It has its place as a business art form, and I'd hate to see it die out. I've made a good living out of acting, but I'm not dedicated to it. I can see how men like John Gielgud and Alec Guinness, who give the work their complete devotion, must get a deeper satisfaction out of it than I do. I have my hand in a lot of business interests. Anyone with as many diverse interests as I have couldn't get that really deep satisfaction out of acting. I could probably out-operate Alec Guinness in any field of business, and I get some satisfaction out of that. These days, because of the international distribution of pictures, my work as an actor involves not only acting in a movie but going on the road with it, all over the country or all over the world, to sell it. After all, I pour the original energy into the acting, and I feel I might as well do the other. However, I refuse to ingratiate myself with the public in ways I don't respect. I haven't given a fan-magazine interview in the past dozen years. But what I will do is go on the road to sell a picture.

During the first few days of work on "Golden Boy," I was so intense I found myself on the verge of a nervous collapse. Then Barbara Stanwyck, one of the stars of the movie, spent night after night, after a hard day's work, rehearsing with me, and she pulled me through. For the past twenty-two years, I've sent her flowers to commemorate the anniversary of the day that work on "Golden Boy" began. That picture was a high point for a beginning; after that things went down. I spent the next couple of years playing ordinary roles in ordinary movies. I didn't feel that my talents, major or

119

minor, were being fully utilized. In 1941, I married Ardis Ankerson, a young actress known to the public as Brenda Marshall. At my request, she gave up acting as a career. She had a three-year-old daughter, Virginia, whom I adopted legally. Ardis and I had two children together—Peter, who is seventeen, and Scott, who is fifteen. Eight months after I was married, I enlisted in the Army Air Forces, and for four years I did public-relations and entertainment duty and made training films all over the country. In 1946, I returned to Paramount, where I got into the rut of playing all kinds of nice-guy, meaningless roles in meaningless movies, such as "Father Is a Bachelor" and "Dear Wife," in which I found neither interest nor enjoyment. By 1949, I had appeared in eleven movies that, for me, added up to one great big static blur. Then, in 1950, I played the part of Joe Gillis, the opportunistic, caddish writer in "Sunset Boulevard," with Gloria Swanson. It was a turning point for me. I not only found the part interesting and exciting but was noticed and liked by the critics. In 1953, I played another interesting part—Sefton, the amoral sergeant in "Stalag 17." I won an Oscar for it. In the meantime, I did assorted odd jobs outside of acting. I worked as vice-president of the Screen Actors Guild. I was Commissioner of Parks and Recreation in Los Angeles. I developed interests and partnerships in businesses such as exporting and importing, aviation, and radio stations here and abroad. I now have a large measure of control over what I do in pictures and how I do it. I receive a percentage of the gross of all pictures I make, pretty much the way Cary Grant and James Stewart do.

Long before I realized the power of the dollar, I had a tendency to express myself. Fortunately, I was able to combine the two. As a boy, I'd see things in movie acting that cried for a better interpretation. I always felt that, with a little study, I could do them much better. Just before I signed my first contract, I was a little vague about it, but I wasn't floundering. I wasn't old enough to flounder. I've always had an idea of what was right for me and what was wrong. In making my first movies, whenever I felt lost or puzzled I had one simple way of working my way out of it. I'd always ask myself, "Well, what would Fredric March do? What would Gary Cooper do?" And it would always solve the problem for me. I'm not like some movie actors, who feel that they must pretend they're just dying to act in the theatre. I've been tempted by it only once, when I briefly thought about doing

"Mister Roberts." Henry Fonda was in it then, and he had some kind of knee trouble. But I didn't replace him, and that was all right with me. I've never pretended I could be an Alec Guinness in the theatre.

Movie acting may not have a certain kind of glory as a true art, but it's acting, and it's damn hard work. You kiss your wife goodbye at eight in the morning, and an hour later you're on a set pretending to be killing somebody or whispering sweet nothings into some glamour girl's ear. It's a terrible emotional drain. It's devastating. The most demanding thing about it is that you must keep up the level of your performance. The way I do it is to think of myself as a reporter. My job is to portray the character and bring it to the audience in a way that will enable them to involve themselves emotionally. I read a script and analyze it. I find that if you develop an attitude toward the character the mannerisms for it come later. You attempt to stay as detached as possible. Then there's a kind of final melting in your mind about a week before the picture is supposed to start. Once you're in it, you're involved in how you're going to develop the character. Once I'm fairly entrenched, I find that the character almost takes care of itself. Then the demands on you are the demands of a particular day of work. It's terribly exhausting. My most difficult roles have always been ones that are unlike me. Still, I've been able to find their motivation acceptable. If you're going to be Gillis in "Sunset Boulevard," for example, you must get it across that there but for the grace of God go I. I may not be able to understand Gillis, a gigolo, but I can sympathize with him. I've found that sympathy is about all you need if you want to act a different kind of person from your real self. When I was doing the part of Sefton in "Stalag 17," I had a really tough time sympathizing with him—the way he used marked cards, and all the rest of his unscrupulousness. What I used to go on was my observation of men like that. I've seen them. I know what they're like. I'm not sure how to explain the talent or whatever it is that makes it possible for me to act by using that approach. Maybe it's just knowing a little more than the next guy. As I tell my older boy, who has some interest in acting, you'll know if you have talent when you get there.

In every man's life, there's a period when he determines how his energies are going to be directed. Every man has a basic problem in deciding that. My decision was, is, and will be to be a good motion-

121

picture actor. Between the ages of twenty-nine and thirty-six, I had a period when I was easily able to handle a lot of outside activities. I don't kid myself that I can still work an eighteen-hour day. I hate to become sloppy. In 1956, I made a picture called "Toward the Unknown," for which I was an actor by day and, by night, a caster, a cutter, and a producer. I'll never do anything like that again. My blueprint is to make one very important picture a year—one that is not only artistically satisfying to me but successful at the box office. Ideally, I'd like to spend six or seven months on my vocation and five or six months on my avocational activities. One of my pet avocational projects is the Mount Kenya Safari Club, which I started with two other men—Carl Hirschmann, a Swiss banker, and Ray Ryan, an oilman from Indiana. We bought the Mawingo Hotel—the name means "The Clouds"—on the slopes of Mount Kenya, outside the town of Nanyuki. We've got sixty acres, with fruit and vegetable gardens, tennis courts, swimming pools, trout streams, and a hundred and twenty servants, and also five hundred adjacent acres, complete with an African village, as well as the prize rose garden on the continent. Our members include John Wayne and Winston Churchill. We're about twelve thousand miles from Hollywood, and about six thousand miles from St. Prex, Switzerland, where I now make my home. From the club, you can get to Hollywood in one full day. These are, after all, times of galloping transportation. I take care of a million things in my import-export business—importing electronic equipment from Tokyo, and things like that. After all that avocational activity, I get back to acting and I feel refreshed.

BURGESS MEREDITH

You have to act with joy, and not mislocate the center of the emotions, which is in the head, not in the stomach. The center of the emotions is right above the eyes.

I was born on November 16, 1908, in Cleveland, Ohio. My father, William George Meredith, was a doctor, but he gave up the practice of medicine early, retired, and moved to Canada. My parents separated then; I was four, and I stayed with my mother, who was the daughter of a well-known Methodist minister in Cleveland. I was the youngest of three children. My brother, George, who was born in 1895, started out as a jazz drummer and later became a farmer in New England; he died in 1960. My sister, Virginia, who lives in Nashua, New Hampshire, and is married to an engineer, is fifteen years older than I am, and helped bring me up. My sister has never missed one of my openings, and she sees every movie I'm in. My parents died in the thirties. I lived in Cleveland until I was eight, when my mother took me to New York, because I had a scholarship to the Paulist Choir School, a Roman Catholic school. In 1920, I entered the choir school at the Cathedral of St. John the Divine, because it was closer to my religion. I was a famous boy soprano in town, and won various prizes for my singing. At St. John, there were about forty students in all, and we had prayers, athletics, and regular school subjects, with very good teachers. The background there was beautiful and cultural, and we were all proud of the cathedral. On Sundays, we sang in the cathedral, which was rather difficult, because the services were often long, and some of the choir boys would faint. The choir music was lovely. I especially liked the Palestrina and Bach things. When I was a student at St. John—and this happened to me at other schools, too—the teachers took a liking to me. When I was about ten, I played the title role in a Paulist School production of "Peter Pan," and got the feeling somehow that I was very good in it. My teachers would speak of it in later years. I had the ability to take on a part quickly. I saw my first play— "Cyrano de Bergerac," with Walter Hampden—when one of the teachers at St. John took some of the boys to a matinée performance. I was fifteen at the time. I remember the strength and power of Hampden's performance. He had one of those big, resonant voices, almost nasal, and utterly magnificent. The nose, the duelling, the balcony scene—it was all very glamorous and moving. Mostly, though, I was influenced by my teachers. The years at the school were a good time for me. My sister was married by then and was living near New York, with her husband, and I was allowed to go out with them. In 1923, when I was fifteen, I started attending the Hoosac School, in Hoosick, New York. It, too, was a church school, but it didn't have much in the way of singing or dramatics. I was head prefect at one time, though I was a sporadic student without much drive. I was very bad at mathematics. I always thought I would be a writer, and I wrote short stories and poems for the school magazine, of which I was editor in my final year. My sister kept all the old magazines for years. One of the great nontragedies of our lives was a fire she had in her house in which all the old magazines were burned up. At Hoosac, too, the teachers liked me. The headmaster recommended me for Amherst College, and I went there. I didn't like Amherst, and stayed there only four months. I was appalled by the social snobbery.

From Amherst, I went to Stamford, where my mother was staying with her sister, and I got a job on the Stamford *Advocate*. I thought it was a good and romantic thing to be a newspaperman. I wrote obituaries and covered Darien for a few months and then decided it was not so good and not so romantic. Then, when I was eighteen, I went to live with my sister, in East Orange, while I looked for a job in New York. After that came a whole series of experiments, of the kind that everybody goes through—working as a runner on Wall Street, selling

neckties at Macy's, a six-week trip to South America on a freighter in a
brass-polishing job. By then, I'd decided that I wanted to be an actor.
I ran across an old piano teacher from the choir-school days, who suggested that I try out for an apprentice job with Eva Le Gallienne's
Civic Repertory Theatre, on West Fourteenth Street, so I went down
there, asked for an appointment with Miss Le Gallienne, and got it.
Right away. She didn't talk with me more than fifteen minutes, and
she said, "Why do you want to be in the theatre? There's no money
connected with it, and we have a long waiting list." But she took me
on. The moment I walked in there, it all felt comfortable and right.
It was just an old, musty, broken-down building, with the dressing
rooms tacked on at the back, and she was running it as a one-woman
enterprise, but it was theatre, and full of atmosphere. Many famous
people were there, including John Garfield, Jacob Ben-Ami, Alla
Nazimova, J. Edward Bromberg, Howard da Silva, Paula Strasberg,
and Ria Mooney, who was in charge of the apprentices and is now a
producer and an actress with the Abbey Theatre, in Dublin. For two
years, I was at the Civic Rep as an apprentice without pay. My sister
supported me in those years, and by the spring of 1930 I was paid
twenty dollars a week. I received lessons in fencing, dancing, and
improvisation, and my constant association with a good repertory
company gave me a kind of training that is pretty special in this
country. I'm not a fellow who can concentrate greatly, and never have
been, but I felt immediately that I could make a go of acting. I enjoyed it. I didn't have many doubts. The main source of stimulation at
the Civic Rep was Le Gallienne. She was a leader, and she was glamorous and talented and full of idealism. We were then on the threshold
of a decade of idealism, and it all seemed so right to me. Le Gallienne
was a very precise director, as she is today. Her fight was a fight on the
side of the angels. It was a very exciting thing for me. We played every
night except Sunday, and we had a new play every four weeks. I felt
I was a part of a living organism. My first speaking part was that of
Peter, the servant to Juliet's nurse, in "Romeo and Juliet." Le Gallienne played Juliet, and was very famous in the role. She was only
thirty-one at the time. She believed in the classics and exposed you to
them. We did a lot of the Russian things, especially Chekhov. She was
always encouraging and helpful and kind, and she had humor. I remember that she charged a two-twenty top for tickets, and never took

125

anything for herself. The Civic Rep embodied an ideal of hers. There's never been anything like it since.

In the summer of 1932, I played a season of stock. I was with three different companies but always in the same part—Marchbanks in Shaw's "Candida." I played it in Mount Kisco and Ivoryton, and then, with Pauline Lord and Tom Powers, in Philadelphia, where first-string critics reviewed it. The critics praised me, extravagantly, and that kind of lit the fuse. I began to feel I wanted to move on. I had an urge to move uptown. Early in 1933, I left the Civic Rep. I gave my notice in the middle of the run of "Alice in Wonderland," in which I played the Duck and the Dormouse and Tweedle-Dee, and I went into a walk-on part—Crooked Finger Jack in Bertolt Brecht's and Kurt Weill's "The Threepenny Opera," then trying out in Philadelphia. "The Threepenny Opera" lasted twelve performances on Broadway, and I didn't get to play in it there at all, because while we were still in Philadelphia I was offered the lead—the role of Red Barry—in Albert Bein's "Little Ol' Boy," which was about the horrors of life in a reform school, and I took it, commuting from Philadelphia to rehearsals in New York until I got my release from "The Threepenny Opera." The play also lasted for twelve performances on Broadway, but I made all there was to be made in the way of reputation out of it. O. O. McIntyre called me "the most thrilling young actor of his day," and Stark Young wrote that my performance was "as near perfection as could be imagined."

I wasn't surprised to be playing leads so soon after starting in the theatre, because I could get right into a part, just as I had done as a boy at school. And I had had good training at the Civic Rep. As Marchbanks in "Candida," I probably had a kind of vitality and realism that were just beginning to come into the theatre. Looking back, I remember that the words used about me were "realistic" and "sensitive." What I did was to believe absolutely in the circumstances I found myself in onstage, so that the play was an actual experience for me and the emotions were real to me. We didn't have Methodology at that time, but later on I sought it. In 1937, after I had starred in "Winterset," I studied with Benno Schneider, who gave lessons much like the ones given at the Actors' Studio now—teaching improvisation, memory of emotions, intention, being able to verbalize what you do, so that you can put your finger on it instead of leaving it to God. Sooner or later, especially if you're in a long run, you have to find a way of putting your finger on what you do. The interesting thing I discovered with Schneider is that emotions on the stage come from your head, and that you have to bring them from there. When I see young actors dragging emotion up from their middles, I try to tell them it's a mistake.

Immediately after "Little Ol' Boy," I was offered several parts. Then and later, I made some dubious choices—too many of them. I had my choice between the lead in "She Loves Me Not" and the lead in "Tobacco Road," and I chose the former. It was a farce comedy by Howard Lindsay, and I had a very gay part. The play was a smash hit, and it opened new horizons for me. I realized I was arriving. You could tell that people recognized me, on the street, in restaurants. I was both glad and worried. I began to wonder whether I was making the right choices for my own development as an actor. My mother died during rehearsals of "She Loves Me Not," and that made it an unhappy time. My father saw the play and liked it. I had been living in a one-room cold-water flat over a plumbing shop on Hudson Street, and now I moved into a two-bedroom apartment on East Sixty-seventh Street, and hired a butler. I didn't have any trouble at all adjusting to the butler. If you have a streak of laziness in you, you know what you want done by a butler. It got complicated a bit later on, though, when I had *two* butlers. Things piled up rather fast. I played in "She Loves Me Not" for a year—in 1933 and 1934—and simultaneously I was doing a soap opera on radio, in which I played a character named Red Davis, whose name was later changed to Pepper Young. In 1934, Guthrie McClintic, who was always interested in the new young actors, had me come up to his office and said he hoped to have a part for me someday. The next year, he asked me to play a small part in a revival of "The Barretts of Wimpole Street," starring his wife, Katharine Cornell. I enjoyed working with them. She was always very warm, very protective, very maternal. If McClintic yelled at me, she'd find some way of touching my arm, to give me reassurance. I found McClintic an extraordinarily effective director. He was a great raconteur, and during rehearsals he'd spend half the time telling you stories, to get you into the spirit of the theatre, of the play, of your part. Then he would get these flashes for the high points of the play, and act them out for you. He did it in a kind of broad caricature, so that you wouldn't imitate him but would see just what it was that he wanted you to do. He was not a man who went into theory. He loved the theatre and felt a tremendous awe of it, and somehow he transmitted it all to you in a way that worked for *you*. After "The Barretts of Wimpole Street," I worked with Katharine Cornell and McClintic again, in John Van Druten's play "Flowers of the Forest." In fact, I was associated with McClintic for several years, and also—in "Winterset," "High Tor," and "The Star-Wagon"—with Maxwell Anderson and Jo Mielziner. After doing "Winterset" on the stage, I went out to Hollywood, for the first time, to act in the movie version. Hollywood has always proved very difficult for me to function in.

In 1932, between seasons at the Civic Rep, I got married for the first time—to Helen Derby Berrien, a girl from Montclair, New Jersey. My second wife was the actress Margaret Perry, the daughter of Antoinette Perry, after whom the theatre award is named. We were married during the run of "Winterset." She was very charming, but that marriage didn't last, either, and we were divorced in 1938. I had five years of bachelorhood during the Second World War, when I was called into the Army Air Forces, where I was assigned to the Air Transport Command but was given time to make orientation films, like "Welcome to Britain" and "Salute to France." My next wife was Paulette Goddard. I'm married now to Kaja Sundsten, a former dancer, and we have two children—Jonathan, born in 1951, and Tala, born the following year. They're lovely kids. We live near Suffern, in a house I built. My wife has a Cessna 182 Skylane, which she keeps at the Teterboro Airport and Spring Valley Airpark, and she instructs student pilots in instrument flying. When I'm working in a play in Chicago or Philadelphia, and have to go to Idlewild to catch a big plane, she flies me around. It makes it handy. Once, she flew me to Westhampton, left me at the theatre, and then told some people she had to beat it back home because she had a turkey in the oven.

In 1938, I embarked on a program of doing a lot of different things, including being acting president of Actors' Equity, which someone should have been but not I. I was fascinated then by the talents of Orson Welles—I still am—and I joined him in his production of "Five Kings," based on "Henry IV," Parts I and II and "Henry V." We thought we'd combine our immortal geniuses, but we shared colossal disaster instead. Our plans didn't come off. Neither Orson nor I was the kind of person who could organize things. I played Henry as Prince and King, and he played Falstaff, but we closed out of town and "Five Kings" never got to New York. I've never known anybody I could have more fun with than Orson. At the time, I was searching for something. I wasn't disciplined. And Orson was so remarkable and refreshing, and had done things with such imagination, like the modern-dress "Julius Caesar" and the all-colored "Macbeth." He was a child of the theatre and was doing new, great things. Those were the days of turning away from the status quo, of finding new forms that seemed to be an end in themselves. I felt myself retreating from the position of conservatism I had settled into with McClintic and Anderson. I was going off with people who felt that acting wasn't important—that what was important was saving the world. The New Deal was so exciting, and there were so many causes to take up and so many committees to be on. There was nothing like the Actors' Studio in those days. Today the actor is working at his craft and isn't ashamed to say that he likes it and that the theatre is a fine thing in itself. Still, in everything I did from that point on, I was learning, and I have never stopped being interested in new forms. The only thing I regret is never having had an opportunity to be exposed to the classic theatre, which I think is sort of right for my nature—poetic, if you like. There was no place I could go for it. I had success fall into my lap when I was twenty-four, and as I look back I feel some sorrow that I didn't go to the Old Vic for classical training. Today there are about ten good British actors for every good one we have here. Great actors get that way by using their muscles on the classics.

In April, 1942, I was granted a leave by the Air Forces to play Marchbanks in a benefit revival of "Candida," by the American Theatre Wing War Service with Katharine Cornell and Dudley Digges. Richard Maney called it one of the ten great productions of all time. In March, 1940, just before going into the Army, I had played in "Liliom," with Ingrid Bergman and Elia Kazan, and in 1944 I was placed on inactive status to play Ernie Pyle in the movie about him, "The Story of G.I. Joe." Also before entering the service, I'd been in the film of John Steinbeck's novel "Of Mice and Men," and later, with Paulette Goddard, I spent three years in Hollywood—another of my regrets. I shouldn't have gone there and tried to beat that racket, though I was in quite a few movies, including "The Diary of a Chambermaid," which I wrote and co-produced. Those of us who came up in the middle thirties were stirred with a pretty wild spoon. We either fell by the wayside or continued up. Elia Kazan went to the top and stayed there. José Ferrer took a longer time getting started, but he got there. My story is a little more hair-raising, because it goes up and down. You have to use your creative abilities; otherwise, they swell up on you and explode. At least a modicum of your talent must be used. When you do things you don't believe in and don't feel, they leave a sour taste in your mouth. If you want to see what I mean, go out to Hollywood and look at some of the people there. What happened to Orson in Hollywood was a tragedy; he attacked Hearst, and anyone who attacked Hearst was bound to be pursued. They got Chaplin, too, in a way. But the real reason for what happened to Welles and Chaplin in Hollywood is that strong individual talent is somehow frowned on there.

I still enjoy trying different things, just as I did when I was with Orson. I am fascinated by the problems of directing. While I was playing in "Major Barbara," in 1957, I started working on plans for the production of "Ulysses in Nighttown," with Zero Mostel. It's always the style of a thing that intrigues me. ANTA turned the project down, saying the play was too off-color, but Barry Hyams, Oliver Saylor, Marjorie Barkentin, and a few other private individuals got thirteen thousand dollars together for the production. It was great fun, and it was all done with our bare hands. When we were trying to think who could play the role of Leopold Bloom, we knew it had to be somebody very special. I'd always been an admirer of Zero's, and when I asked him to play Bloom he was touched. He grasped the part almost immediately. He didn't have to go very far to find it. He seemed to know just what the man was. He is charmed by the characters he plays, and he knows them sympathetically, and he approached the part in a way that made it really bigger than life. His performance was as important as my own contribution, as director, but I wouldn't have traded places with him. We had four weeks' rehearsal, and our group was free of any difficult personalities, which is no unimportant thing. And Zero was a strong leader. It was one of those happy groups. We played in New York for a year and a half, and in the Arts Theatre in London and the Théâtre Sarah-Bernhardt in Paris, and we won prizes for the play all over the world.

I enjoy directing, but I still like to act when I feel it's called for. I find, however, that I'm more involved when I'm thinking of a whole production than when I'm just concentrating on what I'm doing with the inside of a character. I've experienced marvellous happiness three or four times as an actor—in the revival of "Candida," for one, when I felt I absolutely and finally got Marchbanks. Before that, I'd always felt that my parts weren't successful—that I didn't have the right motivation or the right tensions, or else that *something* was off. Finally, as Marchbanks with Cornell, I was satisfied with my performance. Curiously, I felt the same way about Edmund Wilson's play "The Little Blue Light," which I did in 1951, with Melvyn Douglas and Martin Gabel, and in which I played Gandersheim, a kind of homosexual, neo-Fascist Christ image. I also enjoyed playing in "The Teahouse of the August Moon," when I took the part of Sakini for the road. And I was happy in the 1946 production of "The Playboy of the Western World," directed by Guthrie McClintic, when Maureen Stapleton stepped up into the lead at the end of the run and played opposite me. But whether a play comes or goes is not so important to me when it's set alongside a child or a woman I love, or friends, or the life that I lead in general.

EILEEN HECKART

I don't feel the need to be a star. I can walk freely through a supermarket without being stopped for my autograph. That's just fine.

I was born on March 29, 1919, in Columbus, Ohio. My parents were divorced when I was two. My father died when I was about eleven. Five or six years later, my mother married a businessman named Van H. Purcell; I have a brother and two half sisters.

My mother loved movies. She would go to two double-feature movies a day when I was in high school. Before I could walk, she would take me with her. I cut my teeth on Joan Crawford movies. Joan Crawford was always so rich, so beautiful, so lavishly dressed, and she dragged a mink stole better than anyone else. I made up my mind when I was eight that I was going to become an actress. I was attending Girl Scout camp at the time, and one of the Scout leaders told me I had talent. Once, I played in a camp play. I don't remember a thing about it except that the audience laughed. The audience enjoyed me. I smelled blood. That start was enough to keep me going for the rest of my life. We were always poor. I had to work from high school on. By the time I entered Ohio State University, I belonged to five different dramatic societies in Columbus. I decided almost at the

start to be a character actress or a comedienne. I knew I had to be some
kind of actress, and since I wasn't beautiful, I knew I could never
expect to become a leading lady. But I knew with everything in me
that I could act. It took me five years to get through college. I worked
my way through by selling merchandise in Lazarus, a Columbus
department store. They put me in what was called the hot-items section. They had a special sale on hot items every day. I was good at
selling—very fast, very persuasive, very sure of myself. Even now,
when I go shopping I want to grab the sales slip out of the sales
clerk's hand and make it out myself. I gave makeup demonstrations
for Max Factor cosmetics, and meanwhile I did commercials for local
radio stations and, eventually, did drama in radio. I booked fashion
shows into sorority houses and distributed samples of Philip Morris
cigarettes to the other kids. In college, I majored in English and
speech, and I was a very average student. I didn't have time to study.
I had to travel eight miles by streetcar to get to the campus. But I
wanted that degree; I wanted to make good. When your family
doesn't have money, you try to prepare yourself to do anything. I
knew from the beginning that in acting so many start out and so
few succeed. I wanted a cushion. The Max Factor people wanted me
to take a job after graduation demonstrating and selling cosmetics
in Hollywood or on the road. Lazarus wanted me to represent them
as a buyer in books or candy. I turned both their offers down. Getting
through college was a hardship, but I was determined to graduate. I felt
that if I had that degree I could get any kind of job I wanted. I got by
in my studies, and I kept up with all the college dramatics. In 1943,
after graduation, I married a former classmate, John Harrison Yankee,
Jr., who was in the Navy, stationed in Jacksonville, Florida. He's now
an insurance broker. We have three little boys, all under ten, and
we live in New Canaan. My family life is important to me. I love
my three little boys. Recently, I joined the Roman Catholic Church
as a convert, by my own choice. Our boys are being raised as
Catholics. I couldn't devote my life to keeping house. I don't have
that much creativity in the kitchen. Cooking bores me. When I'm
onstage, playing a character other than myself, I feel I'm creating. I
enjoy it. I go out there to play seriously—play to win. I loathe amateurs. It gives me chills to think of myself as part of an amateur actors'
suburban group, laughing and gossiping. Even when I play bridge, I

play to win. Once, on location for "Heller in Pink Tights," I stayed up four nights in a row playing bridge, because I was determined to improve my game. I played seriously. I wouldn't be acting if I weren't acting seriously.

Ten years ago, when I saw movie or stage stars, I'd think how wonderful to have your name in lights, your picture in front of the theatre. Now I'm grateful for my freedom as a character actress, or non-star. In "A Family Affair," the producers said that the show would be thrown out of focus if my name didn't appear above the title, with Shelley Berman's. I agreed with them, but I am still a character actress. The billing just meant that the two leads were equally important in the show. A star has to watch herself every second. When she shows herself to the public, she has to be sure the public sees her as a nice human being. As the star of a show, furthermore, you have to carry the entire responsibility for the show, and every other member of the cast is dependent on you. Being what I am, I have the freedom to accept any role that appeals to me. And my little boys need me to be what I am. I want them to become good citizens. I can spend my time with them, instead of doing all the things a star has to do to keep herself in front of the public—all those things that have nothing to do with acting but that you are obliged to do to keep the public from forgetting you. Stars have to be seen. They have to go to openings of plays that they care nothing about. They have to appear on television panel shows. They have to keep themselves in demand—in demand by all those people somewhere in Kansas who can see them only in movies and on television. They have to do all that extra work, while I'm lounging around in blue jeans with my three little boys.

At college, my first lead was in "Stage Door," by George S. Kaufman and Edna Ferber. I played the lead in George Brewer's and Bertram Block's "Dark Victory," and then in one play after another, for three years. In school, you play everything and believe you're at your best. But New York is different. I came to New York in 1942, just before my future husband went into the Navy. After making the rounds of producers' offices, I auditioned for the Blackfriars' Guild, a Catholic dramatic group, and I did three shows for them. In 1946, I began studying at the American Theatre Wing. The Blackfriars were amateurs. I wasn't satisfied. I kept wandering into one dead end after another. It was tough. You do need something in this business to lean on, something to help you help yourself and accept yourself. All of us in this business know each other so well, and yet it's still possible to get hurt, and get hurt often. The meek may inherit the earth, but the strong survive in the theatre. Acting is not entirely inborn. Only to a certain degree is it inborn. Anyone can become a good technician, become proficient, and have a fairly good life in the theatre. The difference between anyone and a great actor is made up of those moments in the life of some actors in which they kindle a spark—something that makes a moment so real that what they are doing becomes great acting. Marlon Brando will go down in acting history for having had several such moments. Other actors I've watched and admired have had those moments—Orson Welles in "The Third Man," for instance, and Shirley Booth in "Come Back, Little Sheba." Kim Stanley is the best young contemporary actress I've ever seen. When she doesn't get anything onstage from the other actors, she can be almost as great as when she does. And some nights during the run of "Picnic," when others did give to her, she became even better. Watching her operate is an experience I'll never forget. In my roles, unless the situation is a blatantly obvious one I can't tell how I come across. The very friction with other actors brings some actors alive. Actors work on each other's emotions. They know each other, and the better they know each other, the more they have to work on. It wasn't until I got the role of the schoolteacher in "Picnic" that I felt I had got my first big break. Actually, I played the part for eight months before I felt that I really understood it and gave a good performance. I didn't know what I was doing. I didn't think I was any good. I was unhappy. I kept telling myself to respect myself in the part. It seemed to me that others in the cast didn't like what I was doing. I was in a hit, but the kicks were fewer than they should have been. I had read four times for the part before the director, Joshua Logan, finally said yes to me. I was unknown, and he may have thought I couldn't sustain a performance. Logan kept trying to tell me I was having my first success—I was a pro; I couldn't act for a kind of pleasure only; I had to go out there and win. I received two awards for my performance in "Picnic," but the main thing I learned from it was not to rip myself apart over a role. I'm not a natural-born comedienne, like Lucille Ball or Vicki Cummings. I don't have that kind of timing or sense of comedy. My comedy comes from a situation. But I know how to tune in to an audience. These days, I know I can sustain a performance, no matter what kind of house we have—full or small. In "Invitation to a March," a play I did in 1960, I'd get a hand just for the cross—going from one side of the stage to the other in tight purple slacks. Audiences vary. Timing comes from them, not from you. Any time you press or reach for an audience, you lose it.

Every role I've ever played has been somewhat outside me and my life with my husband and little boys. If feeling is real, it's no longer acting. I was strongly affected in myself by only one part—the mother of a child who is murdered, in the Broadway production of "The Bad Seed." I was happy to leave that play; it made me feel sick. There are only a few moments here and there in my acting when I am close to my own personality. But there is a reality I try to establish in my relationships with the other actors in a play. In "Invitation to a March," I was confused during the rehearsals and didn't hear half of what was being said on the stage. I had a talk with the young man who played my son, and we tried to find some way of making our relationship more real, in order to strengthen the performance. Every actor tries to do this. The best Broadway work I've done was as Lottie Lacey in "The Dark at the Top of the Stairs." But the part was beautifully written, and allowed for a full characterization. That helped. And Elia Kazan, the director, had four ideas for me for every one I had. I usually cross out the author's stage directions. Authors should write the words and leave the rest to us. However, three years ago, I went out to California to do "Mother Courage" for John Houseman's Theatre Group, at U.C.L.A., because I wanted to do Brecht. The material is so big and specific. The part of Mother Courage *should* be played by a European. I'm too American. But I had a rapport with that woman and with her strength. I had a lot to give to that role, and I've never worked harder. Brecht says to cut off all emotion in a performance, and to Method actors *that's* news. We're always trying to turn on emotion and to deal with it on-stage. When Brecht confronts Mother Courage with her dead son, he tells you to drain yourself of all feeling and expression. I worked on that scene through three bad performances, but for the last four performances the scene, the whole play worked. To play Mother Courage emotionlessly and to feel those audiences responding in a way I'd never before experienced was unforgettable. Those four performances were the most gratifying of my life.

When I get a new script, I begin by spending days reading and re-reading it and thinking about it. I have no idea, at first, how to play the part. Some actors begin with nothing and gradually build a role. I would rather make a decision after a fifth reading and have it be bad than remain uncertain. I make notations in the script of how I am going to act as the director makes his suggestions to me during rehearsals. I write it all down. Then I have a mental picture of what I'm going to do. But I can't set it until we start the out-of-town try-outs. My greatest satisfaction in acting is that I am able to give of myself. It's difficult, but I like it. And because I like it, it becomes an indulgence. The money is attractive, too. It wasn't at first, but now I don't turn up my nose at money. Also, it takes years of involvement to learn just a little bit about acting, and I'm happy about having learned something. These days, a lot of actors go in for psychoanalysis, because they think it will make them understand their own feelings better and thus help them become better actors. Actors work on emotion all the time. But actors who think psychoanalysis will make them better actors are misguided. They ought to take a look at Garbo. She gives of herself and makes believe simultaneously, compelling the audience to forget the dishes in the sink. An actress is out in the world. The very aliveness of acting makes it attractive to me. I'll never retire.

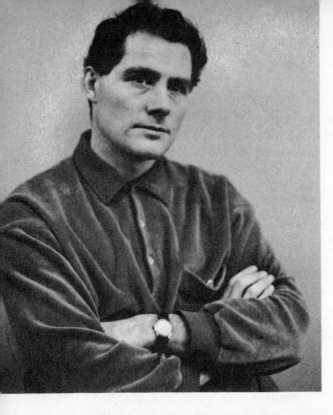

ROBERT SHAW

*So many people in the theatre don't like us to get
down to the bones of a thing. It's been such a fight
for the freedom to do it.*

I was born on August 9, 1927, in Westhoughton, Lancashire, in the
North of England—the heart of the cotton-mill country. My father,
Dr. Thomas Shaw, a general practitioner, killed himself during the
Second World War, when I was twelve. My mother is a remarkable
woman, extraordinarily independent. She was born in Piggs Peak, in
Swaziland, South Africa, and she met my father while she was a nurse
at the Truro Hospital, in Cornwall. She returned to Swaziland in
1953, and now teaches reading and writing to white children in a small
country school there. I'm the eldest of five children. Elizabeth, two
years younger than I am, is married to an English professor at Franklin
and Marshall College, in Lancaster, Pennsylvania, and has four children; Joanna, four years younger than I am, also lives in Lancaster,
and is married to a man who raises money for the college; Alexander,
born in 1932, lives in London, studying pathology, and is married and
has two children; and Wendy, the youngest, born in 1938, is married to

138

a Dutchman, a purser on the Queen Mary, and they have two children. I have four daughters by my marriage, in 1952, to the actress Jennifer Burke. My brother and one of my sisters went to Cambridge, and another sister went to Oxford. After the war, my mother said to us, "All you children are so clever that I'm going to do something, too," and she went off to one of those training centers for people back from the war, and became qualified to teach. My father was unusually talented in many ways. In his younger days, he was a famous Rugby football player and played Rugby football in the trials for England, and also was an amateur boxing champion. He was decorated in the First World War. I am a novelist as well as an actor, and I wrote a bit about this episode in my second novel, "The Sun Doctor." (My first novel was "The Hiding Place.") The day my father killed himself, he told my mother, "I'm going to kill myself." My mother said, "Don't do it in front of the children." My mother says to this day that he didn't mean to kill himself—that he had two bottles labelled "Scotch," one containing poison, and took a drink from the wrong bottle. I was in boarding school at the time—the Truro School, in Cornwall, about a hundred miles from where we then lived, in Keinton Mandeville, in Somerset. The headmaster told me that my father had killed himself, and that he was driving up there and I could come or stay in school. I said I'd stay in school. My father's drinking had been an enormous strain on the family. In the English middle-class milieu we were ostensibly a part of, his drinking was something to be ashamed of. I've spoken with old aunts who were too ashamed to know anything about it. It must have had its effect on me. Even now, I often dream that my father is still alive.

When I was six, my father moved us to Stromness, a small town in the Orkney Islands, north of Scotland. It was a wonderful place for children. It was a tough, simple life. My father was terribly well liked. He was a courageous man, and would go off by boat to visit his patients, even in the stormiest weather. He is still spoken of with great affection in the islands. When I was ten, my mother packed up and took us to Cornwall, where she had lived as a girl. My father moved to Somerset, where he bought the house that Henry Irving was born in. After a while, we joined him in that house, where he was to die. I started going to boarding school when I was eleven, and continued there until I was eighteen. I loved school. I was good at Rugby and I was good at running. In fact, I was a very good all-around athlete, and that always makes things easy for you in an English public school. I was good in classes, too, but I was terribly lazy. I'd work in spurts. I was made head prefect when I was sixteen, and for eighteen months of bliss I had a study of my own, with a wireless. I did a lot of acting in school. I had a great competitive instinct; I was always going on the stage to prove that I was the best actor. I was competitive in general. I never resented it if anybody else was praised. I just wanted what was due me. The most dead-giveaway story about me has to do with something that happened when I was thirteen. We were having Under-Fourteen Sports Day at school. I said to the other boys beforehand, "I'm going to win the hundred-yard dash." Another boy said that I'd be second, and that a boy named Thomas was going to win. We came to Sports Day, and I won the dash easily and Thomas was second. I said to the boys, "I told you I was going to win it." They seemed to begrudge me the victory. That made me feel resentful. All I wanted was my due. From the beginning, I felt that way strongly about acting. When I was twelve, I won the dramatic prize at school for playing Richard the Lion-Hearted in a one-act play. Everybody said I was the only one who could be *heard*. My name was put on a scroll, and there was a lot of applause. For me, at school, and for a long time after that, acting was a matter of showing off. But it wasn't all that simple, because I always disliked people who didn't do it well. These days, I quite often have a great sense of pleasure when I can feel that I am actually communicating something onstage. Truro was a very theatrical school. Every dormitory did a one-act play each term. In school plays, when I was fourteen I played Lady Macbeth, and at fifteen I played Mark Antony in "Julius Caesar." I was the leading lady in these dramatic-society plays for two years; once, I had to play the part of the blond Russian vamp in "Idiot's Delight."

I had one schoolmaster who got me to read all sorts of things—pretty well everything, including all the classic novels. He was just one of those bits of luck one has in one's life. His name is Cyril Wilkes, and I still see him from time to time. He must have been lonely, and that was his life—teaching boys and helping them. He used to take three or four of us to see plays in London. The first real play I ever saw, in the autumn of 1944, was "Hamlet," with John Gielgud, in a repertory production put on at the Haymarket.

Mr. Wilkes took some of us to London during a school holiday. We saw Gielgud's "Hamlet" at a matinée. That evening, we saw Margaret Leighton and Ralph Richardson in "Peer Gynt," and the next day we saw Laurence Olivier in "Richard III" at a matinée, and Alastair Sim in the James Bridie play "It Depends What You Mean" that evening. The third day, we saw Laurence Olivier in the film "Henry V" in the morning, and in the evening we saw John Gielgud again, in "Love for Love." I was quite dazzled. Gielgud made an extraordinary impression on me. I can see him now as he looked in "Hamlet"—that long, angular body in the black costume. That first night, I went back to the hotel room, picked up "Hamlet," and read it from beginning to end. Mr. Wilkes taught French and directed all the school plays. He always had time to talk to the boys. We used to sit in his room until two or three in the morning talking about books and politics. Mr. Wilkes was one of those English liberals of the thirties—a member of the Left Book Club, who had probably thought about going to fight Fascism in Spain but then hadn't done it. He was that kind of teacher. He directed me in the school plays, but he told me not to try to become a professional actor. He said that I had the wrong temperament for it—that I was too rebellious and wanted my own way too much. Later on, I found out that it was his policy to say that to everybody, on the theory that if you're set on doing a thing, you'll go ahead and do it anyway.

Somehow I got through all my exams, and in 1945 I received a scholarship to Cambridge. To fill in the time between Christmas, when I left school, and the start of the university year, in October, I took a job teaching at Glenhow, a prep school, in Saltburn, Yorkshire. I was particularly good at teaching cricket and Rugby, but I taught regular subjects besides—English, French, arithmetic. I still had to take a special Latin exam in order to qualify for Cambridge. Suddenly, the prospect of sitting down to study Latin appalled me. Also, I was rather broke then, and if you wanted to get a bigger grant at Cambridge, you had to agree to stay on and teach for a year at Cambridge, and I didn't want to do that. It seemed to me a good idea to go on to an acting school, so I wrote to the principal of the Royal Academy of Dramatic Art and asked for an audition. When I read for him, he told me that I wasn't talented enough for a scholarship but that I was good enough to get in. I thought I was really good. I knew I could hold an audience. For me, acting was a pleasurable thing—the most pleasurable thing I knew except scoring in a football match. It was much the same kind of thing—not quite the same, though. It gave me the same feeling I used to get walking back up the field after scoring a try, with everybody clapping. What always disturbed me about acting was that you could never prove exactly what you had done, while if you scored a try, there was no doubt about it. I went to the R.A.D.A. for two years—from 1946 to 1948. I didn't do at all well my first year. The teaching was appalling, but one gradually learned from the older actors there; they were wonderful. I couldn't have found a better toughening-up school. If you weren't liked, you only got two-line parts in the students' plays. Toward the end of my last year there, I won a competition for the best actor of the afternoon by playing Lord Byron in "Bitter Harvest" before an audience of agents and managers, and from then on I got good parts in a lot of plays. In those days, I was completely without nerves. I never worried about acting.

In 1948, I was asked to go to Stratford, and I went. I stayed for two seasons, at seven pounds a week the first season and nine the next. I had great energy then, and great attack. I was never one of those actors who don't understand the text. Something that used to annoy me at Stratford was the way actors didn't understand what they were saying. They used to tell me, "I just say the lines." I had great intellectual arrogance. I had no humility then at all. For one thing, I used to try to prove how masculine I was. I would stand in certain ways and attack things very vigorously. In my early years of acting, there was often no relation between what the author had written and what I did. When you're young, you can get away with things like that. You're attractive, and you don't know you're doing it, and you go along on enthusiasm. I was far too outspoken in those days. I had no social graces. If I didn't think I was in a good position onstage, I would say so. In my first season at Stratford, I was playing a tiny, tiny part— the Duke of Burgundy in "King Lear." I was supposed to stand in a tiny corner. John Gielgud was directing, and playing Lear, and I said to him, in front of fifty or sixty people, "I can't possibly give any idea of the majesty of the Duke of Burgundy with my back to the audience." He was so astonished! At the end of the season, he sent for me and said, "I do admire you and think you've got a lot of ability, and I'd like to help you, but you make me so nervous." I suppose we were poles apart in temperament. While I was at Stratford, I went to London to see "The Lady's Not for Burning" when Gielgud was playing in it and was also directing at Stratford. After the play, we drove back to Stratford together. On the way, I told him that I didn't like the play—that I had liked his performance very much but not the play. I said, "That's no way to write plays, and besides a lot of the writing is imitative," and I quoted lines from W. H. Auden, among others, to prove it. I knew quite a bit about poetry, and used to write poetry myself in those days. I was able to substantiate everything I said. I really hated that play, and told him so. It was pretentious, I said. The images were never illuminating. There was no discipline in the writing. There was no economy in the writing. The characters were one-dimensional. It was all sort of a word game. But the play had dazzling costumes, so the public loved it. I think Gielgud was impressed, but wary of me.

I was so anxious to prove that I was the most talented young actor in the company. I thought I was terribly well read. Most of the others at Stratford didn't seem to know anything except theatre. They seemed to me to be so effete, so physically run down. I was quite intolerant of them. I used to be terribly critical of the tendency of so many of the actors to be forever listening to their own voices—all of them, including Gielgud, Diana Wynyard, Peggy Ashcroft. I'd get terribly angry about the way the middle ranks were chosen for their usefulness to the star. It was all so stratified. Very often not the best actor but the most amenable actor would get the job. We had a phrase for that kind of actor; he was a "good company man." Of course, it's now very understandable to me that the director just didn't have the time to bother about the actor playing a messenger or some such tiny part. But in those days I said some pretty silly things. Besides that, I was thoroughly irresponsible onstage. Once, when Alex Davion was playing a courtier and I was playing a gnome in "A Midsummer Night's Dream," at Stratford, I tied the wings of one of the other gnomes to a tree. It was an outrageous thing to do, of course. Afterward, the actor playing the other gnome said it was a very unprofessional thing to do. He was a mild man, and smaller than I was, and I admitted that he was right. I always admit a thing like that when it's pointed out. Nothing frightens me more than a mild man who is righteously indignant. I don't mind it so much if I think he's wrong, but I mind it a lot when I know he's right. We were so bored, though. We thought we should be playing leads. Furthermore, there was an awful lot of dishonest, ritualistic acting that made me want to do rebellious things. In Shakespeare, they'd assume personalities, put on voices, and never grasp the reality of the part at all. In acting Shakespeare, the first requirement is to be real, to present a human being. Of course, you have to have a sense of rhythm—you have to know how to phrase. But the English are so concerned with externals. They're so proud of being able to wear costumes well. I was warned three times at Stratford that I'd be sacked. Edmund Purdom *was* sacked. He and I used to sit in the wings playing chess until it was our turn to go on and open doors, or something. We were full of frustrations. We took ourselves seriously as actors, but we felt that the power was in the wrong hands. One of the older actors we admired and liked very much was Godfrey Tearle, who died in 1953. He used to understand us. He thought we were funny. We could make him laugh at us, and somehow that always seemed to ease the situation.

At Stratford, one night in 1950, Alec Guinness saw me as Conrade, one of the villains in "Much Ado About Nothing," and he came around and said, "My name is Alec Guinness. I would like to compliment you on your performance." He then asked me to join the cast of his own West End production of "Hamlet," produced in May, 1951. For my London début, I played Rosencrantz, at twenty pounds a week. It was my first play in the West End. The play was a famous, disastrous flop, but I liked working with Guinness. He and Godfrey Tearle were the first star actors I felt at ease with. They treated me as an equal. I'm not somebody who is popular, but I've always been able to have four or five people around me whom I can trust. I like to be with people who will tell me the truth as they see it. Now that I know I can be a writer, I don't care as much about success in the theatre, but I do care about maintaining my position. Though I have always been very competitive as an actor, I've never been able to fight a selfish actor or a calculating actor. Now I've simply resolved that I will never again work with anyone I don't like. I've come to understand why John Gielgud surrounds himself with people who are sympathetic to his ideas.

In my first five years as a professional actor, I didn't utter a line that wasn't Shakespeare. I learned pretty fast in those days. One learns taste as one goes along. At first, I forced the charm somewhat. Most actors tend to play for sympathy from the audience, and I think I did it all the time. I was selling myself to the audience—not so baldly as some other people but doing it all the same. In some plays, of course, you've got to sell yourself, because it's up to you to improve on the text. But gradually, over the years, I learned, just by doing it, how to play parts as people would behave, instead of jazzing them up. In the long run, the audience likes it better that way. I always understood it in my mind, but in the early days I couldn't put it into practice. Eventually, I began to be able to weld everything together. For example, in Harold Pinter's "The Caretaker" I played a young man who has had a tragic experience in a mental hospital and, at one point in the play tells what happened in the hospital. I could play that scene for sympathy and get the whole house with me on a certain level, and it took a lot of honesty to do it the way I should, and often did, do it, which was to tell about it as simply as possible. I so respect Pinter. I always had an image of him sitting out in front. I knew how he wanted it played; theatrical effect was not what Pinter wanted. "The Caretaker" was the most wearing play I've ever been in, because I wasn't anything like the character I played. If I dropped my concentration for a second, the play would fall on the floor. I had to listen so intently, and I had to restrain myself so not to play for sympathy, that by the end of the performance I would be exhausted.

One advantage that English actors have over Americans is that they have the opportunity to act much more. Everything I've learned I've learned by doing. From what I've been able to see of American actors, I'd say they are much less secure than British actors. I'm sure part of the reason is economic. There's simply more work to be done in England. There you can do the equivalent of an Off Broadway play and do television at the same time, but here the actor is split right down the middle. If he's lucky enough to have a job acting in New York, he is faced with the choice of staying where he is or going to the Coast to do rubbish television. And actors are treated with more respect in England. Here they seem to be bullied by everybody else. The stagehands are paid more money than they are in England, and they tend to push actors around. American actors seem afraid of their directors—afraid they'll be sacked if they argue with directors. If you're frightened of arguing with your director, you're in a bad way.

In England, producers are prepared to run to half-filled houses and give a play time to build up an audience, but here it seems that costs make that sort of attitude impossible. George Duveen, who runs our Royal Court Theatre, the equivalent of a leading Off Broadway theatre, has said, "We are not here to make money," and he's been criticized for saying it, but I do think that his idea is sound.

After doing "Hamlet" with Guinness, I joined the Old Vic, at the invitation of Tyrone Guthrie, who had directed me as the Duke of Suffolk in "Henry VIII" at Stratford. I played Cassio in "Othello" and Lysander in "A Midsummer Night's Dream," and toured Europe and South Africa with the company. I got married in Rhodesia; my wife was playing a fairy in "A Midsummer Night's Dream," a serving maid in "Othello," and a witch in "Macbeth." In those days, I was sold on Shakespeare. I thought Shakespeare was going to be my theatrical life, and the following year I returned to Stratford. The best part I played that season was Edmund in "King Lear." The rest was frustration, shared with me by Donald Pleasence; we dressed together. At the end of the season, I wasn't asked back. The next three years were a bad period. I was really poor. I got bits and pieces to do. I made my first film, "The Dam Busters," in which I was on the screen quite a lot but had about eight lines. In June, 1955, I played in the London production of "Tiger at the Gates"—the part of Topman, who comes on in the beginning and reports on what Helen is doing in Troy and says "I can tell the sex of a seagull thirty yards off," which is a good line to have in any play. It wasn't a success in London, where we played for eight and a half weeks after taking it on tour for eight and a half weeks. I wrote two plays during "Tiger at the Gates." I'd written my first play while I was in Guinness' "Hamlet"—a verse play about an actor and his girl friend. During those three bad years, I used to borrow money to live on. I never minded borrowing it, somehow, and people never minded lending it to me; we all knew it would be repaid. I made a few more films, and in one, "Hill in Korea," I had quite a nice part, that of a simple country boy. I've never been in a good movie, though. My parts in films have never been remotely as good as my parts on the stage. I also did quite a bit of television work. But I was usually desperate for work. Lying in bed one day, I went as far as to look through the ads for jobs, and I applied for one at the H. J. Heinz factory in London—putting beans in cans. I didn't get the job. They said I was too well educated. They probably thought I'd make trouble. I can remember praying for a job at one point, though I wasn't religious.

In 1957, in London, I made a television series for C.B.S.-TV called "The Buccaneers," in which I played the part of the hero, Captain Dan Tempest. Up to then, I had never earned more than sixteen hundred pounds a year. For the series, I was offered ten thousand pounds for eight months' work. Naturally, I took it. After a while, I began to hate it. I enjoyed the swashbuckling. The captain was a sort of Errol Flynn character, and I'd always admired Flynn in the movies. But the scripts were so bad, and I couldn't go anywhere in England without being recognized. They didn't speak to Robert Shaw any more. They spoke to Captain Dan Tempest. It was slave work. I didn't write a word while I was doing the series. I'd get up at six to go to the studio, and I couldn't get home before eight at night. The conscientious actors in television work of this sort learn all their lines at night. I didn't bother to learn more than the first two lines and the last two lines; I paraphrased the rest. That was the only way to keep sane. It was a cheerful series, however. At least, I was gay in it, and laughed a lot. When in doubt about anything, I'd laugh. I was very good at the fencing, too. I bought my first car, a yellow-and-black 1933 Rolls-Royce. That's about all I bought with the money. I was uninterested in clothes. The week I started filming "The Buccaneers," I had one of my plays produced at the Arts Theatre. Called "Off the Mainland," it was one of the plays I'd written during "Tiger at the Gates," and was based on the Paolo and Francesca story. I played Lazslo Rimini, the lead, myself. It lasted six weeks. We played to half-empty houses. Until the play opened, I thought it was marvellous. One of my friends, Lindsay Anderson, told me that it was bad but that it had flashes of good writing. He said one has to know what one is trying to say, and I didn't. I was probably quite hurt by all this. I was making two hundred and fifty pounds a week filming "The Buccaneers," and I probably decided to take refuge in the commercial world. So I came to America to help promote "The Buccaneers," which not only was being made by an American network but had an American sponsor.

I spent a week in New York, going to a press party at the Stork Club and appearing on a lot of television shows and being in the Macy's Thanksgiving Day Parade. It was all very glamorous and exciting.

Then I went back to London. I was offered a lot of work on television, but it was rubbish work. I turned it down. I took my family and went to live in the country for a bit. Something a London manager had said —that the first act of one of my plays was written like a novel—stuck in my mind. So I started to write "The Hiding Place." One day, Donald Pleasence came to visit me in the country. I asked him if he would lend me some money. He asked why, and I said because I was writing a novel. He lent me a hundred pounds. The novel was a success, selling twelve thousand copies in England and about the same in France and in the United States. I wrote a dramatization of it that was produced on commercial television in England. "Playhouse 90," in America, had a different dramatization of it on television. After the novel, I think I began to grow up a bit. It was a turning point for me. All the competitive thing went when the book became a success.

But as an actor I had become a joke. It was ironic, because people all over England knew me and my name, but to the people in power in the theatre I was nothing. I did some thinking about the way I had behaved at Stratford, and thought, Whom do I like in the theatre? I liked George Duveen and what he was doing at the Royal Court. It was the most interesting theatre in England. I had worked for him at Stratford and given him a bit of trouble. So I sat down and wrote a letter to Duveen at the Royal Court, saying that I thought he was doing marvellous work, and that I was so sorry I had been so stupid. I had an answer in a week, offering me a part in "Live Like Pigs," by John Arden. That's when it all began. I got on marvellously with Duveen and did two more plays with him. All of them were worth doing. I was doing what I could do. I was rehabilitated as an actor. I was in "The Long and the Short and the Tall," by Willis Hall, with Peter O'Toole. It was a hit, and moved to the West End. I played a sergeant in control of a patrol in Burma. It was the best part I had ever had. The acting was worth doing. In that play, I was the father figure, suddenly. Suddenly I was in a position of responsibility in relation to three or four actors more irresponsible than I was. I was actually forced into a position of responsibility. My greatest personal success around that time was in the Jacobean play "The Changeling." I played an ugly servant in love with the mistress of the house—played by Mary Ure—who persuades him to murder her fiancé. He does, and then claims her. They become obsessed with each other, and are discovered, and he kills her. The play was directed by Tony Richardson, and played a limited engagement—two months— to packed houses.

I don't act for the audience now. I act for a few individuals. Pinter, for one. Pleasence, for another. And I act for myself. What I like now is just the work. I don't think I *could* do anything now that I didn't like. I wouldn't mind a sort of Errol Flynn part in an epic, treating it on that level, but I wouldn't be in anything dishonest. Most actors are very vulnerable. It's so easy for them to lose their integrity. You have to learn how to stand up to the pressure of success. All this kind of thing takes so long to assimilate. It was only when I was past thirty-four that I began to prefer the truth.

PATTY DUKE

My biggest problem as an actress is growing. I grow at the rate of one inch a year.

I was born on December 14, 1946, in New York City. My parents, John and Frances Duke, were separated when I was about seven. My father is a cab driver. I don't see him. I have one sister, Carol, who is six years older than I am and works as a secretary for an insurance firm, and one brother, Raymond, four years older than I am, who became an actor before I became one. When Ray was eight, he joined the Madison Square Boys' Club. We were poor then, and lived in a tenement on East Thirty-first Street, and the club was in our neighborhood. He used to come home and tell us about the activities at the club—the boxing matches and the plays and all the rest of the fun. It sounded very exciting. Then, when Ray played the lead in "The Ransom of Red Chief" at the club, someone there recommended him to Mr. and Mrs. John Ross, who specialize in finding children with talent and managing them. When I was about seven, the Rosses, who are extremely kind and serious people, without children of their own, got Ray some jobs to do on television. He'd come home and tell about acting in commercials and how much fun it was to kid

150

around with Paul Winchell and all the other people he worked with. Around Christmastime of 1954, he did a toy commercial that was really something, and then the Rosses got him some work to do in a television series called "Crunch and Dez." It was made in Bermuda, and he went all the way to Bermuda on a plane, and when he came back, he told us how wonderful the plane trip was, and how he had fished in Bermuda and gone swimming, and how beautiful the water was, and he told us about how he had driven a boat. It sounded like such fun to me. I had never seen a play myself. I didn't even know what acting was. I was going to the Sacred Heart School, near where we lived, and we never put on plays except for little Christmas things. After school, I would play in the street with the other kids. Every once in a while, my mother would take us to Coney Island, but I was bored by it. I was smaller than the other kids my age, and usually went around with kids younger than I was. That was boring, too. I knew television and the movies, but I didn't think of them as having anything to do with acting. Acting to me then was something different. Acting was going to faraway places, doing things you never did around our neighborhood, and having fun. I wanted to do acting, the way Ray did. Now that I am fifteen, I realize that everyone has a dream of doing something other than what he *is* doing, but not everyone can do it. I was sure I could. I wanted to become an actress right away. I didn't want to just dream of becoming an actress when I was grown up. So one day Ray took me along to a party at the Rosses', to meet them. I was just eight. The Rosses were very nice. They began to give me training in diction. I love the Rosses. They've looked after me ever since. I now spend as much time at their house as I do at my own.

After a while, the Rosses began taking me around to some offices for interviews. None of the people we saw seemed to believe that I wanted to be an actress. I knew they wanted someone prettier than I was—someone with a round face and blond curly hair and dimples. We kept going around for interviews. After a few months, we got discouraged and stopped. But I knew that the Rosses would remember me if something came up, and they did. When the sinking of the Andrea Doria was dramatized for television, there was a part for a little Italian girl, and I got it. It was my first part. I was nine. I had been discouraged, but when I finally did start acting, it was just as much fun as I had thought it would be. I had to use an Italian accent as this little Italian girl. The Rosses helped me get the accent right. And they kept telling me, "When you are acting, always make a distinction; one part of you is the character, another part is you, Patty Duke. Patty Duke knows what is coming, but the character does *not* know what is coming." My mother in the play had to throw me overboard, but I wasn't afraid. I acted as though I was very frightened, but I wasn't, because I knew I had a nice soft mattress to fall on. In order to seem frightened, I just thought of how I might have been frightened by a height—like the fear of being pushed off a diving board or a snowbank. I always remember the part of me that is the character, as long as I'm onstage. Once, when I was playing the part of Helen Keller as a child in "The Miracle Worker," one of the lights fell to the stage and crashed. It was an accident. Everyone else in the cast and everyone in the audience was scared. Some people screamed. But I didn't. I remembered that I was playing a character who couldn't see or hear, and I kept it up, because we were onstage. I was holding an Irish setter, a real one, and I squeezed it, but no one knew I did that.

For about four years after my first television part, I did a lot of dramatic parts on television, and made other appearances. I was very good at doing British accents. When I was in the television play "Wuthering Heights," with Richard Burton and Rosemary Harris, in May, 1958, I played Cathy as a child. I was the only member of the cast who wasn't really British. I loved doing the British accent. Working with Richard Burton was great, and I loved the beautiful costumes. It was all such fun. In one scene, we had rain. I looked up and there was a big hose with holes in it, and all of a sudden there was rain. In about four years, I appeared in almost forty television shows, including "The Prince and the Pauper," "Swiss Family Robinson," "The Power and the Glory," and "Once Upon a Christmastime," and a number of times in two television series called "Kitty Foyle" and "Brighter Day." And I made appearances on a lot of shows where they kidded around and were kind, and it wasn't even like work—Phil Silvers', Frankie Laine's, and Paul Winchell's shows. I had the most fun of all when I played Tootie in "Meet Me in St. Louis," with Ed Wynn, who played my grandfather. I had to sing and dance. I had never danced before, but Mrs. Ross, who used to be a professional dancer, taught me how to do a waltz clog, and I did it with Ed Wynn. In 1957, I was in a documentary movie, "The Deep Well," with my brother Ray. It was all about this boy who is a delinquent, and his sister. They come from a broken home. It told about this home for children in Pleasantville where children from broken homes go. The film was shown to social workers and people like that. Making it was very exciting, because it was filmed at this home in Pleasantville, and it was the first time I'd gone on location, and Pleasantville was the farthest I'd ever gone from home.

In the summer of 1961, I worked in the film version of "The Miracle Worker." I'd been in a few movies—the documentary with Ray, and "The Goddess," in which I played Kim Stanley as a child, and a couple of others—so I knew a little bit about acting for the movies. Mr. Ross explained that a film and a play require two completely different techniques. He told me about closeups, and how when D. W. Griffith made the first closeup, showing only the face, enlarged, on the screen, the audiences started to scream, "What happened to everybody else?" Mr. Ross also explained how your movements, and so on, are much more confined in a movie. In a play, you have to make things broader, and you have to project more; you have to reach the last row in the balcony with your voice. And another thing he explained was that while everything in a play is done in continuous sequence, in a movie you may shoot a one-minute indoor scene on the sound stage and then shoot the next minute of the film on location four weeks later. It's harder to do, but you learn to do it. Mr. Ross teaches me everything. He works with me until the first rehearsal of a movie or a play I'm doing, but he never interferes with the director. Working with Arthur Penn, who directed me in both the stage and the screen versions of "The Miracle Worker," was a fabulous experience. He's so considerate and patient and kind and gentle, and really fun.

Fifteen months before "The Miracle Worker" was produced on Broadway, Mr. Ross heard that it was going to be put on. He immediately began to plan ahead for it. We knew we were going to get that part. We started to work on it a couple of days a week after school. I would go to his house, and he would read about Helen Keller to me. He bought every book about her childhood that he could get hold of, to find out what she was like. The Rosses both read a lot about her to me, and they told me a lot, too. I learned that Helen Keller loved food and loved to smell flowers. She liked to feel the sun on her skin and to lie in the grass. I'd think about things like that every morning while

153

I was getting dressed to go to school. In the afternoon, after school, the Rosses would sometimes take me to the park, where I would lie on the grass and smell the flowers. After we'd done that a lot, we began working on the blind part. We started by having me keep my eyes closed. Then the Rosses heard that the director was going to want the girl to have her eyes open in the play, so we started practicing it that way. The Rosses made a game of it. I would sit on the couch in the Rosses' living room, looking straight ahead of me, and the Rosses would put something in my line of vision. If I looked at it, I lost. If I didn't, I won. Then we started on the deafness. I would sit on the couch pretending I couldn't hear, sometimes for two hours at a time. Mrs. Ross would come in and ask me if I wanted a Coke, or something, and if I answered, I lost. If I didn't show anything, I won. After we had decided to go out for the Helen Keller part, we turned down a part in "The Sound of Music," although I occasionally appeared on television in a play, like "One Red Rose for Christmas," with Helen Hayes. Aside from that, all I did was go to school and then practice every day that I was blind, deaf, and dumb. We worked for almost a year before I had an audition for the part. At first, the producer and director thought I might not work out, because if I grew two inches I'd be too tall. But Mrs. Ross put two-inch heels on an old pair of shoes of mine and stood me next to Anne Bancroft with the heels, and they decided that even if I grew a little it would still be all right. I was at the Rosses' apartment when the agency representing me telephoned Mr. Ross and told him the part was mine. We were so happy, and we'd worked so hard for it, that now it was here, we cried. It was really great. I've been having fun ever since.

When I'm in a play, I get up at eight-thirty every morning. I go to Quintano's School for Young Professionals, on West Fifty-sixth Street. I get the top marks in my class. I always get all A's in history and French, but I also like English, general science, and earth science. Languages are very easy for me. I like history best of all, though. I want to know why things happened the way they did. I'm planning to go to finishing school and maybe to college, but I'm not sure yet what I'm going to study. I *am* sure I want to stay in the theatre. I love it. My mother and my brother and I live in Elmhurst, Queens. When I'm working, I go to school from ten in the morning until one in the after-noon. Then, if I don't have a singing lesson, I go home or to the Rosses' place. I have two sets of school books. I keep one set at home and the other set at school. When I'm in a play, I may go home after school, if I want to go ice-skating or, something, with the children in my neighborhood, or I may go to the Rosses'. During "The Miracle Worker," I went to the theatre by bus and by subway, and sometimes in a taxi, and then, at the end of the play, a taxi would usually pick me up and either take me home to Elmhurst or take me to the Rosses', depending on how I felt or on my schedule. The Rosses like me to get as much rest as possible, so I try to get to bed by midnight. My mother or one of the Rosses is always with me at the theatre. I found it a lot of fun to act in "The Miracle Worker," even though I didn't get to wear pretty clothes or have my hair curled. Opening night was especially exciting. Everyone was so friendly. What I like about being in a play is pleasing the audience and making them laugh or feel things. Every night there's a new audience. If they applauded the big fight scene in "The Miracle Worker" and if the jokes got big laughs, we'd all know we were going great. If the applause or laughs didn't come—well, we'd just go to work right away and keep working until the applause and laughs came back. The play ran from October, 1959, to July, 1961, and except for the last five weeks, when I left to begin work on the movie version of the play, I didn't miss a single performance. After we'd been playing for several months, sometimes someone in the cast would say, around eight-thirty, "Well, here we go again"—and give a great big sigh. But I never felt that way. Every night was a new night for me.

Best of all, better than being in a play, I love going places with Mr. and Mrs. Ross. Once, they took me on a two-week vacation to Florida. We flew in a plane, and chartered a boat there. It was just as much fun as I'd thought it would be. The Rosses have taken me to Atlantic City, too—to the Barclay Motel, which has a swimming pool, with a plastic dome, where you can swim the year around. In New York, sometimes, we pack some steaks and have a picnic under the George Washington Bridge, or we go to Palisades Park and have a cookout there. That's my idea of fun.

ELI WALLACH

*Acting is the most delicious experience in life. When
I'm supposed to be feeling despair on the stage, what
I really feel is that I'm sitting on top of the world.*

I was born on December 7, 1915, in Brooklyn, in the Red Hook section
known as Little Italy. My parents had a candy store named Bertha's.
Bertha was my mother, who died in 1955. I had just come back from
England, where I had played Sakini in "The Teahouse of the August
Moon" for almost a year. My father is now eighty-six, and lives in
Brooklyn with my brother. I was the third of four children. The three
others became teachers. In Red Hook, we were the only Jews in a sea
of Italians. I grew up feeling Italian as well as Jewish. I attended hundreds of Italian winemaking sessions, carrying boxes of grapes to
winemaking cellars and getting bunches of grapes as a reward. Every
summer from the age of eight to the age of fourteen, I spent two weeks
in a summer camp in Raritan, New Jersey, run as a charity by the old
Life magazine. I made my début as an actor in that camp. When I was
fifteen, my parents sold the candy store and, around the same time,
bought a three-family house on Bedford Avenue, in Flatbush; we lived
on the first floor and were supported by the rent paid by the families

we had as tenants on the two other floors. I went to Erasmus Hall High School, where I was an indifferent student, and unhappy. I never went to dances. I was a miserable adolescent. Across from Erasmus, however, was a Boys' Club, where I played ping-pong and swam. And that's where I really found out about acting. I starred in a play called "Fiat Lux," playing a sixty-five-year-old man who was bitter because he had lost his children and his belief in God. When one of the kids in the audience yelled out "That's Eli!" I wanted to jump off the stage and pot him. I still get sore if I think people don't believe what I want them to believe. It's very important to me that they believe. It gives me an added sense of power, or something. From the time I was a kid, I've never been afraid to make believe. But during my first performance in a role I'm terrified. After the first plunge into the water, I seldom have stage fright.

I graduated from high school in 1932—one of the worst years of the depression. I then went to the University of Texas, where the tuition was thirty dollars a year, which was all I could afford, and majored in history. My family and everybody else I knew told me I should become a teacher, and I agreed with them. I stuck it out in Texas for four years, working at odd jobs and National Youth Administration jobs to pay for my board and room. The university had no Drama Department, but it did have the Curtain Club, which I joined. I swept the stage, painted scenery, and, in 1936, my senior year, played the lead in "Liliom" for one week. At the end of the week, I began to think it might be possible to earn a living as an actor. Zachary Scott was the leading star of the club. He wore a dressing gown with style—with a scarf around his neck—and he looked at home in a tuxedo. I had a kind of built-in hostility toward a tuxedo, and I didn't own one until two years ago, when I was given one. I don't look bad in it, but I don't feel like Zachary Scott.

I graduated from Texas with an A.B., but to teach in New York I needed a Master's degree, and I got it at City College in 1938. While I was studying education, and also Chinese painting, I worked with a little-theatre group, was a playground director in some tough neighborhoods in Brooklyn, did radio plays for WLID in Brooklyn, and read *Theatre Arts Monthly*. After a while, I began to study acting in New York. I was a little guy, and I knew the odds were against me, but I was determined anyway. My family thought I was misguided, but I told them all, "This is what I am going to do." Acting was an avocation in the eyes of everybody but me. My parents' resistance in a way was lovely and wonderful. I guess part of everybody's drive is based on his parents' disapproval and on wanting to show them they were wrong. But in 1938, to please my parents, I went through the motions of taking an exam required by the Board of Education for a city teaching job. I was one of nineteen hundred and sixty out of two thousand who took the test who failed. So I felt free to do what I wanted to do. My sister Shirley was going out with a guy whose brother knew Sanford Meisner, of the Neighborhood Playhouse School of the Theatre, so I went there regularly, on a scholarship. I thought I was terrific. I felt I had great emotions, and believed I could pretend to be anybody. Also, I always felt I moved well onstage—what the books called "the graceful cross." I could bow with great flair. At the school, I learned a kind of rudimentary technique, and because Meisner was one of the first to bring Stanislavski's teachings to the United States, I got my first insight into these, as an antidote to the commercial cliché theatre. In the old-fashioned Delsarte system, actors acted by conventional signals to the audience. By Stanislavski's method, the actor is free to accept a stimulus while he's onstage and to react naturally to it. I loved that. After the first year, the Neighborhood Playhouse dropped students if they weren't satisfactory or promising. They thought I was good. They not only renewed my scholarship for a second year but lent me money— about eight dollars a week for eight months—so that I could keep going with food and cigarettes. Today, I'm on the school's board of directors.

The summer of 1939, I worked as a playground director again, but through James Parke, director of the Curtain Club, I got a part for a week in Locust Valley, Long Island, playing at night in "The Bo Tree," with an exciting bunch of actors that included Richard Widmark and Vincent J. Donehue. The play was about college boys, and my part was that of a young radical who goes to fight in the Spanish Civil War. It was a rounded part, with humor and a lot for me to do, and I loved it. I was ego incarnate. I thought I was a much better actor then than I think of myself as being now. These days, I know too much about the awesome amount of work that must go into making a part your own. But at least, at that time, I had the playground work to go back to during the day, and that was a great leveller.

I drew a low number in the draft, and I went into the Army in January, 1941, before Pearl Harbor. I was in the Army for over four years, as a Medical Corps administrator. I served both in the Pacific and in Europe, and was discharged as a captain. The only theatrical work I did was to organize a couple of soldier revues for hospital patients and staffs. In 1945, I started looking for jobs as an actor. One of my first roles was in an Equity Library Theatre production of Tennessee Williams' one-act play "This Property Is Condemned." Here I was, thirty years old, with ribbons and stuff, and I was playing the part of a boy of fifteen. I liked it. It made me feel good. The girl in the play was Anne Jackson, whom I married in 1948. She's always delighted me. We now have three children and live on Riverside Drive. I have tremendous respect and admiration for her as an actress, and more and more we're getting to appear together in plays. We were in "Major Barbara" together in 1957, and recently played together in "Rhinoceros" for six months. We have a tremendous working compatibility when we're in the same play, and especially when the play means something important to us, as "Rhinoceros" did. On November 13, 1945, I made my first Broadway stage appearance—as the crew chief in a play called "Skydrift," about a plane crash from which the ghosts of the men killed go home. I couldn't raise my voice above the roar of the sound-effect plane engines, but I survived in the play as long as it did on Broadway—seven performances. In 1946, I joined the American Repertory Theatre, and I had a chance to play Cromwell in "Henry VIII;" Spintho, the coward, in "Androcles and the Lion;" minor roles in "Yellow Jack" and "What Every Woman Knows;" and the Duck in "Alice in Wonderland," a part that had been played by an actor wearing skates on his knees. I played it in a continuous deep knee bend but without skates. I also played the Two of Spades and one of the other voices. Annie, my wife, was developing in her acting career, but I kept getting more and more discouraged. It wasn't money I cared about. We were getting along fine on unemployment insurance, living in a one-room, thirty-five-dollar-a-month apartment on lower Fifth Avenue in the Village. But I was always too young or too old or too small—never right for a part. I drove poor Annie nuts with my griping and grousing. At one point, I thought I'd go into medical administration—my old line of work. But in my heart I always knew that if I couldn't act I'd go mad.

I spent a few summers in summer stock, and a lot of weeks in insurance lines, G.I. as well as unemployment. In 1949, I got a part in "Mister Roberts," which I played for two years, and then, in February, 1951, I played the Sicilian lover in Tennessee Williams' "The Rose Tattoo," opposite Maureen Stapleton. I received an Antoinette Perry award for a distinguished feature performance. After a year and a half in "The Rose Tattoo," I went directly into another Williams play, "Camino Real," directed by Elia Kazan. The producers didn't have all the money that was needed to begin rehearsals, and while I was waiting I was offered the movie role of Angelo Maggio in "From Here to Eternity"—the part Frank Sinatra played that launched him on his career as an actor. I felt I should do the play with Kazan, and so I asked the movie producers for the ridiculously high salary of three thousand dollars a week to do Maggio. Sinatra thought I was insane not to try to get the part. Whenever he sees me now, he says to me, "You crazy actor!" But I've never been sorry. What do I need a movie for? The stage is on a higher level in every way, and a more satisfying medium. Movies, by comparison, are like calendar art next to great paintings. You can't really do very much in movies or in television, but the stage is such an anarchistic medium that the mavericks still can come in and do something. I made a gangster film recently—"The Lineup"—working five weeks at ten thousand dollars a week. After that, I felt so guilty about having been paid all that money, and had such a need to do penance, that I went to London and, at a tiny salary, played Elmer Rice's "Counsellor-at-Law" on the B.B.C.—live—with no commercial to break it up, and from there I flew to Rome and gave a lecture to actor-students on acting. I came back to New York, but I still felt guilty, so I did "The Chairs," by Ionesco, at the Phoenix Theatre, for twenty-two performances, at eighty-five dollars a week. By that time, I had expunged my guilt, so I went on TV and played a gangster again.

In 1947, when Elia Kazan, Cheryl Crawford, and Bobby Lewis started the Actors' Studio, I was one of the twenty who were the nucleus of the senior group. Others were my wife, David Wayne, Marlon Brando, Patricia Neal, Mildred Dunnock, Tom Ewell, Kevin McCarthy, Maureen Stapleton, Sidney Lumet, John Forsythe, and William Redfield. I believed, and still believe, it's an antidote to cliché acting. Some people say that the Studio has formalized a style of its own. That is possible. Maybe someday there will be a new movement as an antidote to the Studio. In the meantime, I believe in the Method. Laurence Olivier once said to me, "Isn't it greater artistry when you can communicate emotion but you don't feel a thing?" It's an old argument. A lot of English actors say, "Never mind about all the talking, just get on the stage and do it." We say, "Do what?" Acting is the most alive thing I can do, and the most joyous. The old-fashioned actor develops a facility that is predictable. When he wants to show anger, he'll clench his fists, and so on. We say, "Believe what you act." Naturally, you don't *really* believe, but it does give you a sense of something, and that gives your part life. As the curtain goes up, you're there, and you're willing to let something happen to you. The tendency at first is to absorb so much technique that you abuse it. Only as you mature as an artist do you leave out all the curlicues. You become less ornate and more perceptive. The zenith of the acting craft is when you can leave yourself alone. Each part you play has what can be called a spine—a line. You build a person's wants and needs around the movement of that line. Anna Magnani once told me, "When I do a character, if it's not right a shadow comes over me, because I act from the heart." That's her method, her own means of arriving at a character. She has a technique of her own. She's incapable of understanding any other method. What an actor learns, eventually, is that everyone has to find his own method and has to do what is right for himself. That's all that really matters in the end. The trouble today is that a lot of young people in acting go around saying that they're Method actors, and they don't understand that they are merely technicians, doing what they think is Method. They're losing all the joys of acting. And they're the ones some of our finest actors latch on to as examples of Method actors, saying that these youngsters should stop making such a to-do about creating and just create. Lee Strasberg would be the first to agree with such criticism. He's always told us that a technique is there only to help you, and if it hinders you, don't use it. All good actors aspire to the same end. True simplicity in art is what we all strive for. You use anything you can to achieve that end. If the Method is part of what I can use, I'm for it.

I've used at least a small part of my real self in every part I've ever played. Sometimes you use things inside yourself that you didn't even know were there. When I first read the part of the Sicilian lover in

"The Rose Tattoo," and first read a television play I did about the gangster Albert Anastasia, I immediately knew certain things about these men with my feelings, because I was brought up with Italians like them, and I knew their temperament. One of the Anastasias, as a matter of fact, lived across from the house I was born in, in Brooklyn. The guy became a killer for money. With him, it was a business. That means something special to me. Not that it's all crystal clear. Acting is always looking, always searching out the behavior of people. It's always wanting to know why people do things the way they do. But onstage you're always conscious of the audience. You know you're deluding them. Your own protection, and theirs, too, is the knowledge that it's make-believe, in a darkened theatre.

ANNE JACKSON

I adore finding out about people's behavior, and after
I find out I want to show it to somebody in acting.

I was born on September 3, 1926, in Millvale, Pennsylvania, on the outskirts of Pittsburgh. My father, John Jchekovitch, was born in Croatia, came to America in 1918, at the age of seventeen, and settled in Pittsburgh. He changed his name to John Jackson. He played the violin, the mandolin, and the accordion, and sang Slavic folk songs, and he spoke Hungarian, Polish, and Russian as well as Croatian. After getting his high-school diploma, he worked as a barber and ran a beauty parlor. He died in 1956. My mother, born Stella Murray, was the daughter of a Pennsylvania coal miner and was one of twelve children; she died when I was seventeen. She was always frightened and inhibited, and she was one of those terribly partial-to-the-Irish Irish Catholics. My father was an agnostic. I'm the youngest of three sisters. My sister Catherine, eight years older than I am, is married to a tool-and-die maker, lives in Manhasset, Long Island, and has two children. My sister Beatrice, three years older than I am, is also married to a tool-and-die maker, and she lives in Valley Stream, and has three children. I was the shyest child who ever lived. I loathed my bright-red hair. When I was four, Catherine made me a costume of yellow-and-blue crêpe paper, hung a blanket on our porch for a curtain, and put on a show for the kids in the neighborhood. I recited a corny poem she taught me, which she had cut out of the *Ladies' Home Journal*. Up to then, I'd never opened my mouth, and suddenly I got up there and recited and everybody yelled and clapped. It was wonderful. That's when I became an actress. When I was five, we moved to another little place near Pittsburgh, called Job, just outside the town of Tarentum, where my father had a barber shop. We lived in a little wooden house up in the hills that he'd bought for five hundred dollars. It had no heat and no plumbing. We got our heat from a pot-bellied stove, and we had to carry water from a well, but we were on the edge of a lovely forest and we had a garden, where my father raised beautiful flowers. I walked a mile to get to school. I was good in English, art, and history, and awful in arithmetic. I started going to movies when I was six, at the movie theatre in Tarentum. The first one I saw was "Letty Lynton," with Joan Crawford, Robert Montgomery, and Nils Asther. I couldn't get over the beautiful dress Joan Crawford was wearing—all satin, with fur on the bottom. My sisters had taken me to the movie, and as soon as we got home, we played the whole thing for ourselves; Catherine was Joan Crawford, Beatrice was Nils Asther, and I was Robert Montgomery. From then on, we'd always act a movie out right after we saw it. It was such a gorgeous world. You spent all your time being loved and kissed. Nobody ever washed the dishes in those movies, and the people always died so beautifully.

During the depression, my father couldn't make a living in Tarentum, and when I was eight he decided to move to New York. We lived for two months in an abandoned windmill on stilts in the marshes somewhere in Brooklyn, and then we moved to a tenement on Liberty Avenue, near a cemetery. I went to P.S. 214, then to P.S. 171, and finally to Franklin K. Lane High School. My sister Catherine joined every dramatic club she could find. Beatrice followed, and I got pushed into their footsteps. There was a movie house on Liberty Avenue that held an amateur-night contest every week. When I was ten, I wrote a skit with a girl friend who went to dancing school and was a genius at acrobatics, and we entered a contest. We

pretended we were Dead End Kids, and after some patter my friend
did flips and a tap dance, and I did imitations—of Charles Laughton
in "Mutiny on the Bounty," of Jeanette MacDonald in "San Francisco," and of Katharine Hepburn in "Morning Glory." We won first
prize—three dollars. That clinched it. There was no turning back.
At eleven, I was doing imitations of Shirley Temple. At twelve, I had
a whole Sonja Henie routine. Around then, I had an English teacher
in junior high school, Miss Edwards, who used to write monologues
for me to do, including one as Topsy and one as Anne of Green Gables.
I recited them in junior-high assembly. I recited so much that the
kids got bored with me. Then Miss Edwards introduced me to Shakespeare, and I recited speeches from the tragedies. I was so crazy to
recite that I went to other people's churches to get on their entertainment programs. At fourteen, I played the lead in a school production
of Ring Lardner's "June Moon." I was awful. I felt that the audience
was bored. I knew there was something wrong, but I didn't know what
it was. I didn't do any more school plays. I bided my time.

In 1943, when I was in my senior year, I took part in one of the
auditions that the producer John Golden regularly held for young new
talent. They were attended by agents and directors and casting people.
I got up and tried to do a dramatic scene, playing a woman who
stabbed her husband to death. The man running the auditions called
me aside and said, "Look, you're a little girl. Can't you do something
more appropriate for a little girl?" So I did Miss Edwards' monologue
as Anne of Green Gables—how she was an orphan, and hated the color
of her hair. I was immediately offered a job by George Abbott's secretary to go to the Orient with a U.S.O. show and play in "What a
Life." But I was sixteen, still under age, and my father refused to sign
the necessary papers. He wanted me to finish school. Impatiently, I
finished school and graduated. That summer, I worked as a salesclerk
in a Viennese candy store near Times Square. I knew a boy named
Steve Scheuer—he was a Yale boy I had met at my John Golden audition—and he introduced me to Herbert Berghof, the actor, who was
then with the New School for Social Research, and who became my first
acting teacher. Berghof told me that I should be an actress, that I should
study full time. I went to my father and said, "Daddy, this man says
I'm an artist." My father put me out of the house. Acting, he said, was
a profession for a whore. Catherine was married by then, so I went to

live with her. Berghof helped me get a scholarship to the Neighborhood Playhouse, and in September of 1943 I started studying there full time, from morning to night. My first real part was in the school's demonstration performance of a scene from "Peer Gynt," in which I played the ingénue in love with Peer Gynt. My father came to see me. He didn't say anything to me afterward, but he sat there all the way through.

At the Playhouse, I was battling to be the best. That was all. It was a purely competitive feeling. I didn't think anyone else could act. I thought I was the only one. I was absolutely blind to the needs of everyone else. I was thrown in with other actors, but I was a complete egotist. When I was told that I had to learn to speak well, or that I was showing off rather than doing the part, I was furious. I didn't know how to cope with something like that. I was a monologist. I was a loner. I didn't know the first thing about what it meant to work with other people. The main effect the school had was to shake me up; I began to get my first inkling that the theatre was a group effort. But I didn't wake up completely until much later, and then it was thanks to the influence of Lee Strasberg. He is, I think, a saint for actors. Actors are looked down on by so many people. A young, uneducated actor battles to find strength by using his own abilities. Lee Strasberg helped me find that strength. The reason so many actors and actresses talk about him with a kind of reverence is that they know from tough experience how rare it is to find a teacher who really knows *how* to help them. I had joined the Actors' Studio when it was founded, by Robert Lewis, Cheryl Crawford, and Elia Kazan, in 1948, but the class was too big and I was among those who had to leave; then, in 1950, when Lee was brought into the Studio, I was asked to join again. I have been extremely lucky in being exposed to some of the most dedicated teachers in the theatre—to Herbert Berghof at the New School and Sandy Meisner at the Neighborhood Playhouse as well as to Lee Strasberg. They are all purists and dedicated men. Strasberg makes the actor all-important. He gives the actor a tremendous sense of security. He's an extremely practical man, and he knows how much time it takes to develop an actor. He's the most loving, patient teacher. He levels with you. He knows how to praise the actor; in your worst work he will always find something that is good, even while he is exposing the trickery and the fears that lead an actor to resort to trickery. He always leaves the actor his self-respect. I learned more about acting from him than from anybody else. I started out as an instinctive actress who was absolutely terrified of taking direction and advice. I'd always say, "No, I'll find it myself," and then immediately get into a kind of contest with the director. I learned from Lee how to *listen* to a director. I learned how to take help from a director and not care about whether it was his idea or my idea to begin with; I learned that by working with other people I'd find a way to make my performance as good as possible—the only thing that mattered.

Altogether, it took me over ten years to gain confidence in myself. In 1944, after a year at the Neighborhood Playhouse, I was suddenly offered the part of Anya, the ingénue, in Eva Le Gallienne's road-company production of "The Cherry Orchard," directed by Margaret Webster and Eva Le Gallienne. I put down my fee of seventy dollars and joined Actors' Equity as a full fledged member. Suddenly I was being paid seventy-five dollars a week for sixteen weeks on tour. I'd never been anywhere on a trip, and suddenly I was going to Boston, Chicago, Cincinnati, and all kinds of whistle stops, too. I was completely uneducated. I knew nothing about Chekhov's plays. I didn't even know who *he* was. Eva Le Gallienne was the star, playing Lyubov Andreyevna, and I didn't know who Eva Le Gallienne was, either. Joseph Schildkraut played Leonid Andreyevitch. I had never heard of him. I didn't know that he was a fine actor, and the *son* of a fine actor. I roomed with two other girls, and one of them, Madeleine L'Engle, who understudied the role of Charlotta Ivanovna and appeared in the party scene with me, took me in hand and introduced me to books about the theatre and its history, and to other books. We had discussions; it had never occurred to me before that actors discussed what they called "the author's intention." In the cities, Madeleine took me to museums. The only museum I'd ever been in up to then was the Museum of Natural History—once. I began to get a smattering of knowledge of the arts. And I began to learn something about procedure and routine in the world of the theatre. I missed a cue once in a performance, and although Miss Le Gallienne didn't get furious, or anything like that, she let me know what it means if you hold up the progress of a play. I learned that you didn't call Eva Le Gallienne "Eva;" you called her "Miss Le Gallienne." I learned what respect means, and learned something about how to behave. I learned that when you were on the road you saved your money; you didn't eat much, and if you bought anything, it was a book. None of this was really in my own nature to do, but I went along with the others in order to belong, and by going along I began to develop my own knowledge and taste.

When I returned to New York, I took a thirty-five-dollar-a-month room, with bath and linen service, on lower Fifth Avenue. I began to learn that people can be terribly generous when they believe in you. At one time, when I was practically starving, and couldn't afford a telephone, Sam Jaffe, a very fine actor who lived in the neighborhood, would deliver messages to me about available jobs. Later on, Mainbocher, who had worked on costumes for me for a play, would recommend me for jobs he heard about. I had played in a classic. I had an agent. Now I went and read for what turned out to be a series of smash flops. In February, 1945, I played a hillbilly in "Signature," a melodrama by Elizabeth McFadden, which closed after two performances. I acted with Jessie Royce Landis in two plays that lasted about a week—"The Last Dance," an adaptation by Peter Goldbaum and Robin Short of "Dodsdancen," by Strindberg, and "Magnolia Alley," by George Batson. I was in a flop with Shirley Booth—"Love Me Long," by Doris Frankel. In March, 1946, I was in the Equity Library Theatre production of "This Property Is Condemned," by Tennessee Williams, in which Eli Wallach played the male lead. When I first saw him, I said he was too old for the part. (He was thirty.) I was told by Terese Hayden, a good young actress, who directed the play for the E.L.T., "When you learn to act as well as he does, then you can make statements about people being too old or too young for a part." Three days later, I fell in love with Eli. We were married in 1948. He moved into my room, and we bought a refrigerator and a hot plate. Just before my marriage, I was in the first play I had respected since "The Cherry Orchard." It was the Broadway production, with Margaret Phillips and Tod Andrews, of "Summer and Smoke," by Tennessee Williams, which lasted for a hundred performances and wasn't put on again until April, 1952, when it was produced Off Broadway, with Geraldine Page, and was a big hit. I played Nellie Ewell, the little girl. I had good actors to work with—Margaret Phillips and Tod Andrews—and it was a beautiful play. It was exciting and interesting to play a character who had a mind and knew all about life. After that, I got in on the heyday of live dramatic shows on television. In those days, you'd get a different part to do every three weeks. One week I'd be playing Annie Oakley on "The Quaker Oats Show," and the third week after that I'd be playing a murderess in some mystery drama. In 1951, our first child, Peter, was born. A few weeks later, I was right back in television.

In December, 1953, I was in my first Broadway hit, "Oh, Men! Oh, Women!," by Edward Chodorov. It was a fine comedy, and I felt that in it I was doing my first really good acting. I'd been studying with Lee Strasberg for three years by then, and I had begun to discover something about the exciting process that takes place when, beginning in rehearsals, you really get to work on a part. You get to know the person you play. You protect the character you play. You can make the audience shut up and listen. You show one of the wonders of life—that every human being is different. The rhythm of the character takes over, but you're never mesmerized; you're the one in control. In 1954, I went to live in London for a year, while Eli appeared there in "The Teahouse of the August Moon." After our return, our second child, Roberta, was born. When she was three months old, I appeared on Broadway, with Edward G. Robinson and Gena Rowlands, in "Middle of the Night," by Paddy Chayefsky. Occasionally, I'd bring the baby backstage and leave her in my dressing room, asleep, while I went on. The stagehands sometimes baby-sat for me. It worked out fine. I learned a lot in that play. For one thing, I was still learning how to take advice. In one scene with Eddie Robinson, where he told me—I played his daughter—that he wanted to marry a young girl, it was supposed to be a blow to me. So I wanted to dramatize the point that it was a blow. I wanted to walk away. Eddie said, "No, she would never do that." At first, I was sore. He said, "It's more effective if you don't show them. The cliché is to show them." And he was right. Not because he was an older, more seasoned actor but because he was an *actor.*

I want to be the best actress I can be. I'm competitive about it, but I'm not obsessed by it. When I go to the theatre and see Kim Stanley or Geraldine Page, I'm thrilled by what *she* is doing. At the same time, I work constantly to make myself free to act to my fullest capacity. Playing in "Brecht on Brecht," with Lotte Lenya, Dane Clark, George Voskovec, Viveca Lindfors, and Michael Wager, I have admired

169

them all so much. Viveca is capable of opening her mouth and letting out a scream. I am still afraid to do that. I don't take big chances. For that, you need freedom. Maureen Stapleton has it. Kim Stanley has it. Geraldine Page has it. And, of course, Eli has it. They dare. And Marlon Brando is the daddy of them all in that. He dares and defies, and I love it in him. In all of them. I love them for it.

PAUL SCOFIELD

People talk of magic in the theatre. "Magic" is a misleading word. The pure work is all that matters to the actor. Magic is for the audience to discover. Magic is no concern of ours.

I was born on January 21, 1922, in Birmingham, England, and was taken at the age of a few weeks to Hurstpierpoint, in Sussex, where my family lived—about eight miles from Brighton and forty miles from London—and where my father was headmaster of the Hurstpierpoint Church of England School. I have one brother, John, who is three years older than I am, and who works as a local-government official in Brighton, in the Rate Office in the town hall. I have one sister, Mary, six years younger than I am, who lives with my parents in Hurstpierpoint. My parents, Edward Harry and Mary Scofield, just happened to give all three of us children Biblical names. My father, who has retired as headmaster but still occasionally teaches at nearby schools, is a literate kind of person and also a very open-air man. When we were children, he had us play cricket and other games; he is that kind of schoolmaster. His main interest, however, has always been in teaching. He taught children up to the age of fourteen mathematics, history,

171

geography, and the rest. Our family is still somehow very close, although parents so easily lose track of their children. I live about seven miles north of my parents' village, at the edge of the village of Balcombe, in Sussex—in an Edwardian house my wife and I bought in 1951. I was married in 1943 to the actress Joy Parker, and we have two children—Martin, seventeen, who goes to The King's School, a boarding school in Canterbury, and Sarah, ten, who lives at home and goes to Trevelyan School, a girls' school, in Haywards Heath, about four miles south of Balcombe, and whose main passion at the moment is riding. I recently bought Sarah a horse of her own—absolute lunacy—which we keep at a farm near our house. I ride a bit myself; I learned just in order to ride with my daughter, and now I love it. Sussex is very beautiful. I wanted to go back to that part of the country where I lived as a child, at the foot of the South Downs, in Hurstpierpoint. We lived near wonderful bare chalky hills, where I used to walk. Now we live a little bit inland on the weald, where the plain is undulating and wooded. My wife is not a dedicated actress. Often, she takes a part in a play, many times with me. My children aren't the least bit interested in what I do in the theatre. Children like to forget about their parents' careers, I think, and all the claims that their parents' work makes on them. When I came to America to appear in "A Man for All Seasons," my children stayed in England, in school. It was our first long separation. I wasn't in the least startled to have a letter from Sarah in which she wrote, "I hope you're enjoying yourself in America. I doubt it." It pleases me that the theatre means nothing to the children. I like to leave it behind. I just like to go home. Children eventually get recognized as totally independent creations. They seem to lead the way for you to understand them. It's easy for me to see what they want and what they are. That's the kind of thing actors are so good at—putting themselves in other people's shoes. I'd never lived in a big city for any length of time before I came to America. I'm sort of a country actor. When I'm in England, my schedule is bound up with my family. When I'm in a play in London, I'm part of my family until four; then I catch a train to London. I get to the theatre about an hour and a half before a performance. Commuting from the country is quite hard work but still worth it. I like the silence of the country. I like to be by myself a good bit. Mostly, I walk among the beautiful chalk hills. Professionally, I've never done anything I haven't wanted to do since being in a position to refuse work. I could live without acting, I think. I could very easily work on a farm.

I somehow don't think literally of being born—just of being brought up. I attended my father's school, as a day student, until I was eleven. At that time, it was in a Victorian Gothic building, with an arched stone doorway and imitation church windows. My father is a terribly fair's-fair man, and I was never favored because I was the son of the headmaster. He was very much the disciplinarian in those days, and I got the rough end of both sticks, in a superficial way. The children at Father's school were my friends. I sledged with them on the short grass in the hills, and played football with them, and looked for birds' eggs. I played a great deal of tennis with my brother, who was much better at it than I was. I played a rather defensive game; it wasn't my instinct to rush to the net, and all that. I was not a good student. I couldn't do mathematics. All I seemed to be good at was reciting poetry. At the age of nine, I did the "quality of mercy" speech in a recitation of the trial scene from "The Merchant of Venice," put on at Christmastime. The school was hung with paper chains and holly, and had a general kind of cozy feeling then, at the end of the term. In choosing parts for the boys to do in the play, my father decided that I should be the Portia.

At the age of twelve, I started going to school in Brighton, commuting by train and bicycle to Varndean School for Boys, where I was a leading member of the Dramatic Society. My first part, when I was thirteen, was Juliet. The Romeo was not very good, but my Juliet was a sensation. It's the only part I've ever played of which I can remember every word. It has just stayed. At fourteen, I played Rosalind in "As You Like It." Then my voice went a little low, and I next played Prince Hal in "Henry IV," Part I. From then on, it seemed pretty clear to me that I would become an actor. For a boy who was hopeless at everything else, acting was a tremendous release. I wasn't used to the kind of freedom that doing something well gives one. That made it all the clearer. My parents were sensible about it. They could see that I was totally blank to the sciences and to mathematics, and that acting was a practical thing for me to do. But they warned me about it. "Precarious" is the word they always used about it.

When I was fifteen, I made my professional début, in a touring production of "The Only Way," at the Theatre Royal in Brighton, which is one of the loveliest theatres in all England, with a horseshoe-shaped circle, and red plush and gilt, and all the old theatre atmosphere, pretty much as it has been for a hundred years. It's very much alive as a theatre today. There's always something to see there. The play "The Only Way" was an adaptation of "A Tale of Two Cities," starring John Martin Harvey, who was more or less the Henry Irving of his day. He was making one of his ostensibly farewell tours. They asked for volunteers for the crowd scenes. I turned up at the stage door, was taken on at ten shillings a week, or about thirty cents a performance, and was given a cudgel to brandish in a crowd scene. The play, and being part of it, was awe-inspiring. Sir John had a remarkable style of acting, in the tradition of Irving—highly dramatic and rather operatic—and I was deeply affected. Not that I couldn't sleep at night; hardly anything has ever made me not sleep at night. It was just that one was aware that one was close to something as authentic as the books one read, as authentic as "Jane Eyre." I was in the play for two weeks. At the end, I liked that cudgel they'd given me so much that I took it. I walked out with it under my mackintosh. I still have it.

In my last term at school, I was due to take an examination for my school certificate, but suddenly I was fed up with commuting. I left, and never graduated officially. I was sixteen, and was very much aware of my failure to make headway as a scholar. It was rather depressing, especially inasmuch as my brother was good at school. I was quite fair-haired in those days, the way one sometimes is before going dark. I was round-faced, but I'd already begun to have lines in my face. It's always surprised me that I grew so many of them. I suppose it has something to do with the way the flesh settles down over the bones of one's face. I don't think it has anything to do with what life has done. The time was a year or so before the start of the Second World War. The manager of Brighton's Theatre Royal and the headmaster of Varndean School helped me get a scholarship at the Croydon Repertory Theatre School, in a suburb of London, where I went for two terms. It was all very unnerving. I wasn't at all strengthened as an actor, but I did get on with a bit of practice. I did some public performances, including a big chunk of "Peer Gynt," in which I played the feeble-minded peasant bridegroom. It was the first time I'd done anything that gave me the feeling of bringing a character to life. It was a beginning—the simple business of taking part in productions— and the Croydon brought me into a kind of contact with the professional world of the theatre. Then the Croydon was disbanded. It was a time in England when everyone was being given a gas mask. I didn't know what to do at all. I wanted to get on with some work. I heard of a school called the London Mask Theatre School, which was attached to the Westminster Theatre. There I made my student début, on April 16, 1940, as the Third Clerk and the First Soldier in John Drinkwater's "Abraham Lincoln," starring Stephen Murray. I had hardly been to the theatre at all before I left Varndean School. The first play that touched me was "Desire Under the Elms," put on at the Westminster Theatre, in which I played somebody in the family party. The school was a very lively one. We had good teachers, including Eileen Thorndike, Sybil Thorndike's sister, who gave voice lessons. She had an aptitude for teaching Shakespeare, and because she was a teacher who had been an actress, she communicated an extraordinary love of the work. By showing me her own mastery—which Sybil also has, of course—of the meanings and of the changes of tone necessary to keep it interesting, she was able to make me understand Shakespeare and the value of each word. Sussex has a kind of Cockney accent, and at this point I started gradually to lose it. We had bombs in London in 1940, and the school moved to the country—to Bideford, in Devonshire. I stayed for ten months after the move. It was rather like college life. Teaching acting is a tremendously intangible business, because how can you? Often, a dramatic school is a very difficult place to progress in. But you can find out some technical things, and you do get physical practice. At that time, we all felt the stretch toward John Gielgud, Ralph Richardson, Laurence Olivier, Michael Redgrave, Edith Evans. We had to encompass big scenes of Shakespeare according to standards we were already aware of. But acting is not a job for someone who is good at learning or who has an aptitude for copying. It's got to be more than that. It's got to be positive understanding and illumination. But the school, for what it was, was fine. From a nucleus at the school a theatrical company was formed, in which I played Dan in "Night Must Fall," by Emlyn Williams, and it was a big step forward for me. We went to Cambridge with our production of "Noah," by André Obey, and hoped to start a repertory theatre there, but Eileen Thorndike became ill, and we had to abandon our plans. That was the end of that. It was a sad time.

I still hadn't been called up by the Army. I returned to London, and in running around to agents' offices looking for a job I tracked down Robert Atkins, a splendid old gentleman of the theatre, who had a company called the Bankside Players. He gave me a job, at seven pounds a week, with his tour of "The Taming of the Shrew," which we did for the troops all over England. Atkins occasionally played the lead himself, with Claire Luce, the American musical-comedy star, playing Katharina. I played Vincentio, an old character part. At nineteen, I had the kind of competence that was approved of in those days. I never had any illusions about the quality of the work I was doing. It was a routine thing. I had seen enough theatre by then to know. That job ended after a few months, and through friends of Eileen Thorndike I found my next job, in a very portable tour of "Medea," with Sybil Thorndike and Lewis T. Casson. I was supposed to join the tour in a village near Aberystwyth, in Wales. They were stuck for a man, and I was hired to play a messenger. I'd never seen "Medea" up to the night I reached the village and saw that production, just before I was to join the cast. I was shaken and shattered by it. It had extraordinary simplicity and a kind of magnitude. One recognized that one was seeing something big. The power of the play and the size and range of the emotions in it were clear and overwhelming. The production had a necessarily imposed stark simplicity, because the scenery and everything had to be moved from village to village. It gave the play an extra strength. I was impatient to start work. Before I could even begin, however, I came down with the mumps, and I was left behind in hospital for four weeks while the play went on with the tour.

On my return to London, I searched for work, more or less going where the wind blew me. I went on several tours—one with "Jeannie," by Aimée Stuart, a fragile Cinderella story set in Scotland, and another one with "Young Woodley," by John Van Druten, in which I played Ainger, the head prefect, Woodley's best friend. It was a time of flux in England. The theatre was waiting to see what would happen in the world. At one point, when I was in Newcastle upon Tyne, in Northumberland, it turned out that my Army-application record, which I had filled out in Devonshire, had been destroyed in a bombing, and I was ordered to have another physical examination right there and then. I was turned down for military service on medical grounds; I could only suppose it was because my toes were crooked, since I heard an examiner say I wouldn't be able to wear Army boots. Nevertheless, I happen to be a tremendous walker and have never had a bit of trouble with my toes. So I went on with the tours. There was nothing much to the work, yet there was no other work to be had. It was a lowering time for me; I was trying to achieve a kind of competence, and generally absorbing the feeling of acting, and that's about all. Then Basil C. Langton asked me to join a production of "Hamlet" he was producing and starring in in Birmingham. He had seen me in "Young Woodley," and he asked me to play Horatio. He had temporarily taken over the theatre occupied by the Birmingham Repertory Theatre, whose owner and manager, Sir Barry Jackson, had given up the theatre during the bombings. Margaret Leighton played a court lady, and Joy, my wife, played Ophelia. She was marvellous as Ophelia—better than I was as Horatio. She had just the quality for it at the time, a kind of limpidity. It was a full-length "Hamlet," divided up into two sections, which were played on two successive nights—all very odd, but a splendid production. Life suddenly had purpose for me. It's easy to lose one's sense of direction in the theatre, in the early jobs. Now I found I had a sense of direction, and had an opportunity to develop what abilities I had. I was able to bring some imitative flair to the character of Horatio— some knowledge of another person. I went as far as understanding Horatio's relationship to Hamlet and the rest of the people. It all fell into place. The audience felt it. There was the quality of silence, of intentness, that you get when they're listening and know what you're talking about. You know you've succeeded in showing them something they can believe in. The audience at Birmingham was very good, a very special audience, of the sort that attaches itself to a theatre rather than to *the* theatre. The audience got to know me. I became familiar to them, and that gave me a feeling of sureness. It's a very good feeling for an actor to get—that the audience knows him—and a difficult one to get in the commercial theatre. One of the fascinating things about an audience is that it always takes on a collective character. The kind of audience you have creates an atmosphere. I hate London first-night audiences. They're so cold, and always very unrepresentative. I was braced to hate my first night in America, with "A Man for All Seasons"—which, incidentally, was a better production than the one in London—but it went off with a bang. It was quite intoxicating. I didn't become a focus for the audience in Birmingham. There were plenty of other actors. It was just that I was a contributing member of the group. For most actors in the formative stage, the spotlight is harmful. It makes one set hard too soon, and possibly it makes one become a personality. There's no harm in it if you want to become the kind of actor whose primary concern is expressing your self to the audience. I hadn't, and haven't, any interest in doing that. The point is that if you're a personality to the audience, it becomes increasingly difficult to put yourself in other people's shoes, which is what I like to do. It's a much more interesting job to try to illuminate as many types of people as possible. I'm very, very cagey about my own personality. I've always been very secretive.

Basil Langton took me along on a tour, underwritten by the Council for the Encouragement of Music and the Arts, of Shaw's "Arms and the Man," starring himself. Yvonne Mitchell was in it, playing Raina Petkoff, and so was Joy, playing Louka, the gypsy girl, and I played Major Sergius Saranoff. We had quite a good standard of work. We used to go to factory hostels and give performances before and after night shifts. It made one extremely adaptable. One learned to act under any conditions, and I loved it. At the end of that tour, Basil Langton produced John Steinbeck's "The Moon Is Down" on tour and then in London, in June of 1943. I played a sort of major small part. In one free week between the tour and London, Joy and I got married. I stayed with Basil Langton for another repertory season, at the Theatre Royal in Bristol this time, and played Tybalt to his Romeo in "Romeo and Juliet." I knew the day was coming when I'd be leaving Langton. There was a good standard of work with him, but I was going along hit-or-miss professionally and I felt I had to move on to something else.

When I left Basil Langton, I went on a second factory tour sponsored by the C.E.M.A.—of J. B. Priestley's play "I Have Been Here Before," in which I played Oliver Farrant. In the late summer of 1944, I wrote to Barry Jackson, another splendid man in the theatre, asking him if he could give me a job in the Birmingham Repertory Theatre. At first he said no, and then a place turned up for me and he asked me to come along. My preoccupation at this time was to improve my equipment—mainly my voice, and my use of it. You can train your body as a dancer does, and that's fine, but an actor doesn't dance. I was with the Birmingham Rep for two seasons, and it was there that for the first time I felt I had some power to choose and control what I wanted to illuminate. But it was all done in very embryonic fashion, and was not completely successful. One aspect of it was my finding the most economical way of doing what I wanted to do—cutting out what was unnecessary to do. This may have come as a result of my playing a leading part in a play for the first time— the part of Philip the Bastard in "King John." It isn't simply that one has more lines to speak in a leading part and so one must work harder. In a leading part, one shapes the whole structure of the play. One can't help doing that. Whatever the work of the director, it's got to be done through you. Another aspect was my finding, in most of the plays, the essence of the character; I found that in some odd spot or other it was actually illuminated, so that the character was made alive for the audience. The people in the audience could look and say they recognized that person. They could look and say they saw what the author meant. Not that you see the author's meaning standing there on the stage. The actor should make you forget the existence of author and director, and even forget the actor. If an actor is devoting himself to what he is doing, the talent will be there, but in its least self-conscious manifestation. Some actors have the gift of being able to see and to do things by intuition, without knowing what it is they're seeing and doing. But it isn't enough to see and to do; you must know how to have control over your intuition. And trying to be natural is not the whole story. You find the truth within yourself only about twenty-five per cent of the time. The rest of the time, you find it outside. Yet being observant is a very tenuous kind of process. A great deal of conscious observation is not relevant. It's what remains with you without your having said "This is what I want to remember" that has the profoundest effect. This may be because every one of us carries within himself something of all aspects of human nature. We may know Hitler because in some tiny part of us we're capable of being what he was and doing what he did. It can't all be observation. There are times when I can see more of myself in a part than I can at other times. In 1957, when I played in "A

Dead Secret," by Rodney Ackland, in London, about a murder case of a particularly sordid kind, I took the part of a man who murdered just for money. I found the man a fascinating character, because he was so mean, so narrow, with his mind so shut to life and to humanity. I could understand him. One could make the audience feel great sympathy for him because of his blindness. I found that part very exciting to do, and by then I felt that I had complete control over what I wanted to show. What an actor contributes onstage follows from his craft. His talent is something that is individual enough to be noticed. It is what any actor has to have. Whatever *it* is, it is no business of mine. My business is to have control over what I do.

By 1946, after my two seasons at the Birmingham Rep, I had achieved a kind of technical balance. In addition to "King John," I now had behind me considerable experience in such parts as John Tanner in Shaw's "Man and Superman," and Dr. Wangel in Ibsen's "The Lady from the Sea," and Konstantin in Chekhov's "The Seagull," and also Mr. Toad in A. A. Milne's "Toad of Toad Hall," a show, with music by H. Fraser-Simson, based on Kenneth Grahame's "The Wind in the Willows." Odd as it may seem, a musical is tremendously good experience for technical purposes. Working with music brings you into much closer contact with the audience. You are not confined to the three walls plus the imaginary fourth wall; you include the audience more in the show—a contact that is valuable later for ordinary plays. Once having got that crude kind of contact by singing and playing directly to the audience and not pretending it's not there, you develop a kind of awareness that is with you when you *are* pretending the audience is not there. In so many ways now, I was steaming ahead. I had come to know that too little technical ability results in affectation; one does things in one's own fashion, but ineptly and repetitively, as when one finds that using one's voice in a certain way is effective and then continues to use it that way because it is so effective. If one hasn't got sufficient resources to choose from, one falls back repetitively into the same old ways. I had a kind of routine now, the rhythmic pattern one achieves in one's work as a result of experience. I had had regular practice. Now I was free, and eager to explore.

In 1946, Barry Jackson was asked to be an administrative director for three years at Stratford on Avon, and he asked me and Peter Brook and one or two others to go along with him. It was a very good pro-

fessional opportunity, from a purely practical point of view. I went
to Stratford, and stayed for three seasons. My voice developed, and I
had a chance to act with known and successful actors. I found Godfrey
Tearle particularly helpful; he gave one a feeling of self-confidence,
not by specific encouragement but by the way he treated one in general.
And I must have been influenced in those days by Richardson, Gielgud,
and Olivier, although I had then seen Olivier only in films. I was paid
twenty pounds a week at first, which was quite a lot, and I started on
a new phase of acting. The first character I played was Cloten in
"Cymbeline;" I was able to make this oafish character, who is a little
bit stupid, come very much to life. I was finished with the groundwork
that I had had to lay and that every actor has to lay, and was able to
find the clearest, simplest way of building the structure of the character. Then I played Don Adriano de Armado in "Love's Labor's Lost,"
and the title role in "Henry V," and again I found I didn't have to
waste much time on the technical requirements of the part, and was
free to create the character. I was now exploring aspects of human
nature that I wanted to make clear to the audience. Shakespeare is
particularly well suited to an actor who wants to make his own comment. The lines spoken by Shakespeare's characters mean something
different to every actor, just as everybody who reads a book reads it
differently. In contemporary plays, the actor is much more interpretive of the author's intention. Stratford was altogether different from
Birmingham in many ways. I attracted attention that was national
instead of purely local. Most of the critics gave me notices, some bad
and some good, the latter more or less to the effect that here was a
good new actor who had a faculty for getting under the skin of very
different types of characters. The second season, I played Mercutio in
"Romeo and Juliet" and the title role in "Pericles," and I was able to
consolidate what I had learned during the first season. Between seasons, I got some London jobs that were good for me professionally—
the part of Tegeus-Chromis, the lead, in "A Phoenix Too Frequent,"
by Christopher Fry, and the juvenile lead, Young Fashion, in Sir John
Vanbrugh's "The Relapse, or Virtue in Danger," with Cyril Ritchard
and Madge Elliott.

In 1948, my third season, I was asked to play Hamlet for the first
time. The production was in Victorian dress, and Robert Helpmann
and I played the lead on alternate nights. I played Hamlet again in

1955, in a more conventionally costumed production, which we opened in Birmingham, took to Moscow, and then brought to London. Anyone can play Hamlet. Any actor with facility and technical skill can play him, because the character has such universality. Macbeth is rather more specific. When I was first asked to play Hamlet, I was happy, of course, but I was immediately preoccupied with how I was going to play him. We rehearsed for the play off and on over a period of two months that had been allotted us for rehearsals of the three plays of that season; the others were "King John," in which I played Philip, the King of France, and "The Merchant of Venice," in which I played Bassanio. In 1948, I was an actor with less developed abilities than in 1955, when I had more to bring to the part, and less. The first time, I was much more vulnerable, because I was younger; I had a less sophisticated approach to the play—I was more naïve. In 1955, I had more knowledge and more control over my abilities, and less frailty. One man can play Hamlet only one way. But the first time I wasn't so capable of analyzing what I was doing as I was later. However, I do know that I was temperamentally suited to the part in 1948, when I was twenty-six, in a way that is difficult to recapture. My Hamlet of 1948 was frail. Claire Bloom played Ophelia, and she was so young then that she had a green ration book, the color of the ones given to children; mine was buff. In 1955, Mary Ure played Ophelia. The second time, my Hamlet had more positive assurance and there was probably less of Hamlet in it. The acting was better, the approach was more assured, but something had been lost. If I were to do it a third time, I might learn from the mistakes of the second. That second Hamlet aroused less sympathy, because I was deliberately trying to play it in a more positive way. The Russians were tremendously enthusiastic about the production, however. We played for fourteen days in Moscow. Ours was the first English-speaking dramatic company to have visited Moscow since the revolution. During the run, we were given a large reception by the Artists' Club. The Russians were interested in us, and admiring. I felt a tremendous rapport with them—with their vitality and their warmth and their enormous self-knowledge. You remember foreign voices coming out of faces; you don't remember what was said. But you know. Just as you know when people mean what they say. An actor can always gauge whether he has attention and approval from an audience, of any size. At the reception, we spoke to the Russians through an interpreter. We were all feeling rather tired but were trying to do our best, and the effort to communicate took tremendous concentration and energy. They were so hungry for everything they could learn about us. When we arrived for the reception, one of the other actors happened to tell me that he was so tired he felt he couldn't cope with it. There was a little old Russian actress near us, and she immediately gave us a lecture in Russian. She was such a fierce little old lady. I didn't understand a word she said, but I knew exactly what she meant. She meant that one relies on energy to generate energy. And she was so right. Output in the theatre requires greater energy than anything else I know. Doubt of one's energy is the worst of all. One's output in the theatre requires energy of a sort that is never a factor in family life. Family energy generates itself. Social life outside the family can be exhausting. I don't care much for social life with people in the theatre. I'm rather good at being with people when I want to make the effort, but I'm bad at listening to people when I know what they're going to say. It isn't very interesting, and on the whole it's very draining. The interesting thing in the theatre is the work and working with people. I usually like the people in the work, but I can't go on with them outside the work as long as most actors can. And when I'm working on a part I'm thinking about it all the time, going over all the possibilities in my mind. I like to be alone when I'm working.

After the 1948 season at Stratford, I went to London in a big way, playing Alexander, the lead, in Terence Rattigan's play "Adventure Story." It was a flop, but was artistically successful, and it led to my playing Treplef in a West End production of "The Seagull," with Mai Zetterling, Isabel Jeans, and Ian Hunter. For two years, from 1950 to 1952, I was in "Ring Round the Moon," Christopher Fry's adaptation of a Jean Anouilh play, with Claire Bloom and Margaret Rutherford. During the run of "Ring Round the Moon," I appeared on two Sunday nights in my own production of "Pericles," in London. Then I did a season of plays with John Gielgud at the Hammersmith Lyric Theatre, which is sort of Off Broadway. He and I took the lead parts, and most of the time he directed. We put on "Richard II," in which I played the lead and my wife played the Queen; Congreve's "The Way of the World," with Gielgud and Margaret Rutherford, in which I played my first comic role in London—Witwoud—with a lot of splendid ladies; and Thomas Otway's "Venice Preserved," directed by Peter Brook, with Pamela Brown and Eileen Herlie. Gielgud, of course, was one of the ones we had gone to see and learn from in the early days. He has a tremendous interest in anybody who is new in the theatre, because he cares about new life in the theatre. He is a very considerable person, a genius, who brings life to everything he does. As a director, he never tried to impose his own conception of the role on me, but paradoxically, with an actor as individual and powerful as Gielgud it is impossible not to feel that his way is the way you should follow. He has total mastery of all aspects of the theatre. He participates with tremendous energy in every aspect of a production he is involved in. His knowledge is very stimulating. He has style. Everything he does he informs with a beauty of style, both vocal and physical. But one doesn't model oneself on anyone else. One wants to go one's own way. I'm aware of being referred to by some people as the new Olivier. Every strong new actor is called the new Olivier at some point. How can one be the new anything? I've never worked with Olivier, but I've always admired him.

One of the most important seasons I've ever played in was the one at the Phoenix Theatre in London in 1955–56, with Peter Brook directing. We put on three plays, in all of which I played the lead; one was T. S. Eliot's "The Family Reunion," with Sybil Thorndike, and the others were the "Hamlet" we took to Moscow, and Dennis Cannan's and Pierre Bost's adaptation of Graham Greene's "The Power and the Glory." The program of three plays depended mostly on me, and it was the most that had ever been demanded of me. After the overwhelming experience of seeing Sybil Thorndike in "Medea," I was a bit wary of her, but I found her very down-to-earth and warm and friendly—not the remote type of leading actress at all. One of the most enjoyable plays for me was "The Power and the Glory," in which I played the priest, because I had to go further in one direction than I'd ever gone before. The play presented me with bigger demands on my abilities and also took me in a new direction. The character of the priest was an extremely intricate one—he was drawn as a mess of a human being—and I had to make a truthful character of him somehow. The man was a priest; he was also a peasant. I didn't know how I should make him sound. It gave me an opportunity to work in a completely nonclassical, realistic style, in which I could still use more of my classical training than ever before. In "Venice Preserved," I also had to go further, playing an extremely violent revolutionary. This role demanded that I be extroverted and tough. Up to that point, sensitivity was mostly what had been demanded of me.

In a sense, I feel that I'm part of no group in the theatre. I come sort of halfway between two schools—one exemplified by John Gielgud, with the classic style of speaking, and the other by the Royal Court Theatre, which puts on the work of so many of the good new playwrights. I'm somewhat detached from both groups, although I do come out of the same sort of stable as most English actors, in a general way. There's something about English actors that makes them depend on themselves. I was brought up in the theatre of articulateness. The plays of Shakespeare and Shaw deal with articulate people—people who can express their thoughts. In the plays of Chekhov, on the other hand, everything the characters say has nuances. I don't have a psychological approach to acting; fundamentally, I have an intuitive approach. For me, the totally intellectual approach is never satisfactory. What matters to me is whether I like the play, for one thing, and, for another, whether I can recognize and identify myself with the character I'm to play. My intuition for a part has failed me only once—for the part of Thomas More in Robert Bolt's "A Man for All Seasons," which opened in London in July of 1960. I felt a tremendous warmth toward the character. Then I came to play him, and I didn't know how. As the play is written, it gives nothing more than the bare lines of what the man is saying. It's all in the lines. There is no opportunity for embroidery. I had to start from scratch and just work on facts, making myself totally faithful to what was on the page: More was a lawyer, a man of tremendous faith, a complex and subtle character. Everything in him led inevitably toward a kind of forensic point of view. It was a rather cold-blooded way of ordering one's mind. I found that the part had what seemed like dogmatic exposition. Simply saying the lines for what they were worth would make More sound like a very pompous and noisy man. If I said the lines with all the intensity they seemed to require, he would seem an aggressive man. And he was not an aggressive man. So I had to find a way of making the man sound not pompous and not aggressive. And yet he had to sound strong. If you can see it, then you can do it. First, I had to find the way the man would feel; then I was able to find the way he should sound. Eventu-

185

ally, I discovered that if I used a specific range of my voice, and characteristics of my voice that I had never used before, I might make him sound mild, even though what the lines themselves said was not mild. When I played Hamlet, I used a lot of voice. For Thomas More, I used a voice you wouldn't hear at all if I used it for Hamlet. I used an accent for More that was absolutely a bastard thing of my own. My parents are Midland people, with a very regional accent, and I drew somewhat on this accent and mixed it with some others. The way More sounded just came out of my characterization of him as a lawyer. His dryness of mind, I thought, led him to use a sort of dryness of speech. It evolved as I evolved the character. I would flatten or elongate a vowel in a certain way to get a certain effect I wanted. Not too much happened to the voice as a result of More's being a man of faith and spirituality. One of the great traps in playing a man of spiritual depth is that one is given only a certain number of lines, and if they are not made to sound absolutely true they are likely to sound very self-satisfied and sentimental. The false note is so often struck. Next, I discovered More's humor, and knew that that would be the thing to make him not smug. Then, More was a flesh-and-blood man, with strong family affections. His spiritual attitudes did not put him at all in a backwater of life. He was fully alive and sensual, in the true sense of the word. He used his senses. He enjoyed the things of life—food and wine and the rest. He was reluctant to die. He didn't relish physical discomfort. And he wouldn't want to be hurt. At one point in the play, he says, "This is not the stuff of which martyrs are made." Because you're thinking and feeling all these things, the voice comes out in a certain way. It's constant communication between thinking and feeling. Otherwise, the muscles don't work right, don't take the right shape. One's voice follows the rest. It somehow becomes a willing instrument. I didn't go very far in my idea of how I should look as Thomas More: thin and pale, with a hat on—and a gown on. That's the picture. Actors get into some awful habits through their preoccupation with their faces. You have to look at your face in order to get it looking right, but you get more tired of your face than other people do. As soon as you're in rehearsal, it's necessary to start thinking about what you look like. You're enclosed by the structure of the author's writing. You have to hold back on deciding how you should look until you find what is commensurate with what the lines require. I don't think very often of how I myself look: I've got hair—brown hair with gray in it—and lines in my forehead, lines down past my mouth, and bags under my eyes, and my height is just over six feet. That is the kind of professional knowledge one has.

I find radio a marvellous medium for an actor to work in, and I've done a lot of radio work in England, including reading the whole of "The Fall," by Albert Camus, and Gogol's "The Diary of a Madman." I've played in movies—"That Lady," with Olivia de Havilland, in which I played Philip of Spain, and "Carve Her Name with Pride," in which I played a British spy. I would like to work in more films, if I could be sure of the director. But I've got the stamp of the classical actor, and I don't know whether film people want that. The greater amounts of money to be earned in films are no inducement. The minute one begins to earn large money, one is burdened with so many superfluous and extraneous preoccupations. My wife and I both feel that way. I don't like working in television. It seems to have the worst of both worlds—the responsibility of a play in a three-hour stretch, together with all the disadvantages of the proximity of the camera and the hazards of a mechanical medium. At the age of forty, I plan to play King Lear for the first time. Forty is just the right age to play him. I long ago decided I must play him when I was not too young. Yet to play that kind of old man you need a particular kind of energy that an old man doesn't have. He must be old for the audience, but not an ordinary old man.

WARREN BEATTY

As an actor, I have plenty of time. I'm in no rush.

I was born on March 30, 1937, in Richmond, Virginia, the younger of two children. My sister, Shirley MacLaine, the movie star, is three years older than I am. Until I was in high school, my mother, born Kathlyn MacLean, taught acting and directed plays put on by local amateur drama groups, and *her* mother had done the same. My father, Ira O. Beaty, used to be a psychology teacher and public-school administrator, and is now in the real-estate business. He's a very good violinist, and he might have become a concert violinist if he had taken the gamble as a young man. I changed the spelling of my name so that people would pronounce it "Batey" instead of "Beety." Shirley, who changed the spelling of the name MacLean for the same sort of reason, took dancing lessons from early childhood, and she gravitated naturally toward the stage. All through our childhood, she was bigger and stronger than I was, and it seemed to me that she always knew what she was doing. What I'm doing now is still a little bit of a mystery to me. We were brought up as Baptists, and attended church and Sunday school regularly. To this day, I don't smoke much, or drink. When I had to smoke cigarettes as the dissolute and amoral young Italian in "The Roman Spring of Mrs. Stone," I could do it, but I didn't like it. When I was five, my mother gave me a walk-on part in a play she was directing. I walked across the stage, saying nothing, and that was it. She told me I was very good. My first real acting part came about then, too—in a class play at school, before an audience of parents. It was a Christmas play, and I played the part of one of three toy soldiers under a Christmas tree. All three of us wore soldier suits, and we were required to take a bow to music. I made a big, sweeping bow, the biggest of all, holding my soldier's peaked cap in my hand. I loved it. My mother told me I was very good. I did it right, she said. I didn't waste it. My next part was in another of my mother's productions, the play "My Sister Eileen," put on by her little-theatre group in our neighborhood. I was one of a group of boys who rattled sticks against the grating outside Eileen's basement apartment. I was seven then, and felt I was kind of cute. Everybody in the cast had a crush on the actress who played Eileen. I was the young, young, young one with a crush on Eileen. I got in everybody's way most of the time. Shirley was in that play, too. I thought she was good. My last childhood appearance on the stage was at a local movie house in Richmond, in a stage show directed by my mother; all I know is that I was in there somewhere. Shirley went on working with my mother until she was about twelve. In the summer of 1944, when I was seven, we made a family excursion to New York. We stayed with an uncle in Larchmont and saw a lot of Broadway shows. "Oklahoma!" was the first one. I was thrilled by it. I fell in love with musicals. We bought the recording of the songs from "Oklahoma!," and when we went home, I listened to it over and over. I'll never forget that overture. The next year, we came to New York again, and I asked to see "Oklahoma!" again. My father took me, and left me at the theatre. When the movie version came out, in 1955, I went to see it about a dozen times.

In my early teens, I decided that I didn't want to miss any of the advantages of a normal life. I was an above-average student in high school, and took part in a lot of extracurricular activities. I went out for football and made the first team. I was a letter man in baseball and basketball, and was elected president of my senior class. In high school, I didn't do anything in dramatics, because I considered it sissy. Because of my football record in high school, I was offered athletic scholarships at ten different colleges and universities, but

I decided to turn them all down. I'd had enough of football. Football can get into your blood and ego. The cheers and admiration can go to your head too easily. Besides, I wasn't really passionate about athletics. In basketball, I'd often been more interested in kidding around and having fun than in winning games. I'd never taken anything very seriously. I'd always got good grades without studying. I'd talked vaguely about studying law, but I'd been sort of a goof-off, always clowning around. After high school, I said to myself, "Now I'll do what I want to do," and in 1956 I entered Northwestern University, where I attended classes regularly and joined one of the fraternities. I did two plays in college: "Bus Stop," in which I played Bo, the leading man, and "Under Milk Wood," by Dylan Thomas, in which I played three characters—a clothing salesman, a sea captain, and a poet. After a year, I suddenly realized that I wanted to be an actor, and that I wasn't going to learn acting at Northwestern. In 1957, I left college and came to New York. I lived from day to day. I stayed in a rooming house and got a job as a sandhog at thirty dollars a day. Then I got an easier job—playing cocktail piano at a little restaurant. I had taken piano lessons for a couple of years while I was going to high school, but I'd never practiced; I'd just picked up enough facility to get away with a simple rendition of "Tea for Two."

After I'd been in New York a short while, I started to take acting lessons with Stella Adler. Six months after that, a friend of mine asked me to audition for a "Kraft Television Theatre" play called "The Curly-Headed Kid," and I got the leading role—a rebel, a vagabond, a kid who went from town to town searching for affection and attention. The part came to me easily. I also appeared in "Lamp Unto My Feet," a television series, in which I played a son who couldn't communicate with his father, and a sailor who came home from the service and couldn't adjust to his family again, and things like that—fifteen shows in all, each lasting half an hour. From then on, I belonged to the agents. I signed up with the Music Corporation of America. I did a lot of daytime soap opera on television and appeared several times in a series called "Look Up and Live," and was in a five-part program called "The Family," with Hiram Sherman and Edward Andrews. Very often, I had little more to do than walk across the stage, but I earned about three hundred dollars a week. By this time, I was living in a furnished apartment in the

West Sixties. I also got a job, for an additional hundred dollars a week, playing cocktail piano at a couple of cocktail lounges. It was a lazy job, but I was quite content with it; the only thing that upset me was when a hip saxophone player told me I was a square, musically. I had come to New York thinking I knew everything about acting. But the more I acted, and the more I learned from Stella Adler, the more I realized I had a lot to learn. I auditioned for the role of Artie Strauss in "Compulsion," for Broadway, but Roddy McDowall got it. I finally played the part in winter stock, with the North New Jersey Playhouse, in Fort Lee. Playing this role showed me more clearly than ever that I had a lot to learn. It's easy for me to fall into a state of inertia. I need to be kicked out of it. Progress, after all, comes through conflict. When I'd been in New York for about two years, William Inge apparently saw me in a couple of the television dramas, including one in which I played the part of a student who cheated in high school. Joshua Logan must have seen me, too, because in the winter of 1958 he asked me to make a screen test for his movie "Parrish." He wanted Vivien Leigh and Clark Gable to play my parents in that one, but he couldn't get them, so he abandoned the idea of directing the movie. In the meantime, M-G-M had seen my test and called me to the Coast and signed me to a contract, and then *they* shelved the movie *they'd* had me in mind for. I then met Elia Kazan through William Inge, who was out there working on his screenplay for "Splendor in the Grass," and who wanted me to appear in it. Inge asked me if I'd do his play "A Loss of Roses" on Broadway first, and I agreed. The play was a flop, but I got good notices. I felt it might have been a much better play if we'd had more tryout time with it out of town. As it was, I felt, we were led to depend a lot on clichés. The play deserved more. I'd get laughs at times when I shouldn't be getting laughs. The play was about a boy in trouble, and I didn't think it was funny, but the audience reacted as if I were doing boffo scenes. *Variety* said I was an acceptable actor. I respect the opinions of others, but I knew I could do much better.

Right after the play closed, I played the leading role in the movie "Splendor in the Grass," with Natalie Wood and Pat Hingle, which was directed by Elia Kazan. I worked on the picture from May to August of 1960. From that I went right into "The Roman Spring of Mrs. Stone," with Vivien Leigh, directed by José Quintero. We made it between November, 1960, and February, 1961. Then came "All Fall Down," with Brandon de Wilde, Eva Marie Saint, Angela Lansbury, and Karl Malden, and directed by John Frankenheimer. I worked in that movie from July to September of 1961. All in all, I got a concentrated education in making movies. I felt terribly frustrated when I first saw myself in "Splendor in the Grass" and "The Roman Spring of Mrs. Stone." From every indication, I was very successful. I was very much in demand; I was getting a lot of publicity; I was on my way to becoming what is known as a movie star. But when I saw myself in those first two movies, I realized that if I had done the same parts on the stage I would have had the opportunity to come back and do them again, in a better way, trying to find new meanings in them. In the movies, they were recorded in one way for all time. On the other hand, I knew I was learning how to combat out-of-sequence shooting, how to sustain a performance, and how to come to the set prepared, in my own mind, to play it. In acting, I've always tried to make the most of whatever I was doing, no matter what. My father tells a story about a man who is captured by cannibals in the jungle and is about to be boiled. He says to himself, "There is nothing I can do about it, so I may as well enjoy it."

KATHARINE CORNELL

*I love the pretending, but I've never been terribly
happy on the stage. I've never found it easy to act;
acting to me is agony.*

I was born on February 16, 1898, of American parentage, in Berlin,
where my father, Dr. Peter C. Cornell, was taking a postgraduate
course in surgery. I was an only child. At the age of three months,
I was taken to Buffalo, where my father settled and started to practice
medicine. He was a martinet. I had a very disciplined childhood. In
those days, I wanted to be a trained nurse. When I was eight, my
father gave up medicine to become manager of the Majestic Theatre
in Buffalo. He booked all kinds of touring attractions there. He died in
1948, at the age of eighty-three. My mother, who died at forty-three, was
an amazingly lovely creature and very outgoing. Both my father and
his father were amateur actors. Grandfather Cornell was a friend
of John Drew. My mother was frightened of acting. As a child, I was
gawky and not attractive, and a tomboy. At boarding school—the
Oaksmere School, in Mamaroneck—I coached tennis, basketball, and
drama. I was also the amateur swimming champion of Buffalo. I love
to swim, and do a lot of it these days at my place on Martha's Vine-

yard. I first went to the Vineyard with my maternal grandmother, and fell in love with it immediately—with the sweet smell of fern by the sandy road. I adored my grandmother. I always felt I had a completely theatrical background. Not that I took to the stage as a child. One of the vaudeville acts at my father's theatre was an elephant act, and children were brought out onstage at the end of an elephant act to feed an elephant. Once, I was supposed to go on and give the elephant a bun, but when the moment came to do it I was afraid. My father said I *was* going to do it, and so I was thrust shrieking onstage holding a bag of buns. I threw the buns at the elephant and ran screaming from the stage.

At boarding school, I had a feeling that I wanted to be a director. I wrote plays for the school, designed the sets, and acted in the plays as well as directed. Theresa Helburn came to the school to coach the cast of "Twelfth Night," in which I played Malvolio, and then she coached "Play," which I wrote. After that, I felt I must go on acting. When Edward Goodman, the director of the Washington Square Players, came to the school to help coach one of my plays, he suggested that I try out for the Players. I moved, with my aunt, to New York in 1917 and lived in Miss Pennybacker's Boarding House, at 15 East Thirty-eighth Street. I got along on an inheritance from my mother, and earned about forty dollars over a period of two years, playing bit parts with the Players. The biggest day of my life was when I got a one-line part in a Japanese *no* drama, "Bushido," without pay. I played a Japanese mother, and spoke four words—"My son, my son." I was so nervous I didn't know how to read a part. But I knew the stoicism of that woman, and knew I had to say that line without overdoing it. I grew with this part and made it something of my own. By then, I was talking easily with actors, and I loved them.

During the summer of 1919, I played small roles in Detroit and Buffalo in a touring stock company owned by Jessie Bonstelle, a friend of my family's. Stock is fantastic training for an actor. You have to prepare so quickly to do things. You learn a lot of tricks. The difficult side is that sometimes a stock actor learns the tricks and is never able to get rid of them. I had a pride about what I was doing. Also in 1919, I played Jo in "Little Women," in London, in a production Miss Bonstelle put on there. I felt I was becoming abler as an actress, but didn't talk to anybody about it. I had the feeling for it, the knack and the instinct. In

1921, I made my Broadway début in "Nice People," by Rachel Crothers. I had met Guthrie McClintic a few years before, while I was in stock, and had fallen in love with him. At that time, he had been a talent scout for Winthrop Ames and had written opposite my name in the program, "Interesting. Monotonous. Watch." We were married in 1921, and today live a quiet life. I'm a farmer, basically. I love the early morning. I usually have breakfast at eight, even when I'm working. I have dogs, read a great deal, walk, scrape and refinish wood. Guthrie says I'm always either putting paint on or taking it off. I cook—mostly spaghetti alla marinara. We don't entertain much. After I've finished a long tour, like the one with "Dear Liar," Jerome Kilty's adaptation of the Shaw-Campbell correspondence—sixty-seven cities and twenty-seven thousand miles—I just want to do nothing. That mood may last quite a long while. Guthrie has been a wonderful help to me, has believed very much in me. When I work, I love to work with him. As an actress, what I've had has been an instinct for being somebody else, just as some women have an instinct for doing their own hair. I've never had an instinct for doing my own hair, and I have no instinct about clothes. But I knew I had the acting instinct.

My first big part on Broadway was in "A Bill of Divorcement," in 1921, and then I played the title role in "Candida" in 1924, and in 1925 I became strongly identified with Michael Arlen's "The Green Hat." What you try to do in the theatre is to give a universal picture, through your own eyes and feelings, of the person you play. You try to be, in your own way, what that person would be. You have a feeling about the thing. If you don't feel strongly about a part, or if it doesn't appeal to you, it's a mistake to do it. I loved Candida, but when I read what Shaw said about Candida I didn't think it was anything like the woman I acted. I felt the *maternal* quality of the woman. The only time I met Shaw, he said he wished he'd seen me as Candida and Joan, and I told him I didn't think he would have liked the way I played them. You have to play a part in your own way. It's always a struggle to do it. You have to keep on struggling to get through. Sometimes you accomplish it, and sometimes you don't, but you have to keep on trying to get through, through, through. There are three ways of doing it, in general; you might call them auditory, tactual, and visual. I think I do it in a tactual way. I always have in mind a lovely thing Willa Cather wrote about art's being "a mould in which to imprison for a

195

moment the shining, elusive element which is life itself." It's so wonderful when it happens in acting. When it does happen, a bell rings, but it's very rare. It happened once when I was playing Elizabeth Barrett in "The Barretts of Wimpole Street" for the men overseas in the Second World War. It's a tiny little thing that happens. You then say to yourself, "That was right." Sometimes you can be wrong about it, but when it happens it's wonderful, and usually you're not wrong. Kirsten Flagstad can do it again and again when she sings. Myra Hess can do it when she plays. As an actress, when it happens, I make you confident of me as a human being on that stage. I get a wonderful sense of accomplishment doing that. In the beginning, I didn't want to play Elizabeth Barrett. I thought she was a dreary girl, always lying on that couch. Elizabeth Barrett bored me. I had never read any of her poetry except "Sonnets from the Portuguese." Guthrie, however, thought it was a wonderful part, and read the play aloud to me, and then I began reading about the family. I read six books about the Barretts and Robert Browning, became interested in the father-daughter psychology, and ended up fascinated by Elizabeth.

Sometimes, you read a part over and over, and you get lost in many things you think about it. You flounder around, struggling with it. Little by little, some line emerges—and you've got it. The audience never gets half of what you've thought in your mind. Guthrie felt that Iris March in "The Green Hat" was not at all in my vein, but I always felt I had an understanding of her as a woman. She had a kind of burned-up quality about her. Her whole set had that quality, and I knew it, even though I didn't know the set had and never belonged to it. The play had a seduction scene with Leslie Howard and me. He played it beautifully. My husband directed, and at the point where Leslie Howard said to me, "Iris, Iris, what do you want?," I replied, "You *baby*." And I turned out the lights. My husband said that Howard should turn out the lights and that I should say, "*You,* baby." I said no; I said I had to turn out the lights myself, and I knew it was more natural for me to take the comma out and say, "You *baby*." To me it was an extremely interesting part. She was a disillusioned woman. You had to underplay it and distort it so that people wouldn't laugh at it. You do what is the right thing for you to do in any kind of acting. No two people play the same character in the same way.

You can emasculate a part with *too* much thought. I know that some of the Method actors are fine actors, but sometimes they do think a little too much and I don't understand them. We have a prescribed movement on the stage, and what you do must not interfere with somebody else. You have an obligation to your fellow-actors. Some of these Method youngsters are a deadly bore. It's so exhausting to play with these people who have to talk to their analysts all the time and then come back and tell you what the character is all about. One never knows where they're going to be on the stage. You can't be willful on the stage. You can't be arbitrary. You have to belong to the team. But there are good ones among them, and some are among the best we have. And the art goes around and around, and actors do have to explore. It gets harder to act as you go on. There's more responsibility, not less. You can't ride along on anything you've had. You must always take a part and make it your own. And when you're playing on the stage, every night is an opening night for an audience. Often, you try too hard. It isn't easy for it to come through. You always try to be fresh. I'm still frightened of acting. It's that egotistical thing that makes you want to be so good that turns around and frightens you.

The star thing is utterly indefinable. It's there or it isn't there. Sometimes a star isn't a very good actor, but he has that peculiar quality that makes him a star. It's almost a chemical thing. I know that some great actors have some moments that are so electrifying as to be absolutely delirious. I can't say exactly that for myself, but I do know that some of my moments have been wonderful for me. I worked on preparing "Dear Liar" for five months. It was terrible torture, because I couldn't get that woman. The letters didn't give me the bitchiness of Mrs. Campbell. When you're not good, you just know it. And that is what I call suffering. But I worked on it and worked on it, and I thought, I'm going through with it even if I never act again. I had to find a way of using those letters to bring out what I wanted, and finally I had the feeling that I had done what I wanted. I had done the job as far as it was possible for me to do it. I like to do a job as well as I can.

EDDIE ALBERT

No one but an actor can run the gamut of life's experiences.

I was born on April 22, 1908, in Rock Island, Illinois. My full name is Eddie Albert Heimberger, and I'm the eldest of five children. My parents were both of German descent. When I was a year old, our family moved to Minneapolis, where my father first owned and managed a couple of small restaurants, then gave them up and went into the insurance business. My parents now live in Los Angeles, with my brother John, who works as a mechanic for the Lockheed Aircraft Corporation. My other brother, Frank, works for the telephone company in Los Angeles as a circuit-installation supervisor. My sister Margaret is secretary to a Hollywood lawyer, and my other sister, Mary, is married and runs a ceramic factory in Minneapolis. My father is retired now, and spends his time painting in water colors. I was brought up as a Roman Catholic. I attended St. Stephens, in Minneapolis, and then went to Central High School. At the age of six, I started working, as a newsboy, and I had my own delivery route by the time I was nine. I worked at one job or another—soda jerk, usher, theatre manager—

198

all during my school and college years. I loathed going to school.
I was always disrupting things. When I was in the second grade, I
discovered I had the ability to make the other kids in the class
laugh. One of the nuns would catch me clowning around, making
jokes, and I would get beaten up. I was a real troublemaker. But I
loved getting attention from the other kids. Little by little, during
my childhood, I was singled out for special work in class plays, camp-
fire shows—just the usual small stuff, like playing the Spirit of the
Castor Oil Bean in brown muslin. In one school play, I was the pig
that hid in a churn and rolled down the hill to escape the fox. On
Sundays, I sang soprano in the St. Stephens Church choir. I grew up
in the twenties. All through those years, I was taught that to be
a man you had to be a businessman. You had to work. When I was
in high school, I worked, for thirteen dollars a week, at a soda
fountain from six in the evening until midnight. I never got to
sleep before one in the morning. I was a shy kid. Making other
kids laugh was the easiest way of getting their approval. I played
the lead in the senior-class play, which was part of our graduation
ceremonies. It was the part of the Policeman-Prince in "A Kiss
for Cinderella" by J. M. Barrie. It put me on top of the heap.
The rewards were immediate and unmistakable: the applause, the
newspaper notices, the approval. I graduated from high school with
a bang. I've always envied those people who just go along and don't
give a damn about who approves and who doesn't. I've always been
one of the others.

When I began to plan what I would spend my life at, I thought it
would be business. Prosperity was at its height then. You couldn't
pick up a newspaper or magazine that didn't have some big-business
success story staring you in the face. When I graduated from high
school, I planned to try the same thing my father was doing—selling
insurance. But first I was going to go to college, and to get the
money I spent two years working as a salesman for an uncle who had
a furniture company in Aurora, Illinois. Then I entered the University of Minnesota and started studying business administration. It was
fashionable to study business administration at that time—before 1929.
At night, I managed a fourth-run movie theatre. It still showed only
silents, so I used to entertain between shows, doing magic tricks,
raffling off dishes and other prizes, and occasionally singing popular

199

songs and playing a banjo-ukulele. In my classes, I was always tired. I couldn't concentrate. I slept through my classes. My education plans began to seem absurd to me. I wasn't really interested in business administration. After two years of it, I simply walked off the campus in despair one day. For a while, I worked as manager of another theatre, but I didn't like it, working from noon to midnight; it just didn't seem like a proper businessman's life. Then I went into insurance selling. For extra money, while I was trying to get going in insurance, I joined up with a couple of friends, Herb Nelson and Grayce Bradt, and we did some singing over two Minneapolis-St. Paul radio stations—KSTP and WCCO—as a trio. I was a kind of garden-variety baritone. We sang stuff like "Sweet and Lovely" and "Happy Feet" and "St. Louis Blues." Then Herb and Grayce had an offer from station KMOX, in St. Louis, and they asked me to go along. Since I wasn't doing very well in insurance, I decided to do it temporarily, in order to eat. I had really sold no insurance at all except to my father. So, in 1931, I became a radio singer, at a salary of fifty dollars a week, which was the same pay the two others got. I stayed in St. Louis for eight months. I took some singing lessons, learned something about the technique of both singing and dancing, and developed a sense of comedy, of timing. But I still hadn't decided to go into entertaining as a permanent profession. I lived in a hotel apartment. It was a lush time for us, and we were doing extremely well. But I was not in an emotional position to enjoy any of it. I was bewildered. I was not a happy young man. When I wasn't working, I'd go off and take long walks by myself in Forest Park, a lot of the time walking in the rain, which in St. Louis is nearly always very warm. Eventually, I began to get a feeling for what I was doing. Not only were there the immediate rewards of applause and laughs but I was being paid, and paid quite well. By the end of the year, I'd fallen in love with what I was doing. With the others, I went to Cincinnati, and for the next couple of years we sang as a trio there, on station WLW. Then the act broke up, because Herb decided to drop out and become, of all things, a businessman, managing a radio station down South. It was 1933. Grayce and I decided to come to New York and try our luck here. Nothing happened for a while, but I didn't feel disappointed. I always had the illusion that my next job was just coming up. I lived over a speakeasy—Caesar's, on West

Forty-eighth Street—in a one-room apartment without electricity. I had always read a lot, and I'd read the newspapers by the light of the electric sign—"William F. La Hiff's Tavern"—flashing into the room from across the street. Sometimes, the chef of the speakeasy would give me a handout of cold leftover spaghetti. Every day at noon, I'd go to the Leo Feist office, on Broadway, together with a lot of other guys—some of them would be wearing their tuxedos and maybe carrying their horns—to get bookings, at three or four dollars a night, with pick-up bands in Elks clubs or joints in places like Red Bank, New Jersey. I'd sing and play the guitar. Once, I sang as the Silver Mask Tenor for the Big Ten Polish Pals Dance, at the Grand Paradise Ballroom, in Williamsburg. The silver mask I had to wear gave me a splitting headache, but I sang, and also danced with the ladies, which I was required to do as part of the job. In those days, if it was too late for me to get home, I often slept in a park, or in a saloon. I got to meet and talk with more people than I've ever been able to since I started making some money. I enjoyed congregating with the bums and hoboes. After six months or so in New York, Grayce and I got a job, through a song plugger, doing our act on an N.B.C. weekly variety show called "Morning Parade." We got ten dollars apiece every week for about fifteen beautiful weeks. That led to our getting hired by N.B.C. as a singing team to do a daily show called "The Honeymooners—Grayce and Eddie." We were on every morning at eleven for fifteen minutes, singing duets from our repertoire and carrying on running patter in little scenes with our neighbors, played by various actors. My income jumped to fifty dollars a week. On one broadcast, one of the actors playing a neighbor was sick, and a friend of his, Garson Kanin, played the part. Grayce and I paid a man forty dollars to write some special material for our act, so we could get into night clubs, but he took the money and gave us nothing. We still weren't very sophisticated about it all.

That summer of 1933, I played in summer stock in Mount Kisco. I made my début on Broadway, on January 8, 1936, in a small part in a Zoë Akins play called "O Evening Star," which closed after five performances. In September of that year, I got a call from George Abbott, who said that he was going to produce and direct "Brother Rat," written by John Monks, Jr., and Fred F. Finklehoffe, and that Kanin had suggested me for the leading part of Bing Edwards.

It was that easy. I was hired at a hundred and fifty dollars a week. The play was a huge success. We had a good cast, with José Ferrer, Ezra Stone, and Frank Albertson. But I was still pretty unsophisticated, and I didn't know how to enjoy it. I played in "Brother Rat" for four months, and then I went into "Room Service," in which I played one of the leads. I was in that for a year. I remained bewildered, but not unhappy. Opening nights, though, were sheer torture. My wife, who is the actress Margo, maintains that for me acting is like boxing—a tough contest. She says that I'm Teutonic in that way—that I feel I must always be sweating and suffering. She's Mexican, and the exact opposite of me. Unlike the Teutons, the Latins believe in fun, gaiety, the sheer joy of living. Living and enjoying life go together for them. Margo and I have a son, who was born in 1951, and an adopted daughter, who was born in Spain in 1954. We live in Pacific Palisades, in Los Angeles, with the Pacific Ocean as an extension of our back yard. I'd give up acting in a minute if it ever came to a choice between my family and my career, but I don't think I'll ever have to make that choice. Success is a silly kind of goal. Hollywood is full of people who made success their goal and were more miserable after achieving it than when they were striving for it.

After I'd played on Broadway for a year and a half, I was offered a seven-year standard contract with Warner Brothers, and I took it. I repeated my "Brother Rat" role in the movie version. It was a big success at the box office, but the studio was greedy. "Brother Rat" was a beautifully written script, and the movie was carefully made, but because it was a success the studio immediately made a sequel, "Brother Rat and a Baby," to take advantage of the success, and I was put in that, too. It didn't have the class of the first movie. I was miserable doing it. Then I made two or three other bad movies. I got very upset and discouraged. In 1938, Warner Brothers permitted me to return to Broadway for eight months to play in the Rodgers and Hart musical "The Boys from Syracuse." I played Antipholus, one of the twin brothers, and loved it. Then I had to go back to Hollywood. The next year, I bought a boat, a thirty-nine-foot yawl, and sailed for Mexico in it, with a crew of five friends. I bummed around Lower California and Mexico, and hooked up with a one-ring circus in Mexico for a while as a clown and trapeze artist. In 1941, I planned

to go on an expedition to excavate Mayan ruins on the Isthmus of
Tehuantepec, but the war came along. I wasn't getting much to do
in movies, so I spent my time wandering around by myself. In 1942,
I joined the Navy and went to Officer Candidate School for ninety
days and was commissioned a lieutenant, junior grade. I saw action
in the South Pacific and in the Central Pacific, at Tarawa and other
islands. I was discharged on December 4, 1945, as a full lieutenant,
and the very next day I got married to Margo. We settled down in
Hollywood, and I made more movies, such as "Rendezvous with
Annie" and "The Dude Goes West." At the same time, I started
making educational films—at that time a kind of pioneer work. With
the University of Oregon, I produced "Human Beginnings," a film
for six-year-olds about having a new baby in the home, to help them
over their jealousy. It seems to me I've been searching all along for
things to do that would mean more to me than the commercial
movies I make, most of which I've made to earn a living. When I
was making the movie "The Roots of Heaven," in 1958, I flew from
Central Africa to Lambaréné to visit Dr. Albert Schweitzer. I've
admired his work, and I've tried to help in Meals for Millions, a
philanthropic project he is interested in that makes high-protein meals
available to underprivileged peoples at a cost of two or three cents
a meal.

In my early years in Hollywood, I was pretty miserable, and I often
did pretty hysterical things. I was making more money than I had
ever believed existed. I had made a hundred and fifty dollars a
week on Broadway, and I jumped from seven hundred and fifty
dollars to a thousand dollars a week during my second year in Hollywood, and, of course, I threw it all away. Then, I found myself
questioning my ability to act. I didn't think I was making real
progress. I was successful, but I wasn't a success as an integrated man.
I began to question what an actor really was. With enough luck and
drive, plus intelligence, anybody can become an actor in Hollywood.
Out there, movies are an industry, not an art. I've made about
forty Hollywood movies. I've enjoyed about a quarter of them.
Making a movie requires such a high degree of collaboration. Often,
I find myself in conflict with the authorities. And the industrial aspect
of it is always so important. Money is so much in evidence. Like television, the movies are geared to high ratings.

Acting of any kind is part of the machinery of man's looking at himself and evaluating himself in terms of growth. An actor makes his interpretive contribution to something that—if it's a movie—is seen by millions of people, both adults and children. For me, that in itself makes acting exciting and worth while, provided the movie, or whatever it is, has anything to recommend it. In Africa, while we were working on "The Roots of Heaven," the temperature reached a hundred and forty degrees and members of the company were getting sick all over the place, but I loved the excitement of it. When I worked on the role of the photographer in "Roman Holiday," I always found something new, something stimulating, some new detail of my part that I could study. The drawbacks, of course, are always there. An actor has to worry about so many things that have nothing to do with his acting—like whether his agent is a good agent or a bad agent, or whether to have an agent or not. When I was a kid, I used to pray, "Please, God, make my life interesting." I think He did, by making me an actor. All sorts of roles, whether they were happy or tragic, have given me satisfaction. When I'm playing an unhappy role, the director usually tells me to stay concentrated on it—not to laugh it up on the outside but to make myself feel lousy. That's all right with me. It's all part of life. To avoid pain in life is never to know the joy of life. When you play a part, you're being yourself in some ways. In "Brother Rat," I played the shy-athlete type of fellow, a baseball-playing student. I was new to acting then, and mostly I just memorized the role. Many people who are not very good actors get parts that are so right for them that they make them look like terrific actors, and that's what happened to me in "Brother Rat." All I did onstage was wander around and say the lines I had memorized. In that part, I was an uninteresting, unimaginative, and unresourceful actor, but my appearance was right. In "The Boys from Syracuse," I sang the songs well and I wore the tights well; I had boyish charm and good legs. If you have the proper voice and a good body, it helps a lot, especially when you're starting. I was able to do much more when I had ten or eleven years' experience, and when I played good parts in good movies and worked with good directors. For example, I was able to do quite a lot as the salesman in "Carrie," produced and directed by William Wyler. I had worked as a salesman myself. I knew the manners of salesmen, the façades they built up, their way of dressing. Before I played the part, I read Vernon Lewis Parrington's "Main Currents in American Thought" and then spent months studying the author, Theodore Dreiser—everything he had written. I wanted to know everything Dreiser had ever said about salesmen in any of his writings. I learned that Charles Drouet, the "Carrie" salesman, wore topaz cufflinks, I learned how he selected his ties, and I learned his manner of talking, his brave, hearty way of commanding attention, the forceful personality he developed as the façade he needed for selling. I deliberately avoided the stereotype of a salesman. I knew that the loud, cigar-smoking cliché salesman wouldn't go over with audiences, because they usually know what a salesman is really like. Actually, a salesman can sometimes command attention by standing still in a room. I knew if I played him truthfully, the way I understood him to be, it would have a strong impact on the audience, and it did. I think I was also able to do a lot in the movie "Attack!," released in 1956, when I played a villain—an Army captain who is a coward and who gets drunk and sends his men out to be killed without good reason, and then is shot and killed by one of his own men. I started out, for this part, with a belief that there are no villains. A villain may be an honest, sincere man who is his own victim. The captain I played in "Attack!" was a highly neurotic man, the victim of an authoritarian father, and was unable to act on his own initiative. I tried to make him a well-meaning, unstable person, a man who had been at the top of the academic list at military school but who was incapable of taking any real responsibility in battle. To ease himself over his own suffering, he drank. He refused to send help to the men he had sent out to die, and rationalized his decision by telling himself that the men would die anyway. I felt miserable in this role. I was supposed to. I kept myself simmering with drunken terror throughout the role. Away from the movie set, I worked on the role with the actress Stella Adler, a wonderful teacher, who has an incisive, brilliant way of getting to the heart of a character and to the heart of a script. She taught me to design scenes in accordance with the chemistry of the thing. She shows you how to get at what Stanislavski calls "sense-memory." I have no trouble being miserable for a part—I have so much to draw on.

The more characters I played, the greater my thirst became to enjoy all the facets of life as they have been experienced by all kinds of people. I don't mean I can really feel everything that the character I play feels. I can show what it's like to be an officer or a doctor, or I can go back in time to the twelfth century and get a little of the feeling of what it was like to live in those times—just enough of the feeling to enlighten and satisfy me. In a Western movie, I learn how to ride a horse, and I get to know something of what it was like to live in the open spaces in, say, 1870. Or in a boxing picture I get in the ring with the fighters and throw some punches with them, listen to their speech, find out something about their hopes and their terrors. An actor gets a taste of all this. A taste is often all that you want. To know *deeply* what an actual fighter feels and fears is not for me. Every man is a part of every other man. An actor, similarly, is a part of every role he plays, and every role becomes a part of him.

FRANÇOISE ROSAY

You must believe you are the person you play. Be-
lieve in it—that is the secret.

I was born on April 19, 1891, at nine o'clock in the morning, in Paris,
near the Place Pigalle. My mother, Marie-Thérèse Chauvin, was an
actress, whose professional name was simply Sylviac; my father, Count
Gilbert Bandy de Nalèche, was an Army officer. My parents, both of
whom died in 1948—my father at eighty-five, my mother at eighty-
four—separated when I was about three, and I was their only child.
I have a half brother, Henri, of my father's first marriage. As a child,
I never had a home life. We lived in a huge apartment, where I was
very lonely. It was there, one might say, that I started acting. At the
age of four, with the servants as my audience, I made up little plays—
pretending to be a farmer, pretending to be a lion tamer, putting pots
and pans on my head. Mother would find the pots and pans out
of place, and she did not like it. My mother was very intelligent,
very clever, with great wit, but she was not very motherly. Although she was an extremely good actress, she never became
really famous, because she was always flitting from one thing to
another. She did her best work with a great actor and producer

named André Antoine. I loved to watch her act. When I was five, she took me to Russia, where she played in the Théâtre Michel, a theatre in St. Petersburg that belonged to the Russian government and in which plays were given in French for Czar Nicholas II and the Russian nobility. I do not know why, but the memory from that visit which has stayed with me most clearly is the way the poor people drank tea. They would hang a small piece of rock sugar on a string from the ceiling and swing it from one person to another, and each person would dip the sugar in his cup or take it right in his mouth. I found that ravishing and very painful at the same time.

When I was eight years old, my mother sent me to a boarding school. From then on, it seemed I was always away at school. At thirteen, I was sent to England and attended Norland Holmes, in Hove, near Brighton. I was to be there for only two months but I wrote and asked my mother if I could stay a year, and she permitted me to stay, so I learned English. Then I went to school in Germany, and I learned to speak German. I also attended the Lycée de Versailles. I went from one school to another, and didn't get a degree from any. My mother's ideas were always changing. When I was sixteen, I wanted to sing. I was a soprano, and loved music. I had started to take piano lessons when I was five, and had learned to play quite well. But when I told Mother I wanted to sing, she said, "You are going to act. You are going to work." There was no discussing anything with her. Mother said she would teach me acting, and she did teach me for three or four months. Then I was ready to start acting in the small theatres in Paris. My mother was still acting, of course, so I wanted a stage name of my own. A playwright named Maurice Donnay, who served as my godfather for the stage, gave me advice about taking a name; he suggested I take Francine Rozay, the name of a character in his play "Amants." But I liked my real first name, Françoise, better than Francine, and I liked the spelling "Rosay," so I became Françoise Rosay. My first part was in one of the earliest plays of Sacha Guitry. I got paid nothing the first week, which was a trial period. Then I received thirty-five francs a week—my first real job. I was playing in a small theatre near the house where I was born. Mother came to see me on the opening night. I had the part of a young lady, and I was wearing a long dress for the first time. I could see Mother in the first row, looking at me reproachfully, and I wondered why. Only later did I learn that I had been so nervous that I kept tugging at my skirt and pulling it above my knees—something that was not done in those days.

After a short while, I passed the entrance examination for the Conservatoire National de Musique et Déclamation, where I studied with Paul Mounet, a well-known actor with the Comédie Française. I studied acting there for three years, meanwhile continuing to play in the small Paris theatres—the Théâtre Moncey, the Théâtre Montmartre, the Théâtre National de l'Odéon, and so on. I played all kinds of small parts in the classics by Molière and Racine as well as in modern dramas of the day. During my last two years at the Conservatoire and during the years immediately following, I worked at the Odéon with M. Antoine, the director who had worked with my mother. Antoine was a sort of Stanislavski of his time. He engaged you on the understanding that you would learn everything. You had to do old people, young people, small parts, big parts, classic parts, modern parts, comic parts, tragic parts—everything. At the age of twenty-one, I went to St. Petersburg to play in the very theatre my mother had played in when I was a small child. I was there for six months. Our company played something new every week— twenty-six plays for the season. The nobility liked to see all the new successes from Paris, so we did many modern plays that were hits in Paris, in addition to the classics. We gave several special performances of Molière for an imperial school for the daughters of Army officers, and all the little girls came to see us. When I went to Russia, I was timid. I was frightened. I took my little dog along with me from Paris—a Brussels griffon, the dog that looks like a monkey, which was the fashion then. St. Petersburg was so cold that when people spat outdoors, they spat ice. Everything was wet and gray and overcast. The city was sad, I thought. The architecture seemed to me to be more German than Russian. I did not like St. Petersburg. I remembered that it had been just the same when I was there at the age of five with my mother. People in St. Petersburg were either very rich or very poor. I used to see a concierge trying to sleep on a wooden bench outdoors; his job was to open the door for people, all night long with the temperature fifteen below zero. I was shocked. In the large houses, when I gave food to my little dog the servants would watch, and would grab the scraps of food that the dog left. It was not normal in those days to observe all that and to care about it and feel hurt by it, but I did feel hurt by it. Today, too, I do not like to be in places where I see a great deal of poverty. For example, I do not like Rio de Janeiro, where you see enormous fortunes and terrible degradation and nothing in between. I am not happy in Spain, where one eats in a restaurant and looks through the window and sees people starving. When I was in Russia, I took a trip to Moscow as soon as I got the chance. Moscow I liked much better than St. Petersburg. It was the Russian city *par excellence*. It had a character of its own. There it was wonderful. In Moscow, one could see the sky, and one could see all the beautiful, golden churches, with their spires reaching into the sky.

When I returned to Paris from Russia, I had enough money saved up to move out of my mother's apartment and into an apartment of my own, at 195 Rue de l'Université. It was on the Seine, near the Eiffel Tower, and when I took it there was nothing there—no Métro or anything—and the people of Paris thought that it was the provinces. It was on the fifth floor of an apartment house built around 1880. There was no lift and no electricity and no private bathroom. However, it had a beautiful view—one could see the Palais de Chaillot and Montmartre from the windows, and one could see the sky and the trees—so I took it. Soon after that, I began, at last, to take voice lessons, and then I returned to the Conservatoire and entered the department for the study of opera singing. I studied very hard, and won the first prize for singing and acting, and eventually I was engaged to sing at the Paris Opéra, where I appeared in "Castor et Pollux," "Thaïs," and other operas. But then I became ill for some time and was unable to continue. The voice goes when health goes. Before that happened, however, my singing took me to Lyon, where I was engaged to play the leading role in Goethe's "Egmont"—a part that required an actress who could sing two songs by Beethoven. And there, in Lyon, I met Jacques Feyder, the man who became my husband. He was playing a small part in the play. I still have the *affiche* for that play. We were married in 1917, and he came to live in my apartment on Rue de l'Université. Our children, three sons, were all born there.

Right after we were married, my husband became a film director. He fell in love with films when they were just beginning. I was not considered photogenic in those days, and did not play in films until the talkies arrived, in the late nineteen-twenties. In 1929, my husband was invited to Hollywood to direct Greta Garbo in "The Kiss," and I went with him. We were filled with enthusiasm and excitement. And *voila!* My husband's producer, a man named Al Lewin, suggested, when he saw me reading the script, that I play in a movie based on the Molnar play "Olympia." We stayed in Hollywood, and I went on to appear in twelve other movies, including "The One Woman," "The Trial of Mary Dugan," and "Jenny Lind." We returned to France in 1931. With my husband, I made more movies—"Le Grand Jeu," "Pension Mimosas," "Les Gens du Voyage," and "La Kermesse Héroïque." With Julien Duvivier, I made "Un Carnet de Bal," and with Marcel Carné I made "Jenny" and "Drôle de Drame." I also made movies after the Second World War: in England, "Quartet," among others; in the United States, "September Affair" and "The Scarlet Pen;" in Italy, "Femmes Sans Nom" and "Sur le Pont des Soupirs;" in Spain, "La Princesse Eboli." And in the fifties, in France, I made "L'Auberge Rouge," "Le Long des Trottoirs," "Le Joueur," and "Du Rififi Chez les Femmes." In 1960, I made "Les Bois des Amants," and in 1961, "Le Cave Se Rebiffe." Of all the directors I have worked with, none has been better for me than my husband. I trusted his direction completely. It was always right for me. He loved his work and lived for it, and all the films I made with him I enjoyed.

The Second World War separated me from my husband and my sons. But many other sad and terrible things happened before that. In the early years of the war, my husband and I would stand by our windows and watch the Nazi planes flying past. I felt sorry for the German people, but I despised the Nazis. Then a certain Frenchman, a traitor, using the false French name Ferdonnet, made a number of broadcasts from Germany, speaking against France, and this enraged me. I decided, because I was known in Germany through my films, that I would answer him on radio broadcasts addressed to Germany, and would speak under my own name. I made five radio talks, and was the first person in France to do that—to speak on the radio to the Germans and use one's own name. I never spoke against Germany; I spoke against the Nazis and what they represented to us. I would begin by saying, "I am Françoise Rosay, the mother of three sons." I spoke against the things the Nazis did, and pitied the German mothers for what would eventually happen to them. I received many letters from Germany. They pretended to say things against me, but when I looked under the stamp on the envelope I would find the real message: "Go on, go on with what you are doing." Finally, I was condemned to death, in absentia, by the Nazis. When they began to come near Paris, I went to the South of France, where I acted in sketches written by my husband that were inspired by Ruth Draper's sketches. When France fell, I went to Tunis. After about a week, the Nazis arrived there, and I had to escape again. I made my way through a kind of no man's land until I reached some French troops, who arranged for me to be flown to Algiers in an English plane. I settled down in Algiers, and appeared in plays there. Meanwhile, my husband and my sons escaped from France to Switzerland. When the Allies recaptured Tunis, I went back there, and soon I was flown out again, this time to England, where, separated from my family, I remained until the end of the war.

My husband died in 1948, and today I still live in my old apartment, with my old furniture, and with recollections. All three of our sons now work in the cinema. Marc Frédérix, who has kept my husband's real surname, is an art director; Paul Feyder, who took my husband's working surname, is a first assistant film director; and Bernard Farrel, who chose a name of his own, is an assistant film director, too, and a television director as well. When I am with my children, who know more about the cinema today than I do, I listen; with my grandchildren—I have two—I talk *un peu*. I now divide my time between films and the stage. In 1961, I acted in Sam Spewack's play "Once There Was a Russian" on Broadway, but it closed after one performance. It was my first time in a play in New York. I found it interesting. In 1962, I played the part of a hundred-year-old woman in Michael Redgrave's adaptation of Henry James's "The Aspern Papers," again on Broadway, and this time the play did better. It was the first time I had ever played a woman a hundred years old, and that, also, was interesting. I have enjoyed my experience of acting in New York. I like the audiences here, and if I wish, I can take Metrecal—a wonderful invention. When I want to see what is going on at home, I can go to the Librairie Française and buy *Le Figaro, France-Soir,* and *Le Figaro Littéraire.* Whatever country you act in, you always have to prove that you are a real pro. In our *métier,* we must always remember that each time we have to begin all over again. When you arrive in a new country, the theatre people look at you; when they see you work; they decide. When I hear people say, "She is a real pro," then I know it is all right. To be a real pro is to know your business. But there is more to acting than just that. You must have your own personality, and not copy anybody. In France today, we have too many Bardots. We have big Bardots and small Bardots, fat Bardots and thin Bardots—and they all pout. But still there is only one Bardot. She has something of her own. She was born Bardot.

In our *métier*, when you are just beginning, people are very severe with you. Then, if you have a certain success, you are alone. Either people are too friendly or they say you are bad; it is all very difficult. Yet it is a wonderful *métier*. In "L'Homme Cet Inconnu," Alexis Carrel said that everyone is born with seven personalities but that, only one of these personalities will emerge in a lifetime—which one being determined by such circumstances as whether one is born rich or poor, in this place or that. What is wonderful about our *métier* is that you can show all seven personalities. When I have done a certain kind of part once, I like to change to another kind of part. Whatever one I play, I try to become the person. That is, I become the part in my thinking. I believe in the part, even if I play a tart or a murderer or a woman a hundred years old. In the theatre, I like all the work onstage, and I also like the rehearsals. But I do not like the effect that the audience has on the acting. You wait for them to laugh, you wait for them to cry, instead of concentrating all your attention on the acting itself. It is like being a painter and waiting for the people to come and tell you they like this color or that, dislike this one or that. And, *en passant*, I will say that I do not like to bow. Altogether, acting in films is much better. You do not wait for the public to react. And the day after you do a scene you can study the film and see what you did wrong, so that you can correct your errors as you go along. Whereas on the stage you do a whole performance and then there you are—it is gone, beyond repair.

Whether for the stage or the films, acting ability is a gift. It has nothing to do with intelligence. I have known one or two great actors who were perfectly stupid and yet looked very intelligent on the stage. For the stage, of course, an actor has to have the vocal power and has to articulate; he has to make himself heard and understood. But for any kind of acting you have to observe a lot, and read a lot. And you need great discipline. These days, of course, acting is not always a career. A beautiful young girl can become a star for four or five years without really becoming an actress; she can be enchanting just by being herself. But she does not necessarily think about following a profession. They take a chance, these girls, and if they are lucky they become rich and known. After a few years, they may not go on with their careers. In former days, when a girl thought of becoming an actress, she never thought of making millions or becoming known. She wanted to make a career. Now, because the cinema needs many new faces, a girl may think only a few years ahead and may earn in a few years what an actress used to earn in thirty. When I was starting out and said I wanted to be an actress, it was as one might say, "I want to be a lawyer," or "I want to be a scientist." Acting was a *métier*. I would be a young actress, I would be a middle-aged actress, I would be an old actress, and I would die. Acting was a lifework.

ANDY GRIFFITH

*What I like is to play a character like me. I don't care
for it too much when I have to get away from myself.*

I was born on June 1, 1926, in Mount Airy, North Carolina—an
only child. My parents, Carl and Geneva Griffith, still live there.
My daddy worked in a furniture factory, first running a bandsaw
and then being a machine-room foreman, and now he's retired. I was a
little old white-headed boy, and the other kids made fun of my
blond hair. And they teased me about a birthmark on the back of
my head. My mother told me she had seen a strawberry patch just
before I was born, and she always called the mark my strawberry
patch. We lived in a little old wooden house. We had an old Majestic
radio, which provided our only entertainment, and which gave us
much joy. We heard good country music over the radio. I was raised
a Baptist, and most of my early social life revolved around the church.
Later on, I joined the Baptist Young People's Union and did my
early courting there. I started entertaining when I was in the third
grade at the Rockford Street Grammar School, in Mount Airy. I sang
two choruses of "Put On Your Old Gray Bonnet." The other kids
laughed at the way I sang it and called me "Pandy Andy" and "Andy

215

Gump," from the funnies. Everybody listened to "Amos 'n' Andy" over the radio in those days, and the kids were always yelling to me, "Hey, Andy! Where's Amos?" Kids do that. All it did was make me mad.

I started going to revival meetings as soon as I could walk. The first show I ever saw was when I was five and my daddy and mother took me to Winston-Salem, about thirty-five miles away, to see a road-company production of "Carmen." All that clapping and clanging and carrying on! I sure did enjoy it. At the age of eleven, I played a farmer in a Christmas play about religion put on at the Second Baptist Church in Mount Airy. When I was fourteen or fifteen, I got attracted to swing music, and about that time I went to see a movie called "Birth of the Blues," with Bing Crosby and Mary Martin. In it, there was a man playing a trombone. I had been asking for a musical instrument of some kind, but my daddy couldn't afford it. He fed me and clothed me, but he couldn't stretch his pay far enough to buy me a musical instrument. My daddy worked hard. The people in that part of the country mostly worked for the furniture factory. They were very proud, and so was my daddy, so I couldn't borrow from anyone for a trombone, which was the kind of instrument I wanted after seeing that movie. I was in the Mount Airy High School by then, and I got myself a job with the N.Y.A. sweeping out the school after classes. I started making monthly payments of six dollars on a thirty-three-dollar trombone I had seen advertised in the Spiegel mail-order catalogue. It took me five and a half months, but then I got this trombone, and I was the happiest boy in all North Carolina. It was a tenor trombone—silver-plated. Then I started looking around for someone to teach me how to play it. Just about that time, a new minister, a man named Ed Mickey, came to our town for the Moravian Church, which had a band made up entirely of brass instruments. Many Moravian preachers—going back to Germanic custom—know how to play in a band and how to lead one. Ed Mickey began to make the whole town ring with beautiful music. So I took my trombone to him, and he said he would teach me how to play it. For three years, he gave me a free lesson once a week. Ed Mickey taught me to sing and to read music and to play every brass instrument there was in the band, and the guitar and the banjo besides. I was best at playing the E-flat alto horn.

When I was sixteen, I joined the church, together with my mother and daddy. We had been Baptists, but it was all Protestant anyhow, so it didn't make any difference. I was very happy with the Moravians. All the other band members accepted me. They didn't ever make fun of me. When Ed Mickey had a call to serve another Moravian church, somewhere else in the state, I became the leader of the band until the church could bring in a new preacher. A lot of the people used to point to me and say, "There's our next preacher." I was beginning to get that idea myself. The preacher was the cultural leader of the whole town. When I was a sophomore in high school, our class put on a show fashioned after the Major Bowes "Amateur Hour" on radio. We called our show "Major Knows," and I was Major Knows. Occasionally, I said something I hoped was funny, and a big roar of laughter came at me, and I began to feel great pleasure. It was the first time I'd realized it could please me to be laughed at. I had a teacher—Miss Haymore, who taught English and Latin and had our home room—who was the kind they used to make movies about. She was the one who selected me to be Major Knows, and she encouraged me to go all out for music, if that was what I wanted. She got me to understand that I was really doing something pleasurable not only for other people but for myself by getting them to laugh.

After the Major Knows experience, I relaxed and became an A student. In the summer of 1944, I entered the University of North Carolina, in Chapel Hill. I started out studying for the ministry. I took courses in sociology, and I hated them. I took Latin and Greek, too, and I found the classes long and dull. I missed my music. So I went to Bishop Pfhol, who was the Bishop of the Southern Province of the Moravian Church, and told him how I felt. I asked him if I could get permission to specialize in music, which he granted. I started playing the E-flat bass sousaphone in the college band and singing in the glee club, and I got to fooling around in the Drama Department. They had a group called the Carolina Playmakers, which put on an operetta once a year—usually Gilbert and Sullivan. I auditioned just to get into the chorus, if I could, and was lucky enough to get the role of Don Alhambra del Bolero, the Grand Inquisitor, in "The Gondoliers." When the review of the show came out in the school paper, my performance was referred to as the best. From that point on, I was in every musical show they produced. I began to think

I might be an opera singer, and decided to drop studying for the ministry.

I met my wife, Barbara Edwards, in the Carolina Playmakers. She was a music major, and was an accomplished singer and actress. We graduated together in June, 1949, and that August we were married. Today, we have two small children, Sam and Dixie, and we have a home on Roanoke Island—a few miles from Mount Airy—with fifty-five acres of land, which we bought in 1956. None of us in the theatre can make any permanent plans, but someday soon I would like to move back to Roanoke Island for good. I'd like to farm our land, if I can, and set up a tree nursery for holly and cedar. Most entertainers have something they feel strongly about, and I feel strongly about North Carolina. It's the greatest place in the world for freedom of the mind and freedom of the spirit. You have to see it and experience it to know what I am talking about. I'd like to see our children grow up in North Carolina, on Roanoke Island. For a boy, it's the finest place in the world. There's oystering in the winter, fishing in the spring, summer, and fall, and hunting in the fall and winter. You can get in a boat and go all around Roanoke Island. You can go to Roanoke Sound, Pamlico Sound, Croatan Sound, and Currituck Sound, to mention just a few. Or you can go out in the woods and walk.

While I was in college, I didn't have any notion of how I was going to become a professional entertainer. All I knew was that I wanted to get up there and perform. I spent my summer vacations working at the furniture factory in Mount Airy. It's always been typical of the Southern states to stage historical pageants. I made my stage début in one—"The Lost Colony," by Paul Green. It's still put on every year on Roanoke Island, in a place called the Lost Colony, which is the site of the first English settlement in North America. The pageant is based on the story of Sir Walter Raleigh. For three seasons, I played Sir Walter Raleigh at night, after work in the factory. In my last school vacation, I worked out a combination monologue and comedy routine for a variety show with others from "The Lost Colony," and appeared professionally at the Nags Head Beach Club, about nine miles from Roanoke Island. In a duet with a girl, I sang "It Ain't Necessarily So," and then I did a preacher act, in which I sang a song called "The Preacher and the

Bear." Then, when I wanted to get married, I realized I had no visible means of support, so I took a job as the music teacher at the Goldsboro High School, in the western part of North Carolina. I taught for three years, through the spring of 1952. I wasn't talented at teaching. I couldn't handle the kids. I wasn't a good teacher. It wasn't that I didn't want to be a good teacher, it was that I couldn't do it. I didn't enjoy it. I could very well be there today, *not* enjoying it, but I've been fortunate. I discovered that entertaining and making people laugh was something that I *could* do. Also, I enjoyed it. There's no point in doing a thing if you don't enjoy it. When you find you can do something, it's wonderful. It's like the way my daddy made furniture—the way he'd know how to make sample chairs to look at and show and later make thousands of copies of. My daddy was able to look at that wood and that piece of paper with the plan diagrammed on it and figure out the way to make the seat of that chair, the back of it, the legs, and all, and make all the pieces fit together. It was something he could do, something he learned over the years that can't be described. I'm not in the entertainment business to make money. I've never particularly cared one way or the other about that. I came from a poor background. I was happy as a child. I was happy as a teen-ager. I was happy as a young adult. I never had capital, but I was never unhappy because of that. When I discovered I could entertain, I worked hard at it. It's the only thing I do well. I can't be a company director, I can't be an accountant, I can't make furniture, but I *can* entertain.

While I was teaching high school, my wife was the musical director at the Methodist and Episcopal churches in Goldsboro. In the spring of 1952, we were both studying singing with a teacher named Katherine Warren, in Goldsboro, when a publicity man who was a friend of hers stopped to see her on his way to New York. He offered us a ride to New York in his car and suggested that he set up an audition for us at the Paper Mill Playhouse, in Millburn, New Jersey. We jumped at the chance. That was our first visit to New York. We stayed at the Statler Hotel for a week, and went around to night clubs to watch other performers, and got scared to death by the city— a large, overpowering, frightening thing. At the audition, we lined up with over two hundred other people. Barbara sang "In the Still of the Night," and I sang "Dancing in the Dark." We were turned down. Someone standing around there told me my voice was overly brilliant—almost unpleasantly so. I didn't mind so much. In my own heart, I believed it. So I decided to quit singing and start telling jokes. When our week in New York was up, we went back to North Carolina, by bus. I wanted to go to Florida and look around for something to do in Miami, but Barbara talked me out of it. She said we'd starve to death. So that fall I took out three hundred dollars in teachers' retirement pay that I had accumulated, and we borrowed a thousand dollars, and we bought a used station wagon. We rented a house in Chapel Hill, seventy-five miles from Goldsboro, and then wrote a brochure about ourselves, describing a song-and-comedy act, and got it printed up. We got lists from civic organizations of every convention or dinner that was planned in the State of North Carolina for the next six months. We figured that at least one out of every hundred would have need of entertainment. Pretty soon, job offers began to trickle in. We got into our station wagon and travelled to each and every job. Our usual fee for our act was sixty dollars. Barbara sang Puccini arias and popular standards. I played the guitar while she did interpretive dances. And I delivered a monologue I'd made up, called "What It Was—Was Football." It went over in a big way. There were some civic clubs, and so on, that asked us back for a second appearance. At one luncheon show, after I had done "What It Was—Was Football," a representative of Capitol Records came up to me and said he wanted me to record the monologue for his record company, which I did. We had been paying eighty-five dollars a month in rent for our house, which we hadn't been able to furnish very lavishly, and we had a student boarder who paid us twenty-five dollars a month. Our record started selling all over North Carolina, and then all over the United States, and we began to make enough money to furnish our house and pay off our debts.

We moved to New York four days before New Year's of 1954, with the intention of trying to get work to do in night clubs. Capitol was paying me a salary of about a hundred dollars a week to live on. We lived at the Park Sheraton Hotel, and then we sublet an apartment in Kew Gardens, Queens. My first big, important professional appearance was on Ed Sullivan's "Toast of the Town" in 1954. I felt numb and was scared to death. I was too frightened to do my football monologue the way I was supposed to do it. I was too nervous. It came out amateurish. I couldn't time it out properly. To this day, I can't actually remember doing it at all. But I knew it was a failure. My second professional job was at the Blue Angel. I felt like a failure there, too. In a night club, people are eating and talking and moving around. To control them and command them to pay attention to you and enjoy it is the hardest job in the world. I did "What It Was—Was Football" and other monologues that I wrote, including "Conversation with a Mule" and a couple on "Hamlet" and "Carmen." The night after I closed, Burl Ives opened there. I went to the opening. What I saw was a master at work. Your eyes reflect what you feel. My eyes had reflected fear. The eyes of Burl Ives reflected what he was doing and singing. He sang some of the songs that were my own favorites. He even had a community sing in that supper club—everybody singing "Goin' down the Road Feelin' Bad." I learned a very important lesson from that experience, and that was how to draw and hold your audience, and that a person with something to say has to get the attention to be heard saying what he has to say. After that, I continued with my own monologues and put songs back into my act and went out on the road for two years, working night clubs in the South and Southwest. I learned how to entertain. I would stand there and look at the audience and expect it to look back. I'm always very, very aware of the audience and what the audience is doing and feeling.

In 1955, I was cast in the leading role, Will Stockdale, in the dramatization of "No Time for Sergeants," by Ira Levin, on Broadway. That was my first big chance. I had read the book "No Time for Sergeants," because I'd met the author, Mac Hyman, while I was travelling in the South. I auditioned first for the television presentation of the play, on "The U.S. Steel Hour" in March, 1955. I did my "Hamlet" monologue for the audition and read for the part and walked right out with it. After I had appeared in "No Time for Sergeants" for almost the entire run of three hundred and forty-five performances, Elia Kazan put me in the movie "A Face in the Crowd." When I showed up to work on that movie, it was the first time in my life that I had seen a motion-picture camera. I was petrified on that first day of work. The motion-picture camera is a fantastic instrument. It can record something happening at the moment and it will be there, recorded on film, forever. I worked with some pretty outstanding people in that movie—some pretty fine men and women. Two of them were Patricia Neal and Walter Matthau, who were the first professional actors I ever got to know well. Making that movie was three months out of my life I wouldn't swap for anything. That was the first time I was called upon to play a serious dramatic part. It was the part of a guitar player, a down-and-outer who achieves fame and sudden acclaim. The reviews of that movie in New York were five good and two bad. I learned all I know about acting in making that one movie with Kazan. Now, Kazan knows people; he understands them and knows how to get the best from them. In a movie, or onstage in a play, you talk to the other actors, and you would think that's the most natural thing in the world to do. As a way of saying something, it turned out to be the most difficult thing in the world to do. I could sing along with other folks, or listen to other folks, or enjoy country music or popular songs like "Careless Love" or the blues, but it didn't necessarily follow that I could act or talk naturally with other actors in a play or in a movie. However, in "A Face in the Crowd," with Kazan's help, I acted. Most of my acting came from Kazan. He has a secret. He knows exactly how to keep an actor happy and excited. He treats an actor as though he had hunted all over the world to find him. He makes you feel like a very important part of what is going on. His attention was on me every second. In the very first scene, on a set built just like the jail in Piggott, Arkansas, where I was lying on the floor of the jail asleep, I was supposed to wake up suddenly, turn around, and be like a wild animal. A block of wood was propped under my arm. We took the scene first by having someone pull the block away, so that I would fall. I did it that way and it was filmed. But I had a question. It was in my eyes. Kazan saw it in a second. He called out "Don't move the camera!" and he came over to me. I told him it would be more natural if someone kicked me. Then I would naturally get mad and kick back. We did it that way, and it turned out to be right, and that was the shot that was used. We worked that way all through the picture. I knew the character I played in that movie; he was a drunk, a drifter, and a bum. There wasn't much similarity between him and me in my real life, because I lead a very respectable family life. But from every little similarity there was, and from every experience I had ever

had, Kazan knew how to dig out what was needed. He taught me how
to relate anything I had ever heard or ever read to what I was doing
at the moment for the movie. I'd go over and tell him, "I had an experience once." And he'd say, "Yeah, tell me." Then he'd listen, and
say, "Yeah, that's right, that's right." And I'd transfer that thought to
what I was then doing. Since my experience in that movie, I've tried
to do everything I could to make myself feel any part that I was playing. I'm like a person in back of me, watching me. When I first saw the
rushes of "A Face in the Crowd," I enjoyed watching myself. If I hadn't
gone to see the rushes, I wouldn't have known what I was doing.

In 1959, I went back to Broadway, singing as well as acting in the
musical "Destry Rides Again." I was in the show for over a year, but I
didn't develop much as an actor. It was too much like being back in a
night club. I'm limited as an actor. There are things other actors can do
that I can't do. Other actors can act in a lot of fine things. I know I
can't do the conventional serious dramatic acting. I'm not cut out to be
a dramatic actor. I tried it. I played in "The Male Animal" on "Playhouse 90" in 1958, and I just couldn't do it. There's no point in
doing what you don't enjoy, and if you don't do something well you
can't enjoy it. I have an excellent time now doing my television show,
called "The Andy Griffith Show." It's a weekly filmed situation
comedy in which I star as Andy Taylor, the sheriff in a small Southern
town. Making the television series takes a great deal of concentration, and you have to know what you're doing. But I enjoy doing
the same character every week, and I don't have any difficulty in
getting into that character at all. When I'm supposed to feel happy
or angry or humorous, I'm able to make myself feel those things. I
wouldn't mind playing the same kind of man for the rest of my
life. I would like to continue to give people some small thing to
make them laugh. What I would like to do, whenever I act or entertain, is to say some small truth. No preaching—just to have some small
thing to say that is true.

MARIA SCHELL

There is a powerful drive in any artist to transmit something, to give it form. In the actor, it is the urge to show moments of human existence in their essentiality.

I was born on January 15, 1926, in Vienna, as Maria Margarethe Anna Schell. I am the eldest of four children. My father, Hermann Ferdinand Schell, is Swiss and a Catholic; my mother is Viennese and a Catholic. My father is a fairly successful novelist, playwright, and poet. My mother, Margarethe Schell von Noé, is a former actress who now runs the acting school of the Conservatory of Arts in Berne. Her father was a well-known Viennese psychiatrist named Karl Noé von Nordberg. I have two brothers, Carl and Maximilian, and a sister, Editha, and all of them are engaged one way or another in acting. My parents met and were married when my mother was eighteen and a very promising actress, and they lived with Dr. von Nordberg in his apartment, in the heart of Vienna, on the top floor of what used to be the palace of Maria Theresa. In 1938, to get away from Hitler, my father took all the family but me to Zurich. I was placed in the Convent of St. Odilia in Colmar, Alsace, for a year before joining the others in Zurich. Then I attended the *Gymnasium* in Zurich, but quit at the age of fourteen and went to work as a *Stift,* or apprentice, in a bookdealer's office to learn secretarial routine, including parcel-tying. My father wanted me to have something to fall back on in case I could not get work as an actress. He has always been a very pure, idealistic man, but in this respect he was practical. I have a very sweet family. As children, we were brought up to be independent. When people asked my brother Max as a child what he wanted to be when he grew up, he always said, "Pope." I am religious now in a very private way. My father always taught me that you must try to be appealing by what you are inside, more than by what you put on from the outside. My mother tried to give me acting lessons, but it was impossible. A child somehow goes outside for idols. But my mother did give me the foundation of my self-discipline. From her I learned that what you undertake you must complete to the best of your ability. When I was eight, my parents took me to a hospital, where my grandmother was lying ill, to hear a recital they were giving for the patients. During the intermission, my mother looked in on Grandmother, just in time to see her die. Mother told me of how she closed Grandmother's eyes and then went back and finished the recital. It was my mother who gave me the courage not to be afraid of a powerful dramatic style. In the Greek plays, with her old-fashioned style, she was a wonderful actress. She is now a very good director.

As a child, I saw many plays based on fairy tales. At the age of eight, I starred in one, called "The Princess Searching for a Good Human Being." I played the part of a fool who accompanies the princess to fairyland, called *Schlaraffenland,* where rivers are of milk, birds fly into your mouth, and apple strudel grows forever. My mother tells me that I stopped acting in the middle of the play and started eating apple strudel. I never attended a formal acting school. I do not like being taught. I like to learn by myself. All my life, from the time I was a small child, I felt a desire to experience life as deeply as possible. What made me go ahead in acting was that urge. Today, I have learned that I can go only as far as my body will materialize my thoughts. When I was fifteen, I had my first professional acting job, the leading role in a movie called "Steinbruch," made by the producer Karl Stapenhorst in Zurich. I played a twelve-year-old girl. The next year, I was given my first stage role, the part of Clärchen in Goethe's "Egmont." I created an uproar in the theatre. I stood in the wings trying to *feel* my part, and then I came onstage, opened my mouth, and said, "I'm sorry, but I can't get the feeling," and rushed off the stage in tears. After this fiasco, the manager of the theatre assured me that I was a great comedienne, and gave me a comic role in a play called "Drunter und Drüber," meaning "All Upside Down." Right after that, I had my first real success as a comedienne in "Scamplo," by Dario Niccodemi, in which I played the part of a nature professor's daughter. I was seventeen, and I came to the theatre on the eve of the opening and saw my name being posted up in big letters. I then had the very strange experience of becoming paralyzed. I suddenly grew aware that I was expected to be very good. I became like the centipede with the fly in an old German story. The fly says to the centipede, "I have six legs, and I know how to walk, but you have a *hundred* legs—how do *you* walk?" So the centipede starts to think, and then he becomes paralyzed and cannot walk. I was so afraid. On opening night, I wanted to stay home in bed. My mother made me get up and go to the theatre. She told me something I never forgot: "An actress never fails her audience. If you cannot be good, then you must have the courage to be bad."

From Zurich, I went on to a theatre in Solothurn, Switzerland, where I spent two years, off and on, at a salary of fifty dollars a month, playing in Shakespearean dramas and other classics. Then I found a job in the State Theatre of Berne, at a hundred and fifty dollars a month, and I played in dramas by Shakespeare, Shaw, and Molière. In 1949, I played my first grown-up film role, in a German production of "The Angel with the Trumpet," starring Paula Wessely. That led me to the Viennese theatre, and while I was playing the lead in Elmer Rice's "Dream Girl" in Vienna, Alexander Korda asked me to fly over to London for a couple of days to see him about going into films in England. I visited Korda in his flat at the top of Claridge's, and he asked me to sign a seven-year contract with him, but I said no. I told him I did not want to leave Vienna. He said he would give me four months off each year to be on the stage there. Still I did not want to do it. As I was ready to go back, he said he wanted to give me a few words of advice. We were speaking in German, and he said, "I like your idealism, Maria, but the day will come when you are forty-five, and you will look back, and see that all your hopes and expectations did not turn out the way you thought. And you will wonder, Did I miss my chance, even if it was only a chance to *learn to speak English?*" It was that last question that convinced me, and I signed the contract. In London, I learned to speak English in three months. I played in an English film version of "The Angel with the Trumpet," and then in "The Magic Box," with Robert Donat; "So Little Time," with Marius Goring; and "The Heart of the Matter," with Trevor Howard. I took time off from making these movies to go on several long theatre tours in Switzerland, Holland, and Belgium, playing Gretchen in "Faust," with Albert Basserman, and Nora in Ibsen's "A Doll's House." In 1953, I made a movie in Yugoslavia, "The Last Bridge," and in 1955, in Paris, I made "Gervaise," directed by René Clément. I have made movies in Hollywood, including "The Brothers Karamazov," "The Hanging Tree," and "Cimarron," and I have been in "Playhouse 90" television dramas—"Word from a Sealed-Off Box" and "For Whom the Bell Tolls"—taped in New York. I speak smoothly in English and in French as well as in German. In acting, I can think and feel in whichever language is called for. I was married in 1957 to Horst Hächler, a young German film director who had worked as assistant director of "The Last Bridge." We have a son, Oliver Christian Hächler, born in January, 1962. We live twenty-eight miles outside of Munich, in a newly completed house of natural stone, with a swimming pool, a fireplace, and verandas overlooking the lovely Bavarian hills and the town of Wasserberg, which is a thousand years old.

There is a point in life when one has to make a very clear decision about one's life and sources of life: whether to accept life with all its chaos and disorder or whether to attempt to find harmony in it; whether to take life as it comes or to try to guide it. I think I'm capable of living either way, but the second way is more important to me. For example, when I got married, I decided, This will now have to be part of my own life. Strangely enough, I never *decided* to become an actress. It was always completely natural to me. I want to be part of all of life, of the world, of the universe, and it is in acting that I find a way of being part of all three. That is why I love acting. It guides me to all experience and to all feeling. There is a certain moment in life when you must free yourself from all others. I have now reached that plateau in my life, and I am free of everyone else. It developed this way step by step. In Zurich, when I first got to know the theatre, which was then built up mostly by refugees from Hitler, I was moved by what I saw—by their fantastic teamwork. I admired four actresses—Elisabeth Bergner, Käthe Dorsch, Paula Wessely, and Käthe Gold. Käthe Gold was my idol for many years. In Zurich, too, I had my first experience, in a childish way, of trying to bring some truth to the part I was playing, which was a laundry girl. I knew about Stanislavski, but I had not absorbed his ideas. I devised my own little ways. I went around with a laundry basket in the old town of Zurich, trying to find streets that corresponded to my images. Whatever I had in my head I tried to find, so that I could touch it. I wanted to make it real. The process of forming and shaping had started. Today I don't need so many tangible things to help. It was also in Zurich that I had my very first feeling that I was another person, not myself. I was in a small part, but I was on-stage most of the time during the play. For the first time, the stage became for me another world. Now I have the capacity for concentration, for losing myself, for believing I am someone else. There's not even a second mind that tells me I'm on the stage, only an awareness that tells me where I am going.

It was on the "Faust" tour with Basserman, however, that I had, for the first time, strange and wonderful experiences of the mystical sort. Before the play, I used to sit for an hour trying to concentrate away from myself. I tried not to think, so that everything that was worrying me would go away—all my fears, all my ambitions—so that the confidence that I *was* the girl I was supposed to play would grow within me. Then, one night, I had the feeling that the girl was alive, even though she was only a thought of a poet. And the girl spoke to me. She said, "Oh, I loved him much more." And I knew that for me the girl was alive. I didn't talk to anyone about my experience. All I thought about was how I could transform myself completely into another being's truth. Stanislavski's ideas worked within me. I found my own way of constructing another being out of what I consist of myself—my past, my present, and the circle of my presence. Three girls, German, French, and American, with the same capacity for feeling, will expect and give different things; they will be made profoundly happy, or profoundly unhappy, by different things. Everyone has an inner nationality. I think that I am very German in my urge to make things deeper, in the way small things are large to me. When I am working, all that I think and feel and want, and all that I have learned and experienced, concentrates itself within the limits of the character I am playing. When I read a script, I receive an image corresponding to what I have gone through in life. With what I call my talent, I try to make this image strong—with my heart, my body, my thoughts. My thoughts test it, doubt it, and build it within myself. Then I put this image together with my ability, and the image and the final result get closer and closer together, until they are one. Once in a scene, I try, by remaining as empty as I possibly can, to come to this identification with the character I'm playing. I try then to *avoid* thought. I try to be nothing but the result of what has happened before. I try to live this person. On the stage, there is the advantage of working step by step, growing and developing together with the other actors. In television, there is still a chance for some development, even though the atmosphere is very hectic. In films, you are alone. For the first two or three days, in making a movie, my body still hasn't experienced all the thoughts, feelings, and images, and I am slow and awkward, but then it begins to happen, and I can make the image live. Movies are a wonderful medium. Through a closeup, you can say something with your own heart that is the equivalent of the monologue on the stage. However, in films the image is very fragile; it can be easily disturbed if you don't work toward giving it form. The way I have found to strengthen the image for a movie is to write on the script what the author did not write about the character. In films, I cannot rely on my intuitive feelings of the moment, which may mislead me. I can't talk to myself. I can't rehearse with myself. So I write out my thoughts until the image becomes more and more clear. I like movies, possibly because I have such an urge to make things last. I have learned that good results can come from tension and argument as well as from harmony. Sometimes I disagree with a director. In "Gervaise," I wanted to bring out what there is in the character that touches us today, while René Clément wanted to show life the way it was in those days. I wanted to show how the little things, not the big things, can destroy us, how the small daily failures lead to catastrophe. Clément wanted to show the drama and social life of the time. So we argued, and I learned, and began to understand it in his terms. And now I'd go with blind eyes to work with Clément again. He opened the way for me in so many respects.

Today, I am capable of bending my talent to what the subject calls for. I know how to find the true meaning and structure of a play. I now have the courage to give, to open myself. Actors are artists. I believe that acting is a small manifestation of life. On the stage, we create a concentrated form of life, but it is on a small scale. I don't consider acting essential to life. We are re-creative rather than creative artists. The painter or the writer is dependent only on himself, while the actor is always dependent on others. But each actor has a little workshop inside himself that is his own, and there is something important going on inside actors who really love their profession. Even though every individual is different from the next, I think that human feelings can be conveyed. When the artist gives his feeling form, it is a bridge. Art can transmit something that even people who are close to each other cannot communicate directly. We actors are the very poor artists; still, there is a little space for us. In my own self as an actress, I keep to myself, but I sense the worlds of other people. Each person has his own world. My inner world is the most important thing I have. I try as much as I can to respect people. The world of another person may be a big circle or a small one. What is important is to explore each circle, whatever the size, to the outermost edge. When I am in another person's circle, I am quiet—quieter than I used to be when I was very young. When the moment comes, I can be open. I like to communicate with people, but I need time by myself. Alone, I take in new strength; then I can give it out. It is very much like breathing—in and out.

MAXIMILIAN SCHELL

There are two souls in every actor. One watches the
other. When both are content at the same time, you
have a good moment.

I was born on December 8, 1930, in Vienna, the third of four children
of a Viennese actress and a Swiss playwright, novelist, and poet. My
father was never enthusiastic about the idea of his children's acting;
he felt that acting was too intense an occupation to allow for real
happiness. But my two sisters and my brother and I were all attracted
to the stage and are now acting. I grew up in a theatre atmosphere and
took it for granted. I remember the theatre, as a child, the way most
people remember their mothers' cooking. Acting was all around me,
and so was poetry. I made my début in the theatre at the age of three,
in Vienna, playing a blade of grass in a children's sequence in an
allegorical play written by my father. When I was eight, my father
moved our family to Switzerland, away from Hitler. When I was

about ten, I wrote a play called "Klitos," about the friend of Alexander the Great who always told him the truth about everything, and how one day, when Alexander was drunk, he killed Klitos because he told him the truth. The play was produced by my school, the Humanistisches Gymnasium in Basel, and I acted the part of Klitos myself. I also appeared in a professional play, in the part of William Tell's son. I grew up reading the classics. When I'd read the books of writers like Zane Grey, my father would always say to me, "Why don't you read Goethe?" My father today is not impressed by my acting in movies. For my father, the film is not a real art, and as he is a poet, he does not care about outside success. When I see him, we talk about poetry and writing. I attended the University of Zurich for a year. I was a good soccer player and a member of the champion Swiss rowing team. To earn money, I worked as a newspaper correspondent, writing sports reports for Swiss newspapers. I appeared in many student productions and also found small acting jobs on the professional stage, and played many classical as well as modern parts. I studied philosophy and the history of art. Then I felt I wanted to go away, to learn about life. I continued my studies at the University of Munich, and then I had my Swiss military service for about a year. After that I returned to the University of Zurich for a year and attended the University of Basel for about six months. I then decided, Either you are a scientist or an artist. A scientist is always trying to take things apart and an artist is always creating things and putting them together, and you can't do both unless you're a genius, which I am not. To me it is much more important to look at the stained-glass windows in Chartres and to admire and feel and be stimulated and inspired than it is to figure out the mechanics and workmanship of how the windows were made. Art comes out of chaos, not out of a mechanical analyzing. So as soon as I made up my mind there was no sense any more in continuing to study and in getting a degree. It is like an award; it does not mean anything in itself. If you get an award as an actor—as I did from the New York Film Critics as the Best Actor of the Year for "Judgment at Nuremberg"—it does not mean you are a better actor. A university degree is just a title. I don't think an artist should have a title. It was time for me to concentrate on acting.

For the next four years, I worked in many theatres in the Swiss provinces, and also in Germany, Austria, and France. I spent six months in Munich, with the Kammerspiele Theatre, one of several there that are supported by the city or the state. My older brother, Carl, is acting there now, and in other theatres throughout Europe. My older sister, Maria, is a movie star, and my younger sister, Editha, is beginning to make a name for herself as an actress in Germany and Switzerland. I can't remember when I first saw my mother on the stage, and I can't even remember seeing her *off* the stage when I was a child. My mother has often been called one of the most beautiful women in Europe. I remember seeing her play in "Snow White and the Seven Dwarfs" when I was eight. She played the part of the evil queen. The play was done with music, and it made a strong impression on me. When I was a child, I always took the atmosphere of the theatre, and my being in it, for granted. I didn't especially want to become an actor. Acting is such a reproducing art. What I wanted was to become a painter, a musician, or a playwright; I particularly wanted, and still want, to be a writer. I have written several unproduced plays and one unpublished novel. I can't tell whether what I write is good, but I can tell whether it expresses what I want to express. The world now tries to put everyone and everything into a category. When a play is put into a category, it loses so much—the secret of what it has to say. I suppose I'm an actor and a writer because I come from an acting and a writing family. If I had been the son of a musician, I suppose I would have become a musician. But I *am* the son of a playwright, and now I would prefer to be a playwright.

Still, I love to act. I began to love acting when I played Hamlet in a two-and-a-half-hour television show made in Cologne and broadcast all over Europe on New Year's Day, 1961. It was like falling in love with a woman—my feeling about acting. You meet a woman once, and nothing special happens. Then you meet her again, and after a while you realize you are in love. I had known acting all my life, but not until I acted the part of Hamlet did I have a moment when I knew I was in love with acting. Something in me had told me I was going to play Hamlet someday. When the role came to me, I was ready for it. I felt as if I had known Hamlet all my life. Hamlet belongs to me. Laurence Olivier is best known for *his* Hamlet. It has brought him great success. When I saw it, I didn't like it. Every actor reaches two or three high points in his lifetime. Marlon Brando reached a high point in "A Streetcar Named Desire." Montgomery Clift reached one in "From Here to

Eternity." Olivier reached one in "Hamlet," but, perhaps because I feel so strongly that the role of Hamlet is mine, he seemed to me to be more Olivier than Hamlet. In "Henry V," though, he seemed to be more Henry than Olivier. I've appeared on Broadway once, in an ANTA production of "Interlock," by Max Levin. It opened on February 6, 1958, and lasted for four performances. The play was a flop, but it was an experience I enjoyed. It was interesting to open in try-outs out of town. In Germany we open cold, without tryouts, and you know you have to do it, and the faults make it beautiful.

My first screen role was in a German film called "Kinder, Mutter, und ein General," and then I played in eight other pictures, mostly German. In 1958, I made my American film début as Hardenberg, a strong-minded German army officer, in "The Young Lions," with Marlon Brando, Montgomery Clift, and Dean Martin. After appearing in the part of the defense lawyer in the "Playhouse 90" television version of "Judgment at Nuremberg," in 1959, I played the same part in the movie version, with Spencer Tracy and Richard Widmark. By the fall of 1959, I had earned enough money acting in television here to return to Germany and rent an apartment in Munich. I plan to write and produce stage and television plays in Munich. When I was given the New York Film Critics award for my performance in "Judgment at Nuremberg," I received the most wonderful letter from Maria. It was just two weeks before her baby, and my godson, was born. She wrote: "Now, when you have my letter in your hand, a beautiful day is coming for you. I will be with you, proud, because I knew such recognition would come one day, leading to something even greater and better. Maybe you thought somehow that it would be difficult for me. No. It was not difficult, or if it was, then not more than perhaps for a tiny second—not only because you are close to me but because I count you among the truly great actors, and it is wonderful that besides that you are my brother." Maria and I are very close. When she played in "Ninotchka" in American television, in 1960, she asked me what to do in one scene, and I told her, "Give it all that you are." When I was playing Hamlet, I asked her the same kind of question, and she gave me the same kind of advice. I can act in French, German, English, and Italian, but I like best, and think I am best, acting in English, because I have to think about the meaning of every word. Someday I want very much to produce and act in a play on

Broadway. I still find that the classical figures are the most stimulating. The Greek heroes, an Achilles, a Klitos, are the greatest of all, greater than any of the Western heroes.

Socrates once said, "Know yourself." I do not agree. I think that is bad advice. You should *not* know yourself. By knowing, you take away the secret of yourself. That sentence is one of the most dangerous sentences ever written, especially for an actor. If you are conscious of what you are doing, you are thinking about it, and not doing your best. You are not acting spontaneously. Every actor has a little bit of every other man inside him. And this is how it must be, for it is this that enables him, in each part he plays, to reach what he is or what he is hoping to be. Almost always, the first time I read a script it seems a little silly. It is difficult for me to find any good in it. Shakespeare is different. It is easy to read his plays, and they always seem good. When I was twenty, I played Romeo in rehearsal at Basel. Today, I still find Romeo interesting, new, and different. There will always be some new way of playing him. One of the great tragedies of our time is that we are never willing to admit that anything can be new. We just try to cover up, with our actions, what we don't know. It is very important for an actor to find and touch the nerve of his time. As I see Hamlet, he is a man who knows he can't get the world for himself, or become godlike, no matter what he does. My Hamlet is like a man who has read John Osborne and Jean-Paul Sartre. He is a modern intellectual and a real man, not weak but a very strong man. I think Hamlet is very clear-minded, a very outspoken human being. He loves to go to bars, and he fences. He is a real prince and a hell of a guy. When I played him in Cologne, I made the dialogue conversational. It was as though the words were being uttered for the first time. The production was a very unusual one. We had one very simple set—black curtains, and just suggestions of steps. It was abstract in this way, but we never lost the reality. I think I played Hamlet truly, and in a way that no one else ever had. In playing him, I tried to touch the nerve of our time. Marlon Brando discovered very early how to do this, and it made him the important and successful actor he is today. He knows that in these times an actor can't say "I love you" openly to the girl he loves but has to cover up his feeling of love with some gesture. If John Barrymore—another really successful actor—were alive today, he would do the same, in his own way. He would respond to the times.

An actor has to have success. A great painter can work within four walls, and his work can be recognized after his death. But an actor has nothing to leave. He has to have an audience during his lifetime. An audience wants entertainment, and an actor doesn't want to be boring; he wants to be interesting to his audience. An actor needs those people in the audience who are impressed with what he is doing, and he needs them right away. But he also needs the ninety per cent of every audience that doesn't know what the play means or what the actor means. The actor needs one hundred per cent of the audience. Nevertheless, I don't *play* for the audience; I play for an idea. Going to a play like "The Best Man" is like going to a football game. "Sweet Bird of Youth" made me a little sick. Tennessee Williams is a good playwright, but he is not a poet. The classics are different. The classics say something and offer something more for an evening than watching a football game. But most classics are wrong for the time and have to be brought up to date. In any event, I need the audience to be there. And I need reviews, good or bad. If there were no reviews, the actor would be completely defeated, because the reviews tell ninety per cent of the audience what to think. When I act, I do exactly what *I* want, not what the audience wants. In all my early years in acting, I was not accepted by the audience. The critics thought I was bad, and the public didn't applaud me. All through my years in repertory, I kept hoping to find expression for the secret I knew I had inside me—the kind of secret that Gary Cooper has in "High Noon," the movie that was *his* high point. In Hamlet, I think I found what I was looking for. When I act now, I know how to concentrate on one feeling at one moment in one manner. One of my first true moments in acting was in a small part in a television play called "Child of Our Time," about a concentration camp, on "Playhouse 90," in February, 1959. I played a prisoner of war. The exact point at which I reached my true moment was when I was going to die. Then I knew I wasn't just acting. I was being. At that moment, I knew that happiness lay in being alive. In any circumstances, just to be alive was happiness. This I felt, even though I knew that all of life was a preparation for dying. But, as Herman Hesse says, in every truth lies its contrary, which is equally true.

Just before doing Hamlet, I played in "The Three Musketeers" on American television. I played d'Artagnan, just to prove that I still was not too old to play a dashing twenty-year-old. Then I made three films, one after another: "Judgment at Nuremberg," "Five Finger Exercise," and "The Reluctant Saint." The last movie is the one that is closest to my heart. It was made in Italy and directed by Edward Dmytryk, and in the film I reached what I always wanted to play, a kind of Chaplinesque comedy, very close to Dostoevski's "The Idiot." Everything the saint is is the opposite of an actor's qualities. An actor has to be brilliant and vain, and open himself to the world. This character is humble and modest, and he loves to do low work, to clean the stables and to beg—maybe in the begging the saint and the actor are relatives—and later he becomes a monk. In "Judgment at Nuremberg," I was able to do a good straight piece of acting, but in "The Reluctant Saint" I felt for the first time that I was able to make something strongly my own in a film.

Before I became successful in American films, my best notices from international critics came after I played Hamlet on German television. The notices were overwhelming. When the critics think I'm good, they rave about me, and when they think I'm bad, the same critics tell me I should go back to acting school. Actually, I've never gone to a school for acting, although I've taken speech lessons and classes in fencing and dancing. In Europe, a school isn't needed, because we have repertory theatre to give us experience. Acting talent is something that all children are born with. They naturally play cops and robbers, mothers and daughters. True art in acting is different. To be an artist, you must be lonely. I feel that I must keep my life lonely in order to be as free as possible. I cannot think or act unless I am free, and I cannot be free unless I am alone. So far, I have lived like a hermit, alone, and I expect to die alone. My hours are irregular. I get up at any time—two in the morning, eleven in the morning, five in the evening. My parents have a house in Zurich and a farm in Austria, and since I have my own apartment, I can visit them as I please. The farm has been in the family for a hundred years. There are two hunting cabins on the property, which is surrounded by mountains and forest. My father and my uncle hunt deer there, but I do not like to hunt. I like to walk through the forest by myself. In 1948 and 1949, when I wrote part of my first novel, which I have never shown to anyone, I isolated myself in one of the hunting cabins for three months, without a telephone, without electricity, with heat only from a large open fireplace. I like to work in the woods, cutting trees. I want to continue writing—especially plays. I have a piano in my apartment in Munich, and I play for hours at a time for my own pleasure. After I make a film, I find I need to rest. An actor must have pauses in between work, to renew himself, to read, to walk, to chop wood. Now that I have had success, I find there are some drawbacks—greater demands on my time for myself—but I like it. Freedom I always had, but now the possibilities are so much greater for me to do what I want. When you want to do something that is really in your heart, you keep it there until you do it. I do not like to say what these things are. Picasso would not say, "I am now going to paint something." He would *do* it first. I, also, want to *do* it first.

PAUL NEWMAN

I like all the preparation that goes into acting—the exploratory work, the intellectual stimulation, all the peripheral things. But as soon as I hear "Roll 'em!" for the camera, or the curtain goes up, and I'm committed to exposing myself, I find the experience of literally standing out in front of people to be uncomfortable and sometimes painful.

I was born on January 26, 1925, in Cleveland, Ohio. My father, Arthur S. Newman, ran a sporting-goods store. He died in 1950. My mother lives in Cleveland and comes to New York for all my openings and for visits. My father was Jewish, and my mother was a Roman Catholic and is now a Christian Scientist. I was raised as a Christian Scientist. We lived in the rather well-to-do neighborhood known as Shaker Heights. I have one brother, Arthur S. Newman, Jr., a year older than I am, who lives in California and is going to work as a production or unit manager for my new producing firm. I grew up with the idea that I was going into the sporting-goods store. My whole family, including a couple of uncles, took it for granted. Nobody in my family was connected with acting, although my mother was always, in some way, drawn to it. She used to go to see the plays at the Hanna Theatre, in Cleveland, and was just spellbound by it all. She never took me along, but she used to tell me about it. At the age of seven, I was in a grammar-school play about Robin Hood. A song for the play was written by one of my uncles, Joseph S. Newman. I played a court jester. I didn't like it. I felt as uncomfortable and disturbed then as I do now when I'm onstage. I had one entrance and one exit. I was a big hit. My family was hysterical with pride and admiration. Five years later, I was in a children's play about St. George and the Dragon, put on at the Cleveland Playhouse. I played St. George and poured salt on the dragon. Again I was a big hit. I didn't enjoy it, and I wouldn't enjoy it now: My wife, Joanne Woodward, is just the opposite. Whenever she's acting, she gets a real jolt out of it. Some people get a sense of satisfaction out of their own torment. For me, acting is simply a matter of getting out there onstage—or in front of the camera—and getting the motor running and keeping it going. One trait I've always had is a kind of tenacity in whatever I set out to do.

At Shaker Heights Senior High School, I stage-managed and acted in plays in the usual extracurricular routine, and I remember that one of my big disappointments was not getting the role of the First Gravedigger in "Hamlet." (I got the job of stage manager.) But while I was in high school and college I never considered going into acting as a profession. After graduating from high school, in 1943, I enlisted in the Navy for flight training. While I was waiting around to be called, I attended Ohio University, in Athens, Ohio, for four months, and majored in beer-drinking, though I did manage to wander into auditions for the Speech Department's production of "The Milky Way," by Lynn Root and Harry Clork, and come out with one of the leads—Speed McFarland, the middleweight champ. I couldn't wait to be a pilot, though. I loved to fly. But in July, 1943, I flunked the physical because of color-blindness, and was kicked out of pilots' training. I wound up as an aviation radio man third class on a torpedo bomber, and served in the South Pacific for nearly three years. While I was in the service, I didn't spend one minute thinking about acting. After my discharge, in April, 1946, I went to Kenyon College, in Gambier, Ohio, ninety miles southwest of Cleveland, where I concentrated on economics for a couple of years and then switched to English and speech. Kenyon is one of the most highly respected men's colleges in the country. My days there were the happiest of my life. I managed to get on the second-string football team. I weighed only a hundred and fifty pounds—I weigh a hundred and fifty-six now—but in those days I had a lot of energy. I also used to drink a lot of beer. One high-spirited day early in my junior year, I was kicked

off the team. I hadn't thought about acting in the two years
I'd been at Kenyon, but I had to do something with my spare
time, so I went over to the Speech Department, where they were
holding tryouts for "The Front Page." They handed me the part of
Hildy Johnson. I went on to appear in nine more Kenyon College
plays, including "Charley's Aunt," "R.U.R.," "The Taming of the
Shrew," and "The Alchemist." I was probably one of the worst college actors in history. I didn't know anything about acting. I had no
idea what I was doing. I learned my lines by rote and simply said
them, without spontaneity, without any idea of dealing with the forces
around me onstage, without knowing what it meant to act and to react. I didn't really learn about any of that until I got into the Actors'
Studio, in August, 1952. But I got some measure of local recognition
out of being in the plays.

I didn't have any singleness of purpose about acting until I became
successful at it. In those early days, I was thinking of becoming a
teacher. I more or less stumbled into serious acting. I wanted to run
from the sporting-goods business, and acting was as good a way as any.
People dedicated to an art are usually running *toward* something, but
I was just running away, and where I arrived was the result of a series
of accidents. In 1948, after my junior year, I did a summer of stock at
Plymouth, Massachusetts. Then, in the spring of my senior year at
college, I was offered a room-and-board scholarship for a season of
summer stock at Williams Bay, Wisconsin. My graduation was at two
in the afternoon on June 13, 1949, and by four that same afternoon
I was on the train for Williams Bay. My first part was the soldier in
Norman Krasna's "John Loves Mary." My second was the Gentleman Caller in Tennessee Williams' "The Glass Menagerie." At the
end of the summer, I went to Woodstock, Illinois, near Chicago, and
played a season of winter stock. That spring, I took a job as a laborer
on a farm near Woodstock. In April of 1950, my father became seriously
ill, and I went back to Cleveland. He died in May, and I stayed in
Cleveland, and worked at the sporting-goods store with an uncle and
a cousin and my brother. Then the store was sold. I took on some
odd jobs, including one as manager of a golf range outside Cleveland,
where we picked up golf balls and cleaned them for reuse. I did a
little acting over a local radio station for the McCann-Erickson adver-
tising agency and for the Ohio Bell Telephone Company. In 1949, I

had got married for the first time. My first wife and I had three children; the children now live with their mother. I have two children with my present wife, Joanne. We live in an apartment on Park Avenue. New York is our base of operations. My roots are here now. It's my home. There are a million things I like about the city, and I walk around it a lot, from one end of Lexington Avenue to the other, and up and down Fifth, up and down Second. Joanne and I are pretty self-sufficient. We enjoy being alone together.

By September, 1951, I had had enough of hanging around Cleveland. I decided to go to Yale and study for a Master's degree, so that I would be qualified to teach speech, possibly at Kenyon. I moved my family to New Haven. We lived on the top floor of an old wooden three-family house. I went around New Haven as a salesman of encyclopedias and managed to earn enough to support my family while I attended the Yale School of Drama. I specialized in directing. I heard a lot of talk about acting at Yale. I heard a lot of reverent talk—and rightly so—about the Actors' Studio, in New York. It was the first time I had heard of the Studio. I acted in three or four full-length plays and half a dozen one-act plays, and was also in one of the three major productions of the year, an original play called "Beethoven," in which I played Beethoven's nephew—a very formal guy. The part certainly wasn't anything like the all-American-boy parts I got to do later on. William Liebling, an agent from New York, saw me in the play and suggested that if I ever came to New York I should look him up. So after nine months at Yale I decided to try New York. It was the summer of 1952. I was prepared to try it for a year, and, if I got nowhere, to go back to Yale and get my degree. I had a family. I had responsibilities. Things were a little crowded in New Haven, financially, but I was making out fairly well with the encyclopedias; I once made about nine hundred dollars in ten days. I was committed to the theatre in a general way—not specifically as an actor—but I wasn't going to subject my family to the hanging-out-at-Schwab's-drugstore-in-Hollywood routine. I had no intention of waiting around till I was old and bruised and bitter. I moved the family into a sixty-dollar-a-month apartment on Staten Island. I picked Staten Island because my wife's aunt lived there and would give us a hand with the kids; we couldn't afford a baby sitter. I went around selling encyclopedias on Staten Island. It

was one of the hottest summers I can remember in New York. I had
one decent suit in those days—an old seersucker—and I'd put it on
every morning. I'd start out at eight every morning, take the ferry to
Manhattan, make the rounds of the casting agents, follow up all the
tips in the trade papers, and then get back to Staten Island in time to
peddle encyclopedias. After a month or so, I got two walk-on parts in
live television shows. For one—"The March of Time," in which I appeared as an old man applauding at the inauguration of President
McKinley—I was paid seventy-five dollars. I auditioned for the Actors' Studio—doing a scene as Val Xavier in "Battle of Angels" with a
girl—and, to my amazement, I was accepted. I attended faithfully. I
felt adulation for Eli Wallach, Rod Steiger, Geraldine Page, Maureen
Stapleton, and Kim Stanley, who were at the Studio. But the most I
hoped to accomplish for myself was still to become a teacher of
dramatics. And I still dreaded being drawn back into retail business,
which had given me no sense of accomplishment at all. There's a great
deal of romance in merchandising if you have an interest in it to begin
with. I didn't have it. However, I thought I was a very bad actor. My
body movements were all wrong. I was an untuned piano. I had a lot
to overcome. I discovered that I was primarily a cerebral actor—as I
still am. I began to understand that actors who are instinctively emotional are much luckier. The instinctively emotional actor—like Lee
J. Cobb, Geraldine Page, Kim Stanley, and Marlon Brando when he's
clicking, and also my wife, Joanne—work, I think, from the inside
out. Their emotional equipment is much more readily available to
them.

Soon, I auditioned for Maynard Morris, a Music Corporation of
America agent, and through him I got my first speaking part in a
television play. It was called "Tales of Tomorrow" and was about
a big block of ice that was forming off our West coast. The story
was full of the pulsations of cracking ice, and made one of the
funniest shows in television history. But all I felt was scared to death.
I played an Army sergeant and had two dozen lines to speak, and I
was so overwhelmed by the magnitude of the occasion that all I could
think about was the possibility that I'd drop a line. I didn't, though.
A few weeks before, through Bill Liebling, the other agent, I'd
gone to see William Inge about getting a part in his play "Picnic."
I'd been scared stiff. I'd read for him and thought I read very

badly. Then, a month after that, I read for the director, Joshua Logan, and I came away with the job of understudying the lead, Ralph Meeker. After a few weeks of rehearsals, I was given the part of Alan Seymour, the rich young man who didn't get the girl, played by Janice Rule. So there I was. All I had behind me was nine months at Yale and a couple of months at the Actors' Studio. "Picnic" was a hit. I was paid a hundred and fifty a week as understudy and two hundred a week after I got my part. I moved my family to Long Island—to a two-bedroom, eighty-eight-fifty apartment in Queens Village. I was with the play until just before the end of its run of four hundred and seventy-seven performances.

Even after I had my part in "Picnic," I wouldn't say I was exactly self-confident. While we were out of town with the play during tryouts, I was constantly fearful that the whole thing was going to turn out badly. After the play opened in New York and I had played in it for a year, I began to get a little self-confidence. By then I was even beginning to wonder if I couldn't really make acting my profession and earn a living at it. After doing "Picnic," I went out to Hollywood, under contract to Warner Brothers. I took my family with me, and we lived in a motel in Burbank, near the studio, while I made my first movie, "The Silver Chalice." I have to say "Ouch!" every time I think about it. I played a sculptor who was supposed to model the chalice to hold the Holy Cup. My acting was very, very bad, and I knew immediately that it was bad. It felt terrible. I was uncomfortable with what I was doing. I couldn't handle the language I was supposed to speak. After a couple of weeks, I sent a frantic message to my agent in New York telling him he'd better find me a play to do, to get me back here. I was flailing around, and got a reputation in Hollywood as a very difficult actor. Every time I asked a question, there was trouble. When the movie was finished, I lit out for New York and did a couple of good television plays, one by Tad Mosel and the other by Stewart Stern. In Tad Mosel's script, I played a guy who has an Army buddy whose death he feels responsible for, and when he goes to the buddy's home and meets his mother—she was played by Fay Bainter—he tries to take the buddy's place with the family. I felt comfortable in the part. It was the first part I'd ever played that I found the character for. Luckily, after doing "The Silver Chalice" I had got the job of playing on Broadway in Joseph Hayes' "The Desperate Hours," about a trio of desperadoes who take over a man's home. I played Glenn Griffin, the leader of the trio. In order to get permission from Warner Brothers to do the play, I had to sign a new contract. Instead of a five-year contract to make two pictures a year, I signed a seven-year contract giving them an option for a third picture. I played in "The Desperate Hours" for eight months—at a salary of seven hundred dollars a week—and I continued going regularly to the Actors' Studio. The play was very melodramatic. My part was a flashy one, which I didn't particularly like. The critics liked me a lot in the play, but I don't know why. At the end of it, I went back to Hollywood.

I was lent to M-G-M for my second picture—"The Rack," written by Rod Serling and Stewart Stern, in which I played a soldier in the Korean War who cracks under pressure from the Chinese Communists. I found that movie quite rewarding from an artistic standpoint, though it wasn't a hit at the box office. I then made one movie after another. For Warner Brothers, I made "The Helen Morgan Story" and "The Left Handed Gun." On loan again to M-G-M, I made "Until They Sail." In 1957, I made "Somebody Up There Likes Me," about the life of Rocky Graziano, which did more for my career than any of my earlier pictures. Playing Rocky was great fun. I spent a couple of weeks with him—drinking with him, finding out how he felt about things. I didn't try to imitate him in the part, however. I tried to find a balance between him and me—him as the part, and the part in me. I tried to play *a* Graziano, not *the* Graziano. Right after that, I was lent to Fox for "The Long, Hot Summer," in which I co-starred with Joanne, before our marriage. And I kept on going from one picture to another. In 1958, I played in my first comedy, "Rally Round the Flag, Boys!," for Fox, and I wasn't very good, but trying a new kind of acting at least gave me an opportunity to stretch. Then I was turned over to M-G-M and played in "Cat on a Hot Tin Roof," with Elizabeth Taylor. That was the first of my pictures, except for the one I made with Joanne, that I didn't have to carry pretty much on my own. Before that, it had just worked out, somehow, that I'd never played with a star. In working with Elizabeth Taylor, I was astonished to find that she was a real pro. She's not afraid to take chances in front of people. Usually, stars become very protective of themselves and very self-indulgent, but she's got a lot of guts. She'd go ahead and explore and risk falling on her face. I've made three movies with Joanne since our

245

marriage, in 1958, and we find we like working together. We respect each other tremendously, and if one of us criticizes the other, the criticism is taken as gospel. When we do a scene together, we both know we can't rely on tricks, and if one of us tries to, the other is sure to sound off about it. You have to be married to have that kind of freedom. Marriage is a wonderful area of comfort. In 1959, Warner Brothers got me to make "The Young Philadelphians," with the understanding that it would buy my release to appear on the stage later that year in "Sweet Bird of Youth." After I'd been in the play for a year, I had to start making "From the Terrace" on location here in New York during the day while I was performing in the play at night, and when that was over, I was presented with an opportunity to buy my way out of the Warner Brothers contract. I had to pay half a million dollars for my freedom, but it was worth it. If I hadn't done it, I would soon have had ulcers. There are always limitations in making a movie unless you have control over what you're doing. Today I have my own producing company, with Martin Ritt, the director. It's called Jodell Productions, after the first syllable of Joanne's name and the second syllable of Ritt's wife's name. Some pictures purport to be profound, penetrating analyses of the contemporary scene, and just aren't. If you do a comedy, you know it's fluff; you know exactly what it is. So you grow a bit doing it. But when a picture pretends to be something it isn't, I find it infuriating. I never want to do that kind of picture again if I can help it. A guy has got to come home at night with some sense of accomplishment. In making my own movies, I'll be taking a salary, as if I were working for somebody else. The main advantage is artistic, not financial. I made seventeen thousand dollars for my work in "Cat on a Hot Tin Roof," and two years later, for the picture "Sweet Bird of Youth," I got a three-hundred-and-fifty-thousand-dollar guarantee, with a chance to make more if the picture did very well. I can live very comfortably on my earnings, but I don't have much in the way of material possessions beyond the furniture in our New York apartment, a few paintings, a Volkswagen, and a Lambretta motor scooter, which I use for getting around in the city. I've never put any of my salary into investments. We go out to Hollywood to live whenever Joanne or I have to work there, but we'll never buy a house there. What we want is a place up in Connecticut where we can go in the summertime; apart from that, we want to be as free as possible.

In all the pictures I've made, I've tried to do the best I could. The character of the young lawyer that I played in "The Young Philadelphians" was much closer to me as a human being—and much duller—than Eddie Felson, the character I played in "The Hustler," in 1961. But the characters that are farthest away from my own personality are the ones I feel most successful with. The farther away from me a character is, the more I find there is to dig into. If an actor gets one good script every three years, he's doing very well. I've been unusually lucky in what I've had a chance to do. These days, an awful lot of stuff comes through the door—at least three or four books and six scripts a week. Joanne is the only person whose judgment I trust in helping me to decide what parts to take; it's impeccable. Making a movie is always a challenge to find out whether your intellectual judgments about the character you play are right, and whether the things you do, out of continuity and over a long period of time, blend together to make a consistent character. What you do is limited by your own imagination and your own experience, and to make it all jell is very, very challenging. All three of the main mediums for an actor are interesting, and while I don't mean to slight any of them, I do feel that the best is live television. That gives you everything: having it go non-stop; rehearsals beforehand; all the excitement of the first night. Whatever medium I'm working in, though, I'm always aware of a heavy responsibility to the author and to the other actors. One of the strains of going to the theatre each night is bearing this responsibility, even if you're feeling like death warmed over in your own personal life.

When I begin working on a part, I find that the first things I do are usually wrong. After rehearsals start, however, I find that I get rid of the wrong things bit by bit, until I get the part so that it feels fairly comfortable and fairly right. Nowadays, for movies, I always give a director or a producer three or four weeks for nothing, in order to have a rehearsal period. I won't ever do anything again without rehearsals. For "The Hustler," we had three weeks of rehearsal, using television technique, where you lay out tape on the floor to mark the sets. The motion-picture business is unlike any other in the way it forces you to walk into tight personal relationships and direct, close contacts for a period of three months, and exactly three months, and then—boom!—it's over. From there you walk into another batch of relationships for another movie, and you have close contacts with an entirely new bunch of people. You *have* to see the new bunch, and that leaves you no time to see the previous bunch. When you're like Joanne and me, and like to be self-sufficient, you're in a bit of trouble. Another thing is that we don't feel it's right to burden our two small children with the fact that their parents are movie stars, so we try to keep them away from it all.

There's a tremendous fascination about the idea of acting—trying to be the kind of person you'd like to be, or wouldn't like to be, or think you are. Everybody does it to a certain extent—runs for President or makes imaginary speeches before the United Nations. I love acting in the theatre. I love taking a script apart and trying to find the true person in the written character. The reward of acting on the stage is the continuity. We took three weeks to rehearse the Broadway production of "Sweet Bird of Youth." For the most part, I relied on the director, Elia Kazan, for what I did. He has broad shoulders. His invention, imagination, and patience are extraordinary. He helped me see that I had four things to comment on in portraying the character of Chance Wayne: the beauty of the relationship between men and women; the social disaster of a family that has lost the esteem of others; the fetish of youth and the importance of the fetish in our country; and the loving remembrance of youth. Well, that was a lot. But there were areas of Chance Wayne I never really got, including the aspect of the male whore. So it was always interesting to see what I could do with him. Nevertheless, after ten months of playing him on Broadway it got so that going to the theatre each night was like facing the dentist. I'd try to get to the theatre early. I'd have to have my dinner at five o'clock. Before every performance, I'd drink a couple of jiggers of honey for energy and for my throat; I'd lose three pounds every performance. I'd sack out from about seven to five minutes to eight. Then I'd sit in the shower at the theatre and collect my wits. As I was going to the theatre for my last performance in the play, I thought, I feel utterly exhausted. And all of a sudden I started bawling like a baby. I thought, I'll never say these words again. I'll never have this specific laugh again. I'll never have this kind of quiet near the end of the third act. Never this specific quiet.

LEE REMICK

Everyone has a false image of himself. When I first
saw myself on the screen, twenty-five feet tall, what I
saw was so unexpected that I couldn't look at anyone
else in the picture.

I was born on December 14, 1935, in Boston. My parents were divorced
when I was twenty-one, and both have remarried. My father, Frank
Remick, owns a department store in Quincy, Massachusetts. My
mother, now Mrs. Frank Packard, is an actress under the name of Patricia Remick. She did most of her acting between 1947 and 1957.
These days, she lives in New York but leaves most of the acting
in the family to me. She was a stand-in in "The Millionairess" and
a replacement in "The Small Hours," on Broadway, and also
played in summer stock in Dallas and on the Cape, and appeared
in some television plays. She acted in comedy, mostly. I saw her
a few times when I was a small child, and thought she was marvellous in everything. I have a brother, Bruce, two years older than I
am, who lives in Puerto Rico, where he does soil and sugar-cane research for a sugar plantation. My family moved to New York when
I was seven. I was immediately entered in Miss Hewitt's Classes, then
on East Seventy-ninth Street. My brother and I were taken to the

theatre constantly; I remember that the first thing we saw was Eva Le Gallienne's production of "Alice in Wonderland," with Eli Wallach and Bambi Linn. I took it all for granted, naturally assuming that *all* children went to the theatre. One of the early shows I saw was "Carousel," again with Bambi Linn, when I was ten. Watching Bambi Linn dance as the little girl whose father has died made me cry, and I cried all through the rest of the show. I was a very intense little girl. My mother wanted me to take ballet lessons, because she thought I wasn't getting enough exercise. She arranged for me to take lessons a couple of times a week at a school run by a Russian woman called Mme. Swaboda. It wasn't long before I was taking a lesson every day. I loved it from the start. I went there from the age of eight until I was a tall eighteen. When I was eighteen, I studied modern dance with Charles Weidman for over a year. I decided that I would become a ballerina.

At school, I was a fairly good student in everything except mathematics. At the age of twelve, I joined the dramatic club at Miss Hewitt's, because my mother wanted me to, and I played the part of Mrs. de Winter in "Rebecca." Compared to dancing, acting seemed absurd to me, but there was some fun in dressing up and pretending. I had no notion what I was doing. All the parents and teachers came to the performance, and everybody applauded, and that was that. I hated the dramatic club; it was no fun to play adults in the kind of plays they put on. When I got to the dating age, I had no dates. I thought they were silly. My brother went to the Kent School, in Connecticut, and then to Cornell, and he'd bring his friends home and they would invite me to school dances. I went to a few and hated them. The kids would sit around and talk about who could drink the most and who could do the most popular dances and who was dating whom, and so on. I never knew how to handle myself in large groups of people. I never had anything to say. Nothing really mattered to me except dancing and working at Mme. Swaboda's. As soon as I was old enough to get around by myself, I went to every possible performance put on by the Ballet Theatre or the New York City Ballet. My idols were Alicia Markova, Nora Kaye, Maria Tallchief—all of them.

In March, 1952, when I was in my next-to-last year at Miss Hewitt's, I read in a newspaper that auditions were being held in a midtown rehearsal hall for dancers for the Music Circus Tent, a summer-stock theatre-in-the-round at Hyannis, on Cape Cod. I went and auditioned, without telling anyone. I was sixteen, but I thought I looked past eighteen. There were about sixty boys and girls, in practice clothes. Like the others, I got up, did a few steps, and left my name, telephone number, and age, which I said was eighteen. The next day, to my surprise, I got a call telling me I was one of three girls chosen. I quickly joined Chorus Equity—which has since merged with Actors' Equity— and then told my mother. She wasn't exactly overjoyed, but she didn't object. Then I arranged to go up on a weekend and asked my father to drive me to Hyannis to see the theatre. When we got there, all we found was a big hole in the ground. We hadn't understood that the theatre was a real tent, put up in June and taken down in September. That June, I went to work. It turned out to be a summer of magic for me. We put on nine shows in ten weeks, including "Kiss Me, Kate," "Where's Charley?," "The Firefly," and "Carousel." I was paid about sixty-five dollars a week, and I saved all of it except twenty dollars a week, which went for room and board. Before each performance, we rehearsed from nine in the morning until six in the evening—for the following week's show. I never felt tired. I would have done anything they asked of me. I loved everything I did, everything around me, including my primitive dressing room—a tiny cubbyhole in a cottage across from the tent. The high point of that beautiful, exciting summer came when we did "Carousel." I played one of Enoch Snow's daughters, and I was given my first real lines to say—"My father bought me my pretty dress," and "Your father was a thief." They were my lines, and it was my show. There wasn't anything being done by anyone anywhere, we all felt, that could compare with what we were doing.

At the end of the summer, I had to go back to Miss Hewitt's Classes. My parents approved of my interest in the theatre, but they were absolutely firm about my completing my studies and graduating. Although they were separated, they were together in whatever concerned my brother and me. So off I went to Miss Hewitt's. More than ever, as a result of my sophisticated experience in summer stock, Miss Hewitt's Classes and I just didn't mix. I was even less interested than before in the other students and what they did with *their* time. That fall, I continued with my ballet lessons, and then I started getting calls from producers and directors to read for parts in television dramas. I'd never had an acting lesson in my life, but I'd go down and read and get the parts. It was still the early days of television. We did live one-hour plays. My first big part, in an "Armstrong Circle Theatre" production, was that of a high-school girl, the class brain, who has no dates, and who one day meets a high-school boy who is in the same fix —brainy and no dates—so they get together and then everything is dandy. Things just seemed to snowball for me. I started going to lunch at Sardi's on Saturdays, because that was one of the things to do. One day when I was there, I waved to a theatre director and writer named Reginald Denham. Waving was a thing you were supposed to do at Sardi's. Then I stopped at his table on my way out, and he said to me "Can you act?" I said "Of course." He asked me to read for a part in a play called "Be Your Age," by him and Mary Orr, with Conrad Nagel, Loring Smith, and Hildy Parks. So I had my first reading in a theatre. It was the most frightening and exhilarating thing in the world. There I was, onstage, all alone, under a bright light, with blackness out front, and the sound of voices. I read what they handed me—the part of Lois Holly, a smart-aleck teen-ager who is always shocking her family. From out front, I heard laughs. I loved the sound. I loved the smell of the whole thing. I loved the whole idea of getting up and saying words written by someone else. I felt proud that I could do it. After a third reading, they gave me the part, at a salary of a hundred dollars a week. I told my mother I was in the play, and we were in seventh heaven. The play lasted for exactly five performances in New York. Miss Hewitt's wanted to expel me because of my appearance in "Be Your Age." It led to quite a battle. My mother made a fuss, and dear Miss Hewitt—who is no longer with us—called a meeting of the school board, at which, egged on by my mother, she held that experience in the theatre broadened one, and so on. So I wasn't expelled. Another play, "Time Out for Ginger," had opened a month and a half before ours, and, unfortunately, was about the same sort of thing. But there were agents and producers in our first-night audience, and the phone started ringing constantly, and went on ringing after the play closed. I started getting more television parts. I was in a number of television shows before I graduated from Miss Hewitt's Classes, in 1953.

In the next four years, I appeared in about forty television shows, mostly dramatic plays. I worked in dozens of different parts—a good many of them the lead in a triangle situation. I did a lot of crying on television. I worked with all kinds of directors and producers and actors and sponsors. Just being immersed in all that gave me some idea of what acting was all about. I got a lot of pleasure out of acting, although I never abandoned the idea of dancing professionally; there just weren't enough hours in the day to do both. Actually, I was beginning to find the same thrill in acting that I had found in dancing; they had one aspect in common—that of entertaining. As long as I could entertain in some way, I was satisfied. I did so many television shows that they all run together, somehow. All gave me some pleasure. For the "Kraft Television Theatre," once, I was a piano-playing prodigy, and another time I was a teen-ager in trouble and going around with the wrong boy, who was also in trouble of some kind. I played one of the leads in an adaptation of F. Scott Fitzgerald's story "The Diamond As Big As the Ritz," and I fell in love with the wrong boy in that one, too. Once, I was a girl who lived on a farm during the Civil War and fell in love with a Confederate soldier. In the "Playhouse 90" production of "The Last Tycoon," I fell in love with a movie mogul. In another "Playhouse 90" show, I was a juvenile delinquent in love with a man on trial for his life. I almost always played the part of the sweet young thing in love with the wrong boy— or else the wrong boy was in love with me. After I was in a television show called "All Expenses Paid," in which I played a salesgirl who wins a trip to Nassau in a contest and falls in love with an older man, I had a telephone call asking me to come in and see Elia Kazan, who was going to direct the movie "A Face in the Crowd." I read for the part of the high-school cheerleader in the town visited by the television hero, played by Andy Griffith. I was so thrilled when I learned they wanted me for the part. It felt like something special, mainly because Kazan and others associated with the picture were so highly respected in the theatre. It was the biggest project I'd ever worked in. The scale of it all—the publicity and attention and noise—was impressive. For the movie, I had to learn how to do little pieces of a part at a time. The nice thing was that if you goofed, you had a chance to try again. I learned how to have the piece I was doing figured out and prepared before I got to the set. I was lucky to have Kazan as my first movie director, even though I wasn't able to appreciate fully what he was doing for me until the next movie we made together—"Wild

River," with Montgomery Clift—three years later. I'd been very critical of myself, even on television. Every time I saw myself on the screen, I would cringe. I didn't like the way I looked. I didn't like the way I walked. I didn't like the way my voice sounded. I didn't like the way the various parts of my body were put together. My own image of myself just didn't match what I saw on the screen.

It wasn't until "Wild River" that I was able to be more objective about myself. My part in that movie—of a raw mountain girl, warm and loving, who isn't satisfied with her life and who chooses to follow her own desires instead of what her family wants for her—was my favorite up to then. Working with Kazan on that part was a revelation. He has been an actor himself, and he knows how actors feel. He knows that anyone who is fool enough to get up on a stage or go before a camera is exposing himself in so many ways, and needs someone to give him support and confidence. Kazan always made me feel that I was the only person in the world who could do my part. There's so much to Kazan. He knows how to listen to actors; most actors love to talk, and never have a chance to say enough. He's observant of everything relevant to the actor. He's eloquent, and he knows how to extract the best performance from an actor. Actors confide in him. They tell him things they'd never tell another living soul. Then, whenever it's needed for your performance, he pulls something you've told him out of a hat and hands it back to you, and you know what to do in the performance. My interpretation of the role in "Wild River" was the truest in my experience, and it was Kazan who enabled me to make it true. In one scene, for example, it's raining outside, and I'm in my house waiting for Montgomery Clift, the man I'm in love with. Kazan suggested that I have a towel in my hands while waiting. He wanted me to give the towel to Monty in a certain way. Kazan kept telling me, "It's wet outside, wet and muddy, muddy and wet, wet, wet, and as soon as Monty comes in you'll want to give him the towel." Then, when Monty came in, I don't remember how I did what I did, but somehow I was feeling Monty's wetness. There was a certain feeling in it that couldn't have been there without Kazan. That was only one of a million things he does with actors.

In making movies, you need to be able to rely on your director, because there is no other audience, the way there is in the theatre, or even in live television. In movies, there are so many people trying to tell you what to do and how to do it, and then, when the movie comes out, they are still there, trying to tell you about what you've done. You need the support of the one man who is really in charge of what you do, and that is the director. I like to have an audience whenever I can, though. That's why I like to do live television plays. I hate doing taped television, which has all the disadvantages of live television and of film, and none of the advantages of either. The first thing I think of in considering a new part is whether *I* am going to enjoy doing it. No one can advise me in that respect. Not even my husband, William Colleran, who is a television and film director. He's my worst critic, because he adores *everything* I do. I met him at a party when I was nineteen, and we were married on August 3, 1957. We live quietly in California with our two children—Kate, born in 1959, and Matthew, born in 1961.

I want to try everything in acting. In February of 1960, I played Miranda in "The Tempest" on the "Hallmark Hall of Fame," with Maurice Evans, Richard Burton, Tom Poston, and Roddy McDowall. In "Anatomy of a Murder," the movie I played in with Ben Gazzara and James Stewart, I had to think of my part as peculiar in order to do it, because it was the part of a girl who was fooling around with other men while her husband was facing a charge of murder. In "A Face in the Crowd," I was a high-school girl who was proud of her body and flirted like mad. In the movie "Days of Wine and Roses," I played an alcoholic. That was the first time I'd felt that what had happened to the character I was playing *might* have happened to me— that in every human being there is a certain frailty, and no one is immune. I'm not a martyr to truth. I play within my own limits. And second best to acting a part for which you can draw upon yourself is acting the part of someone you are curious about.

DONALD PLEASENCE

*There comes a moment onstage when you can't deny
yourself and you can't deny the part you are playing.
Somehow these two things come together when you
act.*

I was born on October 5, 1919, in Worksop, Nottinghamshire, which
is D. H. Lawrence country, on the border of Sherwood Forest. My
parents, Thomas Stanley Pleasence and Alice Armitage Pleasence,
were also born in Worksop. It's about thirty miles from Scunthorpe,
in Lincolnshire, where my father was a railway stationmaster in 1919.
The only other person I know who comes from Scunthorpe is Joan
Plowright. Theatrically, the place is a standing joke. It's a town no
one goes to, so you say, "The play did very well in Scunthorpe." My
grandfather was a railway signalman. I have one brother, Ralph, four
and a half years older than I am, and he is a stationmaster at Smeeth
Road, in Norfolk. My father, now retired, is a solid British Labour
Party member, and likes the simple things. He's a keen gardener. My
mother was taken from Worksop to America as a child and was
brought up by her grandfather in Momence, Illinois, which is near
Kankakee. She lived there for about fifteen years before returning to
England. My parents recently came to America together for the first
time, on a three-week holiday. They saw me in the Broadway produc-

tion of "The Caretaker," and then went to Momence, where my
mother found the house she'd lived in as a child. I think she was
pleased, but, like most North Country women, she doesn't believe in
expressing emotional satisfaction. All she said was "Very nice." My
father is the same. If, after seeing me in a performance, he were to say
to me, "You were very good, love," I'd know he had been impressed,
but that's as far as he'd go. My parents' visit to America was rather
marvellous, actually. I took them round to see the sights in a 1955
Oldsmobile, a splendid machine, and they had a chance to spend
considerable time with my wife, Josephine, and our daughter, Lucy,
who was born in May, 1961. I have two daughters by a previous
marriage—Angela, who was born in 1941 and is a student at the Royal
Academy of Dramatic Art, and Jean, who was born in 1944 and wants
to do social science.

Until 1939, I had always lived in railway stations. Now it's becoming usual for the stationmaster to get a house outside the
station. I found the stations wonderful places for a boy, especially
the station at Grimoldby, in Lincolnshire, where my father became
stationmaster when I was about nine. Grimoldby is a village in the
wilds of flat fen country near the sea. It's very attractive country
in a bleak kind of way. My brother and I played in the goods yard,
climbing in and out of freight trucks, and we had animals about—
a pig, dogs, and turkeys. We lived there for about five years. It was a
very happy time. Then we moved to Ecclesfield, right outside Sheffield,
in Yorkshire, and a few years after that to Conisborough, which is a
rather dirty colliery town in Yorkshire. I went to dozens of schools,
including some wretched ones. The main one was Ecclesfield Grammar
School, where I went until I was seventeen, and then quit. My parents
were much concerned about the possibility that I wasn't going to be
clever. Lincolnshire was very backward country educationally—mostly
farming country, with a few industrial towns. By the time I got to
Yorkshire, which is very education-minded, I found that I was somewhat behind in school. I was good in English and literature and
terribly bad at all practical things, like math; science was a closed book,
but I find that I've become rather interested in it now and can understand it. I was good at all theatricals, won a dramatic-reading prize
at the age of fourteen, and was elected a Member of Parliament in a
mock election held at school. I was the Socialist candidate, of course.

I was one of those awful children who go and recite poetry at musical festivals. I had a fairly sunny disposition and was quite personable and probably a bit spoiled and rather horrid. I suppose I recited quite well. From the age of eight or nine, I knew I was going to be an actor. I never considered being anything else. I didn't know how I would do it, but I knew I would. It was a marvellous feeling to stand up on the stage and do things while people watched you. My parents always encouraged me. They had me attend classes in voice production—at two guineas a term, which they could ill afford. At the musical festival that was put on each year by the town authorities, there would be competitions in categories like Verse Speaking for Boys Ages Seven to Nine, and I'd often win the silver medal for my category. To this day, my mother has a drawerful of my medals. The first part I played was Caesar in "Caesar and Cleopatra," at Ecclesfield. I was fourteen. I would have been a very good child actor, I'm horrified to say. Then I lost the knack of naturalness that a good child actor must have. I became too much interested in posing and in making my voice sound beautiful.

We never lived near a theatre when I was a child. Probably the first theatrical performance I ever saw was a local production of a "Miss Hook of Holland" sort of thing. My father took me to the repertory theatre in Sheffield and also to some plays in London. When we went to the Sadler's Wells Theatre, which had been an eighteenth-century music hall, we sat right up in the gods' gallery. The thing that impressed me most as a young boy was seeing a production of "Hamlet," in 1930. I think it was at the Old Vic, where John Gielgud played "Hamlet" for the first time in 1930, but I'm not sure it was. I went with my father. I had never seen a professional Shakespearean production before. It was all wildly exciting. It was so lovely—kind of a wild dream. London itself was so exciting. It was all so foreign, so far removed from my life. My father and I usually travelled to London on an early-morning train, on free train passes my father got from the railway. We'd go round the big shops and look at everything, although we didn't buy much, and once we had lunch at the roof restaurant of a big shop, Derry & Toms. After that, we might go to Mme. Tussaud's or to the British Museum. The first performance of an individual actor that I remember clearly was that of Wilfrid Lawson in J. B. Priestley's play "I Have Been Here Before," in 1937. It was one of those Priestley time plays, in which it turns out that everyone *has* been there before—a quite interesting play. I was eighteen and went to London alone, sitting in the gods', as usual, and I was quite overwhelmed by Wilfrid Lawson's playing of the lead, a businessman. Wilfrid Lawson is over sixty now, and is a great actor, really, who has become a hero to the younger generation of actors, because he has never been allied with the Establishment. In 1953, he made a comeback, after some time out of the picture, with a mammoth performance in Strindberg's "The Father" that set everybody's eyes aflame. He's an interesting figure—a kind of outsider figure, actually.

My background was strongly Methodist, and I wasn't allowed to go to certain films as a young child, and there were no cinemas in the country. I remember seeing a few Chaplin films, including "The Gold Rush." My father wanted to take me to that one, and for some reason I didn't want to go, and was dragged off screaming to see it. I thought it was marvellous when I did see it, of course, and remember vividly the scene in the house on the cliff. My father gave it high praise by saying "Quite good." In my early teens, when the family moved near Sheffield, I became a mad cinemagoer. The American movies of the early thirties, in particular, had a very strong effect on me. I used to devour the gangster ones and the prison ones. In the thirties, I was very much impressed by Hollywood actors like Edward G. Robinson and Thomas Mitchell, but I didn't really appreciate them until later. Actually, I have been influenced very little by most other actors, but James Cagney was quite an influence on me. I was terribly impressed by his relaxation—his habit of standing in a relaxed way. I'm a great believer in relaxation and the necessity for it in acting. When I become tense, I'm at my worst. If I'm having difficulty in a part, my toes tense up and I clasp my hands. If I'm able to relax to start with, then I can create whatever tension I need for my part. Before a performance, I try to empty myself of all tension. Then one is there and one is not afraid to be there. One uses body and mind for the task ahead. There are some actors who believe that they so envelop themselves in their part that they deny themselves completely. For me, it's a matter of the two things' coming together—myself in the part, and the part in myself. Then, there are some actors who use *only* themselves in a part. That kind of acting is a different thing entirely. It has its place, but I wouldn't want to do it. The actor who uses himself is

259

relying on tricks of his own personality—vocal tricks or raising an eyebrow—that always produce certain effects and that have been developed over the years but essentially are still him. Tricks are different from style. There are parts of Olivier's acting—and I happen to think he is the best actor in the Western world—that are uniquely *him*. He has great style, and I admire style, but he always plays the *part*. There's a great difference between exploitation of an actor's personality and individual style. An actor has almost as much right to style as a painter. The three actors who have impressed me most in my life, and all in different ways, are Nikolai Cherkassov, the Russian actor who plays the title roles in "Alexander Nevsky" and "Ivan the Terrible," Parts I and II (all directed by Sergei Eisenstein); Wilfrid Lawson, who combines the best of the old and the new; and Olivier. The important thing about actors in their art—and I personally think that at its best it *is* an art—is that they do use themseves and only themselves, one way or another. You use your own soul. You are absolutely naked on the stage. That is what is so difficult and so exciting at the same time. One can often see a few moments when acting becomes an art, but rarely does one see an over-all performance that is art. It depends on so many outside factors, including parts offered and parts played. A chap might go on playing light comedy in the West End for years, and then perhaps, if he was offered the right part, he might have an opportunity to use his talent in an entirely new and powerful way. An actor can't fully develop himself without a series of first-class parts that are as demanding as possible.

I left school with a year to go, because I became fed up with the difficulty of commuting from Conisborough to Ecclesfield—about an hour's ride on the train. I wanted to go to London and attend the Royal Academy of Dramatic Art—an institution I had known about since I was twelve, when Cyril Maude, who was a friend of an acquaintance of my father's, and who was associated with the Academy, suggested and arranged an audition. At the audition, I recited a long passage from "King John," in which I played two parts—the boy Arthur and Hubert de Burgh, for whose speeches I used a deep voice. It was quite absurd, because they didn't take children in the Academy. They just patted me on the head and told me to come back later. Which I did—five years later, when I auditioned for the one scholarship available that paid fees and maintenance, so that I could afford to go there.

I didn't get it. That meant that I had to find a job. I sat down and wrote hundreds of letters to repertory companies and theatres, and went round to all the theatres I could. Employment wasn't easy to come by in those·days. I couldn't get a job in the theatre, so I spent the next year and a half as a railway clerk at my father's station and then, for about a year, was in charge of my own little station, at Swinton, where I sold tickets and did all the accounts. Finally, I got an answer to one of my letters offering me a job as assistant stage manager in a popular resort area on Jersey, one of the Channel Islands, at thirty shillings a week—about seven and a half dollars—which was enough for me to live on. I jumped at it. My board and lodging cost only twenty-five shillings a week, and after a few weeks the stage manager left and I was promoted to his job and given a rise of five shillings a week. That was in May of 1939. I had never been so happy. I really thought I had arrived. It was my dream come true. I was very good as stage manager, because I had done two and a half years as a clerk and was very systematic and could type. And I played tiny parts and also did general dogsbody—took care of washing up the teacups. We did a different play every week, for an audience of holidaymakers and local people. My first part was as Hareton Earnshaw in "Wuthering Heights," that May, and I was probably all right, as it was a Yorkshire part. I still had an accent. By this time, I thought I spoke quite beautifully, but one night, in my digs, which I shared with a fellow who had gone to public school and had the right— very right—kind of accent, this chap told me I was limited as an actor, because, with my accent, I could play only North Country parts. I then realized for the first time that I would have to learn to speak like a proper gent. Actually, I have a slight North Country accent to this day. Dialect has always been such a terrible problem in the British theatre. It's kept many talented actors out, because they didn't sound as though they'd gone to public school, and until just recently most plays were about proper gents who had gone to public school.

I stayed on Jersey until the Second World War broke out. During what was then called the "phony war," all the theatres in the Channel Islands were closed down for fear of bombardment, and a good many of them at home. I was very politically conscious in those days, and considered myself a pacifist. Gradually a few theatres opened, and I found another job—in a tiny repertory club in

Plymouth, where I played a variety of parts because the company was small. I played the villain in "Gaslight," and I played in a number of light comedies, for which I put gray streaks in my hair and wore a toothbrush mustache to make myself look distinguished. I had registered as a conscientious objector, and while I was waiting to be sent to prison or to an agricultural camp, I answered an advertisement in the newspaper *The Stage,* which was the way to get employment in those days. The ads usually read, "WANTED: ARTISTS ALL LINES TO REHEARSE MONDAY WEEK." So you sent photographs and you exaggerated particulars of your experience. I got a job with a repertory theatre in Workington, Cumberland, which put on two plays a week for six performances each. I played character parts, like a prince in "The Midnight Wedding," an Edwardian play, in which I was called upon to say, "When a man has no proof that his father was his mother's husband, he is called . . . a bastard!" From there, after my investigation by the tribunal for the examination of conscientious objectors, I was sent to work as a lumberjack in the Lake District, near Workington. After six months, I changed my mind about being a conscientious objector, partly because I found that the others in the camp were so callous in their attitude toward the war, and also because by then I had decided that the idea was absurd. After all, I had been strongly anti-Fascist since the Spanish Civil War. In 1941, I enlisted in the R.A.F., and for two years I flew in bombers as a wireless operator. I was shot down over France, parachuted to earth, and spent the next year in a prison camp in northern Germany. It wasn't too bad there. Mostly, the camp was made up of Americans. We had a theatre of sorts. The British senior officers insisted that we put on light comedy, and so mostly we did "Hay Fever" and variety shows and things like that, but I did play in a production of "The Petrified Forest," taking the part of Alan Squier, the part originally played by Leslie Howard. After being released, I spent six months at a rehabilitation camp, a former R.A.F. station at Wolverhampton, because I was supposed to be suffering from malnutrition.

In June, 1946, while I was waiting to be demobilized, I heard that Peter Brook, the director, was holding auditions for "The Brothers Karamazov," adapted by and starring Alec Guinness. I walked in, read some lines, and was engaged for a tiny part, and then got the much bigger part of Mavriky—a very showy little part, very flashy—at seven pounds a week. It was exciting to get back to the theatre after more than five years. I greatly admired Guinness, and loved watching him in his part—Mitya, the elder soldier brother. Guinness is remarkably easy to work with. He gives such a great deal, and he certainly acts *with* you. On the pre-London tour, I unfortunately came down with the measles, and so I missed the opening in London, but I joined the company in London a week later and played for five weeks. After that, Brook asked me to appear at the Arts Theatre, in "Vicious Circle"— the English title of the Jean-Paul Sartre play that was called "No Exit" in America. I went on to play in a verse play, Gilbert Horobin's "Tangent," and then, with Christmas coming and no money in the bank, I took the part of the pirate Starkey in a rehash of "Peter Pan," in London. I played it for six months, and I hated it. After that closed, I was being thought of for parts in London, but I couldn't afford to sit around waiting, so I went up to Perth, in Scotland, and acted in a repertory theatre there for a year. Then, in 1948, I joined the Birmingham Repertory Theatre, where I stayed for almost two years. By now I had acquired class as an actor, and I joined the Bristol Old Vic Company, a permanent repertory company attached to the London Old Vic. We worked in the Theatre Royal in Bristol, a beautiful old theatre, built in the eighteenth century. These were my real years of training. I had ample opportunity to play all sorts of parts, in both classics and modern plays. In September of 1951, the Festival of Britain year, I played in "Saint's Day," by John Whiting, who to my mind is one of the best playwrights in England today. The New Wave in England arrived with John Osborne and Arnold Wesker, and their plays of social realism, but Whiting's play "Saint's Day" is, in my opinion, one of the two best plays to come out of England in recent years. The other one is "The Caretaker," in which I played the part of Davies, the old, discontented, obsessed tramp, for fourteen months in England and then—after making a film —on Broadway for five months. "Saint's Day" is a most important play, but the critics couldn't understand it, and so vented their baffled fury on it. It's about a distinguished writer in his old age—probably his dotage —who has been neglected by the Establishment but is finally about to be honored on his birthday by a visit from a very successful middle-aged poet, who arrives carrying a presentation copy of the old writer's poems. He praises the old man and his work, but meanwhile some soldiers in a camp nearby have deserted. The writer and his daughter and her husband are warned by the local parson—the part I played—that the soldiers are on a rampage. The deserters arrive at the house, ally themselves with the poet, and hang the old man. It is a play of deep religious and philosophical significance, and it is tremendously dramatic. When I acted in it, it was very important to me to play out the character on the stage. Ordinarily, though, I'm not involved, while acting, in what the deeper meaning may be. If you dwell on the deeper significance, it seems to me, you're in danger of playing much too big.

Late in 1951, I came to Broadway for the first time, with the Oliviers, playing the Major-Domo in "Caesar and Cleopatra" and Euphronius in "Antony and Cleopatra." When I returned to London, I was in a very, very funny North Country comedy, "Hobson's Choice," in which I enjoyed great critical success at the Arts Theatre, where I have spent so much of my time. In 1952, though I'm not a serious writer, I adapted Robert Louis Stevenson's "Ebb Tide," and it was a great success at the Royal Court. The following year, I accepted an invitation to go to Stratford on Avon, which was disastrous for me. I was too old to go there on the middle level, which is what I did. In a big soap factory like that, I found myself feeling inhibited about acting. I couldn't act. It wasn't because I didn't want to play in what are loosely called the classics. I did want to. But I felt enveloped, swallowed up, completely blotted out. I think I could cope with it now. I'm more successful now, and more secure, and have a clearer idea of what I want to do. I've always been interested in films. I made my first one in 1954, "The Beachcomber," in Technicolor, in which I played Tromp, an Indian head clerk—a very good part. Working in my first film was very frightening. One had so much to think about at once—the Indian dialect, the completely new medium, all the film things one takes in one's stride now, like closeups, looking at a nut on the camera instead of at the person one is supposed to be talking to, hitting marks that are used to determine the camera's focus on actors, and, most bewildering of all, the lack of rehearsal.

In 1955, I played in a stage production of Pirandello's "The Rules of the Game," at the Arts Theatre, which was a great success. I played Leone Gola, which is my favorite part of all time. It calls for a strange, bitter sort of comedy. I found the play and my role entirely satisfying and wholly engrossing. I'm always very excited about something that is neither clearly tragic nor clearly comic—in the theatre, particularly —and as Leone, a very sophisticated, learned, and rich middle-aged Italian who is a marvellous talker, I had a very interesting opportunity to go from bitter comedy to tragedy. Shallow, but tragedy nonetheless. I went on to play the Dauphin in "The Lark" and the Cockney clerk—one of the best comedy parts of all—in a revival of "Misalliance." I kept getting marvellous notices, but never made any money. At Stratford, where I shared a dressing room with Robert Shaw, and where we'd hear people walk up and down the corridor visiting other people, while nobody came to visit us, we had a self-kidding routine. I would say, "I'm the most successful club-theatre actor in London." Then Robert would say, "Let's get the notices out!" And he would solemnly read Kenneth Tynan's notice of "The Merchant of Venice" saying, "I cannot imagine what Donald Pleasence was trying to make of Launcelot Gobbo, who is not, I suggest, an organ-grinder's monkey." It's very difficult to know when you're successful as an actor. I used to say when I was twenty, "If I'm not successful by thirty, I'll do something else." Then the war came, and I was able to put the limit at thirty-five, because I had lost five years. Then I was noticed, and though I got some marvellous notices, I still didn't know if I was knocking my head against a brick wall. In my country, I'm now very successful in the sense that I can earn a good living. I'm not, however, completely accepted by the Establishment as a leading actor. Most of the time, I have a fairly placid temperament for an actor, but there are weeks when I feel frightfully insecure.

In our world of entertainment, there is no set plan that an actor can follow. When I was very young, my brightest ambition was to play Hamlet at the Old Vic. Now a young actor's brightest ambition is to play the lead, wearing dungarees, in a New Wave play at the Royal Court. Shakespeare is a bit old-fashioned in England now. But he will come back. He's such a good playwright, after all. Back when I was dreamy-eyed, what I wanted most was to play a classical part. Now it's all a hodgepodge. I am loosely involved in what is called the new school, but we have no organization theatre as it exists in Continental Europe, where you can enter a company and stay for life. One thinks enviously about it when one has dependents and is pounding up and down the carpet thinking about how to pay the grocery bill. By and large, the Continental way must be preferable. Still, the situation is better in England, where we have repertory companies in the provinces, than it is in America, where it must be absolute murder. In England, the only way you can get what you want is to be successful first; then you can do the things you want to do. Take Paul Scofield, for instance. He is a brilliant, marvellous actor. He's extremely personable, and he has a beautiful voice and a wonderful, remarkably relaxed presence. He was accepted very early in life as a leading actor, and he's always had a solid life stretching before him. He is, unfortunately, an exception. Generally speaking, the pattern of one's career changes from day to day. One day I am a character actor with a background in the provinces, where I usually played leading parts; the next day I am making a living by working in films; the day after that I am simply one of the best-known television actors in England. That happened in the late fifties. Now, if I meet an English housewife on the street, she'll say, "Oh, the man on the telly!" She doesn't have the faintest knowledge of me as a stage actor or of the play "The Caretaker." The actor's worlds are as sharply divided as that.

For four years before I went into "The Caretaker," I wouldn't act on the stage at all, because I couldn't find anything I really wanted to do. I did an enormous amount of work in television, for which the subject matter is quite good in England. Harold Pinter, author of "The Caretaker," writes original television plays. The programs are not controlled by the sponsors, as they are in America; the sponsors have no connection with what is being written. It's possible to do quite a lot of good work in television, and you don't have to play down to the audience. I've never *enjoyed* acting. It's more of a compulsive thing. I alternate between being terrified and being bored, and yet there's a curious excitement in it the whole time. Television, especially if it's being done live, is quite terrifying. I regard acting, in a sense, as a job, pretty much like being a bank clerk. On the other hand, I always try to do my best. When I was very young, and very bad as an actor, I could find delight in showing off. As I got better, I began to see things more objectively. To play a part like the one in "The Caretaker" and to be an individual success is still exciting. You do have a wonderful mounting feeling when you've got a marvellous part and you can tell that the audience likes it and likes you in it. Then you do begin to walk on air. It's almost as though the thing was running away with you. There are times, however, when what you take for genuine emotion may just be the result of your own impact on the audience. Even then, though, the emotion is a vivid one, and can be used onstage for all kinds of effects. I have no theory about acting, no method, no way, and nobody has ever taught me a way. If somebody could teach me how to achieve a certain look, I suppose it would be nice. As it is, I try to know what my character would do in any circumstances, and whilst I'm onstage I'm totally immersed in the part. But I am never lost in it. You must constantly go back to first principles. If you find you achieve an effect with a certain gesture or intonation or expression, you nevertheless try to do something fresh the very next night. If somebody onstage says a line that is not in the play, you ought to know how to reply. I try to achieve a sort of physical and mental transfiguration, and go on from there. When I first read a part, I don't think of how I will look in it. At least, I try not to. These things come out of rehearsals. I plunge right in, but that's only at the beginning. I try to find a clear line, and then work on the ornamentation. A lot of actors work from ornamentation back—especially film actors. And in weekly repertory we used to have a joke that went, "Is it the week for the mustache?" I hate makeup, putting on wigs and beards, and, whenever possible, I like to grow my own. What is dangerous for an actor is getting an exact physical image and then deciding, I want to look like So-and-So in this part. I don't go to people for my feelings about a part. I always go to animals and birds. For the part of the old, suspicious tramp in "The Caretaker," I thought of myself as an alley cat.

There was quite a lot of comment on my performance in "The Caretaker," and people asked me how I managed to get a look of absolute desperation and terror in my eyes when the old man finally realizes that he is going to be chucked out of the house. The old man at this point comes as near as possible to facing up to himself; he knows it is curtains for him. That look in the eyes arose from sheer intensity of emotion. It arose from very powerful feeling—physical exertion, really—that left me absolutely exhausted at the end. I think I managed to achieve something three nights out of the week. One can come halfway to doing what one is trying to do, provided one is willing to tear one's guts out. Sometimes the whole thing was utterly real to me, even after I'd played it for a year and a half. At other times, it wasn't, and then I had to work all the harder to do it.

CAROL LYNLEY

I never go to see plays. I want to be on the stage, not in the audience.

I was born on February 13, 1942, in New York City, as Carole Jones. I have a younger brother, Daniel, who is studying to become a photographer. My father, Cyril Jones, is from Ireland, and my mother is from New England. I'm a mixture of Irish, English, Scotch, Welsh, German, and American Indian. Both of my maternal grandparents had Indian blood—Connecticut variety. My parents separated when I was a small child. Neither of them has ever had any connection with show business; my mother went to work as a waitress. I was never in a school play. I went to fourteen schools—professional and parochial schools, all over the Bronx—before graduating, in 1959, from the School for Young Professionals. When I was ten, I started working as a photographer's model to supplement my mother's earnings as a waitress. Between us, we managed to support the family. Tuesday Weld and Sandra Dee were also child models in New York at that time, and the three of us often competed, as fairly close friends, for the same modelling jobs. I liked modelling. If I hadn't, I would have quit. I don't do many things I don't want to do. As a child, I had a very active imagination. When I was five, I saw the movie of "The Wizard of Oz" and became hysterical over it, and about the same time, seeing "King Kong," I nearly died. I yelled and screamed, and upset the audience so much that I had to be taken out of the place. When I was sixteen, and was playing in "Blue Denim," by James Leo Herlihy and William Noble, on the New York stage, every time I did the part about going for an abortion I'd feel sick for hours afterward. I started acting for television soon after I started modelling. The agency I worked for would get calls from television producers, and they would· send me out to act in television exactly as they sent me out to model. I was learning every minute, not only about acting but about life. I've never taken a lesson in acting. The good acting schools don't take children under eighteen. They think that children don't need to *learn* to act, and they're right. Children act all the time. Children take the most outrageous liberties with the truth and believe in what they say and do. All that children can learn about acting is voice projection and how to take direction. My first roles in television were bits or walkons. Television plays were all done live at the time I started. I had to learn to change makeup, clothes, and manner, and to run from one set to another, in a matter of minutes. Later on, when I began making movies, I had days in which to do the same thing.

I started taking ballet lessons when I was seven, for two hours a week, after school. I still try to take lessons now. Dancing is a body conditioner. If you're accustomed to dancing and then give it up, you find yourself getting flabby. Dancing helps keep you flexible for acting. It helps, for example, if you have to walk like a child, or like a tomboy, which was the kind of part I played in the movie "The Last Sunset." By the time I was eleven, I was getting a lot of television work to do, and I was so busy that my mother gave up working daytimes in order to be with me. When the television roles started coming in, I thought, I'm in it anyway, so why not try to be the best and get leading roles? It was all very time-consuming. Out of fifty readings, I would get ten small parts. Whenever I was afraid I wouldn't get a part I wanted, I'd think, Well, it's in the lap of the gods, and the chances are ten to one against me anyway. All through school, I was a B student and could have been an A student very easily if I'd worked at it. But I didn't like school. I loved history, and still love it—hearing about it from others or reading about it— but in history class it was only a matter of giving a date when I was asked about an event, or an event when I was asked about a date. I wanted to know about the way *life* used to be. I'm a compulsive reader. As a child, I read everything. I didn't care for "The Bobbsey Twins" and that kind of thing, even though they were big favorites with the other kids. When I discovered the Encyclopædia Britannica, I began to devour it.

As a model, I worked under the name of Carolyn Lee. When I was thirteen, I got a job in the road-company production of Jerome Chodorov's and Joseph Fields' "Anniversary Waltz," and when I applied for membership in Actors' Equity, they already had a Carolyn Lee, so I solved the problem by keeping the same name but dividing it up as Carol Lyn-lee, or Carol Lynley. When I was twelve and had been doing walk-ons and bits for two years, I tried out for the part of Alice in "Alice in Wonderland" for the "Kraft Television Theatre," one of the bigger shows on television. It was while I was trying out for the role that I first realized I seriously wanted to become an actress. While I was reading for Alice, I suddenly began to understand what great enjoyment one could get out of acting. Up to that point, I'd been most interested in becoming a ballerina, even though I knew how hard dancers worked and how comparatively low their pay was. But I'd thought I might combine dancing with doing choreography. My mother, who no longer works and is now a night student at C.C.N.Y., was then still working part time as a waitress, and I was worried about making money. There was something more than that in my new interest in acting, though. The producer—and, for this show, the director— Murray Holland had me read four times for the role of Alice. He wanted me to have it, but finally realized I just wasn't experienced enough to play it. So I wound up playing a page and the Mock Turtle. Robin Morgan got the part of Alice, and went on to play one of the leads in the "I Remember Mama" series. But I had learned about the joy that can come from creating a character as an actress and trying to say something of your own as well as what the author wants to say. Also, I enjoyed playing the Mock Turtle. It was fun. In "Anniversary Waltz," we played Cincinnati, Detroit, and Chicago. I wasn't too impressed with what I was doing. Also, I didn't like those cities. All I would do was sleep and wait to go onstage.

When I was fifteen, I got my first Broadway role. It was the part of the granddaughter of Sybil Thorndike in Graham Greene's "The Potting Shed." I read for the role several times before I got it. When I knew I had it, I decided definitely not only to be an actress but to be a *good* actress. I was still considered a child actress, but I was working in a play that had dimensions quite different from anything I'd ever been connected with before. The other members of the cast were all fine actors, and we had a fine director, Carmen Capalbo. I was terribly excited about having the part and about playing with people who were so professional and so experienced. I loved it all, but I also realized my own shortcomings. I didn't even know if I could be heard by the audience. I learned so much in that play. I played the part for the run of the play—a hundred and forty-three performances—and during that time I really felt that I *was* the granddaughter. From being in television plays, I'd had a tendency to be aware only of the character I myself was playing. In a play, you are forced to communicate with the others; they are right there. You are actually talking to the person you address. I also learned how to project my voice. And I absorbed an awful lot from the others about acting technique. I think my way of acting is a natural one—like the way children act, a kind of natural pretending. I lose all awareness of the audience when I'm in a play. And I never try to imitate any other actress. The worst thing in the world is imitation. When you see actors doing impersonations of other actors, you realize that nothing is as good as the original.

Six months after "The Potting Shed" closed, I got my first movie role—Shenandoe, in Walt Disney's "The Light in the Forest." I began to learn how to do things more slowly than I'd done them in television. I also began to want to do things for myself that would ordinarily be done for me, like makeup. In Hollywood, they have a whole department to make you up, but I make myself up. I got used to putting on my own makeup for the stage and for modelling, and to arranging my own hair, too, so I asked the Disney people if I could do my own makeup, and they let me. For a movie, I take an hour and a half to apply my makeup, compared to twenty minutes for the stage and fifteen for modelling. In putting on movie makeup, I found I could do certain things that would contribute to the role, like putting

dark circles under my eyes. My face is so young and smooth that sometimes it just looks flat under the movie lights and doesn't show enough
character, so I learned to do little things with an eyebrow pencil and to
arrange my hair in different ways to make the character I was playing
come more alive. If your makeup isn't on just right for movies in
Technicolor, you can come out looking blue, so it demands a lot of
attention. It's an additional burden doing your own, but I think it's
well worth it. It helps me. I look at myself in the mirror for so long
that I begin to get a lot of ideas about the girl I'm playing and what
she's like.

About the only preparation I need for a role is to believe in it. I
find that if I believe in it the audience will believe in it. It's easy for
me to believe in a part. I suppose it might be better if I questioned the
role more. I practically always believe I *am* the person I'm playing.
Even playing the writer in "Return to Peyton Place," though I didn't
understand what I was doing, I felt natural in the part. I didn't have
to be a writer to play one; I could pretend I was one. I didn't believe
in the whole movie. I didn't believe in the situations or in the people.
In the middle of making the picture, I got married, so I look back on
the picture through a sort of haze. My husband is Mike Selsman, a
Hollywood public-relations man. He is five years older than I am. We
were married on December 30, 1960. We live in an apartment in Los
Angeles but are planning to move into a house. Mike is Jewish, and I
had become interested in Judaism years before, but I did not become
Jewish when I was married. Mike is the best thing that has ever happened to me. While I was making "Return to Peyton Place," Mike and
I were trying to get married quietly, but something always happened to
create a lot of noise around us. The way I remember that movie is: The
day of my scene with Tuesday Weld was the day of my wedding. I
was married at nine-fifteen in the morning in Newhall, California,
and then I went back to the set and did the scene with Tuesday twenty-
two times.

When I made my next movie, "The Last Sunset," with Kirk Douglas, I learned the terrible hardships that must sometimes be endured in
acting. In "Return to Peyton Place," I had learned about pressure,
because of the way, while I was trying to get married, I was constantly
split between reality and playing the role. We made "The Last Sunset" on location in a small Mexican town. Together with the rest of

the company, I got the local intestinal infection, and we played in hundred-and-ten-degree heat and constantly had to protect ourselves against baby tornadoes. I'd be playing a scene with Kirk Douglas when someone would suddenly push me to the ground, and then I'd learn that a tornado had passed over us. The movie company didn't take caterers along, and in order to get something to eat at our hotel, I had to learn to speak Spanish. I learned enough in a month for basic conversation. My part in the movie was that of a sixteen-year-old girl travelling through the West with her widowed mother and a herd of cattle. I didn't believe in this role, really, so I underplayed it. It was the best I could do, and I think it added a touch of reality to the role. I had to do hard things, like riding among a thousand head of cattle, and leading mules from the back of a horse. What I remember most vividly about "The Last Sunset" is the smell of the cattle. But playing in that movie helped me adjust to my marriage. Because the movie, like most movies, was made in bits and pieces, I began to find it easier to go from being the movie character to being myself. After all, I can't go on being the character when I come home after a hard day's work. I don't think my husband would like it. It's hard, though, to let go of anybody I play. I really get into the part. I'm not much of a watcher of anyone or anything. I hate to watch. I have to participate.

I'm more in command of myself now as an actress than I was when I was fifteen. When you're more in command of yourself, it's easier to create a character. Just the same, acting is inborn. It's instinctive. It can't be learned. No girl can just decide to become an actress the way she might decide to learn to type. An actress is really an entertainer—someone who can make people forget their worries for a while. But I act for myself. Through acting I can experience many things that otherwise I'd be able to experience only through my imagination. And I enjoy it. I enjoy learning things. In "Blue Denim," I learned that even if something terrible happens to you it isn't the end of the world. You survive. And working with different kinds of actors is educational. The male lead in the movie version of "Blue Denim," Brandon de Wilde, was a star. He had been a child star, and he'd had more experience than I'd had as a child actor. But I'd had more experience as an adult actress, so I felt I could meet him on his own ground, in spite of his star billing. In mediocre roles, I can bring a lot of invention to the character. If a character is just true-blue and good—well, I know no one in the world is like her. I try to show that she's not *that* good, even if it's only by putting circles under my eyes. I try to make the best of every role, and if it's hopeless, at least I try to make a different approach to it. In the movie "Holiday for Lovers," I played Betsy Dean, the younger of two sisters, who was so adorable, so good, that no one could understand her. So I'd throw away a line here and emphasize a line there when it was least expected. Actually, there sometimes isn't much you *can* do, especially in a movie. In "Return to Peyton Place," I had a scene in a New York hotel room in which I was supposed to be looking out the window, dressed in a slip, when my editor called on the phone. I suggested that instead of looking out the window, I take a cigarette in a long holder and swagger hippily toward the mirror. The director let me do it my way, and afterward they were convinced I was another Sarah Bernhardt, which, of course, I'm not. I just wanted to do something to make that writer I was playing seem not so cardboard. Acting has many negative aspects. I don't like being stared at at parties. I'm petrified of crowds. But I find that when I'm living in New York, and I get on the subway, if I put on dark glasses and take off my makeup I'm not recognized. I'm free to do my marketing. Acting isn't easy. Being a good actress is as difficult as being a good waitress, but the pay is better.

ROD STEIGER

The actor reminds people of the poetry of being alive.

I was born on April 14, 1925, in Westhampton, Long Island. My full name is Rodney Stephen Steiger, and I'm an only child. As far as I know, I've never seen my father. My parents were divorced when I was about a year old. They had worked together as a song-and-dance team in roadhouse shows. I have no idea what my father looks like, and I wouldn't recognize him if we were in the same room. My background is French, Scotch, and German, and I was brought up as a Lutheran. After I was grown, my mother remarried. Whenever I was in a play or a movie, she and my stepfather would come to see me at least half a dozen times. I grew up in various New Jersey towns—Irvington, Bloomfield, and Newark, among others—where my mother did odd salesclerk jobs to support herself and me. In the evenings, at home, she would entertain me by singing and accompanying herself on an upright piano—songs like "Roses of Picardy" and "Shine On, Harvest Moon." My stage experience in grade school included playing the rôles of Santa Claus and George Washington in classroom productions. I attended Newark's West Side High

School for one year, and then, at the end of 1941, when I was sixteen, I managed to enlist in the United States Navy. I served as a torpedo-man first class on a destroyer in the South Pacific, and in four years I participated in most of the major operations of the Third and Fifth Fleets. I loved the Navy. I was stupid enough to think I was being heroic. I had always been a popular guy with other guys. I was a good softball player in school, and I was the best storyteller in my school gang, and the leader. In the Navy, and for some time afterward, I was in a very disconnected period of my life. I got along fine with the guys, and I didn't worry about anything, but my connection with the world in general was not clear. As long as I could eat and sleep, I didn't think about anything much.

I got out of the Navy with a medical discharge the day after Japan surrendered. I went back to Newark and got a job in the Office of Dependents and Beneficiaries, oiling the check-signing machines and carrying boxes of checks around the office. I got paid twenty-seven dollars and fifty cents a week, take-home pay. After eight months of it, I found it tedious. We had a social group in the office that put on plays. Somehow or other, I sort of got pushed into playing the lead in "Curse You, Jack Dalton." We had a lady director, who told me that I should take acting seriously, and that I had four years of school coming to me under the G.I. Bill of Rights. For the next two years, I studied acting at the New School for Social Research. Then I went to the American Theatre Wing, and later was invited by Daniel Mann to come to the Actors' Studio. I lived on the G.I. Bill—seventy-five dollars a month, plus thirty per cent for disability. In 1947, I got my Equity card and a bit part in "The Trial of Mary Dugan," by Bayard Veiller.

My first real Broadway part was in the Equity Library Theatre revival of Clifford Odets' "Night Music," in 1951, in which I played the part of a fifty-five-year-old detective. I played in over two hundred and fifty live television productions between 1948 and 1953. The climactic point was reached in 1953, when I played the title role in "Marty." Then I went on to playing in movies, including "On the Waterfront," "Teresa," "The Big Knife," "The Harder They Fall," "Cry Terror," "Al Capone," and "Oklahoma!" In 1959, I played the role of the Bandit in the Broadway production of "Rashomon," with Claire Bloom, Oscar Homolka, and Akim Tamiroff. If an actor stays on one level and doesn't challenge himself constantly, he will die. That's why I was eager to do "Rashomon." I like to be a gangster, then play in a Western, then go to Shakespeare. I look to the public to find out how I am in a part. I have great respect for the public. In playing for it, I've been lucky in my selection of parts.

There's no one way of acting. A lot of actors present rehearsals, not performances. They are imitating, not creating. So their acting looks like a bad suit of clothes. Then, a lot of young actors think they're doing Method acting when all they're doing is murdering it. Method is anything that gets you involved personally in the part, so that you can communicate in human terms with the audience. The essence of any art is communication. The need of the actor is to say hello to the audience. I get irritated with some audiences the same as I do with some people, but I haven't lost my faith in their intelligence. Otherwise, I'd be bouncing a ball off a brick wall. The best actors I know are those who try to talk to the audience, make the audience feel and discover feelings—actors who understand their audience and excite it. I find that actors of this kind will be the same offstage as on; they will attempt to do the same thing with anybody.

Actors may be the purest of all artists, because we attempt to reach other people, and to give something to other people through ourselves only. The painter can lean on his canvas, the musician on his violin or piano. The actor has no instrument but himself. The actor is different from other artists inasmuch as his material is intangible. I like to think of the art of acting as an immediate reward and an immediate death. The greater the moment on the stage, the longer the mourning. How the actor achieves his inspired moments is only about three-fourths known; one-fourth is completely unknown. That's one of the things that keep acting so exciting and so uncertain. I've become interested in the way a man can live so beautifully in the fantasy of his art even when he can hardly live at all in the reality of his own life. The actor's highest moments come when his instincts and his intellect meet and together communicate something to someone else. No word means exactly the same thing to every person; an actor must say what the word means to *him*. If he doesn't know, he must find out, or die in a puddle of narcissism. I believe in what I do. In the social structure that exists today, it's so difficult for a person to work at what he believes in and loves and still make a living. If you want to act for no other reason than to be among the happy few who are able to be beautiful in their art, then learn to be honest with yourself and act. For the first twenty-one years of my life, I never thought of actors as being anything but golden people from another world; I didn't know they were really alive. When I was told that people *study* acting, it came as a great surprise to me. I have my own credo for acting. I believe the actor can, through the medium of acting, exchange his discoveries about himself, and his beliefs, with his fellow-man. I believe that any actor who disregards this responsibility, that of truthfully *attempting* to communicate, and "acts for a living," ceases to exist as a creative artist. I know that all of us fail over and over again when we attempt to communicate, but we must always insist on attempting it. If an actor has one inspired moment in a performance, I'd say he's good. If he has two inspired moments, he's great. If he has none, he's going to bore himself to death. The actor really lives for those inspired moments.

I enjoy working in television and in movies as much as I do in the theatre. Each medium has its drawbacks. Live television is the most difficult to do, because you have all the pressure of an opening night in the theatre, and no chance to correct or change what you do. An actor can develop tremendously in live television if he has some background and training. I used to do two or three shows a month, with only five days of rehearsal for a half-hour drama. It was wonderful training and discipline. Unfortunately, live television plays have become a thing of the past. Big money got into television in 1954 and flattened it. But live television is still the closest thing to a repertory theatre, which is the best kind of training in the development of an actor. The essence of playing in a movie is remembering that it's always the picture that is important, not the words. In the theatre, as in live television, you must have the training to sustain your performance. In movies, you can get away with a lot, because you don't have to sustain your performance for more than two or three minutes at a time. If you're only a personality, without talent, and you're photographed right, you can look like an actor in the movies, but the beauty of humanness is always sacrificed for surface appearances. In New York, you're in competition with other actors. In Hollywood, there is always the possibility that you may have to compete with anybody who can be photographed effectively. Wherever an actor is and whatever he's doing, he must maintain his discipline. When your mind is alert, your performance is alert. When you're disturbed or tired, your performance suffers. That's why I'll never stay in a play for longer than six months. There's too much chance that you may start to play it automatically.

The more honest you are in preparing what you're going to present, the more honest you are in playing it. There's a great difference in me when I'm working. I keep more to myself. I get very intense. For the stage, I don't let anybody talk to me for an hour before curtain time. I happen to be what I regard as the nervous type. Sometimes I play tricks on myself to get myself up to the right level. I might come to the theatre early and walk figure eights by myself onstage. After the curtain comes down, it takes me an hour and a half or two hours to unwind. There's always tremendous tension. The trick is to keep interested. If something comes into your mind, your discipline says, "Out—maybe later." You have a responsibility to fulfill at the moment. Once, doing "Rashomon," I was sick with flu, with a temperature of a hundred and two, and I did the part on a pill, and everything was cockeyed. It took everything I had to stay concentrated, but I managed it. For a couple of weeks after that, concentration was easy for me. An actor can't base his art on making pretty poses. Although there's no one way of acting, you have to have talent and you have to be involved. If I had something more important, humanly, to do than acting, I would do it. On one occasion, during a fight with another actor in "Rashomon," I cut his hand and he started to bleed. I looked down and saw another human being's blood on my hands, and I thought, This is a childish way to make a living. I still think that occasionally, but, fortunately, the feeling doesn't last long.

I don't make decisions on how to play a part. I start off feeling wide open to the person I'm playing and to the people I'm playing with. I don't like to intellectualize about it. I try to feel my way. I try to react as well as act. When I was going to play Al Capone, I read his autobiography and the newspapers of his time. I asked myself, "What did this man want?" I decided he wanted to be respected. But there wasn't just one thing that made him be the way he was. He was, to me, a showman, an actor. He wanted recognition. Sometimes my imagination comes into play before I start getting the part, sometimes after. Usually, the way it works, I read the script and reread it, and somewhere inside me it clicks, and there's an "Oh, yes" in a secret place. Sometimes it takes a lot of labor. For one thing, I may not always want the world to see me in a certain guise. I play a game with myself if I get stuck. I walk through a five-and-ten-cent store and associate objects with the part. Say I see a toothbrush; I'll think, How does he brush his teeth? For "The Big Knife," I took a walk and saw a silver tiepin with a question mark on it. In my role as the producer, I wore it throughout the picture. Only *I* knew what it meant—the kid from the other side of the tracks who was always asking himself how to get where he wanted to be. One thing I did for Al Capone was to take out all small gestures. I played it pretty big—I wore my coat draped over my shoulders, and my hatbrim angled—because one thing I felt he wanted was to be big. I wanted the man's natural actions to declare themselves.

One of the troubles with acting is that the more successful you get, the more you have to keep an eye on the business aspects of it. I try not to forget the source of creativity. I'll listen to anybody who wants to talk to me, but after twenty minutes I know I'm going to say, "You're entitled to your opinions, but don't exhaust my life." When the curtain comes down on a play you're in, there's discipline, too, in knowing how to relax. I'm always aware of the danger of being an artist—of making art *all* of life instead of an important part of life. It's the responsibility of every artist to search for new stimuli. You need another person—at least one. I wrote a poem when I was seventeen or eighteen that expressed the idea that another person, in becoming part of oneself, makes one more completely oneself. I believe you've got to be human to act. I don't want my personal life ever to be one of agony, like John Barrymore's. I was married for the first time in 1952, to an actress named Sally Gracie. We were together two years and then we were divorced. I was married again in 1959, to the actress Claire Bloom. We have a daughter, Anna Justine, born in 1960.

All artists have the one quality that is priceless—eternal childhood. The day I walk onstage and don't feel nervous, I'll know my ego has got ahead of my heart. I don't ever want that to happen. I have always done some writing, and I still do as much as I can. I believe that anybody who has in him one sentence that can mean something to somebody else should write it down. I've written two movie scripts. One, "In Time of War," has been sold to Allied Artists. I wrote it with Stanley Shpetner, and will star in it. It tells the story of six soldiers who are destroyed by the Second World War. The other, "The Untold Story," is not commercial, but I hope to make it anyway. The main character in "The Untold Story" is an actor. It takes place in Sicily. The theme has to do with my belief that if a man creates more beauty than he destroys, you must classify him as good; if he destroys more beauty than he creates, you must classify him as evil.

CLAIRE BLOOM

*No matter how great your ambition or how powerful
your need to create something on the stage, there
must be a world outside.*

I was born on February 15, 1931, in London. I have a brother, John,
who is four years younger than I am, and who is one of the youngest
film editors in London. My father, Edward Bloom, was a managing
director of several businesses, including a machinery factory. He died
in 1953. My mother lives in London but spends some time with me and
my husband, Rod Steiger, and our daughter, Anna Justine, wherever we happen to be. My mother was one of nine children, and
all of them were interested one way or another in the theatre.
My maternal grandparents were lovers of music and of the opera,
and of the theatre in all its forms. One of my aunts, Mary Grew,
an actress who now is also a translator of plays from the French and
German, played leading parts in London in the nineteen-thirties, and
toured in "Typhoon" with Dennis Nielson-Terry. When I was about
ten, I came to the United States with my mother and brother to escape
the blitz. At first, we stayed with an uncle on my father's side in Fort
Lauderdale, Florida. After a year, we came to New York. The three of
us lived in one room rented in another family's apartment in Forest

Hills, on Long Island. I attended Public Schools 3 and 101 in Queens. When we had been in Forest Hills fifteen months, my mother became ill, and because we rather regretted the whole adventure, we decided to go back to England, which by then was no longer threatened by an invasion. So we started back on a Portuguese ship, and were stranded in Portugal for three glorious months, where we revelled in the warm climate and the salt air and the peaceful beaches and the neutral atmosphere of the country. We made it back to England when I was nearly twelve. For the next three months, my schooling was a haphazard affair —two makeshift schools outside London, away from the bombings— but in 1943 I enrolled, on a scholarship, in the Guildhall School of Music and Drama, in London. For the scholarship audition, I did a scene from "Saint Joan."

I was a very sophisticated, priggish twelve-year-old. In America, I had always been the youngest child in my class at school, and had fought against getting an American accent. I used to speak in a whisper. I was no beauty, and I was very shy. In Florida, I recognized anti-Semitism for the first time, and since I'm Jewish—though I have no religious affiliation—I suppose that increased my standoffishness. I suppose I set out to do what minorities generally do—prove themselves. The first movie I ever saw, as a child, was "Romeo and Juliet," with Norma Shearer and Leslie Howard. That same year, I saw Walt Disney's "Snow White and the Seven Dwarfs," which I adored. At seven, I saw my first play, which was a pantomime—"Where the Rainbow Ends," about St. George and the Dragon. I loved it. Also when I was seven, I saw "Robert's Wife," with Edith Evans. I remember how Mother and I sat on stools on the pavement, waiting to get into the gallery to see it. I remember the curtain call, and wondering why all the actors stood in line and bowed. I thought it was silly, and I still do. Another thing I saw as a child was a play with men dressed as women and playing women's parts. I hated that kind of thing then, and I still do. Before we went to America, my mother read "Hamlet" to me. I was so petrified of the Ghost that I couldn't sleep and had to keep the light on all night. By the time I was about eight, my favorite play, for some reason, was "Julius Caesar." I suppose I liked all that violence. My mother has always been an idealist about the theatre. In fact, both of us have always thought the theatre was just too marvellous. I do hate the expression "show business." And there's an expression used in Hollywood a lot that I loathe, too—"selling yourself." I was never very good at the whole thing of selling myself. I was quite nasty. In England, I always had bad press relations. I sometimes wonder how I was able to do anything. When I played Ophelia at Stratford on Avon, I used to hate audiences when I'd come out onstage. All the ladies in the audience would do this terrible "Sssss-hiss-hissing-isn't-she-sweet-sss?" I'd hate them for it. But I was seventeen—an age at which one would prefer to be a *femme fatale*. They don't do it any more, fortunately, and I'm glad I'm over that period. I do care about having an audience. I don't want to play to an empty house. But I'm onstage primarily to satisfy myself.

The Guildhall was a reputable school, and I took acting lessons there for about a year. It was all sort of ridiculous—elocution and all that. The Guildhall School offered to renew my scholarship, but I turned it down and went to the Central School of Speech Training instead, because they taught more subjects—costumes, stage design, history of the theatre, and so on. I went there for about a year and then got a job at the B.B.C., playing Ann of Oxford Street in a dramatization of Thomas De Quincey's "Confessions of an English Opium-Eater." The role was that of a sixteen-year-old tart, and I was paid fifteen pounds for one performance. My school was furious about my taking such a job and wouldn't let me come back, so I got a job, a walk-on, in John Webster's "The White Devil," produced by Michael Benthall and Robert Helpmann, in the West End—at the Duchess Theatre. It was my first London appearance. At this point, my father departed for South Africa to see his sister and to seek his fortune, and I had to earn some money. I signed a five-year contract with J. Arthur Rank, for twenty-five pounds a week, disliking everything it represented. I knew then I didn't like being tied down and having to do things I didn't want to do. As things turned out, the only part I ever played under the contract was that of an English aristocrat in "The Blind Goddess," and I was just terrible. I was most unhappy, and they finally released me. In 1948, Benthall and Helpmann held an audition for what they said was a small part at Stratford on Avon Memorial Theatre. It was really an audition for Ophelia, but I didn't know it at the time. If I had, I'd never have been able to do it. I was seventeen, and I got the part. I played it for eight months, alternating it with the roles of Perdita in "The Winter's Tale," and Blanch in "King John," in the second of which, again, I was terrible. I'm always at my very worst in a light part, with nothing to hold on to. But I liked playing Ophelia. I love those parts where you have to read between the lines to find the part. I tried to make Ophelia's mad scene a little less flowery. There are fifty possible interpretations of the role. Mine was based on my feeling that Ophelia was fifteen or sixteen and was very dependent, very high-strung, and that the things that happened to her were things she couldn't cope with—her father killed, her beloved deserting her on the brink of their becoming lovers. I felt that they were never actually lovers. You don't know, because it isn't said in the play; you have to interpret it. The songs Ophelia sings are not the songs of a girl who doesn't know anything about love. On the other hand, she was not a mature woman, or she wouldn't have reacted the way she did to what happened around her. A mature woman *doesn't* react that way. At Stratford on Avon, I was very, very happy. I was on my own, away from home, and I loved being in the country. It was a big, big thrill to know that I was an actress. I wanted to be asked back the next year, but I wasn't. I used to cry and howl at disappointments in those days. But I found that I had the strength, in the end, to take just about anything. And I learned the difference between a disappointment and being faced with real horror.

When I went back to London, in February, 1949, I played Daphne Randall in "The Damask Cheek," by John Van Druten and Lloyd Morris. It was the juvenile lead, a charming, light, easy part, and I was very bad in it. I had known exactly what Ophelia was about emotionally. When you have very little technique, a part that carries an emotion is much easier to play. When I played a light juvenile part, all my mannerisms came out with my nervous tension, and I had plenty of them. In 1949, I got the part of Alizon Eliot in Christopher Fry's "The Lady's Not for Burning," with John Gielgud. I played the part of a young girl and had a lovely little love scene. During rehearsals, I was nervous, and Gielgud didn't like me at all. I was so scared of him. He kept telling me that I ought to have voice lessons—that he couldn't hear me, even on the stage. I was rehearsing for this play while I was still appearing in "The Damask Cheek." Then I got the flu and was out for five days, and I was sure Gielgud would take the opportunity to give me the sack. When he didn't, I became more confident and better in the part. It was a beautiful, beautiful production—

like a medieval tapestry. I came to know and appreciate Gielgud, who is angelic—a quality that is unusual in any man, and especially in an actor. We played in London for eleven months. Then I played Isabelle in Anouilh's "Ring Round the Moon," with Paul Scofield, in a part that everybody wanted, since it was a dream part for any young girl— that of a poor young ballerina who comes to a château and is supposed to stir up jealousy between twin brothers, both played by Scofield. Three weeks after the opening, I had my nineteenth birthday, and I was the happiest I'd ever been.

The world of the British theatre is a narrow, narrow world, and my own world didn't broaden until I made "Limelight," with Charles Chaplin. In Hollywood, I met all kinds of people—writers, directors, producers, stars, everybody. In London, when you're nineteen you're treated as a child, no matter how successful you are. It was completely different in Hollywood. Arthur Laurents, the playwright, had seen me as the ballerina in "Ring Round the Moon," and told Mr. Chaplin about me. In April, 1950, I left London for a week to do a screen test for Chaplin in New York. It was a nerve-racking period. For the test, I was jittery and nervous. Back in London, I got a wire saying that the test was excellent, and that Chaplin would let me know his decision in three weeks. I waited four months. In August, I gave up the whole idea of doing the film, and then, one night, I got a telephone call from Mr. Chaplin at the theatre where I was still playing in "Ring Round the Moon." Chaplin's decision was yes. I became hysterical. I was frightened. To work with Chaplin, the greatest man in the movies! It meant that every ambition of mine as an actress would be fulfilled. I couldn't believe that such a thing could happen to me. Two weeks later, I left London for Hollywood and "Limelight." The whole experience, from beginning to end, was thrilling. It lived up to all my expectations, and more. Everything Chaplin could do for me he did. Just being with him and working with him was marvellous— just realizing that a man of his incredible qualities was interested. Instead of dying of fear, I was able to talk with him. He was interested in what I said. Socially, I had always had great difficulty, but in Hollywood I grew up much more.

My greatest stage success came in 1952, when I played Juliet with the Old Vic Company. The company was on its last legs, facing bankruptcy, when the decision was made to put on "Romeo and Juliet."

We got fantastic notices, and made a lot of money, and the Old Vic was all right again. Then I was asked to stay on and play Jessica in "The Merchant of Venice," which I did. But I was very bad in that part. After that, I made a movie, "The Man Between," with James Mason. After the movie, I fell into the trap of doing the same thing I had done five years before—in this case, playing Ophelia again. It was at the Edinburgh Festival, with the Old Vic. Whenever you do something again, you're open to having it said that you're not nearly as good as you were the first time. And usually the things that you did instinctively the first time, and that made you good in the first place, you don't repeat, because you say to yourself, "My God, I'm years older now." Then, after you get the bad notices, you go back to doing the things you did instinctively. During that 1953–54 season with the Old Vic, I also played Viola in "Twelfth Night," Virgilia in "Coriolanus," Helena in "All's Well That Ends Well," and Miranda in "The Tempest," and then I experienced a difficult period. I started doing a great many things wrong. I had had incredible luck in the beginning, and now I started making a mess of it. I let my career go to pot. I turned down many roles foolishly, including Anne Frank in "The Diary of Anne Frank" and Marcelline, the wife, in Ruth and Arthur Goetz's "The Immoralist." After doing two movies, playing Barsine in "Alexander the Great" and Lady Anne in "Richard III," with Laurence Olivier, I didn't have a thing to do for months. But in October, 1955, I did "Cyrano de Bergerac" on television in New York, with José Ferrer, and that got me back. After that, I played Cordelia in "King Lear," with John Gielgud, in London, and Cleopatra in "Caesar and Cleopatra," with Cedric Hardwicke, on American television. I came to Broadway with the Old Vic in "Richard II" and "Romeo and Juliet" in the fall of 1956. After that, I determined not to play any more Shakespeare if I could help it. I made a couple of movies—"Look Back in Anger," and "Duel of Angels," with Vivien Leigh. At first, I turned down the role they offered me in "Look Back in Anger." They wanted me to play the mistress, and I thought the part of the wife suited me better. Then I reconsidered, decided I was being foolish, and played the mistress. I wanted to play in "Rashomon," because I wanted to get away from the English classics. Now I'm sure I'd rather do modern things. I like doing live plays on television. It's very concentrated, and it's exciting; it's over quickly and you've done it.

287

The most exciting thing in acting is to have a night in the theatre when you're on wings. Craft and skill are satisfying, but having a night on wings is best of all. You must know exactly what you want to do in a part. What you do eventually may be different from what you think you want to do, however. I always start working on a part by reading a script through again and again, and thinking about it. Some people make voluminous notes, but I don't. People think I'm lazy, but I have a fearfully good memory, and I can remember what I want to do. The actors you work with are important in helping you accomplish what you try to do. If you get a good actor to work with, it helps you to be better. If you're with a monster, you have no one to strike sparks from. A director can help you or hinder you. If he's hindering you, it doesn't feel right. If it doesn't feel right, ten to one it isn't right. Your own instinct and taste have a lot to do with the way you feel, and you have to accept them as your guides. You live the role, but I don't believe the people who say they feel it all the time. Twenty-five per cent of you always watches you, no matter how involved you are with the part, and that twenty-five per cent criticizes you and helps keep you in control of yourself. Involvement with the part is essential, but self-pity must never be mistaken for involvement. "I'm so marvellous I'm crying" doesn't mean a thing. When I first read a part, I know as much as I'll ever know about it—what I feel and how I feel it. But you can always develop and enrich what you know. When I did the movie based on "The Brothers Karamazov," I reread the novel many times. I love the books of that period anyway. I discussed one point, very necessary to my characterization in the trial scene, with Richard Brooks, the director-writer, who subsequently rewrote my part in the scene. Playing on the stage takes more energy than any other form of acting. When you do a thing eight times a week, you're tired at the end of the week. It's an inhuman schedule to ask anybody to keep. Other people say they're at their best by the time the Saturday-night performance comes along. Like a greased wheel. But I'm better on Monday. I need my rest. It takes a lot of energy and strength to bring a little beauty into other people's lives.

When I was nine, I wanted desperately to become an actress, and at seventeen I was really playing Ophelia at Stratford, and I didn't care about anything, or take any interest in anything, outside of what I was doing in the theatre. I wasted a lot of years just being ambitious and priggish. I was so ambitious that if I hadn't been successful, it would have eaten me up. When you have that kind of ambition, nothing can stop you. I used to look forward to matinée days, when I could be in the theatre *all day long*. It had such magic for me. Now I find that as I've got older I've really got younger. As a very small child, I was always standoffish. It was in my makeup. I loved poetry, especially Robert Browning's soliloquies. I didn't want to please the public. What I had was the desire to create something beautiful, and it was all-consuming. As all artists do, I wanted to express something inside myself that nobody else had. I had tremendous drive, and at the same time I was appallingly shy. Acting gave me a satisfaction that was to be found nowhere else in my life. The rewards of acting are immediate. An actor's time is now. The transitoriness of acting is what makes people treat it as a second-rate art, as a popular art. But I think it's a true art. It's very hard to act truthfully, but if you have the feeling that you are another person, and you're playing that person, and yet you're in complete control, you're able to express something that is in you and only in you. Yet through being someone else you express the passions of someone else, and you take the audience with you into another world. "Look," you say. "This is what she is." When it happens, you're absolutely on wings. You're carried. You're doing something that is coming out of you and yet you have control over it. You're in the part, and the part is with you. What the author is saying, you're saying aloud for the first time. Sometimes it's there and sometimes it isn't, and when it is, it's marvellous. When it isn't, you have to work, to use what is laughingly called technique. When it is there, it's almost like being possessed. Yet if it worked that way all the time, you'd be a monster. If it happens too often, it somehow seems to go sour. You somehow become a complete narcissist. Sybil Thorndike and Peggy Ashcroft grow more beautiful as they grow older, but Sarah Bernhardt was a complete narcissist, and how it showed on her face! Nobody can disguise it. All that self, self, self! Duse, on the other hand, was an actress who became beautiful through suffering and living. I've seen pictures of her, and I've never seen another face so beautiful in all my life. She had a spiritual quality. She was a woman who lived through her spirit as well as through her body and through her talent. And I've learned that that's what is important—instead of taking from life because "I am I," to take because "I am everybody." It's the safeguard against becoming a monster. I'm glad I found it out in time.

DANA ANDREWS

I believe that all people are half actors.

I was born on January 1, 1909, in the village of Don't, which is now part of the town of Collins, Mississippi. I was the third of thirteen children, five of whom are dead. My father was a Baptist minister, and I was named after a Dr. Dana, who taught at the seminary my father went to, in Louisville, Kentucky. My first name is Carver, after another of the teachers, but I dropped it in college. When I was four, my father moved the family to Waelder, in southwest Texas, and he established quite a reputation for himself as an evangelist in the state. I recently went back to Collins, for the first time since 1913, and visited relatives, mostly on my mother's side, and mostly named Speed. There are hundreds of Speeds in the area—a prolific family, consisting largely of good, solid country folk. Our own family moved to San Antonio when I was five, and about a year later we moved to Rockdale, also in Texas. Then, while I was still in grammar school, we moved to Uvalde, Texas. John Nance Garner, who later became Vice-President, lived there, and a flock of pigeons I kept used to like to settle in his attic; I was always having to go over there and get them back. Uvalde left the strongest imprint on me of all the places we lived in as I was growing up. It was in a wild, colorful part of the state. A friend of my father's joined him in trying to clean up the town, and was shot to death in the street by a crony of the sheriff's, because the sheriff was in charge of an operation to sell bootleg tequila brought in from Mexico. When I was fifteen, we moved to Huntsville, Texas, because it had a state teachers' college, the Sam Houston, where my father felt my six brothers and I could get an education. Four of my brothers attended that college, and so did I. Today my eldest brother, Wilton, is a geologist with an oil company, and, of my other brothers, Harlan is principal of the Bellaire High School in Houston, Texas; Ralph is an oil-company engineer; David is an executive of a warehouse company in Dallas; John is a sales manager in Dallas; and the youngest, William, is an actor—the only other actor in the family—under the name of Steve Forrest. My sister, Mary, teaches school in Houston. I graduated from the Huntsville High School, and immediately enrolled in the summer session of the Sam Houston. I stayed at the college for three years, studying business administration. In my first year, I began working on the side at a local movie house, first taking tickets, then taking tickets and ushering, which included maintaining order among the youngsters on Saturday afternoons. There were two theatres in town, owned by the same man, and right next door to each other. When I was in my third year of college, I became manager of both. I used to watch those damn movies over and over, and after a while I began to take some notice of the way the actors went about their work. It didn't look so difficult to me. I tremendously admired Gary Cooper in "The Legion of the Condemned," and Douglas Fairbanks, Sr., in "The Thief of Bagdad." Also H. B. Warner and Ernest Torrence and Joseph Schildkraut in "King of Kings," and Richard Arlen in "Wings." I felt I might even be able to do better than Richard Arlen. This was before we had any talkies, but some movie companies were experimenting with adding music and sound effects on synchronized phonograph records, which they sent around with the films. I decided to get together a collection of records and use them to provide scores of my own. I even recorded some of my own sound effects. All in all, the results were pretty corny, but any sort of sound was quite impressive in those days. For "King of Kings" we used a lot of sacred-music records. Someone had given me a European record called "In the Garden," and when I played it, it sounded sweet and sort of sad, so in "King of Kings" I used it for the scene in the Garden of Gethsemane. For "The Thief of Bagdad," I used "In a Persian Market," and New York scenes always called for "Metropolis," "Rhapsody in Blue," and "Manhattan Serenade." We always showed a Western movie on Saturday, since that was the day all the farmers came to town, and they didn't care much for a movie with a complicated plot or one about city folks—any more than they do now. It's always been a source of deep concern to me that most people don't like to learn anything new or different. In addition to the feature film, we ran a newsreel and also a two-reel comedy, generally featuring Laurel and Hardy, Charley Chase, or Lloyd Hamilton.

One night, after I'd gone to bed, I began to think about what I wanted to do with the rest of my life. I didn't *like* business. I didn't like keeping accounts, which was what I was learning to do in college. I didn't want to be ordinary. In high school, I had played in some Shakespeare and in two modern plays, "The Microbe of Love" and "Nothing But the Truth." In college, I played in several versions of what the college called "The Sam Houston Drama," and also in "Lady Windermere's Fan," "The Rivals," and "Honor Bright." The director, Dr. Charles O. Stewart, encouraged me to make the theatre my goal. That night in bed, I realized that the only thing I had ever done that made me feel good was acting in those plays. The other students had told me how good I was, and some of them had really appeared to mean it. I had watched all those pictures, and being in movies seemed to be as far away from business as I could get, so now I began to think seriously about movie acting. I wanted approbation, and I wanted to earn it. The idea of making a lot of money was attractive, too. The country was in a depression, and I was in debt. I quit college and gave up my theatre job, which didn't pay much. I was offered a job as an accountant in Houston, and worked there for a short while, and then I became accountant for a large stationery store in Austin. At that point, I decided definitely to try to be an actor. I threw a large party for my friends in Austin, which left me penniless, and then I packed my bags and hitchhiked west to Van Nuys, a suburb of Los Angeles, where my father was then pastor of the Baptist Church. I lived with my family again for three months. At first, I made the rounds of the studios, but I didn't get anywhere, and I ended up driving the Van Nuys High School bus, for ten dollars a week. I was twenty-one years old. Then I went to work in a filling station as an attendant. Making the rounds of all the movie studios in my free time, I came to realize that I was only a punk kid with a little amateur experience, like thousands of other idiots who just walked in and asked for a job, and that I had to get some experience. So I enrolled in the Van Nuys Night School Drama Class, which some of the socially prominent townspeople used as a local little theatre, and where a great time was had by all. I was the only one in the group burning with serious ambition. I joined just as one of the leading men in Bayard Veiller's "The Thirteenth Chair" dropped out. He was the principal of the local high school and couldn't spare the time for rehearsals, and I was offered his part, and took it, even though it was the part of a sixty-year-old man with two daughters and a son, all three of whom in actuality were old enough to play *my* parents. One of the actresses in the play was a wonderfully vivacious local girl named Janet Murray, who had just got her M.A. in journalism at Northwestern University. A year later, on December 31, 1932, I married her. She was an inspiration to me in the days that followed; unlike everybody in my family, who re- fused to recognize acting as a legitimate occupation, she consistently encouraged me. She liked my baritone voice and urged me to become a singing actor, like Lawrence Tibbett. I began to study singing seriously, taking lessons with a local teacher who had sung in the original company of "The Desert Song." Janet and I were very happy. In 1933, our son, David, was born, and when he was two, Janet contracted pneumonia and died. After that, I worked on my music like a maniac, ran two miles every day to build up my dia- phragm, and learned operatic roles in French, German, and Italian. All this time, I still had my job at the filling station. In 1936, I auditioned for an agent named John Columbo—brother of the singer Russ Columbo—and he told me I had a fair voice but couldn't make any money as a singer. Second-rate actors, he said, could earn more than first-rate singers. He suggested that I get some acting training, and I went to the Pasadena Playhouse, and there, after years of blundering around, I began to learn to be an actor.

I started out in small parts in "Julius Caesar" and "Antony and

Cleopatra" during the last year of a three-year festival of all Shakespeare's plays at Pasadena, and then played the intellectual soldier —one of three men doomed to die—in Sidney Howard's "Paths of Glory." It was a highly dramatic part, which gave me plenty of opportunity to shine. It was also a demanding role, and I worked on it with a private coach to get every shading just right. The reviews of that show are still among my most treasured ones. Then, in my next part, that of a simple juvenile in a simple play called "Money," by Aurania Rouverol, I learned a very important lesson when I fell flat on my face. The part wasn't good, but I was much worse than the part. I didn't have the remotest idea how to play a straight part—one that wasn't full of emotional crises. The easy parts, the ones that help you win awards, are those of alcoholics, dope fiends, brutes, and mentally deranged people, because they give you so much to do. However, I slowly began to develop a little technique. Those were hectic days of struggle, filled with intense excitement. There was tremendous satisfaction in working and hoping, in yearning for a part, then getting it and playing it. Playing in movies, later on, never gave me that kind of pleasure.

In 1938, while I was appearing at Pasadena in a small part in Zoë Akins' play "O Evening Star," an agent left a note asking me to come and see him. I did. He arranged a screen test for me on the Samuel Goldwyn lot. Mr. Goldwyn was out of town at the time, but then he returned and saw the test, and, as they say, I was in pictures. After I signed a contract with Goldwyn, nothing really happened for nine months, except that I was financially able to marry Mary Todd, a young lady I had been courting for two years. She had appeared with me in the play in which I fell flat on my face. Now we have three children—Katharine, Stephen, and Susan—and I am building a new house in Rolling Hills, near Palos Verdes Estates. My wife is a very talented actress, but these days she acts—at places like the Pasadena Playhouse— only to have something to do when I'm away. After I'd been with Goldwyn a year, at a salary of a hundred and fifty dollars a week, he sold half of my contract to Twentieth Century-Fox, and I worked for both alternately for the next eleven years. My first movie part, with three lines, was in "The Westerner," starring Gary Cooper. In the next twenty years, I played leading roles in over fifty movies, including "The Ox-Bow Incident," "Laura," "A Walk in the Sun," "Boomerang," "The Best Years of Our Lives," "My Foolish Heart," and a whole string of pictures with titles like "Swamp Water," "Three Hours to Kill," "The Fearmakers," "Enchanted Island," and "Madison Avenue." I don't like to be ordinary. When I was told that my voice would never be among the best, I stopped trying to sing. I once read a Gouverneur Morris short story, "Simon L'Ouvrier," about an actor who is so good that no one can tell he is acting. Once, he spends two years learning Buddhism in order to go to the forbidden city of Lhasa. On his way there, he is crucified and almost dies. Determined to learn his part, he studies for three more years and successfully reaches Lhasa, because no one can detect the difference between the actor and the part. I used to dream of being as good an actor as that.

Every person, whether he's an actor or not, has his own way of communicating with other people. If your personality is unusual enough, you can become a star in the movies. You can't get rid of your own personality. It's going to come through, no matter what you're doing. In certain ways, it's harder to act in the movies than on the stage. The camera is so close. It sees so much and shows so much. It picks up every little thing you do with your eyes and mouth. On the stage, you don't have to be so conscious of every little gesture. On the stage, you can lose yourself in the role more and let what happens just happen. You get a much better opportunity on the stage to develop the character you're playing. Working in the continuity of a play—rather than in snatches, out of continuity, in a movie—gives you a better view of the work as a whole, and a deeper understanding of it. Having an audience right there while you're acting is immensely satisfying. The handicaps you have in stage acting that you don't have in movies are minimal—projecting to the rear of the theatre, remembering lines, playing so that everything is visible and audible to the audience. I replaced Henry Fonda in "Two for the Seesaw" on Broadway for a year, and it was an experience I shall never forget. I didn't miss a single performance—not even one time when I had a temperature of a hundred and three. You can grow on the stage. After a year of playing the lead, I had just begun to understand it, to understand what the author meant me to be. When I started out in the play, I was overemotional. Because I was playing the part of a self-pitying man, I had a tendency to whine. My wife pointed that out to me, and I found that if a man feels sorry for himself, he doesn't have to whine to show it. I stopped whining at once. It's not difficult for me to hide emotion, since I've always hidden it in my personal life. What is difficult is to convey feelings in a quiet and reserved way. Coming to Broadway after twenty years in Hollywood appealed to me. When I came to Broadway, I was looking for a kind of revitalization. I found it. Playing on the stage demands total concentration, and absolute devotion to the part you're playing. I'm unaware of the audience except when it isn't with me. When the throat-clearing, coughing, and squirming start, I know I have to put in a little more effort. I need to get the people back with me. Then I can forget them. In movies, I had been a leading man, and in movies a leading man is usually a man who can do no wrong. I was expected to play pleasantly, to play pleasingly, to play a good man who is always victorious over evil. I've always thought of it as being a boom-boom-boom actor. I'd outshout, outfight, outcharm, out-everything everybody while acting. Meanwhile, the real acting parts were going to the character actors. After all those years in movies, my senses as an actor were dulled. On the stage, it was up to me to hold the interest of the people out there in the audience. I wasn't expected to boom-boom-boom away. I was expected to *act*. That one thing made all the difference. Everything was before me, and the possibilities were endless.

MAUREEN STAPLETON

*Actors are a much hardier breed of people than any
other people. We have to be as clever as rats to survive.*

I was born on June 21, 1925, in Troy, New York. I have one brother,
John, who is three years younger than I am. My parents, both of
whom are Irish-Americans and strict Roman Catholics, were separated
when I was five, and after that my brother and I lived with my mother,
together with my maternal grandmother and three aunts and two
uncles. My mother worked as a clerk in the New York State Department of Unemployment Insurance, in Albany—a twenty-minute drive
from Troy. She still works there, and now my brother does, too. I
made my decision to act when I was five years old, when I saw my
first Jean Harlow movie. I went to movies all the time. Jean Harlow
was so beautiful, and everybody loved her. What the hell, what could
be better? I didn't dare tell anybody about my decision. I minded my
own business. In the parochial school I went to, I would go through
all the expected motions. I happened to be fatter than any other kid
on our block. At the age of twelve, I weighed a hundred and forty

pounds; at thirteen, a hundred and sixty pounds; at fourteen, a hundred and eighty pounds. I had a nice fat, unhappy teenhood. When I was twelve, I informed my mother for the first time that I was going to become an actress. She said, "Sure. Sure." She didn't know that I wasn't asking her, I was *telling* her. I wanted to become an actress because that was the way to be beautiful and rich and to have all the fellows love you. The desire was so strong that it sustained me. I always took it for granted that if you want to be anything badly enough, you just are—that it's simply a matter of enduring. There's a certain time in your life when you have one friend who sheds some light on life for you. For me, that one friend was my Uncle Vincent. When I told him that I wanted to become an actress, he encouraged me. I could tell him anything in the world. I wasn't afraid to say anything to him. Nothing had to be hidden. When I was around him, I always forgot, for some reason, to feel that I was the kid who was fat. He always told the truth, no matter how shattering it was. He was the kind of person who gets very excited about a book. He joined the Navy when he was fifteen, and he died at the age of thirty-one. I was in two plays in high school—"Anne of Green Gables" and "Murder on a Ferris Wheel." In both plays, I took the part of an old lady who was out of breath—or maybe I was out of breath. I saw my first real play when I was fourteen—a stock-company production in Albany of "A Bill of Divorcement." I went crazy. They weren't puppets. They weren't on the screen. They were real people, being kind to each other, alive. I loved it.

After graduating from high school, in 1942, I worked for the Unemployment Insurance Department in Albany as a clerk, for eighteen seventy-five a week. Then I switched to a better-paying clerical job, at twenty-eight dollars a week, at the Watervliet Arsenal, near Troy. By September, 1943, I had saved up a hundred dollars, and I came to New York, determined to become an actress. After two weeks in New York, my hundred dollars was gone, so I got a job, operating a billing machine for the Hotel New Yorker. I knew of a drama teacher in New York—Frances Robinson-Duff—because I had seen her name in a theatre magazine, so I took lessons from Frances Robinson-Duff for a few months and spent five hundred dollars learning the Delsarte system, where everything is supposed to be divided into mental, emotional, and physical categories, with charts under each heading. There were an awful lot of charts. But I was young, and everything was lovely. Then a friend of one of my aunts told me about the drama courses at the New School for Social Research, where Herbert Berghof was teaching night classes, so I registered there. It turned out to be heaven. I roomed with two other girls taking Herbert's course. In the summer of 1945, I followed Herbert and twenty other actors and actresses into the Greenbush Summer Theatre, in Blauvelt, New York. What unbelievable chaos! Twenty-two democratic voices with equal voting power and equal say about doing a different play every week for eight weeks! We acted everything and did everything. Anybody who took time to wash her hair was ostracized. We didn't even have time to eat. Not that we had much to eat. After a couple of weeks, Herbert said to me, "Your work is improving. What are you doing, Maureen?" I said, "I'm washing dishes, scrubbing floors, cleaning toilets." But the question scared me. I asked myself, What *am* I doing? The improvement couldn't be from cleaning toilets. I decided it was because I didn't have time to think. I was beginning to feel my way through a role. I was just *doing* it.

I had the usual couple of years of living off odd jobs, taking lessons, talking acting all the time, day and night, with other actors, making the rounds, and smiling, smiling, smiling. Then, in the fall of 1946, I called up Guthrie McClintic's office to find out who was going to play the lead, Pegeen Mike, in "The Playboy of the Western World." By chance, McClintic answered the telephone himself. I asked my question politely, and he gave me a rude answer, saying that it was none of my damn business. This set me off. Among other things, I told him that I didn't give a damn who was playing it. That did the trick. He turned polite. He asked me to come see him at three the next afternoon. I wound up with the part of one of the village girls and was also made understudy to the lead. It was my first Broadway play. My grandmother, mother, brother, and three aunts came to the opening. For eight performances, in the last week of the play's run, I played the lead. At the beginning of my first performance, I was so terrified I couldn't look up, and when I stood up I had to hold on to a piece of furniture to keep my legs from buckling. It was my happiest terror.

In 1947, I played Katharine Cornell's maid in the touring company of "The Barretts of Wimpole Street," directed by Guthrie McClintic.

It was the best time of my life, going across the country, seeing all the big cities, and working with Miss Cornell and Mr. McClintic. I felt intoxicated all the time just being with the company. The actor who played the father made it easy for all the rest of us, including Miss Cornell, to believe in him. He was Wilfrid Lawson, one of the greatest actors in the world, and all he had to do was just show up and everybody else could get going. Miss Cornell and Mr. McClintic did things in a way that was always considerate, always kind, always thoughtful. Sort of old-fashioned ways that you don't see too much of around these days. I was impressed by them then, and I've found out since—after considerable comparison shopping —that I was right. They treated actors like people. Later on that same year, I played with Miss Cornell again, this time as one of the handmaidens, Iras, in "Antony and Cleopatra." One day, I overslept before a performance, was awakened at home by the stage manager, rushed to a taxi, got dressed as we drove, and arrived at the theatre just as another actress was stepping into my dress and the others were taking their places. As I joined them, Miss Cornell said to me, "I was so worried about you, because I knew how awful you'd feel when you woke up." There may not be a lady like her in the whole theatre.

Around then, I enrolled in the Actors' Studio for study in Robert Lewis's class, with Marlon Brando, Montgomery Clift, David Wayne, Tom Ewell, Thelma Schnee, Karl Malden, Eli Wallach, and Kevin McCarthy. We were one of the first classes in the Studio's existence. In the spring of 1949, I played a small part in Sidney Kingsley's "Detective Story," and that July I was married, at the Municipal Building, to Max Allentuck, the general manager for Kermit Bloomgarden. We had a festive dinner at the Longchamps Restaurant near City Hall, and I just made it to the theatre for the curtain. In 1951, I played the leading role, Serafina delle Rose, in Tennessee Williams' "The Rose Tattoo." I took on the part three months after having my first child, Daniel Vincent. In 1953, I replaced Beatrice Straight in the role of Elizabeth Proctor for the last seven weeks of Arthur Miller's "The Crucible." The following year, in my fifth month of pregnancy with my second child, Cathy, I played Masha in the Phoenix Theatre production of "The Sea Gull." The year after that, I played one Tennessee Williams role, Flora Meighan in "Twenty-seven Wagons Full of Cotton," and in 1957 another, Lady Torrance in "Orpheus Descending." I've played in three movies, "Lonely-hearts," "The Fugitive Kind," and "A View from the Bridge," and I didn't like the experience. I'm now divorced, and I live with my children in an old brownstone, half of which I own, on West Seventieth Street. When I'm working, I go home directly from the play, have a drink and a late supper, and watch the Late and Late Late Shows on television. I try to get eight hours' sleep, because it's necessary for your nerves. Your damn nerves have to be in good condition for this work. I get up at noon. There's always something doing with the kids in the afternoon—taking them to the doctor or talking to their teachers. Whenever I can, I love to play poker. It's very relaxing, like making hooked rugs. I read poetry and other things, but I don't ever broaden. I've been reading the same things over and over since my English Lit. course in high school.

When you have an especially demanding part, emotionally—whatever the hell that means—your own day-to-day living becomes less well integrated. When I work, I get dirty and sloppy offstage. I don't take as much care of myself personally. It could be plain, old-fashioned laziness, but I think it's almost a moral tendency. I feel I don't have to bother as much about matters I don't really care about. Everything is geared to the moment of the eight-forty curtain. In the theatre, I never have to ask myself, Am I *living* the role? There's usually a certain emotional holdover from the stage into your own life, and it can become a physical thing, but you don't have to think about it. The main thing is, you're disciplined, and at eight-forty you're oriented to being somebody else. It's different in making a movie. I found it somewhat demoralizing, not being able to act the way I felt I must act. There are so many reasons for that. For one thing, you sit around for hours, and then, suddenly, you're told you're on. I was never ready. I was too accustomed to the discipline of going on at eight-forty. In the theatre, when you don't have to do one of those guts-away parts, it makes it much easier on your private, away-from-the-stage life. In S. N. Behrman's "The Cold Wind and the Warm," my role, Ida, was easier than the others I've played, because Ida wasn't in turmoil. Her feelings weren't interlocked with the feelings of the other characters. I didn't have to break my neck. In the Tennessee Williams roles I've played, the emotional problems were so great I was living under terrible tension and pressure. That's when you have to call on all that interior jazz. After six months of that kind of thing, you tend to get a little nutty. I got a little nutty in "The Rose Tattoo." I felt anxious *all* the time. After all, just *one* of the things I had to do in that play was the scene with the priest, where I clawed at him, tore at his clothes, screamed, and carried on. Something like that in one *day* of anyone's life is quite enough to happen. You do that, among other things, every night, over and over again, it's bound to take a hell of a lot out of you. It forces you to keep yourself on an emotional track full time.

The prospect of becoming stale in a part is quite frightening. You mustn't let yourself become like a record. Yet, at the same time, you've got to be sure that that other person you become is going to be finished at the end of the play. Everybody, after all, wants to be something and somebody. In acting, it's yourself becoming something else and somebody else. It's making believe all your life, and who says there's anything wrong with *that?* If you're lucky, you *become* the person you're playing. Every performance, you do new things, just as you do all the time in real life, where you never do anything exactly the same way twice. Someone like Marlon Brando is so complete a talent he can draw on things inside himself for what he needs. He has more equipment for doing that than most people. If it isn't there, the director has to find something to help you put it there. The assumption is that emotionally people are all alike, so that nothing you do is really alien to anybody else.

I like to read a play not knowing what part I'm up for. When I do know, I can't focus on my own part at all. There's something that almost blinds me. The part is like a blank space. Fear sets in immediately, and I then read the play over several times. In certain plays, when you start work you can make a strong emotional identification right away, or get some sort of over-all picture of the characterization. Then it's like a construction job. I often draw on other people or on experiences that illuminate some part of the character. Then I add things as I go along. I once worked with a woman who turned to me suddenly, in the middle of a rehearsal, and cried, "Now we're getting the pants on!" It *is* like getting dressed. After a while, as you go along, you find that all things dovetail. The director is a guide. If I don't trust a director, I pretend to listen to him but I muddle through by myself. Once you set the things you do and make them mean certain things, you then respond to the stimuli you yourself have set up. Then you *feel*. You might set it up as a combination of mind and feeling, but the feeling usually takes over. Crying is easy. I watch "Lassie" on television and I cry. I watch an old man carrying an icebox up two flights of stairs and I cry. Bobby Lewis says, "If crying were acting, my Aunt Rifke would be Duse." All you have to do to cry is set up the stimulus that will trigger the mechanism, and off you go. Laughing is much more difficult. On the whole, it's very, very hard to do a true laugh. It's that way in life, too. You hear a lot of laughter but very little real laughter. The usual laugh is more like a nervous mannerism. A real laugh is so real you have no control over it. It's quite beautiful.

I believe in the toughness of actors. I have a feeling of genuine pride in actors as my people. We're called egomaniacs; we're thought of as children. The people out in front are regarded as heads of state, but actors are supposed to be irresponsible, stupid, unaware, and a kind of joke. They're accused of having big egos. Well, the actor's ego is no different in size because he's an *actor*. Actors don't need half as much of that flattery malarkey as some people think they need, and they need much less than a lot of other artists. A writer or a painter or a musician can go off into a corner and lick his wounds, but an actor stands out in front of the crowd and takes it. Actors are up for exposure night after night. Yet actors are expendable, like cattle, because so few jobs are available. Actors spend years and years being treated like dirt. They're constantly in a state of debasement, making the rounds of casting directors and having to look happy and great. I made the rounds for years, but I wasn't good at it. But then *nobody* is. You need a very strong stomach. You need a sense of the business as a whole, so that you don't get lacerated every time somebody tells you you're lousy. You need strength, and no matter how strong you get, you always need to get stronger. There's never a guarantee you'll go on working. A show will always close, sooner or later. If I'm not working, I just consider myself somebody who is waiting to go on working. It's the only thing you can do. Your aspiration to act is so great, so deep, so complete, that you give yourself not ten years, not twenty, but your whole lifetime to realize it.

RICHARD WIDMARK

*Your personality, for the most part, is what the movie
medium draws out and uses, but somebody who really
knows his craft can act, as well as appear, in movies.*

I was born on December 26, 1914, in Sunrise, Minnesota. My father
had a general store there, then later became a travelling salesman. I'm
a mixture of Swedish, Scottish, English, and Irish strains. My parents
were divorced in 1941. I had one brother, Donald, four years younger
than I was, who was a pilot in the Second World War and who died
right after the war. Our family moved around a lot when I was a child.
We lived in Sioux Falls, South Dakota; Henry, Illinois; Chillicothe,
Missouri; and Princeton, Illinois. Princeton was where I graduated
from high school and where I discovered that I was a pretty good public speaker. My grandmother started taking me to movies when I was
three, and I was movie-crazy from then on. As a boy, I never admitted
I liked acting, because it was considered sissy among my friends.
One of my earliest favorites was Harold Lloyd in "Safety Last."
My grandmother was nutty about Tom Mix, who played cowboys,
and Thomas Meighan, a matinée idol of the time, and I began to
worship them, too. I used to go to movies about three times a week.
Later on, I worked as doorman at the movie theatre in Princeton and

saw scads of pictures. After high school, I went to Lake Forest College, in Lake Forest, Illinois, on a scholarship. I took a pre-law course, and was active in the Drama Department. I appeared in about thirty plays, all of them modern. It was after playing the lead in Elmer Rice's "Counsellor-at-Law," in my sophomore year, that I began to think I'd have a go at acting for a living. I met my wife, Jean, at college, but we didn't get married until 1942. After graduating, in 1936, I took a job there as an instructor in the Drama Department, at a hundred and fifty dollars a month; I directed plays and acted in them for two years.

In 1938, I came to New York, where Jean was by then attending the American Academy of Dramatic Arts. A man I had gone to school with was producing radio soap operas, and he gave me a part playing a gas-station attendant in "Aunt Jenny's Real Life Stories." It was the heyday of radio, and I went on to play in a lot of fifteen-minute soap operas—"Big Sister," "Joyce Jordan, M.D.," "Front Page Farrell." Also, I got to belong to an inner circle of actors in New York. Getting launched was easy for me. Too easy, perhaps. That's probably why I never got that dedicated feeling. I never considered myself a dedicated artist, and don't now. I've never had the feeling I'd die if I didn't get a certain part. Just the same, I love to work, and I work hard. Acting has always been my work, and it's part of my life. When I was working in radio, Jean and I were married, and we had a Bronxville house with a swimming pool. I was making fifteen or twenty thousand a year, and I'm probably the only actor who ever gave *up* a swimming pool to go out to Hollywood. Radio acting is not acting, and it can be dangerous to an actor. I'd be playing an upset young husband, say, in something like "Life Can Be Beautiful," on N.B.C., and wind up in a gale of emotions at 11:58, then rush downstairs by elevator and taxi over to C.B.S., where something like "Big Sister" went on at 12:15, and at 12:17 I'd come on playing an upset young lover in another gale of emotion. There'd be no preparation, no thought—only four minutes in the morning when you'd read through your script. You'd do a lot of radio shows and develop a super-facility at reading lines. Fortunately, I was aware of this; I knew enough about acting, about taste, about perform-ance, and I knew the kind of actor I wanted to be. In my adult years, the man I have admired most in acting is Spencer Tracy. What an actor should be is exemplified, for me, by him. I like the reality of his acting. It's so honest and seems so effortless, even though what Tracy does is the result of damn hard work and extreme concentration. Actually, the ultimate in any art is never to show the wheels grinding. The essence of bad acting, for example, is shouting. Tracy never shouts. He's the greatest movie actor there ever was. If he had wanted to go the classic route, he could have been as great in that field as Laurence Olivier. I've learned more about acting from watching Tracy than in any other way. He has great truth in everything he does. You can arrive at truth in acting only through concentration, which in the movies is most difficult to achieve. I've always wanted to be as good as Tracy is, and I'm still trying.

I suppose I wanted to act in order to have a place in the sun. I'd always lived in small towns, and acting meant having some kind of identity. I started working on the Broadway stage in 1943. Because of one of the largest eardrum perforations on record, I was turned down three times for the Army. I'd never had any formal training for the stage. I'd never played any Shakespeare, and I still haven't. Also, I was never a joiner. I don't like actor groups, which I think can be terribly destructive, especially to a kid. In my first role, at a hundred and fifty dollars a week, I played an Army lieutenant in F. Hugh Herbert's "Kiss and Tell," which was produced and directed by George Abbott. After that, I played in "Get Away Old Man," "Kiss Them for Me," and "Dunnigan's Daughter," and in the Chicago company of "Dream Girl." No matter what I did on the stage, I always tried to keep the radio work going. I actually derived certain things from radio —the self-reliance and confidence that come from sheer experience, and the concentration you have to develop working in a small physical area. On radio, I played parts pretty well typed—a lot of young, neurotic guys. I began to enjoy a lot of things about acting when I started working in stage jobs—building up a part, getting it all set, discovering how to maintain control.

From the beginning, what I always had in mind was eventually to go to Hollywood. I wanted to act in movies more than in plays. Now I find the greatest fascination in the production end of movies. My idea now is to do two movies a year—one for a big company, and one I produce myself. The first movie I did was "Kiss of Death," made in New York in 1947, *before* I went out to Hollywood. I did it strictly for fun, but in order to do it I had to sign a seven-year contract with one-year options with Twentieth Century-Fox. Between 1947 and 1954, I made about twenty movies for Fox, including "Panic in the Streets," "No Way Out," and "My Pal Gus." But I knew I had to get away from Fox, where I was being switched around from movie to movie without getting a chance to do much that I liked. I didn't sign another long-term contract. I now work as an independent. I have a farm and ranch, where I grow barley and raise cattle, between Santa Barbara and Los Angeles, and a house in Brentwood. Every day, I go to my business office, which I maintain at the Universal-International studios. I have my own film company, called Heath, which is my daughter's middle name; her first name is Anne, and she's sixteen, going to high school and, thank God, not acting. Occasionally, I'll go to one of those Hollywood parties, just to see the birds and bees all decked out, but I'm a firm believer in keeping business separate from my home.

My first movie, and my part in it as a laughing murderer who pushes an old lady down some stairs and kills her, practically gave me a phobia. I'd never seen myself on the screen, and when I did I wanted to shoot myself. That damn laugh of mine! For two years after that picture, you couldn't get me to smile. I played the part the way I did because the script struck me as funny and the part I played made me laugh, the guy was such a ridiculous beast. I was doing "Inner Sanctum" on radio at the same time, and I remember reading the "Kiss of Death" script to some of the guys and saying "Hey, get a load of this!" and laughing, it was so funny. And that's the way I played the part in the movie. Movie audiences fasten on to one aspect of the actor; they hold on to a piece of your personality for dear life, and decide what they want you to be. They think you're playing yourself. The truth is that the only person who can ever really play himself is a baby. You seldom learn to act in movies. I learned the fundamentals on the stage. In movies, you learn to do things on a minute scale, and there's nowhere to go from there. If you start in the theatre, you can learn later how to scale things down for pictures. Movie acting, however, is the most difficult kind of all to do. Theatre acting is a breeze by comparison. The fact that you're working on comparatively short fragments in a movie, out of context, and that you have to make them all add up to a whole is difficult enough. But then you have all the mechanical paraphernalia around. True movie acting is such a rare thing. You find a lot of effective performances, but it's hard to think of anyone except Spencer Tracy who has really had a whole career of superb

307

acting in movies. He discounts it, but you have to have pride in what you're doing if it's going to be really good, and it's obvious that he has it. When he's doing a part, it's bang on the nose. The older you get, the less you know about acting but the more you know about what makes the really great actors. In each succeeding movie, you're virtually starting all over. The actor is tested again each time. If you're successful, you've been there, they've seen you, and they're measuring you against the time before. Actors are a little lonely in that regard. It's *you* out on the stage or on the screen. The reaction is to *you*. The motion picture is a popular art, demanding a mass audience. They're the ones reacting to what you do. The result you see on the screen is a combination of actor and director, in most cases. There's no way of distinguishing between what the director does and what the actor does. You can't tell by the result on the screen how it came about. Most directors are good mediocrities; there's a dearth of really good ones. There are very few really good moviemakers altogether.

When I'm reading a script for the first time, I read it for story. As you go along, you see something in your part. Once you start, it's kind of with you all the time. You can be out driving a tractor on the farm, and the part is with you. It demands constant absorption. That aspect of it is pretty much as it is with a play. I learn my part first off, line by line. My wife or my daughter cues me. I learn the whole thing by rote, and then it's out of the way. You don't have to think of the words; they just come. For my recent movie "Judgment at Nuremberg," it took me six weeks just to learn the lines of my part. Rehearsals are for common movement, but you get little time for that. If we had three or four weeks of rehearsal for movies, it would make a tremendous difference. I've got be up on a tough scene weeks before I do it for the camera. It's tricky. You have to have the over-all idea of what you're going to do firmly entrenched. Then, making one scene match another is tricky, too. When you stop at 6 P.M. Monday and pick it up again at 4 P.M. Thursday, you need to be absolutely in control of what you're doing if you want it to match. Memory counts a lot, and, fortunately, I have a very good memory.

What makes acting exciting is that real spark you feel. For me, the spark is a kind of elated feeling. You're zigging up in a jet. It's wow! When it's not there, it feels like walking in mud. The audience always sees or senses that spark, too. It's there. Nobody can explain it. A lot depends on your fellow-actors. When I'm in a scene with Tracy, I play to him. He's the greatest listener in this business. It's a very elusive thing. Somebody can be looking you in the eye and he's in Timbuctoo. You can only *feel* it; you can't know it intellectually. Tracy plays Judge Dan Haywood in "Judgment at Nuremberg," and I play Colonel Lawson, an attorney. I look at this guy, and something goes. He doesn't talk much about acting, but he knows it all.

VLADIMIR SOKOLOFF

*Acting is the only way I am able to live. I want to
be everybody, and I want to be everything. One life
is not enough.*

I was born on Christmas Day, 1889, in Moscow. My mother died when I
was born. My father was a schoolteacher. I have an older brother and
sister, but I have not seen them or heard from them since I left Russia
in 1923. I was brought up by a wealthy merchant, a patron of my
father's school, who took me into his own family of five boys and a girl,
and who gave me everything—education, travel, care, love. I learned to
read at the age of three. As a child, I also learned to speak French and
German. I started out wanting to be a bear when I grew up. Such an
enjoyable prospect—lying in warm fur, in a warm den! Then I wanted
to be a beggar, roaming the country, extending a hand, and having
people give me bread and milk. After that, I wanted to be a clown. I
studied gymnastics and juggling, and then I discovered that I did not
have the necessary strength and health to become a clown. I in-

vented my own pantomimes, imitating cats and birds, and put on skits for the entertainment of my patron and his family. I wanted to be an actor, but the idea was taboo. My patron wanted me to become a brilliant professor. I was small and looked Oriental. The old family nurse would tell me, "Dear child, you are ugly, but you will get everything, not by the way you look but by what you have inside." The mother of the family was different. I adored her. She always told me, "You are not ugly. You are funny."

At seventeen, I attended the University of Moscow, studying philosophy and literature, but after a year I wanted to go to the Moscow Art Theatre school. More than a hundred young men applied for auditions each year; only seven or eight were chosen. Stanislavski himself was at my audition. Instead of reading a story or reciting a poem, as the others did, I gave a little act I had composed in which I read a newspaper as various contemporary characters in Russian life would. Stanislavski told me, "You have something, but we cannot accept you, because you do not look healthy or strong enough. Get stronger and come back next year." I burst into tears. He then agreed to put me in a second-string school, taught by the student actors themselves. So every day I would leave home to go to the university, and from there I would go to the theatre school. After three years, the strain was too great. I became ill with tuberculosis. I had to tell my patron what I had been doing. He sent me to the Crimea and the South of France to recover. I gave him my word I would forget the foolishness of acting. But after my recovery I broke my word and joined the school again, appearing in mob scenes in Moscow Art Theatre productions and attending the regular theatre school. I appeared onstage in heavy disguises, but one day I was recognized, and there was a big scandal. I felt like a scoundrel. But I moved out of my patron's home and got a room for ten kopecks a week—about twenty cents. I was very happy. I got a Ph.D. degree in literature from the university, and in 1914 I became a professional actor.

I adored Stanislavski. I worshipped him. But I wanted a different approach for myself in acting. I wanted the miraculous, the fascinating, the romantic theatre, with more music and more staging. I felt I could play anything, but my heart from the beginning belonged to the theatre of Molière and Shakespeare. I found my kind of theatre when I joined the Kamerny Theatre, the first theatre founded as a departure from the Moscow Art. My first important part was the buffoon in an old Hindu play, "Sakuntala." Then I directed "The Taming of the Shrew" and played the lead, and married Elizabeth Alexandrova, the actress who played Katharina. Life was good. Life was wonderful. Then there was the revolution, and all theatres were closed. There was no food. There was no fuel. I went to Molvitino, in the country, about six hundred miles from Moscow, and lived there for sixteen months, fishing, picking mushrooms and wild berries, getting healthy. I put on a production of Tolstoy's "The Power of Darkness," with peasants as the actors and peasants as the audience. It was a powerful experience— the closest I have ever come to being at one with my audience. In 1920, the theatres in Moscow were opened again. Actors were given privileges in the way of living conditions and in obtaining food. They were considered useful as propaganda for the revolution. In 1922, I thought of myself as an actor who should be limited to doing broad comedy, but Isadora Duncan, who had opened a school for dancing in Moscow, told me, when we met, that I should play tragedy. She had a tremendous influence on me. She was a revelation to me. A great person in life. Not only a dancer but a tragic actress. She had immense generosity and understanding of art. She was the only person I had ever met who was not a conformist. To me, she was the personification of the great artist. She was to be an inspiration to me for the rest of my life.

In 1923, I went to Vienna with the Kamerny company, playing the Dauphin in Shaw's "Saint Joan," and parts in Ostrovski's "The Storm" and in an adaptation of G. K. Chesterton's novel "The Man Who Was Thursday." We set out to tour Germany. In Dresden, I was in an elevator that fell into the basement of the theatre during the second act of the Chesterton play, and I broke my right foot and right leg. I stayed on in Germany for eight months for treatment. I played occasional parts, in German, such as a ninety-year-old rabbi in "The Dybbuk," in which I could wear a long robe, limp, and carry a cane. I was playing such a small part at the Kleines Theatre in Berlin when Max Reinhardt saw me and asked me to join his company. I played Puck for him in " A Midsummer Night's Dream." I loved Reinhardt from the start. Perhaps he was the greatest man in the theatre in my experience. Stanislavski was a pedagogue; he was always explaining things to you in words. But Max Reinhardt always gave you the *feeling*. He was the

greatest director of all. He was shamefully misunderstood and mis-
treated when he came to America. He was a born magician. Every actor
I know who worked with him fell in love with him. My years with him
were more than enjoyable; they were incredibly fruitful. He loved
character acting. He loved actors. I once said to him, "Professor, why
don't you act?" He said, "I act in all of you."

I played in Germany in the twenties, and made my first movie there,
a silent film, in 1925—Berthold Viertel's "The Adventures of a Ten
Mark Note," in which I took the part of the ragpicker who finds the
bill. In 1927, I was in New York briefly, on tour with Reinhardt's company. In the thirties, I went to France and took French-speaking parts
in French plays. I also went to Hollywood, making German versions of
movies, to be shown abroad, but I did not care for the life, and returned to Germany and France. In 1937, I came to America again and
acted under contract with Warner Brothers in "The Life of Emile
Zola." In 1938, in New York, I played Robespierre in "Danton's
Death," with Orson Welles—a part I had played in German with
Reinhardt's company in Vienna and in New York in 1927. Then I
made many Hollywood movies, in which I played Chinese, Japanese,
Malayans, Filipinos, Hindus, Italians, Spaniards, Czechs, Mexicans,
and Germans; only twice have I played a Russian. One day in 1947, in
Hollywood, I got a call to come to New York to play in "Crime and
Punishment" with John Gielgud. I was so excited. Here I had just
finished making one of those movies about narcotics and had played
a Chinese narcotics commissioner. Now I was offered the part of
Porfiri Petrovitch—the prosecutor who from the beginning feels
that Raskolnikoff, played by Gielgud, is guilty of his crime. I
tried in the play to catch him in a very subtle way, without being
too aggressive but working on his conscience. I loved the part. I had
never met Gielgud before, but I had seen him in "Hamlet" and
thought he was brilliant. I have always thought that, besides being a
splendid actor, he is a poet. That is the element I like in him. I consider him in every way much deeper than almost any other actor.
From the moment we started rehearsals, we understood each other.
Seldom have I felt such ease as I felt rehearsing with him. There were
many fine actors in the cast, including Lillian Gish, who played
Katerina, and Dolly Haas, who played Sonia, the prostitute in love with
Raskolnikoff, and the whole play was one of the most satisfying I have

ever done. Gielgud from the beginning always asked us whether we felt all right, and in every way he offered such gentlemanly coöperation. He is so generous, so considerate of his fellow-actors—a gentleman on the stage. He made me feel, It is so simple for me to play this part. We were rehearsing half-voice one day, very quietly, when suddenly we saw one of the producers, Robert Whitehead, standing in the orchestra. He asked us, "Why don't you rehearse?" And Gielgud laughed and said, "We *are* rehearsing." Because our dialogue was running so smoothly, so naturally, and with such conviction, Whitehead thought we were just talking to each other. Gielgud stands almost alone as an artist. After every performance, he would gather the company together on the stage and make remarks about the night's performance. He wasn't the director, but he felt a responsibility for all of us. We played "Crime and Punishment" for forty performances, and every performance to me was just like a first performance. Gielgud and I had three big scenes in which we were onstage alone together. Gielgud is so flexible, so hospitable to every nuance you give him, that there was always something new to find in what you yourself did. I enjoyed the way he would take it and answer it. In our three big scenes, I felt as though we were playing tennis with the audience, the ball going to the audience and then back to the stage, and it was almost as though Gielgud would say, "Vladimir, you take it," and then the ball would go to the audience again, and then back, and I would say, "You take it, John." We were playing doubles with the audience, and we always won. It is such bliss to act with a man like that.

Every actor has, as a gift from God, his own method. My particular method is to go first by the sense of taste—physical taste. I actually have a physical taste for every part. Then I go by the other senses—hearing, seeing, touching. Thinking comes much later. Thinking comes when you have already molded the part you are playing. You should analyze the part, but not too much. One of the poets has said that every art must be a little stupid. An artist should not be overly intelligent. My method, without thinking, is to follow the path of physical truthfulness. The way I ate the soup in "The Power of Darkness," which I played again in New York in 1959, I was not pretending, I was doing it. And the audience believed in me a hundred per cent. From then on, no matter what I did, the audience believed in me, because I had already won them. Max Reinhardt always said it is the task of the character actor not to disguise himself but to reveal himself. The simplest way is the truest way. You start to think only when the part has reached a certain age. It's like a child—he's not ready to think until he has reached a certain point of development. When you are building a part, that point is in the last dress rehearsals or after the first few performances.

In 1934, I was sitting with Stanislavski in Paris, in the Bois de Boulogne, and he was reading to me from "An Actor Prepares." He said to me, "Sokoloff, if you go with Max Reinhardt to America, if you want to help youngsters, forget all this theory. Don't apply this. Don't pay any attention to this. Everything is different in America. The education. The psychology. The health. The mentality. Even the food is different there. We needed this book to open actors up in Russia. In America, it is different. They don't need it there. If they try to use it, they will unnecessarily spy on themselves, asking 'Do I feel it or not?' Tell them, 'In America the actor is free.' " Stanislavski tells actors to observe. I do not believe in observing too much. Eighty per cent of observations are wrong. People do *not* look like what they are. There is only one exception I know of—Albert Einstein. I once observed a man I decided was a mortician. Who did it turn out to be? Igor Stravinsky! The clown Grock was my idol. I was supposed to meet Grock in a restaurant. I had never seen him without his clown makeup and costume. In the restaurant, I saw no one who could be Grock. I saw a dull-looking white-haired man with gold-rimmed spectacles who was sitting with a fat, typically middle-class wife wearing diamonds. *That* was Grock.

However, I have great curiosity about everything. That is the only thing that keeps an actor's acting alive. When the weather is good, I take walks. My wife died in 1948, and I am alone a good deal. But everything I see gives me something. I see a girl with a charming smile. I see a child with a doll. A new tie in a window. A passing cloud. Every day, when I am in New York, I go to some museum and absorb the loveliness of what they have there. Every day, I find at least one beautiful thing. It is invaluable to me as an actor. An actor has a peculiar structure as a human being. For me, the world is divided into two parts, and the dividing line is the footlights. You must know at every given moment on the stage not what you feel but what you want —what Walter Huston used to call your "intention." I love to watch children when they play. They are acting all the time. They are making their own world the way they feel it should be. Acting is childhood hidden under the cape.

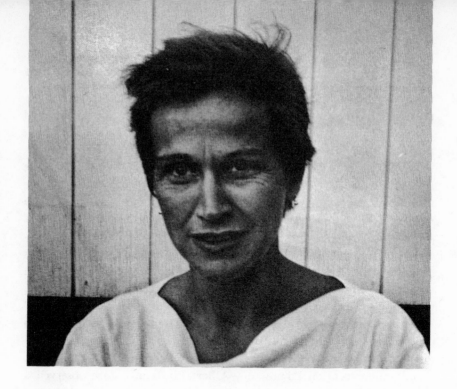

KIM HUNTER

Onstage, I can use a lot of aspects of myself that aren't available to me, because of shyness or various other complications, in my real life.

I was born on November 12, 1922, in Detroit, Michigan. I have one brother, G. Gordon Cole, eight and a half years older than I am, who lives in Minneapolis and works as a captain for one of the big commercial airlines. My real name is Janet Cole. My father, Donald Cole, was a refrigeration engineer. My mother had been trained as a concert pianist and used to accompany choral groups in public performances, but after she got married she gave it up, because she had two children to raise. My father died when I was three. Seven years later, my mother married Bliss Stebbins, a retired businessman who lived in Miami Beach, and we all moved down there. When I was about ten, I began to go to movies. The first really impressive movie I saw—when I was eleven—was "The Sign of the Cross," with Fredric March, Claudette Colbert, and Elissa Landi. I found it an incredible experience. It seemed to me then that movies came out ready-made;

it never occurred to me to make a connection between acting and the movies. I led a kind of solo existence in my childhood. Each summer from the time I was eleven until I was sixteen, we spent several months at Grand Lake, Michigan, where my stepfather owned a hotel and a cluster of small cottages, one of which we lived in. Each summer, there would be different families living in the other cottages, always with a lot of boys but no girls. My brother had friends, and I got the notion that girls were rarities and boys were rather expendable. The place was wild and woodsy, and I would go off for long walks by myself. During my first summer at Grand Lake, I came across an old libretto of "Cavalleria Rusticana" in my stepfather's library. It had a rhymed English translation facing the Italian text, and I took it to one of the vacant cottages and sat down in the living room and read it all the way through. I couldn't get over the rhythm and beauty of the words, and the wonder of thinking that live people got up on a stage to sing those words. I immediately felt inspired to write a play of my own. It took me two weeks. I called it "Helena"—the most romantic name I could think of at that time—and it was probably fairly similar to the libretto of "Cavalleria Rusticana." As soon as I got back to Florida, I got a couple of girls from school together and said "Let's write plays," and we started writing our own plays. It then occurred to me that I might act in plays as well as write them.

Not long afterward, I began to study acting with a woman in our neighborhood named Charmine Lantaff, who had worked in New York as a drama coach and had set up a kind of acting school, with lessons available to children and adults, in her own home in Florida. My mother was all for it. She backed me in every way. She arranged for Miss Lantaff to give me three lessons a week, in voice technique, theatre history, and theory—a lot of theory. In my spare time, I studied on my own. At first, I was very shy. It frightened me to get up in front of people to read; I could do it for Miss Lantaff, and only for Miss Lantaff. I spent hours discussing the theatre with her, and she led me beyond my natural capacity to act things out. I was her best pupil. I had the child's notion that since I was able to please Miss Lantaff, I could win the world's approval by doing the same thing for large groups. My mother didn't have the attitude that she wanted me to do what she had failed to do, or anything like that;

she simply knew that she had had a gift that had never been utilized, and she wanted me to utilize mine if I felt I really had it. When I was sixteen, I had my first big theatrical experience, reciting a monologue at an entertainment given by the student council of Miami Beach High School to raise money for the school. I was asked to give the monologue because the students knew about my acting lessons. I chose "The Waltz," Dorothy Parker's short story about a wallflower at a dance, to adapt as a monologue. I didn't write it until the morning of the day I was supposed to give it, hoping against hope that something would come up to get me out of it. There was an awful feeling inside me that I didn't want to do it. I just didn't want to perform for anybody. I nearly panicked waiting to go onstage. I didn't think I'd make it. But then the training and discipline I'd got from Miss Lantaff took over, and I leaned against a pillar onstage and went through with the monologue, and everybody clapped. After that, with Miss Lantaff's encouragement, I participated in two school plays, and performed in plays put on by Miss Lantaff for women's clubs. I took every role I could get. In my senior year, I was given the leading role in the graduation play, Clifford Goldsmith's "What a Life." My mother came to see me in it, and said I was good, and encouraged me to keep working at it.

After my graduation from high school, in June, 1940, there was nothing for me to do in Florida. By that time, Miss Lantaff had started a summer-theatre company in Hendersonville, North Carolina, so I went up there and joined it. I lived in a girls' summer camp nearby, and at the theatre, which was called the Old Mill Playhouse, I played ingénue roles. We put on a different play every week for ten weeks, and I played most of the leads. In the fall, I went back to Miami Beach and worked as an apprentice with the Gant Gaither Theatre, a local group that imported professional stars. I got only bit parts to play. Then I joined the Theatre of the Fifteen, a group in Coral Gables, where I played Cecily Cardew in "The Importance of Being Earnest." In the summer of 1941, I went back to the theatre in Hendersonville, this time with the Coral Gables group, and we went on to play a season in Baltimore that fall. Then we went back to Coral Gables for a full winter season. I played the ingénue in "The Male Animal," "Is Zat So?," "The Man Who Came to Dinner," "The Philadelphia Story," and others. My pay consisted of my board and room. Quite a few of the members of the Coral Gables group had come from the Pasadena Playhouse, in California, and one of them, a young director, left to go back there. Soon various wartime restrictions made it impossible for our stock company to survive, and in May, 1942, we broke up for the duration. I again went back to Miami Beach, and worked for the American Red Cross. I thought, fearfully, of coming to New York to try my luck here, and I wrote to the young director in Pasadena and told him this. He wrote back and suggested that I come to Pasadena instead, to audition for one of the student groups at the Pasadena Playhouse. So in November of that year I went to California, and got the ingénue part in a Playhouse production of "Arsenic and Old Lace" and another sort of ingénue part in "The Women." About a year later, on the West Coast, I met a captain in the Marine Corps, William Baldwin, and we were married. It was one of those wartime marriages; he was sent overseas, and when he returned, after the war, we both knew we had made a mistake, and were divorced. We had one child, Kathy, who was born in December, 1944. She hasn't seen her real father since she was three. He has remarried and has several other children. I am now married to Robert Emmett, who writes television situation comedies and has adapted material for television and the stage. We have a son, Sean, who was born in 1954. Both children take my being an actress for granted. My children belong to the theatre, just as my husband and I do. We're never away from it. We live next door to the Cherry Lane Theatre, in the Village, and our bedroom wall adjoins the wall of the stage. We hear the rehearsals, the performances, and the applause, even in our sleep.

In 1943, an agent who had seen me in Pasadena and wanted to represent me got me to sign a seven-year movie contract with David O. Selznick. I never made a movie for him, but he was the one who got me to change my name. Janet Cole was not theatrical enough, he said, and besides there were a lot of other Janets around, including Janet Gaynor and Janet Blair. I was delighted, because I loathed my name at the time. I tossed in "Kim," a name I admired longingly—the name of Magnolia's daughter in "Show Boat." After Selznick had arranged to lend me to R.K.O., the secretary of an R.K.O. producer came up with the name "Hunter." Selznick put the two together, and there I was. All I ever did for Selznick, however, was to appear in Ingrid Bergman's role in screen tests for actors trying to get minor roles in "Spellbound." I was lent out by Selznick to other studios, and made "The Seventh Victim" for R.K.O., "Betrayed" for Monogram, and "You Came Along" for Paramount. I have only a vague recollection of what the movies were about, but a clear one that most of them were labelled "B." The one big point that had been impressed on me was that the movies magnified every movement a hundred times—a statistic that affected me so powerfully that I became afraid to move at all. What really mattered to me, though, was that I was earning a living for myself and my baby. Then J. Arthur Rank, in England, offered me a contract and the role in "Stairway to Heaven," and Selznick dropped my option and I was free to work for Rank for six wonderful months—from June to December, 1945. I left the baby with my mother and went to England. It was quite an experience, being in England immediately after the war, working with good actors, and working with Michael Powell, who is a wonderful director. When the six months were up, I went back to California. By 1947, I'd had enough of sitting around in California, and I decided to return to summer stock. Through a direc- tor, I was offered the leading role in a summer-theatre production of Rose Franken's "Claudia," in Stamford, Connecticut, for a week. I got my mother and Kathy into our Buick, and we drove East.

One night during the week of "Claudia" in Stamford, a representa- tive of the producer Irene Selznick came backstage and told me that there was a possibility that I might read for the role of Stella Kowalski in the new Tennessee Williams play, "A Streetcar Named Desire," after the role of Blanche had been cast. It was a nutty conversation, and I promised to call him before I accepted another job, and then put it out of my mind. As things worked out, we took "Claudia" to play in Detroit for a week, and when I arrived there, I found that the Irene Selznick office had wired to ask me when I could be in New York to read for the part. I was impressed by the play, but I was still such a baby that I didn't know how seldom parts like Stella came along, and I didn't quite realize the significance of it all. I thought it was a rather good play, but I was so eager to do a play in New York that I would have tried for the role even if I had thought the play was bad. Actually, my ability to judge a play has never been very good. I had been offered another summer-theatre job, playing Cathy in

"Wuthering Heights" up at Lake George, in the Adirondacks, and between "Claudia" and "Wuthering Heights," on a hot, sunny, beautiful afternoon in late August of 1947, I went over to the Henry Miller Theatre, and, with Irene Selznick, Elia Kazan, and Tennessee Williams in the audience, I went out onstage and read two scenes from "A Streetcar Named Desire." I read without any idea of how to play the part. Irene Selznick said just to make it loud and clear, so I tried to make it loud and I tried to make it clear. The stage manager read the part of Blanche with me in the opening scene, where she comes to stay with us, and then he read the part of Stanley in a first-act scene with me. During the readings, the reaction around me was so strong—I could feel the way they were breathing out there—that I began to think it was an exceptional play. I was told to go back to my hotel—they would call me. I was staying at the Beekman Tower Hotel, so I went back there, sat down on the bed in my room, and looked out the window for a couple of hours. Then the telephone rang, and I was told "It's yours." I was so excited I couldn't stand it, but I was afraid to tell anybody, and besides I didn't know anybody in New York to tell. My mother and Kathy were in Detroit, visiting my brother. I got on a train and went up to Lake George, where I forgot about Stella and just concentrated on playing Cathy in "Wuthering Heights." After a week of that, I joined my mother in Detroit, and we drove back to California, packed up, and moved to New York.

Rehearsals for "A Streetcar Named Desire" started on October 1st, in the rehearsal theatre on top of the New Amsterdam Theatre. I'd met Marlon Brando a day or so before that. He seemed like a very nice young man, and very shy, but no shier than I was. We rehearsed for three and a half weeks. I learned more during those three and a half weeks of rehearsal than I had learned in all my life up to then. Every day there was something new. The way Elia Kazan, the director, began the rehearsals by having us sit and read and search until we had established the relationships between the characters was a revelation to me. Up to then, I had gone on sheer instinct. Now I was really learning something. Marlon and I were the most insecure ones. We were the untried members of the cast. Marlon kept saying, "They should have got John Garfield for Stanley, not me; Garfield was right for the part, not me." Of course, Marlon was just wonderful for the part. One absolutely extraordinary thing about Marlon, which makes him my favorite actor of all time to act with, is his uncanny sense of truth. It seems absolutely impossible for him to be false. It makes him easier to act with than anybody else ever. Anything you do that may not be true shows up immediately as false with him. It is a tremendous experience to play in relationship to him; he yanks you into his own sense of reality. For example, one thing that made it all so real during my year and a half with the show was the way Marlon played the scene where Stanley goes through Blanche's trunk. Stanley has found out a little bit about her at that point in the play, and is starting to question her, and he begins to go through the things in her trunk, while Stella tries to protect her sister's belongings. Marlon never, never did that scene the same way twice during the entire run. He had a different sort of attitude toward each of the belongings every night; sometimes it would lead me into getting into quite a fight with him, and other times I'd be seeing him as a silly little boy. I got worn out after many months in the play, but I never got bored, even though it was hard and painful after a year to keep it fresh, to keep myself stimulated, to make it live.

Even before rehearsals started, the newspapers began building up the play. Irene Selznick kept advising us not to get overconfident about it—just to treat it as a nice little play. After a while, the play got so much publicity that we had to work hard against overconfidence. Then we began to feel that even if it was the greatest play ever written we couldn't live up to the reputation it had before it opened anywhere. We kept ourselves closed up like oysters. I was young and impressionable, and though I found the role of Stella challenging, I felt like a scared rabbit. But Kazan got me to working rather than trembling. I didn't understand Stella until he began directing me in the part, and then I began to find her. By the time the play opened on Broadway, I had learned all I could from the outside—from others—about Stella, and after that I kept discovering new things about Stella from inside myself. The New York critics were all terribly enthusiastic about the play—except George Jean Nathan, who had no patience with Tennessee Williams' work—but the critics don't help you learn anything about your part. You learn by yourself, from playing the part. The longer I played it, the more I discovered by myself about Stella. One thing you discover is that you never quite come to an end of discovering. If the playwright writes well and makes it possible for his characters to live, you learn more about the character each night you play it. It's like learning more about a girl each time you see her, even if she's your closest friend. I played in "A Streetcar Named Desire" from December, 1947, to June, 1949, and then I played Stella in the movie version. I won so many awards for the part that I became known just for that. It's a wonderful part. For one thing, it's such a fully written part. It's always easier and more interesting to realize a character that is written fully. Very few writers know how to write parts for women to play. Tennessee Williams does it better than any other writer I know of. He gets the character of Stella across in his writing. Most writers become sentimental or overly romantic when they're writing about a woman, and that makes it difficult for an actress.

My basic aim as an actress is to bring a part to life. There are times when a playwright will depend on the actor to convey a thought or an emotion, or illuminate a thought or an emotion, because the writer feels that words won't achieve it, and might even muddy the meaning. Sometimes a writer will say to me, "*You* do it." He may deliberately underwrite a part, because he won't know how to convey a certain moment. For example, in a television play I did in 1955, called "Portrait in Celluloid," I was supposed to be a witty, all-knowing, all-understanding female. But the part seemed to me to be underwritten. The character's place in the play was clean and clear but not completely conveyed by the writer. Once during rehearsals, when I asked Rod Serling, the writer, how to convey the woman's feelings, he said to me, "*You* do it, with a look." That sort of thing is easier for an actress to do for the camera than onstage. The camera, either for television or for a movie, can come in for a closeup and catch the look that will convey the meaning. Onstage, the playwright can't get away with the slightest neglect of duty. In film scripts, you often find long passages of instructions for the actors. In essence, they tell you that the camera will come up close and express what the writer couldn't express.

In acting, there are no rigid rules. After you start rehearsing, various unpredictables usually come to light. I start out by getting acquainted with my part. I cling to the clues I find even when I'm at home. On my way to a rehearsal—and, later, each time I'm on my way to the theatre—I start the ball rolling by bringing the character to life physically, picturing to myself how she appears. Once the preliminary work is done, I get terribly subjective about a part. I can't trust what I think of the character intellectually, so I have to trust my instincts. If I get myself involved emotionally and then am able to blend what I feel with what I think, I can go ahead and do it. After a while, subtle alterations have to be made here and there, and everything starts to become molded, and I grow confident in the part. I carry the part with me at all times. For instance, after three weeks of rehearsal for "Write Me a Murder," in which I speak with an English accent, I began to use the English accent and English expressions automatically. At that point, I'm bringing the part home, and my family gets in on it. The more I bring home with me about the character, the closer I know I'm getting to the character. Then, when my husband and my children start picking up the speech and mannerisms I have created, it feels legitimate.

No matter what I happen to be doing during the day, I am always waiting for the evening's performance to start. I can be sending my laundry out or planning a meal or taking Sean to the museum, but I'm still with my play and with my part in it. I somehow seem to become a better person when I'm acting in a play every night. My family life becomes more harmonious. I'm less restless in everything I do. My husband finds me easier to get along with. In my early days in stock, I knew only the bare minimum about acting, and it was all such a ball. I had no problems. What I didn't know didn't hurt me. I knew I had to get on the stage and off the stage, and I knew a few things about each part. My feeling of obligation to the audience went only as far as realizing that I couldn't rehearse in front of them. Plays were geared for one week in one town. I was young and romantic, and found it exciting. I could mess up my part, but it wouldn't make the play a flop. Today, I know that my name is on the marquee to draw people into the theatre. It's my job to convey whatever the playwright has written and to do credit to his words and to him. If anything I do unbalances the playwright's concept, I feel that I'm cheating the audience, and I can't stand that feeling.

Acting is unquestionably an art. Duse was a creative artist, who could find meanings in plays that no one had ever found before. An actor takes an author's words and infuses life into them. Many actors today are merely interpretive artists, but they can be more than that. It takes more than talent, or even a capacity for greatness, to do it, however. It takes learning, training, guidance, and experience. What you use in acting is everything you are as a human being. Every actor has his own key to acting. You use what works for you. You use what was used before Stanislavski was born. Coquelin once said that if you cry onstage, the audience will never cry. When Elia Kazan directed "A Streetcar Named Desire," he told us to fight our tears, because in real life people try to hold back tears, and that would be more truthful. There are people today who say that what Coquelin really meant was that *unless* you cry the audience will never cry. It's a continuing argument. I don't know which is true. To judge by my own experience, if you cry real tears, the audience does seem to cry, too. Whatever the technique, your aim must always be to achieve command over the audience.

HAROLD SCOTT

In the twilight zone I'm in, known as up-and-coming,
you go to great lengths to build versatility, but no
one wants it. Everyone wants types.

I was born on September 6, 1935, in Morristown, New Jersey, about
thirty-five miles from New York City. My father, Harold Russell
Scott, Sr., is a doctor—a general practitioner—in Orange, New Jersey.
My mother is a housewife. I'm an only child. No one else in our family
is remotely associated with the theatre. My mother's grandfather played
the harp beautifully, and also played seven other instruments, and my
mother's brother played the piano. I'm a pretty good bass-baritone.
We moved to Orange from Morristown when I was nine. My father
is the only Negro ever to be appointed to the staff of the Orange Memorial Hospital, in Orange, and the Presbyterian Hospital in Newark.
He wanted me to go into medicine, and when he first heard that I
wanted to become an actor, he was furious. When I was ten, he had a
little white coat made for me that was identical with his, and I used to
hang around his office wearing it and charming the patients. It would
have been easy for me to go into medicine, but by the time I was fourteen I knew that I didn't want to be a doctor. I wasn't brought up as a

Negro. In Orange, we lived in a mainly white middle-class neighborhood of one-family houses. Our house was within a block of an all-Negro school, but my parents didn't want me to go to a segregated school. I was sent to a school in another zone, and was the first Negro in that school. I never had any trouble there, but in my neighborhood I was once chased by some other Negro kids, who called me a "nigger." I ran to my father's office and asked him the old question, "Daddy, what's a nigger?" He had an immediate "conference" with me about it. He took me on his knee and explained that one might expect to encounter this sort of thing from time to time in one's life, and that the best thing was not to get angry but to understand what was said and to rise above it. My parents were always having conferences and discussions with me. As a child, anything I wanted had to be discussed—what it was I wanted, why, and what I was going to do with it. The talks were endless, and occasionally took all the joy out of my hopes and plans. I began going to plays when I was eleven. Noël Coward's "Present Laughter" and "Annie Get Your Gun," with Ethel Merman, were the first ones I saw. I was deeply affected by the whole aura. And I was fascinated by the special nature of props onstage—mirrors with soaped faces, and things like that. We lived across the street from a movie theatre, and going to the movies was a weekly ritual, but movies didn't mean very much to me. It was the theatre that drew me.

I attended public schools until I was fourteen, and then I went to Phillips Exeter Academy. I had applied for admission to four or five leading Eastern prep schools and had been accepted by all of them except Exeter, so my parents decided that Exeter was where I had to go. In order to become eligible for admission, I had to take summer courses in English, mathematics, and French, lasting about eight weeks. I prepared at Exeter's own summer session. As far as I know, I was the third Negro ever to be admitted as a freshman to Exeter. The second, Monroe Dowling, was a year ahead of me; he's now a medical interne in Detroit. The first Negro had been admitted twenty years earlier. I loved Exeter. The way the place is set up, you have to grow up, you have to learn to take care of yourself. I was not an honor student, but I was good in whatever interested me—language, writing, speech— just as I still am. I was not good in anything that had to do with figures or science. It was my father who unwittingly got me started as an actor. He always told me that it was terribly important to learn how

327

to speak. He felt that a well-read man should be a well-spoken man. He was interested in city and state politics, and he believed that a man should know how to present his point of view objectively and intelligently. When I was fifteen, he suggested that I take a course in public speaking, so I did, and then, also at his suggestion, I took up debating. In my third year at Exeter, I tried out for the Merrill Prize Speaking Contest, in the dramatic division. I wanted to recite "The Tell-Tale Heart," by Edgar Allan Poe, but "God's Trombones," by the Negro writer James Weldon Johnson, was suggested to me by one of the teachers. I got huffy, but I agreed to do selections from it, with a chip on my shoulder. I did two poems from it and won the prize—twenty-five dollars. I have since recorded all the poems on a record. In my senior year at Exeter, I auditioned for "Captain Brassbound's Conversion," one of Bernard Shaw's potboilers, and got the title role—sort of a half-Arab pirate. It was my first real part except for Christmas plays in grammar school. I played it for two performances. It was marvellous. I loved the excitement, the whole feeling. Suddenly I felt that I had some status. Other boys were successful in athletics or other things, and although I was a good athlete, too, I felt that acting was something only I could do in my own special way. Then I was asked to try for the Merrill prize again. It had never been won twice by the same person. This time, as a previous winner, I had to write my own piece. I wrote what I now think is a little piece of slop, about a modest man and his simple faith in God, and I won the prize again. At that point, I decided that acting would be my profession. In my Exeter years, I loved to go to the theatre alone—as I still do. One of the few indulgences allowed me was the theatre. I'd come home for weekends and go to a Saturday matinée, then to a movie, then to another play after that, and make the last bus back to Orange around midnight.

I went to Harvard, and graduated in the class of 1957. I originally planned to major in philosophy, and then, in the middle of my sophomore year, switched to English literature. I wasn't a strictly A student. I proved that I could make the Dean's List once, and then it was no longer important to me. My main interest at Harvard was in the theatre and acting. I was one of a nucleus of five people who took it all very seriously: Steve Aaron, who later worked as an assistant to Ingmar Bergman; Glenn Jordan, who directed "Another Evening with Harry Stoones," an Off Broadway show, in 1961; and two others, who are now actors—Colgate Salsbury and D. J. Sullivan. In my freshman year, I immediately gravitated toward the Harvard Dramatic Club. That year, I played three tiny parts in "Marco Millions." I was in my glory. It was the first time I'd gone and read for a part and been cast right away. In my sophomore year, D. J. and Glenn spearheaded the founding of the Eliot Drama Group, primarily for the purpose of putting on classics. I was involved, one way or another, in about thirty productions at Harvard. I played enormous and wonderful parts—Edmund of Langley, the Duke of York, in "Richard II" and Oedipus in "Oedipus Rex," both with the Eliot Drama Group, and the title role in "The Emperor Jones," in the New Theatre Workshop of the Harvard Dramatic Club, for which I had to dye my body black and cut my hair very short to make myself look more of a Negro. In my senior year, John Eyre produced the American première of "Deathwatch," by Jean Genêt, at the Pi Eta Theatre in Cambridge. I played Maurice, one of three characters in a prison cell. It was an astounding success; we played twice a night for a week and made money for John Eyre, who, in association with Richard Barr and Clinton Wilder, later produced "The Death of Bessie Smith" Off Broadway. We were then invited to give "Deathwatch" at the Yale Drama Festival, which we did for one night, and after that a director named Leo Garen asked me to repeat my role in New York. I very delightedly said yes. I felt I was actually going to be able to arrive in New York with a *part*. I graduated from Harvard, went to Europe for the summer, and rushed back to New York expecting the play to be done that October. Actually, it wasn't done until a year later. In the meantime, I suffered through a dry spell. I lived at home with my parents and sat by the telephone waiting for calls— from producers, from directors, from casting people, from anyone. It was a terribly crushing time. My parents were dubious about my course. I told my father that I just had to try it, that I'd been told marvellous things about my acting at Harvard. I told him I'd never been panned. We agreed that I deserved to have a three-year trial period. I said, "If somebody I respect pans me during that time, then I will abandon acting and I will go to law school." Today, now that my parents have *seen* me as an actor, they are wildly enthusiastic about the whole idea.

In the fall of 1957, through a friend, I got my first New York job, for ten dollars a week, in a non-Equity, Off Broadway production of

"A Land Beyond the River," at the Greenwich Mews, as a replacement in the last two months of the play's run. I played a young lawyer taking a desegregation case before a court. Then, to earn money, I worked, at a dollar an hour, for a firm called Marketing Impact Research, Inc., doing various kinds of surveys. In September, 1958, I was in an Off Broadway musical, "The Egg and I," in which I played Albert, Ma and Pa Kettle's son—the romantic interest in the show. Finally, on October 9, 1958, "Deathwatch" was put on at Theatre East, and ran for nine weeks. It was my first Equity show, and I was paid the going rate of forty dollars a week. My parents have always subsidized me in my career as an actor. Without that help, it would be impossible. Any young actor who wants to go on must either have an independent income or get financial help from somewhere. For my performance in "Deathwatch," I won the Obie Award for the Off Broadway Distinguished Performance of the Year. That was the first real evidence my parents had that I had some merit as an actor. After that, I was invited back to Cambridge to appear, as a professional actor, with a group of undergraduates doing "King Lear." I played the title role for eight nights and was paid two hundred dollars, plus expenses. Then I had another long dry spell—an entire summer with nothing to do.

On February 22, 1960, I made my Broadway début, in "The Cool World," at the Eugene O'Neill Theatre. The play lasted two performances. I played Chester, one of a group of juvenile delinquents in Spanish Harlem who becomes the kept boy of a wealthy white man. I had one long scene—fifteen minutes—in which I explained to my friends why I was doing what I did. For this part, *Variety's* poll of drama critics named me one of the most promising new actors of the year. In March of 1960, I played the part of Tiphys, a pirate captain, in an adaptation of Friedrich Duerrenmatt's "The Jackass," at the Barbizon-Plaza Theatre. It lasted one night. In May, 1960, I played in an Equity Library Theatre production of "Dark of the Moon," as John, the witch boy, for one full week. Edward Albee's "The Death of Bessie Smith" was performed one afternoon that June at the Actors' Studio, which I was attending at the time, and I played the part of the young Negro orderly at the hospital where Bessie Smith's lover tries to find help for her after her auto accident. That summer, I was in "Program One," produced by the Theatre for the Swan at the Gate Theatre, on Second Avenue. I was in three one-act plays: as the character Death in "Santa Claus," by e. e. cummings; as First Musician in "Calvary," by Yeats; and as the King in "Escurial," by Michel De Ghelderode. That repertory season lasted thirteen performances. On March 1, 1961, I opened as the orderly in "The Death of Bessie Smith" at the York Playhouse, at the Off Broadway minimum salary, then forty-five dollars a week, and I closed with it on January 7, 1962. Ironically, this part was the smallest part I'd had in my entire career. I'd been playing very challenging parts up to then, so this was a great blow to my ego, and I had to find a way to do the part and not resent doing it. It was a matter of getting used to a situation you have to live with. I was helped by something I came across around that time while I was putting my old college scrapbook together. It was a review in the Harvard *Crimson,* by a young critic named Thomas Schwabacher, of my performance as the Duke of York in "Richard II," my first sizable part at Harvard. Schwabacher wrote of me, "His acting is the best in the entire production, and he makes the agony of York's divided loyalty to both Richard and Bolingbroke clear in every line and even the dejected shuffle of his steps; Scott proves that a comparatively minor part can assume major importance in the hands of a skillful performer." After reading that once more, and pasting it in the scrapbook, I decided that if I'd done it once I could do it again.

All in all, things have come easily to me. To a great extent, it's a matter of luck, of being in the right place at the right time. I hope to achieve some kind of true prominence in the theatre, to become, I suppose—in American terms—a star. I think this is quite likely to happen, because there are enough unusual things about me to make me unique—though that can take you either way, can be a hindrance or a help. The fact that I've been trained in playing the classics as well as contemporary plays, and that I sing as well as act, and that I'm equipped to do character work as well as play juveniles should help me to achieve something eventually. Versatility is a wonderful thing once you're a star, but not before. After a while, in auditioning for parts, you form a kind of audition-interview personality. My particular difficulty is that I'm not dark enough to play an African and not light enough to play a white. Not many of the good parts are designed as Negro roles.

I go to the theatre constantly—usually alone. I feel obliged to talk about it if I go with someone else, and I'm not good at discussing performances. It's much too personal. You understand what's wrong with a performance, but how do you make somebody else understand? For the same reason, I find it difficult to try to study acting. When I tried studying acting with some New York teachers, I found I was being encouraged in bad habits, encouraged to indulge myself. Although it sounds egotistical, I really feel that I can learn more on my own. I'm fascinated by people. I understand people, and it gives me great satisfaction, in acting, to use what I know about them. It's always been easier for me to see what other people are like than to see what I am like myself, so I enjoy the transformation onstage; I completely enjoy becoming another person. What throws me is when another actor isn't playing with me—won't look me in the eye, won't listen, isn't picking up his cues. Once you're onstage, you have to care about getting to the audience. As an actor, I feel that I give an audience some knowledge and information that it might not otherwise receive.

Building a character is for me a long, agonizing procedure. I'm often able to follow through on my initial impulses in filling out the emotional life of the character, discovering what propels him, but then I spend an endless amount of time taking the role apart, figuring out how this person will walk, speak, and dress, and what his gestures will be. It's only after I get a sense of what his emotional life is like that I begin to work on the externals—the voice, the walk, the gestures. Does he talk with his hands, or does he seldom move his hands? Usually, someone who is very inhibited does a lot with his hands. The part of the orderly in "The Death of Bessie Smith" is one of the most difficult I've had to play, because it is terribly underwritten, or seemed so to me. I had to be the one to fill in the gaps, to find reasons for his behavior that were not suggested in the script. There was nothing written about the orderly's background outside the hospital. What I had to go on were stage directions indicating that he is cowardly and frightened. Since many of his lines are interrupted, giving him no chance to finish what he is trying to say, I had to go to work and figure out what he *is* trying to say. At the outset, I read the script over and over again. The most important thing I ultimately found out about the part resulted from the author's going back repeatedly to the fact that the orderly is frightened. But you can't play simple fear or simple weakness; it makes a part dull. So I had to find some way of acting the part. Together with Rae Allen, the actress playing the part of the white nurse, I worked on the idea that the orderly was sexually attracted to her but couldn't ever touch her or say anything openly. Still, he could stare at her body. In that way, I found something to play against. By using the sexual attraction, I was able to show the boy's fear. The description given of the orderly is that he is clean-shaven, trim, and prim—that's all. I had to decide that he is terribly concerned about his appearance; his trousers must be pressed, his nails must be absolutely clean. Onstage in that play, I'd listen intently to the other actors. I wouldn't read a line exactly the same way two nights in a row, or take the same pauses, or have exactly the same reaction to someone else's pause. At the end of a performance, I would usually feel depressed. I don't like curtain calls. If the audience is ecstatic, it reminds me that I am an *actor*. If the audience is stunned or indifferent, it's difficult for me to get out of character. Either way, it's hard to flash a smile and say "It's me."

MICHAEL REDGRAVE

I prefer the fiction and fantasy of acting to the truth,
but I hope I use truth in experiencing fiction and
fantasy on the stage.

I was born on March 20, 1908, in Bristol, England, while my mother
was on tour with some melodrama or other. Both my parents were
actors, and there have been others in my family, going back to the
middle of the nineteenth century. They were, generally speaking,
what we would call "touring actors." Those were the great days of the
touring actor. I was christened at the age of six months in Melbourne,
Australia, where my parents were on tour, acting together in various
melodramas, including "The Sign of the Cross." My mother continued
acting, in supporting roles, until a few years before her death, in
1957. My father, George Ellsworthy Redgrave, who was known professionally as Roy Redgrave, was, I am told, a very fine actor. When I
was two, I was carried onstage in his arms, and that was my first
stage appearance. A year later, my parents separated and my mother
took me back to England. My father stayed on in Australia, and I
never saw him again. On the boat going back, my mother met a rich
tea and rubber planter, whom, years later, she married. I tagged around
with my mother, living in various theatrical lodgings or with various
relatives, and since I didn't know what a home was, I didn't miss
having one. I didn't have a real home till I was nine, when we

moved into a big house in London with my stepfather. He was a very kind man, and I respected him, but we were never closer to each other than we were on the day of my seventeenth birthday, when he said, "You know, you and I don't talk the same language." I was a precocious child in the usual ways: showing off, dressing up, always getting up little plays—all the signs of somebody who ought to act. But I was never stage-struck as a child. The only time I ever felt stage-struck was at the age of thirty-four, when I was an Ordinary Seaman in the Royal Navy on brief leave in New York during the Second World War. Ruth Gordon took me on a theatrical tour of the city. The last night in town, on my own, I paid a dollar for standing room at "The Corn Is Green," with Ethel Barrymore. I had bought an autograph book in Macy's, and I took it backstage and asked Ethel Barrymore to sign her name in it. I had been disappointed in the performance for the first few minutes. Then something happened that does suddenly happen with great performers—you get up on their plane. I thought she was marvellous, and I was stage-struck. It may have been because, for the first time in my life, I felt *outside* the theatre. I was a successful actor, but all that was behind me. There was a war on, I was in an Ordinary Seaman's uniform, and I was stage-struck.

My stepfather sent me to Clifton College, where I played in the "School play" each summer and in the "House play" each Christmas— and wrote one of the House plays myself. From fourteen onward, I was playing everything from Lady Macbeth to Captains Absolute and Brassbound. Whenever it was possible to get up an amateur production, I'd do it. Though I was born into the professional theatre—there were members of the family acting for much longer than anyone now living can remember—I didn't, as they say, "turn pro" until I was twenty-six. My mother didn't encourage me to think about acting as a profession. More than once she told me, "It's no life for a man unless you're very successful at it and unless you intend to give something *to* it, unlike most people, who just want to get something *out* of it." At the age of sixteen, I grew two inches in one term—almost to my full height, six feet two and a half—and that was another reason my mother discouraged me. I outgrew my own strength. I'd tire easily. I have a very good constitution, and I look younger than my age, but I still tire more than I'd like to. I always go to bed for a little while at some time in the afternoon or early evening. I think every actor should do that, even if he only lies down on the floor for twenty minutes and shuts his eyes. Physical vitality is something you have to conserve if you're to be at the top of your form when the curtain goes up. I was a very slow student, but I scraped into Cambridge, where I did a good deal of acting and writing. I wrote stories; I was a drama critic and a film critic; I edited the *Cambridge Review,* and I started a literary magazine that kept alive for two years; I wrote poems. When I left, I fancied myself as someone who might work in a publishing house, but my only commercial asset was my university honors degree in modern languages and English literature. I decided to take up tutoring, and, to get away from home, applied for a job in a grammar school in North London. I wrote for a testimonial to a man who had been a master at Clifton and was now the headmaster of Cranleigh, a public school, and he wrote back asking me why I didn't come there instead. I told him I didn't intend to be a teacher. He suggested that I try it for two terms. I did, and stayed three years. I produced and designed all the school plays and acted in them, having a wonderful time with such plays as "King Lear," "Hamlet," "As You Like It," and "Samson Agonistes." I enjoyed teaching, enjoyed sometimes catching the imagination of my students, but I was bad at what we call the donkeywork. One day, I took my French class to London to see a French repertory company, La Compagnie des Quinze, do "Noah" and other plays. Suddenly I had a revelation. I understood, for the first time, what it was like to be a member of a repertory company, without big stars but with a general style of acting. After seeing this company, and the way its members worked together all the time, I could see how the repertory company was much bigger than the sum of its parts. I decided that I wanted to become a director. I immediately determined to leave Cranleigh, and I gave notice. I wrote to the Old Vic, and had an audition. When, after a long wait, I had not yet received any contract, I wrote to the Liverpool Repertory Theatre, one of the best companies of its kind in the country, and asked for an interview, and on my way to take the night train to Liverpool, I stopped off at my mother's house and found a contract from the Old Vic. In Liverpool, the director and producer of the repertory company, William Armstrong, a Scot and a wonderful man, said he had no room for me but told me not to give up hope. He would "let me know." I brought the Old Vic contract tentatively out of my pocket. "When will you be able to let me know, Mr. Armstrong? You see, I have to let the Old Vic know." He was astounded. "How much are they offering you?" "Three pounds a week." "I'll give you four," he said, and I returned to my schoolmastering by another night train. I was blissful, but it did occur to me later that had I lied to him and said seven pounds a week, he might have said eight. Anyway, after three months I was playing leading parts and he put my salary up to six. At the end of my first season, I met Rachel Kempson, who came to us from Stratford as our new leading lady. Ten days later, we became engaged. Her father was headmaster of the Royal Naval College, Dartmouth, and we were married in the chapel there.

I made my first professional appearance on August 30, 1934, playing a small role, that of Roy Darwin, a smooth New York operator, in "Counsellor-at-Law," and spent two years with the Liverpool Repertory Theatre. I was an ambitious, arrogant, conceited young man. I wanted to play everything. I took it for granted that people should offer me everything. And everything began to come so easily to me I took it for granted that it would go on that way. Actually, I've never been out of work except deliberately, for a holiday, since I started. While I was playing in Liverpool, Tyrone Guthrie offered me a contract for the 1936–37 season with the Old Vic, where I played Mr. Horner in "The Country Wife." I found myself playing with Edith Evans, Ruth Gordon, and an all-star cast—Laurence Olivier was to join the company later—that was destined for New York. I was invited to go to New York with the company, but Edith Evans was staying in London to play in "As You Like It" at the Old Vic. She said to me, "You don't want to go to New York. Wouldn't you sooner stay here and play Orlando in 'As You Like It'?" There was not a moment's doubt in my mind that I wanted to play Orlando to Edith Evans' Rosalind. She had only to look at me. Odd that my eldest daughter, Vanessa, is at present performing in London as Rosalind. I have two other children, Corin William—named after two minor characters in "As You Like It"—and Lynn Rachel. All three of my children intend to work in the theatre. I was more influenced by Edith Evans than by any other performer. I was very much in awe of her. She asked me, "What kind of actor do you want to be?" I was taken aback by the question. Then she asked, "Do you want to be like Johnny? Do you want to be like Larry? *What sort* of career do you want to have?"

Suddenly I realized that she was suggesting that—if I put thought, passion, and labor into it—I might indeed *be* like Gielgud or Olivier.

For me, Edith Evans has the authentic magic. Claptrap word though "magic" may be, it's the only word for the stage. When she comes onstage, the stage lights up. She's a very strict person about her own profession and is without any of the nonsense. She's a real and dedicated artist. Her art is her life. Everything she does on the stage is interpreted through her own morality. It's the way Picasso paints. It's the way Beethoven composed. It's the thing the great artist has that makes him different from other people. I don't mean morality in a pettifogging way. I mean moral values, without which nothing is achieved and nothing is created. Part of it is caring enough about what you do to achieve something beyond the mundane. One reason for the great influence Edith Evans has had on me is that she accepted me in the early phase of my career. Until you act the great parts in theatre literature, you really don't know what acting is. Orlando for me was a great part. I was twenty-eight. Edith Evans was forty-eight. I had been married about a year, and Rachel and I had just had our first child. But none of that seemed to have anything to do with my special life on the stage as Orlando. We played for something like five weeks in repertory, and then we took the play to the West End and played it for three months, which was pretty good for a Shakespeare run. Acting with Edith Evans was heaven. It was like being in your mother's arms, like knowing how to swim, like riding a bicycle. You're safe. The late Michael Chekhov said once that there are three ways to act: for yourself, for the audience, and to your partner. Some of the newer theorists say if it's true for yourself, it's truthful, which is not so. The majority of actors act for themselves or for the audience. I believe that the only way to act is to your partner. As a partner, Edith Evans was like a great conductor who allows a soloist as much latitude as is needed but always keeps everything strict. Strict but free. Never is anything too set, too rigid. The stage relationship always leaves enough room to improvise. For the first time in my life, acting in "As You Like It," I felt completely free. For the first time, I felt completely unself-conscious. Acting with her made me feel, Oh, it's so easy! You don't start acting, she told me, until you stop *trying* to act. It doesn't leave the ground until you don't have to think about it. The play and our stage relationship in it always had the same shape. It was entirely well proportioned, and yet in many respects it was all fluid. In the forest scenes between Orlando and Rosalind, she would encourage me to do almost anything that came into my head. Yet if I had done anything excessive, she would have stopped it by the simplest means. Somehow it didn't occur to me to do anything excessive. For the first time anywhere, onstage or off, I felt completely free.

The second great influence on my acting life was Stanislavski's book "An Actor Prepares." I had read "My Life in Art" and thought it was all very fine but a little fancy. Then I read his other book, and for the next six months I was terrifically upset by it. Edith Evans won't have anything to do with theory, of course. Everything she does, she does naturally. Stanislavski himself would have said, I'm sure, that he wasn't teaching anything new—only a codification of what all good actors did instinctively, without having to think. So many people who talk about Stanislavski don't understand him at all. What I got wrong at first was to think that you should take him literally, by the letter, when you must take him by the alphabet. You've got to soak yourself in it.

Michel Saint-Denis, director of La Compagnie des Quinze, was another very strong influence on me, beginning with the first time I saw his repertory company, when I was still a schoolmaster. He is one of my heroes. In 1937, I joined John Gielgud's company at the Queen's Theatre and played Bolingbroke in "Richard II," and in the same season I played Charles Surface in "The School for Scandal" and also Baron Tusenbach in "The Three Sisters," with Gielgud, Peggy Ashcroft, and Alec Guinness. It was directed by Saint-Denis. He was, and still is, a great director. Of all the directors I've ever worked with, he is the one who best understands the style inherent in any good play. There's a style for Shakespeare and a style for Chekhov, and Saint-Denis has a sense of this. When Gielgud, who had cast me as Andrei, came to me and said he was sorry but Saint-Denis didn't see me as Andrei and wanted me to play Baron Tusenbach, I was abashed. After three days of rehearsals, Saint-Denis said, "I don't know how well you know the character of Baron Tusenbach, but he is without any personality, and yet you seem to be trying to make him have personality." I said, "But surely an actor must try just that." But he said no, the whole point was that this man doesn't make much sense when he talks. "Nobody listens to him," he said. I was so dismayed that I just mumbled the part, and Saint-Denis immediately said, "That's it. That's the way this man should talk." When Saint-Denis formed a new repertory company, at the Phoenix—with a nucleus from the Gielgud group—I continued working with him for a season, and my cup of happiness was full. He took the most scrupulous care with everything he did. I had utter belief in his judgment. I believed in him the way a man believes in his priest or psychiatrist. I revered him. I still do.

We had something very special when we were doing "The Three Sisters." I felt, We don't have to worry, we have something beautiful here, and if the audience doesn't like it, that's just too bad. For the audience. I've felt nearly the same thing since, but not often. It's the kind of feeling you get when everything comes together perfectly. That does happen, you know, but mostly in permanent companies. I'm sure it happened with the Moscow Art Theatre, the Abbey Theatre at its height, the Théâtre National Populaire. At Stratford, one achieves it in one or two productions during the season. I'm sure Joan Littlewood had it occasionally in her Theatre Workshop. I made my first movie at this time, during the day, while acting in "The Three Sisters" at night. I didn't take to movie-making at first, though I love it now. At the time, I signed for pictures reluctantly, with Gainsborough Pictures. The pay was tempting. Nobody prepared me in the beginning for the horrors of picture-making. Nobody explained it to me. I think I got the contract by doing a test for which I didn't give a damn. I was playing with this wonderful galaxy at night and let everyone know it during the day. Naturally, Alfred Hitchcock, the director of the picture—it was "The Lady Vanishes"—did everything to take me down a peg. My second picture, "Stolen Life," was with Elisabeth Bergner, a great actress and one I adored, and although the picture was not very good, I enjoyed making it. The director, Paul Czinner, told me that films could do something special that stage acting could not; there was a spontaneity that the camera could catch when you were first feeling your way in a part, before it became too polished. On the stage, one would work for weeks to achieve a certain thing, but the movie camera could catch something early that was more effective on the screen than the polished thing. One of the movies I enjoyed doing most was "Dead of Night." I also enjoyed "The Browning Version" and "The Dam Busters," and there have been a number of others that have caught my imagination. But I confess that many of the pictures I have made I have accepted because the money they brought me helped me to choose in the theatre only the parts I liked. "Dead of Night" is the one of the films that many people, oddly enough, seem to remember me for. I played the role of a mad ventriloquist. The director of my sequence in the film was Alberto Cavalcanti, and something happened, the kind of thing that happens when a particular actor meets a particular director who excites his invention in a particular part and works with him on a give-and-take basis. Perhaps it's too easy an answer, but I've always believed to a certain degree that the effectiveness of a film part depends on whether you can say in one sentence, or on a postcard, what the part is. For example, about my part in "Dead of Night" you can say, "It's about a ventriloquist who believes his life is controlled by his dummy." And everyone then is able to say "Ah!" I don't think you can describe Hamlet on a postcard. A film has a more immediate impact than a stage play, which is not necessarily an advantage for the actor. Hamlet leaves a deeper impression on you when played on the stage than any role I can think of in a film. There are differences in the satisfaction I get in acting in the two mediums. Some of the most exciting moments in the theatre come in rehearsals, when you're first discovering or exploring a part. The camera can catch these early moments on film. But in the theatre you go on for several weeks making natural each time what would otherwise become stale. During rehearsals, you find the little truths, and as time goes on, you can work to enlarge your part without making it seem enlarged. I made two films in Hollywood in 1947—"Mourning Becomes Electra," which didn't come off as a story told through a lens and "Secret Beyond the Door," directed by Fritz Lang. Hollywood was all right for three months, but when I stayed on to make the second picture, I couldn't take the publicity, the status symbols, and all that foolishness.

Every part is different, and every new part demands new and fresh consideration. I try to beware of the overly intellectual thing in approaching a part. Some parts I feel I can get in a flash. That's when it's most dangerous. Every good actor knows immediately whether a part is sympathetic or not. But I'm very scared of parts in which I give a good first reading. I think I have a quickish intelligence, but it's dangerous to go on a radio actor's intelligence, which is the knack of giving a good first reading of a part. Nevertheless, some of these parts have turned out to be the best things I've done; others I didn't get right until I had tried them in several ways. When I first saw the Graham Greene play "The Complaisant Lover" in London, where the part I took on for the Broadway production was played by another actor, I didn't take to the play or the character. Then, after I'd read it, I was attracted to it and I said I'd do it. The character is a dentist, an extrovert, and a farceur who plays practical jokes. I am not notably either an extrovert or a farceur, and I don't like practical jokes, so I had to get to work and work hard in a special way on that one. I asked my own dentist quite a lot, and I bought a dental-association tie and wore it in the play. I found out how much money dentists make, on the average, because in preparing for any role I investigate the character through the method of social realism. One must be aware of the financial pressures on that kind of character. I tried to determine such things as whether the dentist in the play could afford to have his own wine cellar, which he can't, or whether he would send out for wine. Then, for some reason, I thought he should have a mustache, and because I couldn't think of any dentist I knew who had a mustache, I asked about until a dental technician told me she knew one. So I had a mustache made to wear. Later, I decided I would not wear a mustache. In any case, I wouldn't grow one. Then I changed my mind again. I'm the sort of actor who is helped by a bit of disguise. Paradoxically, a bit of disguise can help to show that aspect of yourself which is essential to the part. Like a lens. I don't like to wear my stage personality all day. It should be something you look forward to assuming in the evening. There have been times when my parts affected me in my real life, but I discovered that it's bad for the part when that happens. Mostly, it happened some years ago, when I misinterpreted Stanislavski and thought it a good idea to *live* the part. Now I never play a part for more than eight or nine months, because I want to prevent it from affecting me too strongly.

It's important to have failures as well as successes as an actor. The theatre is commercially tied to success. Therefore, to be able to perform, the actor must be in successes, and that leads him to pursue a false ambition. I've made films sometimes to have money in the bank. One hopes, of course, to give one's best to everything, and turning a sow's ear into a silk purse is not such a bad proverb to go by, but the truth is that not all plays or films inspire you to the same degree, and the imagination is not liberated in the same way. What inspires me is belief, of one kind or another—and I don't mean just theatrical belief, because actors have to make believe. Even in melodrama, there has to be some reality. It may have a false premise, but it must proceed logically outward toward truth.

If I couldn't act, I'd like to be a writer first of all. I could *just* be a writer, but a mediocre one. I've written three plays. I'm no great shakes as a playwright, but my first play, "The Seventh Man," a one-acter about Arctic whalers in the eighteen-nineties, written in three days when I was with the Liverpool Repertory, is still performed. My second was a children's play, and my third—a good play, I think—is an adaptation of Henry James's "The Aspern Papers," which I directed in London. There are Sunday painters. I'm a Sunday writer. In acting, however, a mood, an emotion, an idea, or a theory can be conveyed more quickly, more succinctly, with more immediacy, than in any other art. That's the peculiar advantage the actor has. Acting is the most immediate art of all. The audience is either caught up entirely or not; it's now or nothing.

BEN GAZZARA

Actors have eyes and ears. We know we are on the stage; we see the curtain go up; we see the audience out there. But once in a while, if we are lucky, we get lost, for a few moments, in the part we are playing, and then we can reach the heights.

I was born on August 28, 1930, in New York City. My real name is Biagio Anthony Gazzara, but my family always called me Ben, or Bennie. My mother is the youngest of ten children of a Sicilian family named Cusumano. Her brother Mike migrated to America in 1900 and had brought all but one of his brothers and sisters over here by 1903. He eventually opened a bar called Mike's, at Second Avenue and Thirty-ninth Street. This was a neighborhood full of Italian immigrants, and it was where the family settled and where my parents met. I have one brother, Anthony, who is five years older than I am, and who works as an executive at the New York Athletic Club. My mother was forty-five when I was born. My father, himself one of twelve children, was a moody man who drank a lot. He worked at bricklaying, carpentry, and other skilled jobs. We moved frequently, from one cold-water flat to another, but we always stayed in the same neighborhood. Between the Gazzaras and the Cusumanos, there were over two hundred members of our family in the neighborhood. We were inclined to hang around with each other. We ate together in one another's houses, drank together, and had parties together, and, of course, there were always funerals and weddings, too. Family or no family, I felt very lonely as a small boy. Then, when I was six, I joined the Madison Square Boys' Club. It was the center of social life for all the kids in the neighborhood, so I went along with the others. I played punch ball and basketball and other games in the gym, and we were shown movies—Laurel and Hardy comedies, and so on. When I was about twelve, some of the boys in the group told me they had joined what was called the drama section of the club. A former actor named Howard Sinclair had charge of the dramatics. My voice had just changed, and was very deep, and apparently the boys told Sinclair about that, because one day when I was playing punch ball in front of the club Sinclair stopped on his way in and asked me if I wanted to be one of seven Arabs in a play he was putting on. At first, I said no, but he persuaded me to give it a try. So I was one of seven Arabs in a play called "The Gods of the Mountain," by Lord Dunsany. All I had to do was wear a sheet and wait around for alms, and then die at the end. It didn't mean much to me, but I nevertheless decided to join the drama section.

A little later, Sinclair, who had become interested in me, cast me in the leading role in Justin Huntly McCarthy's "If I Were King." At rehearsals, he would tell me about his own experiences in the theatre, and I began to dream of becoming an actor. I had found a goal. Also, I began to enjoy the attention I was getting because I was doing the play. I started counting on it. Every day after school, I would wait for seven o'clock, when Sinclair arrived at the club. Sinclair was a very handsome man, with Anglo-Saxon features—different from the Latin faces I was used to. He was tall and lean, with silvery hair and a mustache, and I considered him cultured and strange. Coming to know him was like finding a new father, from another world—a kind of world I had only dreamed about before. His world seemed strange and new and wonderful to me. It was as though I had found a new home. Before I knew it, I was playing the leads in all the plays we put on. It was marvellous to get Sinclair's approval and to feel his enthusiasm.

345

I really began to live on the stage. The theatre stimulated me in a way that was entirely new to me. Sinclair would tell me about actors like Eleonora Duse, Sarah Bernhardt, and Edwin Booth, and I would daydream about putting on makeup and costumes, and hearing the applause. By the time I was fifteen, I had definitely decided to become a professional actor. Whenever I felt doubts, I would tell Sinclair about them, and he would say he was sure that I would have a place in the theatre.

I attended a parochial school—a Carmelite school, Our Lady of the Scapular—in our neighborhood, and then went to Stuyvesant High School. I disliked high school, and after about two years of it I left, without telling anyone at home. I was a truant. I spent the next fifty-six days wandering around New York, going to the movies to see the actors who had become my favorites—Spencer Tracy, Clark Gable, James Cagney, and Edward G. Robinson. In another way, I was also fascinated by John Garfield. He was the first actor I had seen in the movies who felt close enough to my own life to be reachable. Eventually, I told my mother that I had left school, and said I would return to school if I could go to a small uptown coeducational parochial school, where I thought I would feel more at home. So I went to St. Simon Stock, in the Bronx. I still wanted to be an actor, but I felt that I needed an education. When I was sixteen, Sinclair left the club, and my interest in dramatics began to lag. One summer during high school, I worked as a soda jerk at the Whelan's drugstore at the corner of Forty-second Street and Vanderbilt Avenue. Another job I had during high school was running an elevator in the Hotel Shelton, on Thirty-fifth Street. I graduated from high school in 1947.

That fall, I entered C.C.N.Y. night school, with the intention of studying engineering. I had put aside any thought of acting as a way of earning a living. For six months, I worked during the day for a shop on Canal Street as a silver replater and buffer, and was able to bring home twenty dollars a week. Next, I worked in a place that made slipcovers for furniture; my job was to prepare the piping for the slipcovers. At the end of my first year at the night school, a boy who lived in our neighborhood told me about Erwin Piscator's Dramatic Workshop at the New School for Social Research. One night, he took me with him to watch one of the productions of the New School. It happened to be one that Piscator had supervised himself—"The Flies," by Jean-Paul Sartre. I was stunned by the theatricality of what I saw. Piscator believed in the epic style of theatre. I was impressed by his use of music, and his use of film on the stage, and his use of lighting to make a very small stage seem enormous. It was unabashed theatricality. I decided to quit night school and try to join the Workshop. Not having money for tuition, I auditioned for a scholarship. I did a few scenes from "If I Were King," "They Knew What They Wanted," and "Seventh Heaven" for one of the teachers, a man named Raiken Ben-Ari, and I got the scholarship in September, 1948. I stayed there a year and a half. Studying with Ben-Ari, who had come from the Habima Theatre, in Moscow, I was working with a man who himself had worked with Stanislavski and Eugene V. Vakhtangov, and I began to learn that there was a craft of acting. Piscator directed me only once—in "Macbeth," in which I played the part of Malcolm, one of Duncan's sons. Piscator believed that it was the purpose of the theatre to educate. He knew every aspect of the theatre: acting, staging, directing, lighting—everything. About that time, I began to go to Broadway plays, and I began to hear reports of something else in the theatre—a departure from the Piscator school of acting. In 1948 and 1949, the talk in class and everywhere else that students of acting got together was about the newly founded Actors' Studio.

The first play I saw on Broadway was one that astonished me— Tennessee Williams' "The Glass Menagerie," with Laurette Taylor. Her acting impressed me so deeply that I went back to see the play five times. I had no way of knowing it then, but now I realize that I was watching a truly great performance. It was the only great acting I had ever seen until I saw John Gielgud in "The Ages of Man," in 1959. Six months after "The Glass Menagerie" closed, I went to see Williams' "A Streetcar Named Desire." I thought it was the most exciting play I had ever seen. All the performances were good. Kim Hunter's acting impressed me enormously, and Marlon Brando's got me terribly wrought up. I reacted strongly to the raw emotion, the animal vitality, in his acting. I found something new and poetic in all the characters in the play. I had heard at the Dramatic Workshop that Marlon Brando and Kim Hunter had gone to the Actors' Studio, and I decided to audition for it. My first audition, which I passed, was for Daniel Mann. I did some scenes from "Night Music," by Clifford Odets, for my second audition, for Lee Strasberg, Elia Kazan, Cheryl

347

Crawford, and Mann, and I was accepted. Around the same time, I got married to a former child actress named Louise Erickson. We were divorced four years later.

I went to the Actors' Studio regularly for three years, and I still go occasionally. In those years, I don't think I missed a single session. I felt inspired—almost the same way I had felt as a kid with Sinclair. Also, once again, I had a place to go that felt like home. For the first time, I began to see action myself. In 1953, we did Calder Willingham's "End as a Man," first at the Studio and then at the Theatre de Lys, in the Village. I played the lead—Jocko De Paris, a monstrously rebellious student in a horribly discipline-ridden military college in the South. I felt wonderful in my part. I felt wonderful onstage. The play was great, and so were the notices. Then the play was moved uptown to the Vanderbilt Theatre, and I felt that my career had really begun. "End as a Man" ran, altogether, from September, 1953, to January, 1954.

In March, 1955, I opened on Broadway in Tennessee Williams' "Cat on a Hot Tin Roof," in which I played Brick. When we opened in Philadelphia, I felt that the rehearsal period—three and a half weeks—had been too short. I felt that I had only a shell of a performance—that there hadn't been time to produce valid results. During rehearsals, Elia Kazan, the director, and I had worked on the part enough to create certain mannerisms, but I felt that that was all. I wasn't able to analyze what was wrong with my performance, but friends who were in the audience told me I sounded sonorous and inhuman. I started to retrace my steps after the opening in New York, which actually meant I was rehearsing in front of the audience. I stayed with the play for seven months, but I never felt the part as a real experience. My words were measured, vocally precise, and empty. When I was supposed to show anger, it was the vocalization of anger rather than the experience of being angry. Later that year, I got the part of Johnny Pope, a dope addict, in Michael V. Gazzo's "A Hatful of Rain." At that time, if I wasn't crying or hysterical onstage I thought there was no drama to my role. Now I realize that simpler behavior can be more touching. I began to find this out during the run of "A Hatful of Rain." After playing Johnny Pope from November of 1955 to June of 1957, the play closed, and I went to Florida on location to make the movie version of "End as a Man," called "The Strange

One"—my first movie. Then I rejoined "A Hatful of Rain" on the road. Six months later, in Milwaukee, it came to me that even in a part as serious as this one there was room for humor, and that one must be less rigid and look for humanity. My love scenes with Vivian Blaine, who for part of the run played my wife, became more real. The love for the wife is there, even though the man has the dope addiction. I found I could catch the attention of the audience by pleading with her quietly.

The best Broadway part I ever had was in "The Night Circus," in 1958, with Janice Rule, whom I married three years later. I had the part of Joy, a young man who is running away from life. The play lasted for exactly seven performances. In addition to appearing on the stage, I've played leading roles in about twenty television dramas, including "Moony's Kid Don't Cry" and "Body and Soul." I would like to be able to say that television is good training for an actor, but I don't believe it. It doesn't offer an actor enough opportunity to develop. I accept television roles, however, because it's necessary for an actor to keep acting—just as any man has to keep working. When I was offered the role of Lieutenant Manion, the moody young Army officer, in the movie "Anatomy of a Murder," I had many doubts. I walked the streets wondering whether to accept it. The role would be too easy for me, I felt. Like television, it wouldn't give me enough to do, enough to solve. I finally decided to accept it, because I thought it was important for me to be in a successful movie. This one had all the elements of a smash, including Otto Preminger, a popular producer-director, and the big box-office name of James Stewart, and that's what it turned out to be. But its success didn't affect me in any way, because I didn't have enough of the responsibility for carrying the movie. As the star of the show, James Stewart had that responsibility. He is a bankable star, and was counted on to bring in the dollars at the box office, and he did. I had nothing to do with it.

Nothing is pleasanter than doing something successful. But successful acting isn't necessarily good acting. An actor needs success in order to get opportunities to be good, so he concentrates on achieving success, and in the process he may lose whatever it is that has made him good. In the movies, if an actor's success comes when he is just starting, he is in danger of becoming a business expert and a tax expert. If his devotion is to how much his last movie has grossed, he is in danger of stopping, and never developing as an actor. Instead, he may just repeat what won him attention the first time. He loses the desire and the patience and the will to work at his craft, so he ceases to grow as an actor. I feel I'm a much better actor now than I was a few years ago; I find that the more I do, the more colors I can use. When I started, I was locked up, in many areas. I came out rebellious and hostile, which was the way *I* was. Then I found other colors: humor, romantic feelings, and what I call my middle—human—register. I take parts wherever they are. Right after making "Anatomy of a Murder," in 1959, I went to Coral Gables, Florida, and played in "Two for the Seesaw" for two weeks in stock. The following summer, I played the title role in "Epitaph for George Dillon," by John Osborne and Anthony Creighton, all over the summer circuit—the Cape, Westport, Ogunquit—continuing to explore the part in each performance. I feel freer now—more my own master. Even movies are changing; one can be more selective, and one doesn't have to live in Hollywood. I've made only one movie, "Reprieve," in Hollywood. In the summer of 1960, I went to Italy to make "The Passionate Thief," with Anna Magnani and Toto. I played a professional thief who tried to pick the pocket of a rich man on New Year's Eve. Magnani and Toto kept getting in my way and preventing the theft. It was a divertissement after all the heavy roles I had been playing. My next movie—"The Young Doctors"—was made in New York in 1961. I played a young doctor, upstanding and idealistic, in conflict with an older doctor, played by Fredric March. I loved that story. It had a mellow tone, and the conflicts the young doctor underwent were external, for a change, rather than internal.

I married Janice Rule in November, 1961, and we live in a seven-room apartment on Riverside Drive. When I'm not at home and not in the theatre, I like to spend time at P. J. Clarke's bar, nursing a beer. I feel happy when the place gets crowded.

JANICE RULE

When I'm onstage, I usually just want to be quiet, but the audience gets me going. I know the audience is expecting something from me, so I try to live up to it.

I was born on August 15, 1931, in Cincinnati, the fourth of six children. My father, John C. Rule, is a dealer in industrial diamonds, and now lives, with my mother, in Vallejo, California. My parents have always moved restlessly from one place to another. When I was about eight, we moved to a suburb of Chicago called Glen Ellyn. We lived in a white frame house on a quiet street at the edge of town. I shared a room with my sister Kathy, who is one year older than I am. Now she is married, has three children, and lives in Pasadena, California. My sister Anne, two years older than I am, is also married, also has three children, and also lives in Pasadena. My sister Emily, four years younger than I am, is one of twins and is married to Denis Sanders, a movie director in Hollywood, and has two children—not twins. Her twin, Ralph, lives in Seattle and works for a pharmaceutical company. Charles, three years older than I am, and the eldest of us, is married, has one child, and lives in New York except when he is singing in the chorus of touring musicals. He often sings in the choruses of Broadway shows. I was always closer to him than to anybody else in the family. He wanted to become an opera singer, and he taught me to love music. I was raised as Catholic, and as a child I sometimes thought about becoming a nun.

All four of my grandparents lived in Springfield, Missouri, where my parents were born, and when I was a child, I used to visit them every summer. These visits were the happiest time of my life. My parents were never enthusiastic about my becoming an actress. When I was ten, I was more interested in ballet than in anything else in the world. At home, I was forever dancing to records of Strauss waltzes— the only classical, or semi-classical, records we ever had. I went to the movies every Sunday, but I wasn't crazy about them. The only one I went to see more than once was "The Great Waltz," with Luise Rainer; I liked it because it had Johann Strauss music I knew. I was always up on my toes, and my parents liked showing me off to the neighbors. I kept asking to take lessons, and finally, that year when I was ten, started in at a school in Glen Ellyn. It was held in a kind of loft, about eighty feet by forty, and was run by Mme. Sonya Dobrovinskaya, who now teaches in New York, and comes to my opening nights. I took an hour-and-a-half lesson every night, and practiced by myself for half an hour, and also spent about an hour helping teach the younger children. I kept that up for four years. Saturdays, I'd take lessons all day. Mme. Dobrovinskaya used to watch over me like a mother. I always wanted to be like Melissa Hayden, but I was never strong. It was always a great struggle for me to maintain my strength. In my senior year of high school, in Chicago, I studied ballet four hours a day and practiced in between lessons. At first, my paternal grandfather paid for the lessons. My father thought that ballet was frivolous but all right for a girl. My grandfather died when I was fourteen, and then my mother managed to pay for the lessons out of our grocery budget. My brother Charles used to take me to see ballet in Chicago. He'd keep track of everything coming to Chicago on tour, and we'd always be first in line to see Alexandra Danilova or Alicia Markova. Mme. Dobrovinskaya's daughter was dancing in the biggest night club in Chicago, the Chez Paree, and when I was fifteen I got a job dancing there, too. I worked there for several months, at a salary of about fifty dollars a week. I'd get home at three o'clock in the morning. Danny Thomas was playing the club at the same time, and after the late

Saturday-night show we'd go to Mass together. He used to tell me I ought to get out of the night club and go to college. He said he'd send me himself, because the Chez Paree was all wrong for me. But I told him that I wanted to be a dancer and would do anything to stay in dancing. Actually, I hated night-club work. I would come out to do my special toe dance, and the people would take one bored look at me and then turn their backs and start eating and drinking and talking. One night, Monte Proser, one of the producers of the musical "High Button Shoes," came to the Chez Paree and saw me. He offered me a job as a dancer in the chorus of the road company of the show, then in Chicago, and I grabbed it. My salary went up to seventy-five dollars a week, but it wasn't the money that was the important thing. It was being in a musical show, which meant being in a real theatre, with an audience that had come there for the purpose of seeing the show. The company starred Jack Whiting, Audrey Meadows, and Ellen Hanley, and my brother Charles got a job with the company as a singer. After I'd been in the show for a few weeks, Charles took me to see my first play, "A Streetcar Named Desire," with Uta Hagen and Anthony Quinn, at a matinée on a day when we weren't performing in "High Button Shoes." We were both floored by it. It was pretty hard to go back to "High Button Shoes" after that. Shortly afterward, we went to see "Medea," with Judith Anderson, and that was pretty powerful, too. But though I was impressed, I didn't think in terms of doing that kind of thing myself.

Around that time, my parents moved to Antioch, Illinois, so I moved in with a family in Chicago whose daughter I'd known in ballet school. At the same time, I enrolled for my senior year in a professional children's high school—a high school for working children. When I'd been in "High-Button Shoes" for four or five months, the company moved on to Philadelphia, and Charles and I went with it. With my earnings, I bought my first fur coat, a mink-dyed muskrat. We were with the show for four weeks in Philadelphia, and then it closed. Immediately after the last performance, Charles and I took a late train for New York. That was where we both wanted to be—where we wanted to study. I'd been dreaming of studying at George Balanchine's School of American Ballet. I moved into a small room in a small hotel on West Forty-sixth Street and started taking lessons at the School of American Ballet. I was quickly disappointed. It was rigid and cold, with eight or ten teachers, none of whom took any special interest in me. In Glen Ellyn, I had thought of myself as the belle of the school; here everything seemed to be mechanical, and there was no flexibility in the teaching. It was exciting to be in New York, but the excitement was all bottled up inside me; I was wholly involved with myself and what I was doing. The only person in the city I knew besides my brother was Jerome Robbins, the choreographer of "High Button Shoes," whom I had met right after I came to New York, through Monte Proser. I looked him up, and he told me he was planning to do the choreography for another musical, Robert E. Sherwood's and Irving Berlin's "Miss Liberty," and promised to give me a job dancing in it. He suggested that in the meantime I try out for the Copacabana line, and recommended me to the club's dance director. I was hired— one of eight dancers in the line. I was there for about two months, appearing in production numbers. I'd come out in a scanty costume and a very ornate hat, and sort of flow about the stage. You had to know *something* about dancing in order to do it, but it wasn't dancing. After that, I went into rehearsals for "Miss Liberty." One night during the Philadelphia tryout of the show, in a dance number in which I was lifted by three other dancers, one dancer was late in setting me down, and I broke my ankle. I had my ankle in a cast for three weeks and was out of the show for six. I became very restless, and felt I had to do something. A friend suggested that I use the time to study acting with a teacher named William Hanson, who gave lessons in his apartment. I still hadn't thought much about acting. In those days, it seemed sort of immoral to me to be glamorous. Compared to ballet, acting seemed highly undisciplined and very frivolous. I kept on with the lessons just to be doing something. When my ankle was better and I rejoined the show, I continued to study acting. I wasn't exactly inspired, but I wanted to be prepared to try it if the dancing didn't work out. After seven months in "Miss Liberty," I became a member of the chorus of the musical show "Great to Be Alive!" and was also understudy to Bambi Linn. A little later, I was offered a seven-year movie contract, with options, with Warner Brothers. I had been making seventy-five dollars a week in the chorus, and under my Hollywood contract I started making five hundred dollars a week. It was as simple as that.

I arrived in Hollywood one morning in the fall of 1950, and my agent met me at the airport. That afternoon, he took me over to the lot and introduced me to two of the Warner brothers and to other executives and some of the writers. We got off to a friendly start. I moved into a one-room apartment in Burbank, right near the studio, and then I reported for work on my first movie, "Goodbye, My Fancy," in which I played a college student, the young daughter of a college president, played by Robert Young. A congresswoman, played by Joan Crawford, returns to the college, her Alma Mater, to take additional courses and renew her acquaintance with Robert Young. That first day, I began to feel uneasy. It suddenly occurred to me that I had never *acted* before. The director, Vincent Sherman, asked me to start crying. Well, I had never cried in front of anyone in my entire life. It was part of my upbringing not to do a thing like that. The director kept saying, "*Start crying, start crying,*" and I couldn't. I kept saying, "I can't do it." It went on this way for a while, and suddenly I did start crying. The director said, "That's it, that's what I want. Let's shoot it." That's the way I became an actress. When the movie was finished and I saw it, I thought I came out looking terrible. When I first arrived in Hollywood, everybody said about me, "She's pretty, but can she *act?*" After the picture came out, everyone said, "She looks terrible, but she *can* act." I now adore seeing movies, but I've never been in a good one myself or felt I did anything good in the ones I have been in.

I appeared in "Starlift" for Warner Brothers, then broke my contract and signed with M-G-M, for which I made "Holiday for Sinners," with Gig Young and Keenan Wynn, and "Rogue's March," with Peter Lawford. On the whole, I found that life in Hollywood was deadly boring. Everyone in the community was involved in the motion-picture industry. No matter how a conversation started out, it eventually got around to the subject of picture grosses. The only good thing about my life in Hollywood was a little-theatre group I heard about, headed by Arthur Kennedy. I went around there, and started studying with Michael Chekhov, the actor and teacher. Everything I learned was elementary—how to attack a scene, and things like that—but it all deepened my interest in and respect for acting as a profession. In 1952, on vacation from the studio, I came to New York, and was sent by an agent to see Richard Rodgers, who was getting ready to start rehearsals for his musical "Me and Juliet." I told him that I was hung up in

Hollywood, that it was disastrous for a young person, that I'd gone out there not really wanting to go, and that I was miserable there. Rodgers talked to one of the Metro executives and got the studio to let me break my contract. I felt as though I'd been freed from jail. Rodgers hoped I might work out in a part in "Me and Juliet." He sent me to a voice teacher, and I tried to work on my singing, but I didn't think I was making much progress. Then Rodgers sent me over to meet Joshua Logan, who was holding readings for "Picnic," by William Inge, which he was producing with the Theatre Guild and was scheduled to direct. I didn't know anything about anything in those days. I had no Broadway show-business friends, except for Jerome Robbins and Rodgers, who has always been very kind and fatherly to young people. Logan gave me the script of the play and I looked it over that night, and the next afternoon I read for the part of Madge Owens before Logan, Inge, and some Theatre Guild people. That same day, Logan told me the part was mine. Then he told me that before I read for him, he hadn't planned to go ahead with the play, because he couldn't find the actress to play the part, but that after I'd read he could "see" the character of the girl. Then Kim Stanley came on and read for the part of Millie Owens, the kid sister, who was supposed to be fourteen. I'd never seen her before. She came on looking much too old for the part—she was almost twenty-eight—but after one reading I knew she was perfect. We hit it off from the very start. I felt her strength.

I didn't really like "Picnic" after the first reading, yet something about it attracted me. There was something Inge was saying about pretty girls that hit home. It was that most people treat pretty girls as pretty girls and nothing else—as though nothing could be wrong if a girl was pretty, so she had no right to be miserable. The play ran for four hundred and seventy-seven performances, and I was with it almost all the way. Every day, it seemed, gave me some further revelation about acting. At that time, I was a beginner. Today I can think of things I did in the play that I had to work so hard for then, and I realize that they'd be easy for me now. There was a kind of frantic grabbing at anything—at some memory of something, perhaps—that might give me the feeling I needed for the part. Now I know how to build a part in a more stable way. I discovered that acting enabled me to do things that I could never do through dancing. Acting gave me an opportunity to develop empathy. I was—and still am—inarticulate in my real life. A pretended life, I discovered, could be much deeper than a real life. I really began to live in my acting. There was a long stretch in the run of "Picnic" when I played the whole thing off Kim Stanley. She was the first person I'd ever acted with who made me feel that acting was a dignified profession. I began to respect what I was doing. After the play had been running for a few months, most of the actors in the cast had gone pretty dead, but not Kim. She's a very alive person on the stage. You know she's alive to whatever you do. Acting with Kim is like going into a room full of people and finding one person you have a feeling of rapport with. At one point in the play, I said to Peggy Conklin, who played my mother, "It's not enough to be pretty." It was hard for an audience to sympathize with a girl whose only problem was that she was the prettiest girl in town. I felt that the audience wasn't with me. But Kim and I believed that these two sisters were very vulnerable to each other. Kim helped me to develop in a rounded fashion what the two sisters felt for each other. Just in chatting with her about the characters, I began to understand what the sisters might have been like *off* the stage. We worked out what kind of things they would have liked and disliked, and what would have amused them. Kim's lines were right for her. Every time she spoke to me onstage, the audience would laugh at me derisively. I felt in the beginning that the character I played was being hurt by her gibes. I wanted the audience to feel sympathy for me, and like me, so I drew on things inside myself to make it seem that the older sister felt inferior in some way but was inarticulate—was hurt by the younger sister but was unable to defend herself. Kim was the only one in the whole play who understood what I was trying to do, and she played along with it. It made her part even better. And after a while the audience stopped laughing at me.

When "Picnic" closed, in 1954, I felt somewhat lost. I went up to Maine for a rest, but I couldn't stand the quiet. I couldn't unwind that quickly, and had to come down to Boston. My next play was "The Flowering Peach," by Clifford Odets, based on the story of Noah's Ark, in which I played Rachael. After that, I was in "The Carefree Tree," a Chinese play about peace, by Aldyth Morris, at the Phoenix Theatre. It was a flop, but I thought it was very sweet. Then I went down to Acapulco and made a film, "A Woman's Devotion," with Ralph

Meeker, for Republic, and not long after that I made another film, "Gun for a Coward," with Fred MacMurray. I read a lot of plays, and in the summer of 1957 I played the leads in "Bus Stop" and "Ondine" at the Olney Theatre, in Olney, Maryland. Following that, I did a great deal of television—one show after another. Late in 1958, I appeared on Broadway in Michael V. Gazzo's "The Night Circus," with Ben Gazzara, whom I married in 1961. I have two small daughters—Kate and Elizabeth—by a previous marriage, to the writer Robert Thom.

It gives me marvellous satisfaction to make an audience react to a situation as if it were real. Then I feel wildly alive. And you have the advantage of knowing that you can drop that life if you don't happen to like it. What is most difficult for me is playing myself. When a director says to me, "You are everything this character is, just be yourself," and I try to do it, I feel I'm exposing every part of myself. Sometimes I find myself thinking how wonderful it would be to be a salesgirl and have the peace of knowing exactly what you would be doing day after day. Actually, though, being a salesgirl would be deadly for me. What really interests me is the essence of life, rather than life itself. I would rather live at a heightened level than have to live the dull, commonplace life of the average person, and onstage I can do just that.

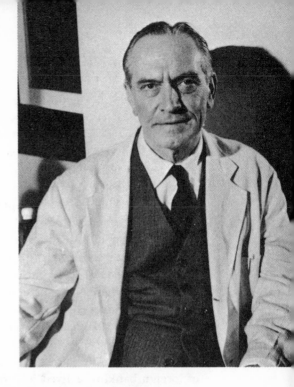

FREDRIC MARCH

I do the things the guy who wrote the play has written.
A writer should write. An actor should act.

I was born on August 31, 1897, in Racine, Wisconsin. My father was in the wholesale hardware business, and he was a very devout Presbyterian Church elder. My mother, whose maiden name was Marcher, was a schoolteacher. My real name is Frederick McIntyre Bickel. I was the youngest of three brothers; one of my brothers is now dead, and the other, John M. Bickel, is a retired vice-president of the Carrier Air Conditioning Company. Jack gives wonderful talks before Rotary Clubs—something I could never do. My father used to tell us stories when we were little boys, and he played a marvellous Santa Claus at church socials. The very first time I appeared on a stage was when I was eight and played a little page in a church festival. After that, I gave poetry recitations at church and in grade school. For some reason, I favored a poem called "Poor Little Mose." I went in for oratory at my high school in Racine, and won the Wisconsin State Oratorical Contest in 1915 with, God help me, a speech by Henry Grattan. When I was about ten, my father took me and my brothers to see Maude Adams in "Peter Pan" when the touring company came to Racine. Also, I always used my dimes to go to see stock-company productions and vaudeville shows with other kids. I saw plays like "Wedded but No Wife" and "My Partner." I had a natural desire to get up and be seen and to show off, but I never thought of myself at that time as a potential actor. However, in 1916, when I went to the University of Wisconsin, where I majored in commerce, I began to take part in amateur theatricals. I spent a couple of summers working in the Manufacturers Trust Bank in Racine, intending to become a full-fledged banker someday.

In the spring of 1918, I left college to join the Army. After a three-month training course, I was commissioned a lieutenant in the artillery, and for the last few months of the First World War I was stationed at Fort Sill, where I taught equestrianism. After nine or ten months of service, I returned to the university, and I graduated in 1920. In the summer of 1919, I had worked for the National City Bank in New York. Then, in 1920, I was sent to take a one-year training course, with about thirty-five other guys, for the National City Bank's program of foreign banking. I lived in a rooming house in Brooklyn run by a sweet old landlady, an ex-vaudeville actress, who was nutty about actors and was always talking about acting. She said I should become an actor. Before the training course was two months old, I had an emergency appendicitis operation. I went under the ether thinking that I wanted to go on the stage. When I came out of the hospital, I asked the bank for a year's leave of absence, notified my family of what I was going to try to do, and started making the rounds of casting offices. I still go to the annual picnics held by my old bank pals at the Sleepy Hollow Country Club, in Tarrytown, New York. The big joke every year is "When is Bickel coming back?" At any rate, as an aspiring actor, I beat the pavements, posed as a model for Charles Dana Gibson, Neysa McMein, and others, and worked as an extra in a movie, called "Pay the Piper," with Dorothy Dickson, that was being made in Astoria. I also found an agent. Then I played for one day in the movie "The Great Adventure," with Lionel Barrymore, again as an extra, for seven dollars and fifty cents, seventy-five cents of which, of course, went to my agent. I then took lessons with Mme. Eva Alberti, a great teacher of acting, who had taught at the American Academy of Dramatic Arts. She'd make me do life studies—imitations of people I'd seen in subways, for example—and she called me "son." She'd say to me, "The world is your workshop, son." Everything she told me came as a revelation. She once told me, "Son, if you don't come off the stage feeling you want to go right back on again and do it better, there's something wrong."

I made my first professional appearance, as Fred Bickel, in December of 1920, playing the two-line part of the Prompter in the David Belasco production of Granville Barker's adaptation of Sacha Guitry's "Deburau." I also understudied the juvenile lead, which I got to play for one week. Then, as Frederick Bickel, I played a good part, in "The Law Breaker," by Jules Eckert Goodman. In 1922, I went to Dayton, Ohio, for a season of stock—twenty-two weeks, and a different play each week. I didn't know how to relax when I acted in those days, but even so acting wasn't difficult for me, because I was playing young men my own age. I have found out since that relaxation is the prime requisite for acting. In those early days, I'd lock myself in my bedroom and read my lines, getting the feeling and outlining the feeling for myself. I'd been pretty good at memorizing ever since I was a kid. And I suppose I did just naturally a lot of what the Method people talk about so much today—digging into your own past for clues to characterization. In 1924, when I was appearing in Chicago and throughout the Midwest in a play called "Tarnish," with Patricia Collinge, I changed my name, because I found out there was a pretty well-known German comedian named Bickel.

In 1926, I met the actress Florence Eldridge, who had just played Daisy Fay in "The Great Gatsby," and we were married the following year. In 1927 and 1928, as a general-utility actor, I toured for the Theatre Guild, playing supporting and minor roles in "Arms and the Man," "The Guardsman," "Mr. Pim Passes By," and "The Silver Cord." I was doing what I wanted to do. One of my first big leads on the West Coast was the role of Anthony Cavendish—the John Barrymore character—in "The Royal Family," both on the stage and in the movie, which was called "The Royal Family of Broadway." The experience was a tremendous one for me, and the effect on me of the character I played was very powerful. For a while, it was hard to break away from it. While I was in the play, my wife used to tell me I was being John Barrymore around the house. Ordinarily, the character doesn't really take you over. When the curtain comes down on a play, that's it.

There's so much mumbo-jumbo about acting. Spencer Tracy, one of the finest actors of our time, once told me, "I just learn my lines." Laurette Taylor really explained the way it is for actresses when she told me, "I just pretend." Little girls, particularly, know what it's all about. They do Method acting naturally. Some of the best actors are the ones who aren't too crazy about it. Jack and Lionel Barrymore didn't like it. They used to say they didn't respect it. Lionel did etching and composing, and Jack was originally a caricaturist, and they enjoyed doing those things more than acting. Lionel used to tell me, "All you do is listen to the other fella and then you answer him." Another time, he told me, "You sit on a hot stove, you burn your behind, you jump up." The Barrymores didn't think about it too much. They just did it. Another one like that is Spencer. I'm nuts about Spencer. Working with him in anything is always a real joy. I think I'm a ham who likes to act in whatever there's a chance to act in. Live television is the hardest acting to do. Tape is less frightening. I don't have too many years left in my life, and I like to travel, and I'd rather do a picture and get it over with than do a play. From November, 1956, to March, 1958, my wife and I played in Eugene O'Neill's "Long Day's Journey Into Night," and that was too long. I've made close to seventy pictures, beginning with "The Dummy," in 1929, and including "Jealousy," "Footlights and Fools," "Ladies Love Brutes," "Paramount on Parade," "True to the Navy," "Manslaughter," "Dr. Jekyll and Mr. Hyde," "The Marriage Playground," "Smilin' Through," "The Sign of the Cross," "The Eagle and the Hawk," "Design for Living," "Death Takes a Holiday," "The Barretts of Wimpole Street," "Les Miserables," "Anna Karenina," "Anthony Adverse," "A Star Is Born," "Nothing Sacred," "The Buccaneer," "Susan and God," "Bedtime Story," "The Best Years of Our Lives," "Death of a Salesman," "Executive Suite," "Alexander the Great," "The Man in the Gray Flannel Suit," "Middle of the Night," "Inherit the Wind," and "The Young Doctors." I never watch my own movies on television. I don't like to stay up late, for one thing, and, for another, I'd find it depressing. I learned about the importance of relaxation when I started making pictures. The director of "The Marriage Playground," Lothar Mendes, was the first person to mention it to me. He said, "Freddie, when I say 'Camera,' all it means is—relax." When you are watching a play, the actor on the stage you go along with is the one who's most relaxed. Some of us older actors are very much inclined to tense up.

Younger actors, the ones devoted to the Method, have the ability to relax. It's a terribly important element.

What I enjoy is working on a scene until I finally get it right. It's fun to know you're hitting it. There are advantages in being in a long run. You should see plays after they've been around for a while if you want to see the best performances. It's the relaxation again. The actors are more relaxed in their parts. When I first consider a part, I find myself judging the play as a whole. Simultaneously, I try to decide whether I can play the part, whether it's dramatically interesting, whether I feel I can make it make sense. It's a mistake, I think, to go for parts, as some actors do, instead of for the play as a whole. I'll never do a part in a play or a picture that makes me lose my self-respect. Two of the best plays I've been in—both with my wife—are, I feel, "Long Day's Journey Into Night" and Thornton Wilder's "The Skin of Our Teeth," and the best movies are "The Best Years of Our Lives," "A Star Is Born," "Dr. Jekyll and Mr. Hyde," and "Death Takes a Holiday." In a way, though, I've liked everything I've been in. I'm kind of a dimwit. I just like to act.

ANGELA LANSBURY

*When I'm onstage, I often think, What the hell am
I doing here? I realize that I want to go home.*

I was born on October 16, 1925, in London. My father, Edgar Lansbury, who was a lumber merchant, died when I was nine. My mother,
the actress Moyna MacGill, had earlier been married to Reginald
Denham, the actor and producer, and I have a stepsister, Isolde, four
years older than I am. We used to put on dances and imitations together for the family. My mother now lives in Hollywood and does
quite a bit of acting on television. She's a far more ambitious actress
than I am. She wanted me to become an actress, but she could never
by any stretch of the imagination be called a stage mother. Her best
period as an actress was in the early twenties, when she succeeded
Madge Titheradge as Desdemona to Basil Rathbone's Iago in
"Othello," in London. She played Lady Brockhurst in Sandy Wilson's
"The Boy Friend" in the 1954 Broadway production. I have two
younger brothers—identical twins. Edgar Lansbury, who lives in
Weston, Connecticut, has designed scenery for the stage and is now
producing an Off Broadway play. Bruce Lansbury lives in Hollywood
and is a production executive at C.B.S. and is writing a play. Both

are married and have children. One of my grandfathers, George Lansbury, was a famous politician of the twenties and thirties; he was leader of the Labour Party—the Opposition—from 1931 to 1935. As a child, I was taken to large political rallies. When my grandfather spoke at the Albert Hall, I would stand, along with several thousand other people, and sing "Jerusalem." It was awe-inspiring. As a little girl, I thought I might become a politician. My grandfather was a strong supporter of women's suffrage. One of the first bits of acting I did, when I was seven or eight, was an imitation of what I thought women's-suffrage leaders must be like, for the family. It started me off on being a bit of a wag. I've always had an ear that picks up accents and speech mannerisms. I was a morose little girl at times. I was very sensitive, very easily hurt, and I would cry when my mother left me to go to the theatre. And I would retreat into make-believe. From the time I was eight until I was twelve, I'd go for days pretending to be other people. I was also terribly stubborn. And I'd do all sorts of things just to make people laugh. I was born under the zodiacal sign of Libra, and I'm a pure example of a Libran; I see both sides of every question, unfortunately and fortunately, and I long to break away from the course I'm forced to stay on, and light a few bonfires. My mother has always had a wonderful spiritual quality—sensitivity, an understanding of people. When she is working, she has a sense of well-being and accomplishment. Acting is a thing that she feels she needs to do, and she can't understand my attitude. She works on scenes from Shakespeare all by herself, for herself, whereas I am strictly practical and won't lift a finger unless I get paid for it.

In 1935, when I was ten, we moved to Hampstead, on the outskirts of London, and I attended the South Hampstead High School for Girls. The headmistress, Muriel Potter, was the sister of Stephen Potter, and Stephen Potter had been my father's best friend, which is how I happened to go there. Stephen Potter and my father had played cricket together—something Englishmen do on weekends. When the war started, the schools were all moved out into the country, but I didn't want to leave home and go to boarding school. I was a great homebody. So Mother said, "Look, are you interested in studying acting?" I said, "By all means, anything, but don't make me go to boarding school." So arrangements were made for me to continue my studies at home, with a tutor, and to attend evening classes in diction, dancing, and singing. After six months, Mother said, "Look, if you're really interested, you should be going to a proper dramatic school." I loved the idea. It seemed very glamorous to me. In 1940, I attended the Webber-Douglas School of Singing and Dramatic Art, in Kensington, on a scholarship—my first part was as a lady in waiting in a school production of "Mary of Scotland"—until August, when things got hot in the war. That was right after Dunkirk, and everything looked black. We had no ties to keep us in England. Some distant cousins in Brawley, California, were instrumental in getting us evacuated to America. My mother and my small brothers and I came to America late in the summer of 1940, sponsored in this country by Charles T. Wilson, a Wall Street businessman, and his wife, with whom we stayed for a while at their summer home on Lake Mahopac, in New York.

In September of 1940, I enrolled in the Feagin School of Drama and Radio, in Rockefeller Center, on a scholarship arranged by the American Theatre Wing. I didn't know what the pickings were in schools, and I didn't care. I lived from the fall of 1940 through the spring of 1941 in an East Ninety-fourth Street town house with a terribly kind family named Mr. and Mrs. George W. Perkins. I had breakfast and dinner there and took sandwiches to school. I was fifteen and very grown up. English girls *are,* for the most part. By the fall of 1941, we had moved to a one-room apartment on Morton Street, in Greenwich Village, and the boys were going to the Choate School; eventually they both attended U.C.L.A. In the spring of 1942, Mother went off to tour Canada with Anna Neagle in a variety show for the R.C.A.F. units training there. At the Feagin School, I became a character actress. In Congreve's "The Way of the World," I played Lady Wishfort, who is supposed to be sixty, which was starting off on a weird foot. After that, I played a leading part—Lady Windermere. I never had any trouble making an ass of myself. I had a sort of comedienne thing about me. I was never the ingénue type—luckily, since there were too many girls who looked like ingénues. But I would have been a character actress in any case. It was my bent from the beginning. In comedy, you automatically lose your own identity. You characterize away from yourself. In comedy, I am able to recognize the humor in life and relate it to myself. It has something to do with my having a sense of humor of my own. I tend to see the funny side of things always. It interests me. Playing the mother in the movie "All Fall Down," I had an opportunity to play a composite human being—to make you laugh and cry at the same time. To be funny, I've always realized, one must be deadly serious.

One of the other students at the Feagin School, Arthur Bourbon, who studied by day and danced at night, said to me one day, "Angie, you ought to do an act." He worked out an imitation of Beatrice Lillie singing Noël Coward's "I Went to a Marvellous Party" for me and then set up an audition for me with an agent, and in the summer of 1942 I found myself in Montreal with a job in a night club called the Samovar, at a salary of sixty dollars a week. I roomed with a Yugoslavian singer known professionally as Blanca, who was also on the bill. She is now married and has a couple of kids. She was a wonderful, peasantlike girl, and she taught me a great deal—how to put on makeup, how to do my hair, how to dress. When I first arrived, I stayed alone at a place called the Ford Hotel, where strange men knocked on my door at night. Arthur Bourbon had told me to stay there, because it was the cheapest place. I was very innocent, very green indeed. When older men made advances, I didn't know what they were doing. I moved to a rooming house. The night club was always filled with R.C.A.F. men. It was a bit of home to them, to see an English girl making a fool of herself. When I received my first salary check, I sent most of it to my mother, who was still on tour. The job lasted six weeks, and then I went back to New York, where the twins had returned from a summer on Long Island. I packed them up and sent them back to Choate. At the end of her tour, Mother had gone to Los Angeles, and she wrote saying how much cheaper it was to live—about twenty-eight dollars a month for a one-room apartment. (We had been paying forty-two dollars a month for ours, in New York.) And the movies were there. So I joined her. We went round to all the studios looking for jobs, but we didn't get anything. At Christmastime, we both got jobs in Bullock's Wilshire, the department store. Mother was in the toy department and I was a wrapper. Mother soon got fired, because she spent too much time playing with the toys. After the holidays, I was kept on, as a saleswoman in cosmetics. They thought of training me to be a buyer, but I was no good at mathematics. I could never figure the retail and wholesale prices. In June, 1943, a struggling young actor I knew, named Michael Dyne, who was being considered for the title part in the M-G-M movie "The Picture of Dorian Gray," told me they were looking for a young English girl for the cast. I got the afternoon off from the store and went out to M-G-M and saw the casting director. I was sent on to see George Cukor, who was going to direct "Gaslight," with Ingrid Bergman and Charles Boyer, and I was told I would be tested for the part of the Cockney maid for that movie, instead. Mother helped me prepare for the test, which I made during a week's vacation from the store. First, I was given a costume from Character Wardrobe, and then they took a lot of trouble with my hair and makeup. They padded me out to make me look bigger. I did a scene with an actor named Hugh Marlowe, in which Nancy, the maid, sort of seduces the character later played by Charles Boyer. It was a scene from the play that wasn't in the movie. I can't say I was frightened. I was terribly interested in how it was all done. After the test, they said I was too young. But Louis B. Mayer insisted that they put me under contract. So I signed a seven-year contract, with options, with M-G-M, at a salary of five hundred a week. I had been making twenty-six a week in commissions at Bullock's. I called them up immediately and quit, over the telephone. Then Cukor took me for the part of Nancy after all.

It's strange, but I've never worked in England. I'm a pure product of American movies. I celebrated my eighteenth birthday on the set of "Gaslight." They had a lovely cake, and the stars were wonderfully sweet to me. I thought, Well, this is making movies. I never felt I was that rare-orchid kind of thing. With me it's always been a matter of being ready to work at nine o'clock and achieving what I can. I happened to see "Gaslight" not long ago on television. I was amazed. I thought, My God, how did I have all that assurance? I have much less assurance now. In those days, I suppose, I went ahead on trust. There's always been joy, exuberance, and fun in movie acting, but I have never been blinded by it. I had an opportunity to do all the things that would have led me to the glamorous side of a screen career, but I didn't seem to want that. At M-G-M, I came in at the end of a very lush period. L. B. Mayer was always terribly nice to me. He always seemed interested in how the family was getting along. He wanted to put my brothers under contract, but Mother wouldn't have it, and we both felt that it wouldn't be fair to do that to the boys.

I was always able to go and chat with L. B. Mayer—mostly about the family or about the movies. I suppose I was an enigma to him. When Dore Schary became executive vice-president in charge of production and studio operations, in 1948, I began to get lost in the shuffle. Anyway, once I was settled in, I found being under contract terribly confining. From 1943 to 1950, I made thirteen movies, including "If Winter Comes," "State of the Union," and "Samson and Delilah." The year after "Gaslight," I also did play in "The Picture of Dorian Gray"—as the young girl, Sibyl Vane, who is seduced by Dorian Gray. It was a lovely part, sort of the antithesis of Nancy, the maid, who is a bit of a heavy. I sang a song as Sibyl—"The Little Yellow Bird"—and for some reason it has always been associated with me since.

I was married for the first time in 1945, to the late Richard Cromwell, the actor. The marriage lasted nine months, and, thank goodness, did a great deal for me. I learned the meaning of marriage and a lot of other things, and I had a better idea of what it was all about when I was married again, in 1949, to Peter Shaw, a William Morris agent, who is now executive assistant to Robert Weitman and Benjamin Thau at M-G-M. We live in Malibu, in a house overlooking the sea, and have two children—Anthony, born in 1952, and Deirdre, born in 1953. I also have a twenty-year-old stepson, David. In 1952, when Anthony was six months old, I started doing a six-week season of summer stock in the East, playing in "Remains to Be Seen," by Howard Lindsay and Russel Crouse, and "Affairs of State," by Louis Verneuil. Anthony slept all over the place. We trouped round together. I did it because Peter and I were sort of struggling along, and one could make a thousand dollars a week in summer stock. After that, I did a lot of acting for television—half-hour films based on W. Somerset Maugham short stories and things of that sort. It paid awfully well and didn't take me away from home. Actually, I prefer making movies to acting on the stage, because it doesn't take so much out of you. I like that. Stage demands are so stringent. You're thinking about the part all the time. I hate the idea of having people see me and think I'm not very good. I worry about it all night. The mechanics of it worry me, too—whether I'm going to have a cold, and so on. You've got to be absolutely up to pitch to play on the stage. I have a great sense of responsibility about it. Maybe that's the reason I can't enjoy it. It means pushing all the way.

I have a split life, and being an actress is a very small part of it. My role as a mother always comes first with me, and the making of a good life. That to me is Number One. I've always had to be shoved into acting. Because I've never had the ego or whatever it is on my own, my moves as an actress have not been brought about by me. They've been the result of my being talked into it by producers, writers, agents, my mother, and my husband. I find myself wanting to stay home all the time. Living the life of an actress has always been difficult for me. If I feel I'm going to sacrifice the children to it in any way, I don't want any part of it. Other actresses may make acting their whole life; that's what they want, and they put wonderful labels on it. It's never been that driving thing with me. My children have recently begun to understand just what the hell Mother is doing. I'm not too comfortable about it. I hope my son doesn't want to do it, too. It's a terribly unsatisfactory life for a man, when you think of a struggling young actor with a wife and babies to support. I wouldn't wish that on anybody. My daughter has an awful lot of the ingredients of an actress in her—mimicking, an awareness of the peculiarities of people —even though she's still shy and gauche, as little girls are. Acting on the stage, as far as I'm concerned, is very hard work. I've always had parts where I'm screaming or talking my head off. But I've never felt a compulsion to woo and hold an audience. Some actors say they love to hold an audience in the palm of their hand—then they absolutely taste the nectar. For me, the compensations are different. To have a chance to perform something well and be successful in it is satisfying. Then, when you get a letter, as I do occasionally, from someone in the audience, saying, "You gave me the greatest enjoyment I've had in the theatre in five years"—*that* is tremendous.

When David Merrick, the producer, sent me the play "A Taste of Honey," in 1960, I said no at first. I couldn't imagine how to arrange it domestically. I didn't want to leave Malibu for New York in the winter. I wanted to hole in, garden, cook, and just generally be at home. Then I had a call from the director, who said what a wonderful part it was—the part of the girl's irresponsible mother. Then Merrick came out. He's a very persuasive man, but I made very steep demands. He met them. So then I had to do it, and I got terribly enthusiastic. When I first read the play, I read it objectively, which is how I ordinarily read a play for the first time. Then, almost immediately,

I put myself in the part. I'm a pretty good judge of my own capabilities—the things I'm best at. If the ingredients of a character are totally understandable to me, if I know the character, if I know people like the character, I know I can play it. I can work myself up. I agreed to do the play for only six months, however. I moved Anthony and Deirdre to New York, and we sublet an apartment on Fifth Avenue. Some nights, in playing a part onstage, I can give the part more validity than I can on other nights. It's pushing all the way, however, and especially when the audience has mass ennui. Everything I do is the same in every performance. It's set. But there are some nights when I have an extra impetus, especially if I feel I'm ringing bells with the audience. If I give it that extra push some night, it may not always mean it's a better performance. I go on technique. You get it set and it goes along. If you try to do too much, the more you do, and the more you try to win an audience, the more it turns away. It works that way, somehow. You have to go on technique. You can't live it night after night. Creative interpretation counts for a great deal, but if you maintain that you can't say a line until you *feel* it, to me that seems to be lack of discipline. Born actors are like sponges. They go through life soaking up idiosyncrasies and storing them up in themselves—all the little bits and pieces of what people are and what people do. When I act, it's completely apart from *me*. It's like putting on a suit of clothes that doesn't belong to me but fits me.

I like acting in movies better than on the stage, because you don't have to keep on and on with it. I'm a traitor to the cause. I don't indulge myself in the enjoyment of acting. I have a tremendous sense of duty about the theatre. For instance, I have a strong sense of guilt about being late. I become all professional as soon as I leave my home —as soon as I have my coat on and am on my way. I feel I have to be early. And if I don't put the makeup on just right, I worry about it all night. I have a great sense of responsibility. Maybe that's the reason I can't enjoy it. Actors are accorded the open door. It's amazing that this welcomeness has survived as long as it has, especially with television and the constant exposure. I should think it would have waned, but I find that the actor is still accepted by everyone everywhere. I have a tremendous urge to retreat from acting. But when you're a woman and you're recognized as an actress, you feel that if you give it up, you may lose your attractiveness for your husband, and for your friends; you're afraid of replacing it with just being a house-wife. My greatest gratification in acting, now that I'm older, is simply that I get to play some fantastic parts. The key, I think, is that I seem to ring a bell with women. They do understand the way I get at them in my parts, and portray women not as famous stars portray them but as women are. Movies are now beginning to take a more realistic approach to life and its problems, and this is in my favor. In the past—the era of the thirties and forties—women were portrayed in a too narrowly defined way. There were no nuances in a script. A woman was a *woman;* a mother was a *mother;* a femme fatale was a femme *fatale.* The parts have more appeal for me now. However, when it comes to stage parts I feel so often that it isn't worth it—all the necessary splitting up of the family, and being away from my husband. When everybody pushes me to do it, I feel, Oh well, all right. But I don't want to wait to be happy. I want to start being happy now.

ANTHONY QUINN

On the stage, you have to find the truth, even if you have to lose the audience.

I was born on April 21, 1916, in Chihuahua, Mexico. My father's father came to Mexico from County Cork and was, according to my mother—who now lives in Los Angeles, is a social worker, and keeps half the Mexican population of the city alive—a blond and blue-eyed version of me. My mother, who is an American, is also blond and blue-eyed. I have a younger sister, Stella who is married to a screenwriter named Martin H. Goldsmith. My father was tall—six feet two, like me—and adventurous and talented. He tried to work at everything—bullfighting, railroading, painting. Right after I was born, my father was conscripted in the Mexican revolution. Everything around us was blown to hell. My mother took me and walked four hundred miles in seven months to El Paso, to get away from the fighting and to look for my father, who was reported to be in the north. We stayed in El Paso for two years, living in a shack near the river. My father found us in El Paso. When I was four, we headed for California. At five, I was working with my parents in the fields near San Jose, picking walnuts. We lived in one migrant camp after another—beautiful years for me, in a way, because I remember how all the people used to sit around campfires, playing guitars, singing, eating beans from a common kettle. It was all quite wonderful. Then we moved to Los Angeles, where my father got a job taking care of the animals at the zoo on the lot of the Selig Polyscope Company. Our first home in the city was a one-room shack near the railroad tracks—a horrible, marvellous room, with a piano box for our dining room. My grandmother —my father's mother, who was a Mexican and who lived with us— and I slept next to a wood stove. My father was embarrassed about the poverty and dreariness around us. He painted colorful pictures on our windows to make the scene look better. My father had no fear. One of the animals he took care of was a panther that I fell in love with and who was in love with me. I'd go to the zoo and stare at her for hours. Then my father got a job as a cameraman at Selig. He worked with Rudolph Valentino and Ramon Novarro. As a kid, I wanted to be a priest. Until I was twelve, I was a very pious young boy. I believed in the Lord to the letter. When I was thirteen, my grandmother got very sick, and Aimee Semple McPherson came to see her and made her well. After that, I started preaching for Aimee Semple McPherson and playing the saxophone for her at meetings. When I was twelve, my father died. We were so poor that I had to make the cross for my father's grave. I became the man of the family. I quit grammar school, and became foreman for the Camarillo Apricot Growers Association until a truant officer found me and sent me to junior high school for a year. Then I got a job as a foreman in a mattress factory. My hands to this day show the marks of being chopped up by the springs in the mattresses. I shined shoes and sold papers for extra money. I had little education, and I thought I had three choices for a career—to become a gangster, a prizefighter, or an actor in the silent movies. I was literally tongue-tied until I was nineteen.

When I was fourteen, my mother remarried. I couldn't accept my stepfather. I went to live with my grandmother in Los Angeles. When I was eighteen, I wanted to join a local drama group, but it wouldn't accept me, because of my speech impediment. I had an operation to correct it, and paid for it on time over the next five years. But I was a nervous kid. I was tall and scrawny. I always looked old, even when I was a kid. I went in for boxing, and got five dollars for a fight, and also got my nose broken. For a while, I even worked as a janitor for my stepfather, who had a window-cleaning business, and later I cleaned windows for him. Then, when I was eighteen, I met a girl at a party, and when I met her mother, the mother took me in hand. She educated me. She made me read a book a week. To this day, because of the routine she made me follow, I can't go to sleep until I've spent an hour reading some book or other. This woman got me to listen to classical music, to understand philosophy, to appreciate life. At night, I went to the little drama group. They had accepted me after my operation but still wouldn't let me talk, so I mostly played pantomime parts. Through a friend, I got a small part in a movie called "Parole," with Alan Baxter. When I told my grandmother I was in a movie, she said, "You are going to be a great actor." She was pretty sick by then, but she kept telling me she wasn't going to die until she had seen my movie. I had to carry her into the Pantages Hollywood Theatre for the opening, because she was too weak to walk. I was just a face in the movie, but I got notices in reviews in *Variety* and the Hollywood *Reporter* as "a face." My grandmother died a week later.

After that, nothing happened in my acting career for a while. With the son of the woman who was educating me, I hopped a freight train out of Los Angeles, and we went to Arizona and Colorado. I spent six months working on ranches or as a dishwasher in restaurants. While I was in Ensenada, just over the border in Mexico, I read a notice in a newspaper saying that Cecil B. deMille, at Paramount, was looking for Indians to play in "The Plainsman," starring Gary Cooper. I took the next freight back to Los Angeles, shaved with Borax soap in a gas-station washroom, and applied for a job as an Indian with deMille. He asked me if I was an Indian, and I said yes, I was a Blackfoot. Being Mexican, I may actually be part Indian. He asked me to say something in the language, and I made up some gibberish, and he said I would have to learn to speak Cheyenne. When he asked me, I told him that I rode well, although I had never been on a horse in my life. He gave me the job and a four-page single-spaced monologue to learn, in what was supposed to be a Cheyenne version of English. I got an allowance of ten dollars a day, which I used for riding lessons. The monologue I learned for that movie served me well for the next twenty years, in all kinds of movies. I used the same accent for Chinese dialect, Hawaiian dialect, and never got a single complaint. During the filming of "The Plainsman," I objected to the way I was supposed to deliver this monologue, as though I were addressing ten thousand Indians. I spoke up and said I thought I should address my remarks to Gary Cooper. The various assistants around deMille said he should fire me, but he said, "The boy is right." He let me do the part the way I thought it should be done, and he then tried to place me under personal contract to him. I turned the offer down. I met my wife, Katherine deMille, while I was making "The Buccaneer" with deMille. When I first asked her for a date, I didn't know she was his daughter. A few months later, we were married. I was twenty-one. We have four children: Christina, who is studying business administration; Kathy, who is in Germany with M.R.A.; Duncan, who thinks he wants to act; and Valentina, the youngest, born in 1952, who is very musical. At the time of my marriage, I was making two hundred and fifty dollars a week, but I was terrified that I'd be dubbed deMille's son-in-law. I didn't want to be at the same studio with him. I wanted out. That led to a rupture between us.

The year before I was married, I lived off and on with John Barrymore, who was sick at the time. He gave me the suit of armor he had worn in "Richard III." He told me that I should be a stage actor. I liked making movies, but the important thing for me was to get away from Paramount. I was a very intense young man. I felt I should try everything, do everything. So I broke my contract, went over to Warner Brothers, and got a small part in "City for Conquest," with James Cagney and Arthur Kennedy. I began to go from studio to studio. I have always been in the process of being discovered. That's the way it was for me then. I didn't mind playing Indians, but a lot of the other parts I was in made me unhappy. I was frequently the leading man's friend or a gangster. I didn't feel I was getting anywhere. I played in a pirate picture with Tyrone Power, in "The Ox-Bow Incident," and in "Guadalcanal Diary." Then I was in another Western. I felt useless. I felt, Christ, nothing is happening to me. How long can

I go on, being at one studio after another and not making it at any studio? In 1946, the doors began to close. Then Sam Wanamaker asked me to play in a Broadway production of "The Gentleman from Athens," by Emmet Lavery. I grabbed it. In Boston, Elliot Norton, the leading critic there, called me the greatest actor he had ever seen. The play folded after seven performances in New York, and I was stuck. But I had tasted the theatre. What with Norton's review, I felt that all was not over. I had no money left. I was broke. Then I was offered the part of Stanley Kowalski in the road-company production of "A Streetcar Named Desire." I signed to play it in Chicago for six months. I lived in a four-flight walkup behind a stable. After the first six months, I felt I still hadn't made it on my own, and I stayed in the play for another six months, and then, because I felt I hadn't yet solved any of my problems, I stayed for another six months after that. We brought the production to the City Center, in New York, and got glowing notices. When I returned to Hollywood, my salary was way down. I played in "The Brave Bulls" for peanuts. Then I played in "Viva Zapata!" and felt, for the first time in movies, that I was doing the kind of acting I wanted. I still wasn't making much money, but I made a deal with myself; I said, "The hell with it. From now on, I'm not going to be just anybody." I won an Academy Award in 1952 as Best Supporting Actor for my performance in "Viva Zapata!" I began to feel that maybe it hadn't all been for nothing. I had an offer to make three pictures in Italy with Dino De Laurentiis and Carlo Ponti. "La Strada," in which I co-starred with the Italian actress Giulietta Masina in 1954, was brought into the company by me. They produced it reluctantly. I took an interest of twenty-five per cent in the picture instead of a big salary. If I had kept my interest in that movie, which made millions, I would be a rich man. However, my agent at the time saw the movie and thought it would be a flop, so I sold my interest in it for twelve thousand dollars. But things were starting to happen to me. I made a lot of money playing the part of Paul Gauguin in "Lust for Life," and I won another Academy Award for it, and I made several other pictures that did well.

Then came another step in my life. Whether I was making a lot of money or not, I felt I was in a rut. When I was offered the part of Henry II in "Becket," with Laurence Olivier, on Broadway,

I decided it was time to start a new phase of my life. Olivier is the greatest actor in the world, and I had a chance to play with *him*. I felt strongly that I had to come out from behind the tree. Playing gangsters was always very painful to me. I was using only fifteen per cent of myself in those parts. I was just renting my face out. Until "Becket," "La Strada" had been my greatest single accomplishment. But the theatre was a real challenge to me. The happiest period of my entire life was when I was rehearsing for that play. After it opened, I looked forward every night to going to work. I was very excited by the thought that I was going to learn something new each night. I've never felt so *used* in all my life. I have never been happy unless I was using the greater part of myself, and this play gave me the chance to do so. Oddly enough, it was my son Duncan, then fifteen, who got me over the last hump and into the play. I was afraid that more would be required of me than I would be able to deliver. Just before the opening, I developed laryngitis and wanted to give up, but Duncan told me, "You're going to have voice enough to do this play, because this play means more to you than anything else you've ever done." Well, we opened and got rave notices.

In the theatre, you play to the audience. In moviemaking, the director is your audience, and if he's pleased, you feel you've done your job. In the theatre, you've got a whole new crowd out there every night. You can become mesmerized by the feeling of acceptance you get from them. You have to keep yourself in check. Sometimes you have to step on a laugh, if you know it's a bad laugh you're getting. Only the amateur actor looks to make himself feel good. The pro takes his work seriously and has a constant awareness of the battle to tell the truth. A bad actor feels good after a performance, but the pro feels only the responsibility for finding the truth, no matter what. Some actors say "How much of me is like this part?" and others say "How much of me is *not* like this part?" I always try to see myself in the part. You create your own propulsion for going onstage each night. Olivier is a dedicated actor. His standards are extremely high. He is a model of discipline. But I have to work differently from the way he works. He finds the truth offstage and brings it with him; I try to find the truth onstage. I'm searching for it; he's already got it. The closest thing to acting is bullfighting or boxing. It's a matter of adjusting to the other man's blows. You're so busy adjusting it's difficult to think of anything else. Your images control your movements. It's a way of life—the same all over the world. The actor is an artist. He comments on life constantly. He's a true creator. No one has more latitude to create than an actor. I can conjure up all the images I want, with perfect freedom, and what are the words until I say them? Before I go onstage, I experience the tremendous thrill of knowing that I will feel love, hate, anger, and will transmit them to the audience. My objective is now clear. What I want to do is to create, to say what I have to say.

JASON ROBARDS, SR.

On the stage, actors have a rapport that is one of the most precious things in their life. Other actors lean toward you and look into your eyes and talk right into your heart.

I was born on December 31, 1892, on a farm in Hillsdale, Michigan, a town with a population of five thousand, about eighty miles southwest of Detroit. I was the youngest of three children. My brother, Frank, Jr., who was seven years older than I was, died at the age of eighteen. My sister, Rolla, who died recently, was always interested in painting, sculpture, and the other arts. She married a bank teller, settled down in Hillsdale, and then encouraged me to get out into the world. My mother had taught school, and my father, who quit school after the eighth grade, was self-educated and worked as a farmer and post-office inspector. We had the usual Middle West hundred and forty-seven acres, with corn, cows, and chickens. My father was a very voluble man, always mixed up in politics, and, as a former strong Republican, he shocked everybody by becoming Teddy Roosevelt's campaign manager in Michigan for the Bull Moose Party in 1912. He was a natural pantomimist. My mother could look out of a window and see him standing way across a field talking to somebody, and from his gestures she'd know exactly what he was talking about. She was a gentle, sensitive person who couldn't ever stand a lull in conversation, she'd get so embarrassed. When I was fifteen, we moved to Saginaw for a couple of years, because my father had been transferred by the post office. My mother's sister, who taught school in Saginaw, lived with a family named Beach, whose son Louis, later a novelist, had written to New York for the catalogue of the American Academy of Dramatic Arts. I got to looking it over one day, and it set me thinking. I'd taken part in some home-talent theatricals. I'd always been musical; I had sung in our Episcopal Church choir as a soprano and could play almost anything by ear on the piano. When we moved back to Hillsdale, I graduated from high school and then I took a job working for my brother-in-law as a cost clerk, for a salary of nine dollars a week. At night, I sang, for a dollar a night, in Hillsdale's nickelodeon, which happened to cost ten cents. Accompanied by a piano, I sang songs illustrated by colored slides. They were the most terrible things you ever saw—the fellow and the girl sitting on a bench with the big yellow moon behind them. My son Jason and I have given many a wonderful party at which I played the ukulele and sang. Those songs always put Jason in stitches. Jason likes to have me sing the old tear-jerkers, like "The Road to Yesterday," and "Dear Little Boy of Mine," and "Pansies Mean Thoughts and Thoughts Mean You." I'd sing twice a night, and in between I'd watch a movie, like "Ramona," with Mary Pickford, or "The Deerslayer," with Wallace Reid. It was 1910 and 1911, and if you were making fifteen dollars a week, the way I was, you could save a lot of money. So I saved up, and, with some help from my sister and brother-in-law, I went to New York in the fall of 1911 to enroll in the American Academy of Dramatic Arts. It was a pretty strange move for a boy from Hillsdale, Michigan. I lived in a rooming house on West Fifty-seventh Street, which cost fourteen dollars a week. My tuition was four hundred dollars for six months. It was the greatest experience of my life. I learned all the basic things of my craft, which is all a school can give you anyway. You can't *teach* anybody to act. That's why I insisted, when my son Jason said he wanted to be an actor, that he go to the Academy, too, and he did. My classmates included Edward G. Robinson, William Powell, and Joseph Schildkraut. The class ahead of ours had Guthrie McClintic.

We were all pretty green, but you immediately got the feeling at the Academy that acting really is an art, that it's not a gay, flamboyant life but a way of life and an art. Basically, all the good actors know that. They have that as their belief. It's implanted in them. We had classes in speech; diction; life study, which meant going out and looking at people on the street and on the subway; dramatic reading; and so on. We acted in plays directed by the late Charles Jehlinger, the greatest of them all. There's no doubt in my mind that acting is an art, because it is handling the most vital thing in the world—human behavior. The writer sees something contained in his own mind and puts it down—and God bless him for it. The musician *hears* something in his mind and puts it down. The painter *sees* something and puts it down. What all these artists do is *engraved* somewhere. But acting is a living thing. The actor creates a living human being not himself. What you create as an actor isn't yourself any more than what a painter creates. The painter is himself; he isn't Mona Lisa. The actor creates something and brings it onto the stage. Then he carries it five steps and it's gone, and he's himself again.

Everything you do on the stage has to come from your mind. As soon as you start to do it, however, you begin to feel it. All of a sudden the lines leap out, and you find a new meaning. Even after you've been doing the same part for months, the lines jump out at you, and you're always finding new and additional meanings in them. When you start to build a character, you have to think it out: What is the author saying? How does your character relate to the others? Then you start going into very minute details, and suddenly there's a click. And you know why. You can *feel* it. You get it from yourself, from your own soul, and you get it from the other actors. It's never a routine. And always, inside yourself, is the suspicion that you might be wrong. Any time an actor thinks he's always right, he'd better examine himself. You have a sense of behavior that tells you what to do, and you work with that, together with a well-defined, well-thought-out point of view. At all times, you're interdependent with the people you're acting with. Always, you have a deep respect for the audience. They came for enjoyment, and you've got to give it to them. Some audiences are so sharp, so wonderful, so inspiring, you work accordingly. They give you so much.

All I knew when I started going to the Academy was that I had to do it. I had to act. My father, who just didn't want me to be an actor, said he could get me an appointment to go to Annapolis, or was willing to send me to the Michigan Agricultural College and give me his farm. It was tough to turn that down, but I had to. Then my father kept after me to become a lawyer. "That's acting, too, in a way," he'd say. Actors weren't held in great repute in the Middle West. But I couldn't be turned away from what I felt I just had to do. After six months at the Academy, my money ran out, and I couldn't continue, so I got a job with a show on the road, understudying the lead in "The Country Boy," by Edgar Selwyn. I was pretty bad. I'd had no actual experience. I still had ahead of me the things you sweat over for the first few years, including appearing before an audience. We were ten weeks out on the road, in Davenport, Iowa, when the leading man got sick. I had got to the theatre early that night—as I always still do, because I like to adjust myself to the feeling of the part. When I was asked if I could go on that night, I said sure. When you're nineteen, as I was, you always say sure. So there I was, a leading man.

The next year, I toured again in the play, as the lead, up to the Canadian Northwest. I was back in New York for one day, and was offered the lead in the road tour of a comedy called "Excuse Me," by Rupert Hughes. I played a young Army lieutenant, and it all took place in a Pullman car on the Union Pacific. But I knew I needed more experience, so I went into stock to get it. I was in a different play every week. I played old men and young men, rich men and poor. I specialized in what might be called hands-in-the-pockets juveniles. I was making fifty dollars a week, and acting in places like Lowell, Massachusetts, and St. Louis, and Salt Lake City. I met my first wife, Maxine Glanville, in Salt Lake, where she was visiting her brother. She was from Portland, Oregon. We were married in 1914 and had two sons: Jason, and Glenn, who is an electronic engineer with Western Electric and a very solid citizen in Winston-Salem, North Carolina. I have a daughter, Laurel, by my second wife, Agnes Lynch. Laurel works in a California bank, is very beautiful, and doesn't care about acting. I sometimes look at her with both wonder and regret.

My first Broadway play, in 1917, was "Turn to the Right," a light comedy by Winchell Smith and John E. Hazzard, in which I played the heavy, a rich man's son interested in making trouble for the poor young hero. My salary had grown by then to seventy-five dollars a week. Then I played a lead, the part of the prosecutor, in Winchell Smith's and Frank Bacon's "Lightnin'." In 1922, I played with Madge Kennedy in Frank Craven's "Spite Corner," and in Chicago I played Chico in Austin Strong's "Seventh Heaven," with Helen Menken. I loved that play. It represented the growth of man, from sewer to sunlight. When I came up those stairs to that little Helen Menken, with her carroty hair, I could feel what it meant to the audience. The play went to the West Coast from Chicago, and I went with it. I didn't return to the Broadway theatre until thirty-five years later, to play in Budd Schulberg's and Harvey Breit's "The Disenchanted," with Jason, late in 1958. I had four studios bidding for me when I first went out to Hollywood, and that, in those days, was enough to stop me from coming back to New York. My first year in movies was disastrous. I signed with Universal, because they offered me the most money—seven hundred and fifty dollars a week. Making movies was a new experience for me. It was exciting and different. A lot of it meant working outdoors, on location, and getting up at seven o'clock in the morning and acting, a routine I wasn't used to. In those days, the hours weren't regulated at all. They used to work you around the clock on weekends, in what we called the "midnight follies." I made two movies, "Stella Maris," with Mary Philbin, and the first of a series of Cohen-and-Kelly movies, in which I played a Kelly, a young motorcycle officer. Each of my movies took six or seven weeks to make. After that, for the next thirty weeks, I was idle. In 1926, I was lent to Warner Brothers, which put me under contract. I was in "The Third Degree," with Dolores Costello, and in three of the early Rin Tin Tins. Then I vegetated again. But I couldn't leave, because I was under contract, and besides I needed money. By now I had a house in Beverly Hills, a maid, two cars, a wife, and two children. Then talking pictures came in. I had been filling in my time playing in local stage productions, and there I was, right in front of them, an actor who could talk, so they grabbed me. I started making one movie after another. I was in "The Gamblers," with H. B. Warner; "On Trial," with Lois Wilson; "The Isle of Lost Ships," with Virginia Valli; D. W. Griffith's "Lincoln," with Walter Huston and Una Merkel, in which I played Lincoln's law partner; "Paris," with Jack Buchanan and Irene Bordoni; and the movie version of "Lightnin'," in which Joel McCrea played his first big part, the prosecutor, my old role, while I played the heavy.

In 1959, after doing a play again on Broadway, I didn't like the idea of going back to work in Hollywood television movies of the conveyor-belt kind, but sometimes you have to go back to all those "Cimarron City"'s in order to live. I'll never forget what Jason said to me when I

I was going to be in that play with him. "This isn't any father-son deal," he said. "We're two actors together, and we won't give an inch." Real life for an actor is in the living theatre. There is *nothing* that compares with the living theatre. It's like telling a story and having someone to *listen* to you. If there's no one in the room who cares what you say, if your only audience is the cold camera eye, if you bobble a line or slur a word and there's a mechanic to yell "Cut!" and you do it over again, you feel more and more that something important is being taken away from you. In the living theatre, you have the challenge right there with you—this is it, hot or cold, for better or worse, this is *it*. The audience out there cares—cares what you're doing, cares to hear what you're saying, cares to respond to what is happening on the stage. Why, in movies I've walked in at the start of a picture and not even known the people I was playing with. The important things were the lights, the dollies, the cold camera eye. The other actors had never seen me before, and I had never seen them. We'd have that little embarrassed thing where we all said our names. Then we'd have a run-through. Then the camera would shoot it. In less than a day, you pick up your script, put on your makeup, get your wardrobe, and meet your fellow-actors, and then the machine gets to work on you. In the old days of quickies, I'd make a full-length feature picture in one week. How does that compare with being in the *theatre?* With four or five weeks of careful rehearsing, people looking into each other's eyes—real, living people? You're in a state of well-being. You can't find it in any other way. Everything else is blotted out. It's plain joy. It keeps you alive. Jason's elder boy, Jason III, is twelve and likes acting, too, and has already been in grammar-school plays in New York. Jason and I talk about getting up a play for the three of us to be in together.

MARGARET LEIGHTON

Trying to see other people from the point of view of the character you play forces you to have a little perception about the other people, which, ultimately, is all that life is.

I was born on February 26, 1922, in Barnt Green, Worcestershire, England, the eldest of three children. In Birmingham, which was nearby, my father was then in the business of selling cotton to retailers, but in his late fifties he got into steel, because the cotton shortage during the Second World War made it necessary for him to set to and find another means of making a living. In my childhood, when he was in cotton, I used to go to his office and come home with a collection of little samples of cloth. Today, my brother is in the steel business, and lives in India. My sister is married to a businessman in England. I grew up in a middle-class suburban neighborhood. I was a bored child. I went to a school connected with the Church of England College in Birmingham. In the holidays, I was taken to Church of England Children's Special Service Mission meetings at the seaside, and by the time I was eight I had begun to sing at them. They were held on the beach at Borth, in Wales, where my family rented a cottage each summer. Theology students would come there for their holidays. They were undergraduates, in their early twenties, but to me they seemed like elderly gentlemen. We children would build a pulpit out of sand and decorate it with shells and flowers. It was a rather jolly time. It was all for a child's religious education—reading the Bible and singing hymns. I sang all the solo parts. It didn't occur to me that anyone else could do it. I must have read the whole of the Bible by the time I was twelve. From around that time, I never expected to do anything but go on the stage. Before that, I had talked about becoming a lawyer. But I couldn't imagine growing into the dull life of the Birmingham suburbs. In 1938, when I was sixteen, I left school at the end of the summer term and joined the Birmingham Repertory Theatre. That September, I was given my first part—Dorothy, the Cockney maid, in "Laugh With Me," by Adelaide Phillpotts. It was quite a good part, and I was terribly frightened. I kept giggling nervously and acting rowdy during rehearsals, and then I cried all through the first three weeks of the play. In the part, I was supposed to laugh all the time, which is quite a difficult thing to do, especially if you're terrified, but I managed to get out a series of strangled wheezes. Anyway, I stuck it, and began to learn something about the discipline of the theatre. I lived at home, in our suburb. My family didn't take my ambitions very seriously. When I first started, the idea of getting up and saying two lines in front of an audience, or even in front of the other actors, nearly killed me. It seemed entirely different from giving recitations. I'd try my lines out at home, saying them in front of my mother, and that eased me into it a bit. My mother became quite a devotee of the theatre. She used to make my costumes and listen to me for hours at a time without ever getting tired. I did all sorts of bits and pieces with the company, and then, when I was nineteen, I played my first lead, the role of Lady Babbie in "The Little Minister"—the first time I really had responsibility for a play. Acting was something I enjoyed. All this time, I was living in a blissful vacuum. I didn't think about anything but acting. I didn't know about anything else. I wasn't interested in anybody or anything outside of the theatre. I found everything in losing what I suppose I might call my own identity and becoming what I was intended to become in the plays. That kind of bliss decreases with experience—and, indeed, it must, as you become better equipped and grow more aware of the hazards. In those days, I wasn't aware of audiences—only of what *I* was doing. Today, if an audience is quiet I know whether it's because everybody is asleep or is interested. You can feel it, mostly. A quiet audience is either dead quiet, which means that it's listening, or restless quiet, which means that it's not. To act in the way one did as a child, disregarding the audience, would be complete self-indulgence. One is there to satisfy, in whatever way one can, the people who have paid for their tickets. But as a young actress I was far more self-absorbed, as most young actors and actresses are, than I think I am today. I had far less acute critical faculties.

I spent six years with the Birmingham Repertory Theatre. They were good years, when almost everything I did was enjoyable. I had offers after a while to go to London and appear in plays, but some un-canny instinct told me not to accept them. It was probably the only clever decision I've ever made in my life. I didn't have an agent in those days. I wasn't interested in making more money. I lived at home, for one thing, and, for another, my final salary was the top one, nine pounds a week, which to me was untold wealth. Those years in reper-tory were the only time I have ever fully lived for the theatre, as actors are thought to do. When the war came along, I was allowed to stay in the theatre, instead of being called up, as other women were. In my sixth year at Birmingham, another instinct told me that it was time to move on, before the audiences got tired of me. That is a thing that is especially apt to happen in provincial repertory. It's something like playing tennis. You're never going to improve if you play with the same partner all the time.

Some friends advised me to go to London and see a man named John Burrell, the chairman of the newly formed board of directors of the Old Vic Theatre Company. I didn't really know anything much about the Old Vic then. I did an audition for him, and he asked me if I would book three seats at the Birmingham Rep for the next matinée. The two other seats, it turned out, were for Laurence Olivier and Ralph Richardson. It was 1944, all but the end of the war. Both Larry and Ralph had been in the Fleet Air Arm, and they had decided to re-form the Old Vic as a permanent company in London, using as many veter-ans as possible. In May, 1941, the Old Vic's theatre, on Waterloo Road, had been hit by a Nazi bomb. During the war, the Old Vic

toured in England. What I didn't know at the time was that that season had been designed for Larry and Ralph. In the first season, Ralph
played the title roles in "Uncle Vanya" and "Peer Gynt," and Larry
played Saranoff in "Arms and the Man" and the Duke of Gloucester
in "Richard III." When one was playing a leading part, the other took
a small one, just to appear in the same play; for instance, when
Ralph played Peer Gynt, Larry took the part of the Moulder of But-
tons. Another thing I didn't know at the time was that Burrell and
Larry and Ralph wanted to know how I would fit in with the rest of
the company. The other actress they were interested in and got that
year was Joyce Redman. At the Birmingham matinée, I was playing
the part of the daughter-prostitute in Pirandello's "Six Characters in
Search of an Author." There was no sound from the audience during
the performance, no sound at all from in front. I thought, My God,
it's terrible, I'm terrible. I found out later that the Birmingham
audience had recognized Larry and Ralph, because both had played
there. It was an awfully small theatre, with a capacity of four hundred.
The audience was absolutely transfixed by the sight of Larry and
Ralph, and wasn't even watching me. Larry and Ralph came round
later with Burrell. We had tea, and they asked me to join them at the
Old Vic. I said I had one more play to do in Birmingham, and they
said they'd arrange to work around it. I was reasonably frightened at
their invitation.

I stayed at the Old Vic from June, 1944, to April, 1947, leaving to
appear in James Bridie's "A Sleeping Clergyman," with Robert Donat,
in June, 1947, in London. They were three extraordinary years.
Sybil Thorndike was in the company the first season, and I acted with
her in "Arms and the Man," "Peer Gynt," and "Richard III." She has
always been for me one of the most wonderful people in the theatre.
She's absolutely unique. She's completely tireless—never too tired to
help other people, to talk with you when you want to talk. She's really
saintly. I used to sit in her dressing room between shows. She'd give
me some tea, and I always felt I could tell her anything. She's always
been most generous, particularly with younger actors. The theatre in
so many ways is slightly megalomaniacal—the antithesis of Sybil.

My first appearance with the company was as Raina Petkoff in "Arms
and the Man," in which we opened in Manchester, and in which I
acted with both Larry and Ralph. Then we opened in London, and I

made my début there in "Peer Gynt." I played the Woman in Green, the evil influence on Peer Gynt. It was a big, spectacular production, directed by Tyrone Guthrie, with a lot of stylized dancing, and so on— a wonderful production, really. Acting with Larry and Ralph was like starting all over. It made everything I'd done before seem like reading telephone books. They were very kind to me. They didn't grumble. I felt I was very unskilled. I was very shy—pathologically shy, actually. I'd never worked with London actors before, and I was painfully unsophisticated. London was a world I was quite unused to. I appeared in only one new play, "An Inspector Calls," in addition to classics like "Uncle Vanya." I loved, and still love, playing Chekhov. It suits me. It suits the way I behave on the stage. Chekhov is tragicomic in a most subtle way and on a very civilized level. It's what appeals to me more than anything else—that combination of being very moving and being very funny. When I was twenty-two, I played Yelena in "Uncle Vanya," and, at twenty-eight, Masha, the unhappily married sister, in "The Three Sisters." The part of Masha was my favorite of all.

In looking back at the roles I've played, some of them seem to me to have been insipid. All I knew at the time, though, was that I was acting away for dear life. As soon as the role was over, I forgot it. Until I was twenty-five, I did nothing but work. Then I got married, to Max Reinhardt, a book publisher. I still went on acting. I still went on working. I still had no friends outside the theatre. I went home with the script, and that was all. When I was thirty, I looked back and felt that I had had nothing at all. I was divorced six years after my marriage. Around that time, I began to feel bored with the theatre. In some ways, it was like a kind of strait jacket. I felt that especially when I was playing Shaw. I would get into a certain role as it had been written by Shaw—written in a special way, so that there was only one way of acting the part. That one way was right and any other way was wrong. Roles like that don't give you much elasticity. Shaw writes musically, as though for an orchestra. As an actor, you're simply one musician in the orchestra, and, as such, you can't go off suddenly on your own. You must play it the way it's orchestrated. It was something, however, to discover that there was a correct way and an incorrect way of playing a part in the light of what the author had intended. And that, I must say, helped me become more workmanlike. I learned how to build a role into a solid structure based on the written words in the play. But I missed having room to explore the character.

Acting is delicious in anticipation but more delicious in retrospect. I don't always know if audiences like me. I worry about boring them. I enjoy acting, but the special feeling of enjoyment that comes when you get caught up in a part is rare. You're lucky if it happens once a month. The moments come suddenly. Suddenly you're able to swim through a scene. It happened to me occasionally when I was playing in "Separate Tables." Three times, in fact: the last night of the run in London, in 1956; at the Actors' Fund benefit in New York; and my last night in New York. It may be that I knew it was the last time or the only time, that I wouldn't have another chance, and so I knew that whatever I wanted to do, I'd better do it quick. I can enjoy doing a part without being terribly glad about it. I don't clap hands, and all that. I find it very exciting working with an American cast. American acting has a·sort of guttiness, a complete giving up to the acting that the young actors do here, and this is an enormously vital thing. American actors, on the whole, are much more perceptive about adhering to the truth. They make more effort to seek out the truth than English actors seem to do. English actors have more adroitness. Technically, they're better equipped. But American actors—not stars, especially, but the people in little parts, coming on with a tea tray and that sort of thing—never fake it up. It's a matter of trying to find the truth. Without this effort the theatre can become anemic. There could be a lot more of that sort of thing in England.

When I'm in a play, I spend in-between times waiting to get to the theatre. I always get to the theatre an hour and a half earlier than is required. One has to be absolutely at one's best, and to do that one has to turn everything into preparation for it. I can't eat before a show. I have a light lunch, and after the show I finally have a warm meal. One thing I can always take, physically, is bad weather. When you're brought up in England, it's easy to take heat or cold or fog or rain. I don't go to the theatre very much as part of the audience. It makes me ill—I have claustrophobia—to be in a crowd of people. And I find myself identifying with the actors on the stage in a way that is exhausting. It's absolute purgatory for me to go to an opening night. When I was younger, I worked harder and liked it better. I lived inside the theatre. Now I work differently and more effectively. When you're starting, your energy is different. Not that I would want to be eighteen again. It's not a very enviable age, energy or not. The way you feel has tremendous bearing on what emerges in a part. Health is very important. It's awfully hard to inject anything into a part if you feel miserable as hell. It's the churning up in acting that makes it tiring. Only a phenomenally strong man can play Macbeth. He's got to be extraordinarily fit. The role of Macbeth is demanding in every sense; it never lets up.

Once I accept a part, I feel relieved for the moment that the first important decision has been made. After that, I always think, I've got it now; I wish it were over with. One thing I hate is having to decide whether to do a part, although, actually, when I first read a script, I know immediately whether I want to do it. One *smells* it immediately. One thing that puts me off in reading a play is getting too strong an impression of the author—feeling that the author is intruding upon the play. If I find myself thinking that I know what sort of chap the author is, I know it's a bad play. In all bad plays, you see what sort of chap the author is; that is, you have to think about it. Finding the right part doesn't really mean that the part is right for you; it's more that you are right for *it*. Some plays need more homework than others. You do a lot of homework on all of them, but you pretend that you don't. More homework is required when the language is complex, difficult, with lots of colors. When you start to work on a part, it's easier if you know how you're going to emerge. But it's often more exciting if you don't know. When I start to work on a part, I read it over and over, and one little bit after another falls into place. Then I begin to see a moment truthfully. I work up to that moment, and then I work away from it. Such moments are why you want to play the part. When I was asked to do "Separate Tables," in which I played two roles, I had exactly nine days in which to study the characters, and it ordinarily takes that long just to learn the lines and the moves. I was too tired to think about what I was doing. I just did it. I've been in more plays than I can count in repertory and on English and American stages over a period of almost twenty-five years. I've been forced to examine closely, and appreciate, every character I've played.

I've found that it's fatal to regard acting as necessarily fun. It's marvellously exciting, but one ought not to regard it as something necessarily pleasurable. A lot of acting takes the form of self-indulgence. I remember one time when I was playing Ellie Dunn in "Heartbreak House" in Birmingham, the tears were streaming down, and I was tearing the place apart. Once you get taken hold of, it's easy to let go and go on that way, but it's not acting. The director stopped me. He caught me between scenes and said to me, "You're here not to enjoy yourself but to give pleasure to the audience." One must know that before taking a part. I've made terrible mistakes in accepting some roles and turning down others, but some good is bound to come of doing, rather than not doing, any role. The most successful actors are actors who simply keep acting. My theory is either do it and don't talk about it or don't do it and don't talk about that, either. Finding the right play is of the first importance. Good judgment is needed in selecting roles. The judgment *can* be someone else's, but I have always had to use my own. It requires a dogged perseverance to act.

I admire Edith Evans for her taste, her discrimination, her selectivity, her restraint. I admire Laurence Olivier and Ralph Richardson and John Gielgud for the same qualities. I've been lucky in having had the opportunity to act in plays with all of them. Laurette Taylor was great. There was no chichi about her. She was a human being who imitated no one. I somewhat resist being confined to what the author says I must be, but I suppose authors have to reduce feelings to something that is acceptable to mass audiences. The most important thing in acting is truthfulness—to life and to the author and to the style of the play.

ANTHONY PERKINS

*The delineation of character may have been done
originally by the author, but you go out there onstage
and frost it with yourself.*

I was born on April 4, 1932, in New York City. When I was five, my
father, the actor Osgood Perkins, died of a heart attack, at the age
of forty-five. After living in New York for a while, my mother and I
moved to Boston, where she worked as head of the Stage Door Canteen.
She's interested in the theatre, because of my father, but she's not an
actress. We lived in Brookline. I attended various schools in the
region—Brooks School, North Andover, for a couple of years, then
the Browne and Nichols School, in Cambridge. From the age of five,
I wanted to act, but I was ten before I had the feeling I had to do
something about it, and it wasn't until I was fifteen that I felt I was
ready to start. Then I played in "Junior Miss," by Jerome Chodorov
and Joseph Fields, at the Brattleboro Summer Theatre, in Vermont.
I became single-minded about acting in high school, where I nevertheless went in for athletics and played tennis, because I hated to be in-
doors. My mother was keen on my finishing my education before I got
too deeply involved with acting. She wanted me to be educated, so that
if it turned out I didn't have ability for the stage I could do something
else. She felt there was no sense in rushing me. When I was eighteen,

I went to Rollins College, in Florida, where I majored in history and English literature. I joined a fraternity, and talked girls and sports cars and records. I was one of the few guys in the fraternity who cared about the theatre. The college had a pretty high-powered Drama Department and two theatres. I was happy at Rollins. I enjoyed the Drama Department. The two teachers in charge of it, Wilbur Dorsett and Howard Bailey, got me to learn the fundamentals of playing on the stage—walking, facing front, developing facets of a character. I got a chance to play parts in "Harvey," "The Warrior's Husband," "The Importance of Being Earnest," "The Madwoman of Chaillot," and many other productions. I was still too inexperienced to get to play a leading man, so I played parts like the thirty-five-year-old reporter in "Goodbye, My Fancy." There was something wonderful to me about acting on the stage. Instead of really acting, however, I was performing in an outgoing, senseless rush at the audience, using my appeal, taking advantage of easy situations, being charming and lush. Acting, I was to learn later on, is more circuitous. It takes thought, consideration, real construction.

After I had been at Rollins for three years, I hitchhiked to California and made a screen test for a movie called "The Actress." The following December, I worked in the picture, in the role of Jean Simmons' suitor, and since I was on Christmas vacation, I missed only one week of school. I returned to Rollins for one term. Then I came to New York and got myself transferred to Columbia University, because I thought that when the picture was released I'd get acting jobs in television on the side while finishing college. I played in some television dramas, put on by the "Kraft Television Theatre," "Studio One," and others—usually those family plays, in which I was the boy with hair falling down over his forehead. Before graduating, I auditioned for Elia Kazan for the part James Dean got in the film "East of Eden." Although I didn't get that part, Kazan hired me to play in "Tea and Sympathy," with Joan Fontaine, on Broadway, when John Kerr left the play. I played the part of the young man for thirteen months. Then William Wyler chose me to play one of Gary Cooper's sons in the movie "Friendly Persuasion," for which I was nominated for an Academy Award. After that, I made more movies, including "Fear Strikes Out," with Karl Malden; "Desire Under the Elms," with Sophia Loren; "The Matchmaker," with Shirley Booth; "Green Mansions," with Audrey Hepburn; "On the Beach," with Gregory Peck and Ava Gardner; and "Psycho," with Janet Leigh. I found Hollywood terribly hard on the nerves. In movies, you feel thwarted. No rehearsals, just meeting your fellow-actors, and then you're right in production. It was in "Friendly Persuasion," however, that I first realized what acting could be. When I watched Phyllis Love and Mark Richman work, I saw the difference for the first time. When I worked in "The Actress," I didn't learn. In all the time I played in "Tea and Sympathy," I didn't learn. But I saw Phyllis Love on the set of "Friendly Persuasion" making copious notes and then I heard her asking the director all kinds of questions, like "What time of day is it supposed to be?" So I started to wonder about what I was really doing, and I'd say, "What time of day is it supposed to be?" Then the lights began to go on, and I was learning about Method acting. I began to learn to rely less on intuition and to study the architecture of a role. It's easy, as a young actor, to depend on your intuition, which often leads to an inaccurate motivation for the character you're portraying. I began to get a reputation for being a director-botherer. After "Friendly Persuasion," I made "The Lonely Man," and by that time I really understood the Method. I worked with a girl named Elaine Aiken, who was an absolute slave to the Method. The movie was a Western—with Jack Palance as a retiring gunfighter—and together Elaine Aiken and I finished off Henry Levin, the director, with our questions. Usually, I'm a great believer in what a director tells me. I'm very malleable.

Of the various kinds of acting, I prefer the stage. I played the part of Eugene Gant in "Look Homeward, Angel," by Ketti Frings, and the part of Gideon, the young man, in the Frank Loesser musical "Greenwillow." After Hollywood, being on the stage felt great. You can't separate the actor from the circumstances in which he works. When you act in a picture, the director can threaten and bully you or else let you do it your own way and then just cut it out of the picture and not show it at all. The only way to keep control over what you do is to act on the stage. Once you walk out there, nobody can shout at you or pull strings and get you to jump. Once you're out there acting, you're doing it on your own. Life in Hollywood is corrosive for the actor. The minute you're through making a picture, you're an actor out of a job. It's over. If you're a big star, theoretically you have no worries, but even if you're the kingpin, all you can do is play croquet or see that your kids don't fall in the pool. For the half-way stars in Hollywood, life is really tense. I just can't fit into the Hollywood march. I've never been able to swing there. All that talk about values and yappety-yap. Getting up at six, driving out in fog and smog to the studio. All those people who nibble at you like hungry piranhas. The sluggishness of the studios. Everything overcome by a kind of sleeping sickness. Even in the acting, you think you've done something but it turns out to be not what you expected. I don't like to go into a movie unless I can work with the very best director, of my own choice. Being good in movies is like doing heart surgery. It's great for some people. The fine thing about Broadway is that if you're in a hit you can play in it for a year. Even television is better for an actor than Hollywood movies, especially if you're making a nice, comfortable series. At least, that way you're steadily employed. However, for myself, I want something more than steady employment from acting. An important man in one of the big movie studios in Hollywood once said to me, "You're going to make good pictures and bad pictures, and if something doesn't come off, we'll just look at each other and say, 'It's only movies.'" I was shocked. Of course, some movie producers don't take that attitude at all.

I'm very happy as an actor. Every night I perform on the stage is a creative experience for me. When I'm in a play, I look forward all day long to appearing in the play at night. Even if I have a lot on my mind or don't feel well when I get to the theatre, as soon as I hear my cue I feel all right again. I feel absolutely at ease in a fiction of some kind. I might come unglued if I couldn't act. Acting is built in, dependable, acceptable. When I first became a little well known and had a day when I was feeling down, I'd actually say to myself, "Well, I think I'll go out for a walk and be recognized." There's even something to that. Onstage, you feel you can make the audience listen to you and watch you. When I played in "Greenwillow," we'd get terrible houses—only a handful of people on some nights. I always liked that. The audience would be feeling terrible; they'd be wishing they hadn't come, because nobody else came. But I always felt I could bring them out of it. I always felt that if there were five or ten people out there, I could give each one my individual attention. The real purpose of this particular medium, after all, is to stir people, to touch them. You're on a raised platform taking up a small area in front of which is a larger area with a lot of seats and people in them.

397

Before that, you're sitting in a cubicle putting stuff on your face to make it look darker. Then you get on that raised platform with some other people and you try to reveal situations and emotions, you try to inform the audience and to enlighten it. When you walk out there, you think of nothing but the application of yourself to your part. You can't deny your own feelings; you must believe in the emotions you express, but you have to keep some detachment. If another actor is near you, you can't walk right into him. You submerge your own personality, but you can't ever lose yourself entirely in the part. If you're playing the part of someone in love, for example, you can't make your voice a whisper, as you might do in real life. You can't do that onstage, or your response is lost. Every night when I go out onstage, I remind myself to keep my responses fluid, to keep them really moving. Whatever is said to me, I can really respond. I never walk out feeling rigid. Although I never push my responses, I do try to coax them. I learned that from Kim Stanley, who once said somewhere, when she was in "Picnic," that acting is like playing the piano or the guitar; no matter how good you are, you're never as good as you can be—you never realize the full potentialities of your instrument, which is yourself. I believe in Method acting, but I've always been afraid to audition for the Actors' Studio. They might say no.

When I see my mother, we don't talk very much about acting, although she's given me some very sound advice on how to get my own way and still not be difficult. Before I went into one of my leading roles on the stage, she told me, "If you're the star of a show, you've got to be just right. That's your responsibility." Nothing is as raw as a play rehearsing. It's also at its most exalted level then. That's when it's most involved, and you can't clutter up your life with outside problems. In "Look Homeward, Angel," I was almost fired in the beginning because I seemed inattentive. I have an undisciplined appearance. I can't stand still too long; I want to get on with it. On reading a script for the first time, I see myself in a part in two ways: first, the qualities in the part I can dramatize through the application of my own personality, and, second, how I can enhance the part with aspects of my own personality. Once I've done a part right, I just assume I'll do it again. One of my stage directors taught me that the best acting is spare acting, the sparest, with the smallest gesture, the greatest economy. I've learned how to mete it out.

SIMONE SIGNORET

Acting creates the illusion of life, because what you give is out of yourself, but if you give everything in yourself to the acting, you miss your own life.

I was born, to French parents, on March 25, 1921, in Wiesbaden, Germany, during the French occupation after the First World War. My father, André Kaminker, who recently died, was Jewish; my mother, whose maiden name was Signoret, is Catholic. My father was a charming, brilliant man, a little superficial, and not meant to be head of a family. I grew up with two younger brothers—Alain, who became a film director and was drowned while making a film about fishermen, and Jean-Pierre, who is twenty-eight and is a professor of Latin, French, and Greek in a *lycée* near Paris. When I was two, my father, who knew five languages and was a professional translator, moved us to France, to Neuilly-sur-Seine, a fine middle-class suburb of Paris, where we tried to be middle-class and failed. I always wanted my family to be average, to be like other families. Our family had the appearance of being average, but we were not. After my mother, an educated woman, took me to the Comédie Française to see the classics, I never wanted to be anything but an actress. When I was fifteen, I started to read a lot, and the next year I went to England for three months as a paying guest on an English poultry farm. I arrived ahead of another French girl guest, and by the time she arrived, I had a little bit of English, so I translated for her, and thus began to learn a lot of English. I have never lost my English. Recently, when I made a French movie called "Les Mauvais Coups," I was able to do my own English dubbing for a version to be shown over here. I like to do that, but since a lot of the subtlety is lost in any dubbing, I also like to feel that people here will have the opportunity to see the original French version; in such cases, both should be available. At eighteen, I took my last examination at the *lycée* three days after the German occupation of France began. It was a black period for the family. My father, who was already in his fifties, nevertheless went to England, on June 18, 1940, to join de Gaulle as an officer, and did a great deal of interpreting, writing, and broadcasting for the Free French. As the eldest, I felt I was head of the family. I felt responsible for my mother and my small brothers. In some ways, it was the best thing that has happened to me in my whole life, because it led me to get into an entirely different social group. I learned typewriting and took a job typing for the *Nouveau Temps*—a pro-German newspaper. It was disgusting. I might have become a collaborationist myself, because at that time I had no conscience about anything; I must say I was quite tough. But through my job I met a new group of people, the people of the Saint-Germain-des-Prés of wartime. There were only three cafés to go to and no big lights in the district, and it was wonderful. I met actors who were not famous but who were interesting and exciting people. Some of them worked as extras in films. I discovered people who were success-haters. And with them I found a little bit of myself. They showed me good books, and they introduced me to the avant-garde and to new feelings about life. In those days, there were two kinds of people in Occupied France—those with the wallets, in which they kept all the tickets for bread and meat for themselves, and the others, who never had wallets and who never had tickets, because they gave them away to other people. I discovered the difference between these two types of people.

When I was twenty, although I was tough, I was also very shy. Then I became an extra in films, and something broke inside my shyness. My new friends taught me to regard acting as an honest job. They told me it was all right to want to act, all right to leave the typing job. Before that, I had never said anything to anybody about acting. It was stirring in me, but it was a secret. I thought that *everybody* had a need to be an actor but that it was a dream you shouldn't talk about. I found out that it wasn't such a ridiculous thing, that you could really do it as well as dream it. These people who were my friends taught me such a lot about life and about acting. Now they are getting older, and they are on the bitter side. They talk of nothing but Brecht and Ionesco, and they despise anything that is light. But in the early days they were very helpful to me in my life and in my career. For a young actor to be an extra is very frustrating but very good for him. You learn to be on time for appointments. You are treated anonymously, and it is good for your health to be lost in the crowd. Also, you see a lot of actors acting. The first film I worked in as an extra was "Le Prince Charmant," in 1941. I was paid a hundred and seventy-five francs—or about four dollars—a day, for a week's work. On my first day, I was frightened and disappointed. The scene was an elegant bar, but I had nothing elegant to wear, and because it was wartime there was no makeup. The producers wanted the women extras to wear spring furs. As a result, the extras who had spring furs stood near the camera, and I, since I had no furs, was put in the background. In 1942, I was in the chorus of a bad stage version of "Oedipus," called "Dieu Est Innocent," for fifteen francs a day—and I started to learn about acting. After two months, however, I was fired, because I was giggling too much onstage. I learned that one must have the discipline not to giggle onstage, and I went back to extra jobs in movies. The quality of movies was very low in those war days. I studied acting with a magnificent woman named Solange Sicard. With her I learned quite a lot, and one most important thing—never, in French, to put stress on a verb. Only phonies do that.

My first real movie part was as a prostitute in "Les Démons de l'Aube," made in 1945. I was married to a director, Yves Allegret, and was pregnant when I made the movie. When my baby, Catherine, was twenty-one days old, I was hired by Jacques Feyder to play with his wife, Françoise Rosay, in his movie "Macadam." I will never be as happy as I was the night I was chosen for the part, when they called me and told me. Again I played a prostitute. Françoise Rosay is very handsome, very elegant, and very wonderful, and I was very much afraid of her. She took me aside and gave me some good advice: You can't act unless you know your lines upside down. I call her "Madame" to this day. She says "*tu*" to me. I worship her. Feyder taught me how to act with natural gestures and not fiddle with objects for no reason. He taught me how to be relaxed. The picture came off superbly for me. The other actors were already known. It is always the newcomer who steals the picture, and I was new, so I got all the attention. I was on top of the world. I was immediately offered a part in an English picture, "Against the Wind." It took four months, and I was away for four months from my baby. When I came back, she didn't recognize me. It was a horrible moment for me. After I had been married for seven years, I met Yves Montand. It was 1949. I was on holiday in Saint-Paul-de-Vence, in the mountains between Cannes and Nice. He was playing on tour there. As soon as I met him, I fell in love with him. I left my husband and my home, which was bad. I left my child, which was worse. People didn't like it, but I had to do it. I started to live with a man who is a performer, which was a complete change in my life. Before I married Yves Montand, I had never made a picture without signing up to do another, but Yves wouldn't be happy if I worked all the time, so I decided that I would do only what I liked very much, and I have since made very few films. My daughter Catherine lives with us now. I remember that when my mother called for me at school, she would be dressed to look like a maid, because we did not have a maid. When I've called for Catherine at school, I've tried to look like any other mother.

I like my life today. I feel I must be careful and not do too much acting, because there is always the danger that I might forget my own life. If you take that path, you find yourself with nothing. Yves is a wonderful performer. I admire him very much. We are almost always together. If you give everything to acting, you are embroiled in a constant fight for a bigger part, a better part. There is no time to live. You get old and you still want to be young. That is not life. A woman is a fool if she does not learn this. I was lucky, also, to learn before I was thirty that you cannot show emotion as an actress if you have never experienced it. It is like showing the grand passion for a man. You cannot do it if you do not feel it. There are some actresses who are always taking and taking in life and never giving, and they live entirely in their acting. That may be the only kind of satisfaction they are seeking, but to me they look lonely and frantic. When I am making a picture, I never feel relaxed. When Catherine is ill, it always seems more important when I am not working. It frightens me that I don't feel as anxious about these things when I am working. Any woman who is an actress should be able to feel frightened by this. If she doesn't, she should change by the time she is thirty; otherwise it is too late. I was happy about the prizes that came to me for my acting in "Room at the Top," and it was one of my happiest days when I was given the Academy Award for it. I had decided very carefully to make that movie, just as I had decided only after great thought to make "Casque d'Or" and "Diabolique." What was for Yves and me the greatest enjoyment was when we played together in Paris, in Arthur Miller's "The Crucible," on the stage, for one year. For Paris, a run of one year is enormous. People came to the theatre to see the play who had never before gone to the theatre. Yves drew them there. In France, a popular singer is a big hero, as a football star is in Brazil or a bicycle champion in Italy. We loved the audience we got. We never grew tired of the play for one second. We lived in an apartment across the street from the theatre we played in. Sometimes, at seven o'clock, we would feel, Oh, not tonight again, but once we got into the theatre we were happy. I prefer acting on the stage to acting in films, where you do the part in little bits from day to day. You can't leave the part while you are making a movie; if you don't hang on to the character completely, you can lose it. But on the stage you start to be the character at nine o'clock, and as soon as the curtain comes down, it is finished. It is out of you. You can go back to your life.

ROBERT PRESTON

*Next to acting myself, watching other actors gives me
my greatest joy.*

I was born on June 8, 1918, in Newton Highlands, Massachusetts. My
full name is Robert Preston Meservey. I was lucky in having young
parents, Frank and Ruth Rea Meservey, who married before they
were twenty-one. My father now works in the office of a coat-
lining business in Los Angeles. I have one brother, Frank, Jr.,
twenty-two months younger than I am, who lives in Los Angeles,
is married, has two children, and works for a beer distributor. When I
was two years old, my parents moved from Massachusetts to California,
and went to live in my maternal grandparents' house, in Los Angeles.
My grandmother was a strongly matriarchal type, and she had
decided to move the whole family out to California for the sake of
my grandfather's health; he was believed to have tuberculosis. My
father was working as a billing clerk for American Express, and it
didn't matter to him where he worked. To him, a job was a job. My
grandmother bought a large old white frame house in Lincoln Heights,
the poorest section of East Los Angeles. She thought a sanatorium was
going to be built there, because the region was higher than the rest

of the city and was considered good for people with respiratory ailments. Eleven people—my grandparents, my parents, my brother and I, and my mother's two brothers and three sisters—moved into this house. The neighborhood was predominantly Mexican, and when I started going to school there, I found I was the only white American. I was also younger than the other children in my class. All in all, I felt strongly that I was a member of a minority group. It made a listener out of me. I hung around bashfully, listening to what everybody else said, and I've been a very careful listener ever since.

Both my parents always worked, and so did my aunts and uncles. We had a fluid household; everyone came and went as he pleased. I'd come home from school and find only my grandmother there, cooking oyster stew or some other New England dish. I'd go out and hang around in the houses of our Mexican neighbors. Poor as they were, they had furniture and other possessions that they'd brought from Mexico, and I loved the way their homes looked—the velvet table scarves with hand-painted designs, and all the rest. There was always a strong, wonderful aroma of tortillas cooking in oil. I got to like their food better than oyster stew. My mother worked at the Platt Music Corporation, one of the leading music stores in Los Angeles, which carried everything from grand pianos to harmonicas. She was manager of the phonograph-records department, and was the foremost authority on records in town. That was before the day of the disc jockey. Every record-company representative or song-plugger who came to town would get in touch with my mother. Sometimes she'd dress up in a beaded gown and pat me on the head and go off to attend a record-company convention at the Cocoanut Grove. A lot of important movie people bought records from my mother, and she knew their tastes. At home, we had a Victrola—one of the early models, with the big horn and the picture of a white puppy dog on it. Mother was a pianist, and could play just about everything. When I was seven, the family bought a second-hand upright piano for me to take lessons on. It cost seventy-five dollars, and had supposedly belonged to Russ Columbo, the singer. I took lessons for four years. There was always music in our house. Both of my uncles tried to play the mandolin. When I was fourteen, my parents took my brother and me and moved into a house in a predominantly Italian neighborhood. I still have a working knowledge of both Spanish and Italian. When

I've had to play a Spanish or Italian role, I've never had a problem with the dialect, because I listened so carefully as a kid. Our neighborhood cobbler and barber had wonderful tenor voices. Mr. Bellin, our grocer, played the zither. On warm summer nights, all of us would get together, sitting around on front stoops, and play and sing. I learned to play the guitar and the trumpet, and to belt out arias from operas. I could sing "Vesti la Giubba!," from "Pagliacci," and the tenor part in the quartet from "Rigoletto." I also learned to sing "O Sole Mio" in both Sicilian and Neapolitan dialect. The only one in our family who is not musical is my father, who more or less goes for Lawrence Welk.

My mother always brought home the latest records and made the rest of us listen to everything she enjoyed, so I heard records of John Barrymore doing passages from Shakespeare long before I could appreciate them. Still, I always liked to listen. I began to prefer listening to records of music to playing my own. My mother started taking me to see plays, put on by touring companies, when I was about eight. She'd hear about the plays in the music store, and she decided that it was important for me to see them, even if I didn't know what they were all about. After school, I'd wait for Mother outside the music store, and when she got through work, off we would go. One of the shows I remember best is the original production of "Tobacco Road," with Henry Hull. When I was ten or eleven, I used to sit around for hours with the school janitor, a former Shakespearean actor, who was about seventy years old. He'd nail me after school and talk on and on about the theatre. I learned a lot from him. About the Broadway theatre in 1918, about the Hungary of Ferenc Molnár's time—things like that. My idea of homesickness isn't for a place to go back to; it's for all the things I've heard about or read about. There are times when I'm not sure whether some of my experience is my own or things I've read or heard about.

Almost every kid takes part in little school plays, and I did that, and also took part in little plays at the Episcopal Church. I started going to movies and vaudeville shows regularly when I was ten. Vaudeville teams—Kolb & Dill, for instance, and Weber & Fields—were in their heyday then. I'd watch them and learn their routines and then do imitations of them for the kids in the neighborhood. A number of us kept little black books of the jokes we heard in vaudeville. Ernie

Sarracino, who was one of my friends all through school and is now a character actor, still has a fat collection of these jokes. I attended the Abraham Lincoln High School in Los Angeles, and each year, in my English class, I competed in the acting of passages from Shakespeare's plays. Class winners would compete with the winners in the other schools in the city. I had a great advantage, because I'd spent all that time listening to recordings of John Barrymore. I was Shakespearean champ of my school three times—as Julius Caesar, as Polonius, and as Hamlet. When I was a freshman, my English teacher was a man named E. J. Wenig, who also headed the school drama department. His love was Shakespeare, and he imparted his love of Shakespeare to me. He got me to play leads in Shakespearean productions and in "Clarence," "The Goose Hangs High," and a lot of other items in the Samuel French catalogue. E. J. really led me to share his own love of acting. I never thought about doing anything else. He was right for me, and I was an apt learner, and everything went smoothly. I took that for granted. E. J. knew about every acting group or theatre company in or near the city of Los Angeles. He had a sidekick named Hegner, who made our costumes at school and did our makeup. The living room of Hegner's apartment was filled with racks and racks of costumes. He could have outfitted the entire Old Vic Company with them. He and E. J. were both wonderful guys. I graduated from high school when I was sixteen, but E. J. wasn't letting go. He told me about the Elizabethan Stock Company, a group headed by Patia Power, Tyrone's mother, which had come up to Los Angeles from San Diego. E. J. told me they were casting for some roles in "Julius Caesar." I was a pretty good Julius Caesar for my age, so E. J. took me over to the company director to read for the role. I had already reached my present height—six foot one. So I read for the role and got it. I played opposite Ty's mother. E. J. had always told me, "In doing Shakespeare, just remember your iambic pentameter." I remembered it, and I played the role for several weeks. I was paid about seven dollars a week, and then, for some sordid reason or other, the company folded.

In 1934, we were hit by the depression. My father lost his job. It never entered my head even then that I could do anything but act. E. J. had contacts all over, and he took me to the Jewish Forum, a theatre group putting on "He That Is Greatest"—a play about a modern-day Robespierre. The star was a famous old professional character actor named Josef Swickard. He was so old he couldn't hear, and he took his cues by reading lips. Eventually, he committed suicide, jumping off the big "HOLLYWOOD HILLS" sign. Each letter was as big as a building, and I think he jumped off the "D." The play was so far to the left that it was practically anarchistic, but I never asked who was behind it, or even who had written it. My only concern was that my part, that of a young anarchist, was good and I was allowed to play it. From that point on, I began to mingle with all kinds of bohemian and semi-bohemian groups, and also with a lot of wealthy people living in Hollywood Hills who wanted to sponsor plays. I'd go along with groups giving auditions at some of the luxurious homes of wealthy people to raise money for plays. We'd be served a good lunch, take a swim in the pool, and spend some time lying around in the sun, and then we'd do our stuff. It felt good to me just to get out on the lawn and show what I could do.

Then my father went to work for the W.P.A. in San Bernardino, putting up high-tension lines for the government, at much lower pay than he'd been getting, so I had to buckle down and get a job to help out at home. I became a clean-up man at Santa Anita Park, picking up cigarette stubs and sweeping the aisles in the mornings, and parking cars for the patrons in the afternoons. I got ten dollars a week, plus tips. Will Rogers would always give a good tip, and Clark Gable was always a cinch for fifty cents. That was big money in those days, and the other parking attendants would fight with me to get him. He always flipped the coin to me. I spent two seasons at the race track, and toward the end of that time I started going along with some members of my clean-up crew who were rehearsing for readings for plays at the Pasadena Community Playhouse, not far from the race track. There were no performances at the Playhouse on Sunday, and open readings were held then. A director and actor named Thomas Browne Henry gave me my first chance to read. After that, I got one small part after another at the Playhouse. I kept my job at the race track for a while, but finally the acting crowded it out. The Pasadena Community Playhouse and the Pasadena School of the Theatre consisted of five theatres: the Playbox, which was probably the first theatre-in-the-round in the country; the Junior Stage and the Senior Stage, which were used mostly by junior and senior students, respectively, in the Playhouse School of the Theatre; the Laboratory Theatre, for trying out new playwrights; and the Main Stage, the largest, which was used primarily by established actors and postgraduates. The community gave the Playhouse wonderful support. I was one of the established actors, and the Main Stage was my hangout. The big ambition of the students at the Pasadena School of the Theatre was to be cast in a play with established actors at the Main Stage. In 1940, I married one of those students, Catherine Feltus, who had come to the school from Indiana. We had met three years earlier in T. S. Eliot's "Murder in the Cathedral," when I played one of four knights and Catherine was one of twelve members of the speaking chorus. Thomas Browne Henry played the Archbishop. Then we acted together in "Night Over Taos," by Maxwell Anderson, in which I played the heavy and Catherine played the ingénue. My wife and I have always had a special feeling for the Pasadena Playhouse. In 1946, we went back there together for a summer festival of its greatest hits and played in Victor Jory's version of David Belasco's "The Girl of the Golden West;" Catherine took the leading part of the girl and I was the bandit.

After we were married, Catherine had no burning ambition to keep on acting, so we decided to have just one career in the family. My wife enjoys what I do. We live in an old converted carriage house on two and a half acres of land in Rye, New York, on Long Island Sound. We take care of the grounds ourselves, and we enjoy our privacy. I have my own woodworking shop, and my wife is an excellent cook. We have no children. Catherine's judgment of plays and movie scripts is unusually good, and I depend on her opinions. We may argue about the merits of a script, but I've never done anything she hasn't approved of.

In the spring of 1938, when I was playing the part of Harry Van, singing and dancing, in Robert E. Sherwood's "Idiot's Delight," at Pasadena, a Paramount lawyer named Sidney Justin, who lived in Pasadena and saw most of our plays, suggested that I try out for the movies. Everett Crosby, Bing's brother, who knew my mother and was sort of my agent, took me to see a talent expert at Paramount. The talent man took one look at me and said to Everett, "I told you to stop bringing me truck-drivers." So I went home and decided to forget about the movies. But the next day I received a call from the executive producer of B pictures at Paramount, asking me to come back for a test, which I did—the day after that. It turned out that there was a feud going on between the producer of B pictures and the talent man, and the producer wanted to use me to prove that the talent man was incompetent. For my test, I did a comedy scene from "Idiot's Delight" and a Killer Mears sequence from "The Last Mile." I did tests all day long. The result was the best thing I've ever done for the movies. I wound up with a contract for six months, with options, at a hundred dollars a week. The producer of B pictures had proved something or other, and the talent man was fired. But I wasn't given anything to do. Paramount might have forgotten all about me and dropped my option after six months, but I decided not to just sit around waiting. I did another show at Pasadena. Whenever actors talk about how important it is to be in the right place at the right time, I always think it is better to be in *some* place at *some* time, doing *some*thing. Late in 1938, I heard that Robert Florey, Paramount's best cameraman, was going to direct a movie called "King of Alcatraz," with J. Carrol Naish, and was looking for someone to play a sailor. I went after the part and got it. Lloyd Nolan and I played two sailor buddies, brash young guys, on leave. It was a good part for me, and I was lucky to have a good man to act with. Nolan is generous and kind, both as a man and as an actor. We spent eighteen days shooting the film. By the second day, I felt so much at home I forgot all about the camera. B pictures in those days were very much in demand. Very often, people going to a double-feature bill, which was the usual thing, would like the B movie better than the more expensive A movie. Many of the B products had very good actors and turned out to be sleepers. People would sit through the A and enjoy the B. For me, the acting in the movies was the same kind of acting I'd always done. The main difference was that I had to learn how to stay within range of the camera. Acting wasn't a big problem then, and, actually, I've never made a big problem of it. In the early days, there was nothing to fear. You'd usually have another movie to make after you'd finished one. In my early movies, there wasn't much difference between me and my parts. In "King of Alcatraz," Lloyd Nolan and I were rivals for the hand of Gail Patrick; we went ashore, went to a bar, got drunk, returned drunk to our ship, and were chewed out by the captain, played by Harry Carey. As an actor, I was simply the author's means of getting to an audience. I knew what my character said and thought and did, because I knew what I said and thought and did.

My second movie, "Illegal Traffic," had me cast as a criminal. In my third, "Disbarred," again starring Gail Patrick, I was an assistant district attorney. My next one was "Union Pacific," with Barbara Stanwyck and Joel McCrea, and in that one I got started playing the role of a charming Western rascal. I've played all kinds of villains in the twenty-four years I've spent acting in movies. Very often, I've found it more satisfying to play villains than to play heroes. I made four movies with Alan Ladd—"This Gun for Hire," "Wild Harvest," "We Are All Heroes," and "Whispering Smith." I understood and enjoyed all the villains I played. The only villain I ever refused to play was the one in the Cecil B. deMille picture "Unconquered," because the part had no shadings; he was just a villain. After my villain period, I made about a dozen other movies in fairly quick succession, including "Beau Geste," in which I was one of three brothers—Gary Cooper and Ray Milland were the others—who joined the French Foreign Legion, and I got to play a bugle and die in the end; "Moon Over Burma," in which I was on a teak plantation somewhere east of Rangoon, fighting with Preston Foster over Dorothy Lamour; and deMille's "Northwest Mounted Police," with Gary Cooper and Madeleine Carroll, in which I was in love with Paulette Goddard. Then, there was "Reap the Wild Wind." One sequence was an old ship on the high seas. John Wayne and Paulette Goddard were on the ship, along with Raymond Massey, the chief heavy, and me, the assistant heavy, who were interested in the ship's cargo in an underhanded way. About the only role I've ever played that I didn't believe in but let myself be talked into doing was in "Typhoon," with Dorothy Lamour. She wore a sarong, and I had to wear one, too. It didn't feel right. It embarrassed me. I played a rum-soaked rotter left on an island by mutinous members of a pearl-fishing expedition, and was discovered by a beautiful maiden. I didn't like any of that. The only reason the movie was called "Typhoon" was that another company had already made one called "Hurricane." I received the most fan mail for "Typhoon" I had ever got in my life. It made me wonder. In 1942, soon after making "Reap the Wild Wind," I went into the Army as a private. I eventually served as a captain in Army Air Force Intelligence, in the European theatre of war, and I came out in 1945.

After the first blush of enjoyment at seeing myself on the screen, I gradually became more objective about myself. When I'd go to see myself in a movie, it would be almost like watching another actor. Luckily, I've never had a burning desire to exercise absolute control over what I do. Movies are the director's medium and his fun. It's the director who cuts and pastes and makes you come out one way or another. I've heard some directors say, "Give me So-and-So and let me shoot two hundred and fifty thousand feet of film and cut it the way I want to cut it, and *I'll* give you the performance." People in Hollywood still talk about the way John Ford took over Victor McLaglen in "The Informer" and got what he wanted out of that wonderful face. Generally, you have to trust your director, even though you know he makes mistakes. As a movie actor, you really have no choice. Still, it helps in the movies, as well as on the stage, when you work with actors who know exactly what they're doing. I loved working with Gary Cooper. People refer to Cooperisms and Cooper tricks, but I always found him to be a tremendous actor. In "Beau Geste," I was supposed to discover him dead. I was so convinced by his acting that I kept saying, "Speak to me, Coop! Speak to me." I wasn't bored while I was making most of my movies, because there was always some little thing I could do with a part. My first movie after I got out of the Army was "Wild Harvest," in which I played a member of Alan Ladd's wheat-harvesting gang. After that, I did two and occasionally three movies a year, including "The Macomber Affair"—based on Ernest Hemingway's story "The Short Happy Life of Francis Macomber"—in which I played Francis Macomber, and Joan Bennett, who played my wife, shot me instead of a lion, because she was in love with the guide, played by Gregory Peck; "Blood on the Moon," with Robert Mitchum and Barbara Bel Geddes, in which I was a Western heavy again; and "Big City," in which I played a Protestant minister, Danny Thomas played a cantor, and George Murphy played an Irish Catholic cop, and we all became fathers to Margaret O'Brien, a foundling. As Thomas's mother, Lotte Lehmann sang "God Bless America." Some of my later Westerns were "Tulsa," with Susan Hayward a female wildcatter, in which I helped her bring in a gusher; "The Sundowners," in which I was a talented heavy who sang and played the guitar; "My Outlaw Brother," in which I played a Texas ranger; and "Best of the Badmen," in which I framed Robert Ryan on a murder charge as a reward-hungry detective. In "The Bride Comes to Yellow Sky" episode of the film "Face to Face," I was a small-town sheriff; in "The Last Frontier" I was a colonel at an old Western fort, and Anne Bancroft, hidden under a blond wig, played my wife; in "How the West Was Won" I was a wagon master in Cinerama, and everything that had ever happened in any other Western ever made happened again, good or bad—wagon trains crossing the country, fights with Indian tribes, camping out, and vying with Gregory Peck for the hand of Debbie Reynolds. I had sporadic relief from Westerns in "When I Grow Up," in which a little boy thought his parents were too severe and ran away from home, and I was his father who drove out into a storm to find him and later died of pneumonia trying to show the boy that he loved him; and also in "The Dark at the Top of the Stairs," with Dorothy McGuire as my wife, in which I was a harness salesman who lost his job because of the horseless carriage. In 1961, I made the movie version of "The Music Man," playing the role I created on Broadway—the con man selling musical instruments to the townspeople of River City, Iowa, and getting his foot caught in the door for the first time in life because he'd fallen in love with the local music teacher.

By 1951, I'd begun to feel I was in a casting rut. I wasn't under contract to any studio, so I came to New York to do some television. Then I was offered a part in an English film called "Cloudburst," and I grabbed the chance to work in England. While I was there, I somehow began to feel more confidence in myself as an actor, and when my wife and I returned to New York, it seemed to me that the city was teeming with vitality, and we decided to stay here. Since then, I have appeared in ten plays. The first of them was a revival of Ben Hecht's and Charles MacArthur's "Twentieth Century," in which I replaced José Ferrer as Oscar Jaffe, in 1951. After that, I opened as Joe Ferguson in a revival of "The Male Animal" at the City Center, with Elliott Nugent and Martha Scott, and we were such a hit that we moved to Broadway and played there for the next eight and a half months. I then played in "Men of Distinction," by Richard Condon, a flop that closed after four performances; in "His and Hers," by Fay and Michael Kanin, with Celeste Holm; "The Magic and the Loss," by Julian Funt, which was another flop; "The Tender Trap," by Max Shulman and Robert Paul Smith, with Kim Hunter; "Janus," by Carolyn Green,

THE PLAYER: ROBERT PRESTON

with Margaret Sullavan—later replaced by Claudette Colbert and Imogene Coca—which played for two hundred and fifty-one performances; and "The Hidden River," by Ruth and Augustus Goetz, with Lili Darvas. I also made appearances in Philadelphia one summer in "Boy Meets Girl" and "The Front Page."

When I'm on the stage, the one thing I never lose sight of is that I'm an entertainer first of all. When I replaced José Ferrer in "Twentieth Century," I went to see him in the show the last night he played it. I realized that he was a powerhouse in the role, and that there were certain things he had established in the part that I couldn't change. I had to play almost an imitation of him, because the others in the cast were so dependent on every little thing he did. If I had changed things, it would have thrown the whole show off. My main obligation was to see to it that the audience was entertained. However, in December of 1957 I created the role of Harold Hill in "The Music Man" on Broadway. He's my character. Other actors may be playing him in musical tents across the country for the next ten years, but I have the satisfaction of knowing that I created him. I played Harold Hill for two years and one month, which was the longest run I'd ever been in. It was also the first musical comedy I'd ever done. When the author and composer and lyricist, Meredith Willson, and the producers, Kermit Bloomgarden and Herbert Greene, started looking for someone to play the part, they tried several well-known musical-comedy performers and found that each one wanted to add something of his own to each scene—something characteristic. So they started getting actors to read for the role. At the time, I was doing "Boy Meets Girl" in Philadelphia. One night after the show, Kermit Bloomgarden came backstage and asked me if I'd like to try out for the lead in "The Music Man." It didn't surprise me in the least to have this visit from Bloomgarden; I'm never surprised to see him in the audience anywhere in the country. I found the part of Harold Hill very comfortable to fit into. After the kind of training I'd had as a kid, the songs in "The Music Man" seemed simple and easy to do. The minute I hit the opening number for Willson, he loved it. Harold Hill was just right for me. He was a slugger, a one-punch guy, not the kind of fellow who has to pile up points in round after round. I thoroughly enjoyed being in "The Music Man." I knew I was in a hit, and it gave me a feeling of security, which must have shown up in my performance. Playing to an audience coming to see a comedy has certain advantages. They come expecting to laugh, so they help you do the part. You don't have to work so hard to get them. But you have to play each show as a separate performance; there's no way of tape-recording what you did the night before. I never allowed my performance to become mechanical.

If you face each new character you play with new understanding, you become a better actor. When I begin learning a part, I don't know exactly what I'm going to do until rehearsals start. I use externals a lot in creating a character. If you have to play an old man, you put on an old man's underwear and a shawl, and sit in a rocker, and, by God, you're going to feel like an old man. If I'm aware of a feeling of discomfort in myself, I know there's something wrong with me in the part. Sometimes talking to the director can help me overcome this feeling of discomfort. But I try not to think a lot or talk a lot about a role. Too much talking can kill it. You can talk a character right out of existence. Sometimes I lock myself in a room and go through a whole part in front of the only person I can't lie to—myself. Starting from the fact that no matter what role I play, it has to be fun, untrammelled fun, I try to find out what's wrong. One way or another, I get to feel comfortable in the part. I like to arrive at the theatre early. Usually, I can't wait to go on. All the trepidation is just fine. A little nervousness simply adds to the excitement. All that kind of thing serves to bring the playing to its peak. I love actors, and I follow everything the other actors do. I go to most of the shows on Broadway. I find something good in every show. No show is all bad. I enjoy what I do, and feel lucky that I can do it.

WALTER MATTHAU

An actor must have senses that are spongelike and soak up everything, and that means he's vulnerable. This very vulnerability can make it tough for him to work in the highly commercial, competitive field of the theatre.

I was born on October 1, 1920, in New York City. I have one brother, Henry, who is two years older than I am, and who is an Army-Navy-surplus jobber. My father was an electrician and odd-job man who worked as a process-server in the last ten years of his life. He loved music and art and debates, and spent his money on classical records. He left home when I was three, and died in Bellevue Hospital when I was fifteen. I grew up on the lower East Side, where we moved every few months, or got evicted, because we didn't have money for the rent. I lived in cold-water flats until I was twenty-eight. When I was a very small child, my mother worked in the garment district and would leave my brother and me, for a dollar a week, in the Daughters of Israel Day Nursery, on East Fifth Street; at night she'd pick us up and take us to a cafeteria for potato soup. I went to P.S. 25, Junior High School 64, and Seward Park High School. In high school, I had my full growth, six feet three, but I weighed only a hundred and twenty-five pounds, because of some nutritional deficiency. Even though I was the kind of kid who never bothered anybody, I'd keep having fights with guys who picked on me because of my skinny look.

At the day nursery, I was in a religious-festival play when I was four. I knew then that I liked to get up in front of people and do things. When I was five, I would do an imitation of our landlady coming to collect the rent. That always used to break my mother up. In grade school, I used to recite poems in assembly. I had a high soprano voice. When I was eight, I had a teacher, a Miss Creeden, who told me my voice was beautiful. She had her hair pulled back in a bun, and she had a sweet, soft face and wore glasses. She was always smiling at me when I recited. As I got older, my voice got louder and better. In junior high school, I found out that I could make the other kids laugh with my imitations of movie stars. I played my first role in a real play at a settlement house on Second Avenue—a toff in "A Night at an Inn." Soon after that, at another settlement house, I played Polonius in "Hamlet." When I was eleven, I started working for the candy concessionaires, selling ice cream and soda pop in most of the Yiddish theatres along Second Avenue, for a fifteen-per-cent commission on all sales—places like the Second Avenue Theatre and the Public and the National. I worked in those theatres for five years. I got to see many of the leading Yiddish actors, like Julius Nathanson, Herman Yablokoff, and Michael Rosenberg. I watched the way they worked. The idea of becoming an actor was lurking somewhere in my head. The Yiddish actor who made the strongest impression on me was Michael Rosenberg. The minute he walked onstage, he had his audience. He brought a whole world out with him. He was just a little guy who wore wigs and beards—very unprepossessing offstage—but he was the most interesting actor I've ever seen. He had electricity. I learned something of what I know about comic timing from him. I played bit parts in Yiddish musical comedies, which were actually tragicomedies with music, with marvellous actor-comedians, like Leo Fuchs. I earned fifty cents a night, f   seven performances a week. I soaked up everything around me just being there. I used to feel wonderful in the theatres— with the actors talking to each other, the girls changing costumes, the smell of stale smoke, the dampness, the upholstered chairs, the musty rugs, the buzzing in the audience, and the dead silence just before the curtain went up. During intermissions, I'd run out to the audience and sell my ice cream and soda pop, which netted me about two dollars and

417

fifty cents for a good week, in addition to what I earned as an actor. I was in a play called "The Dishwasher," with Herman Yablokoff. In the first act, I played an immigration officer who hit Yablokoff over the head and made him blind. In the third act, I took the part of a cellist in the orchestra Yablokoff was conducting when, in the middle of a concert, he suddenly regained his eyesight. In "Sergeant Naftula," I played a soldier in a pinochle game in the trenches during the First World War, and I'd say, in Yiddish, "Four hundred," after another player said, "Three-fifty," and Leo Fuchs was a kibitzer who, when a bomb landed on us, said sadly about me, "He never would have made it." It always got a tremendous laugh. Once, I played an old lady wearing a shawl in a play called "The Organ Grinder."

In high school, I didn't go out with girls very much, and I refused to go to dances. Instead, I read plenty of Shakespeare. I'd lock myself in the bathroom and read the plays and poems out loud to myself for two or three hours at a stretch; I liked the sound of them. I managed the campaigns of kids running for office in the student government, and every time I got up in the school auditorium to make a campaign speech, the audience would start to laugh even before I opened my mouth. There was always something about the way I stood or looked or sounded. When I graduated from high school, in 1939, I did odd jobs as a file clerk under the National Youth Administration and worked as a boxing instructor for the P.A.L., and then I joined the Civilian Conservation Corps as an axeman. I was sent to Belton, Montana, where I gained weight, broadened out, and started smoking cigars. In 1940, I went to work for the W.P.A. as a basketball and boxing coach, for twenty-three dollars a week. I tried to get into the Federal Theatre, but I found that I was ineligible, because I had never done any professional acting. Then I tried to join the Dramatic Group of the National Youth Administration. I auditioned by reciting "Casey at the Bat" and was turned down by a teacher, who told me I should learn a trade. I then worked for a year or so as a cement-bag hauler. In April, 1942, I enlisted in the Army. I was trained in the Army Air Forces radio school in Savannah, Georgia, then joined a heavy-bomber outfit in Salina, Kansas. I was a radio operator at Attleborough, England, and then a Link-trainer instructor, and I served in France, Holland, Belgium, and Germany as a radio operator-cryptographer. Then I was shipped back to the States, to Reno,

Nevada, where I was in the Air Transport Command, and in 1945 I was discharged, in Sacramento, California. I returned to Reno for a few months, working as a Railway Express hand, and there met a Red Cross worker who told me I ought to go to school in New York under the G.I. Bill of Rights. I came back, and when I heard that the Dramatic Workshop of the New School for Social Research, run by Erwin Piscator, was at the old President Theatre, a block and a half away from Madison Square Garden, where I liked to hang out and watch the hockey and basketball games and the fights, I decided to go there.

There were nice people at the school, and every month there was a check from the government. It was simple. And I began to soak up more of the climate of acting. Gradually, it started to sift down into something I could use. Piscator was a weird, eccentric man, but he knew more about the theatre than almost anybody else around at the time, and there were two terrific teachers there named Raiken Ben-Ari and Brett Warren. Piscator would come around two days before the opening of the plays we put on every couple of months. He'd redo everything the director had done. I began to get more of the real feeling for acting from him. Once, I was playing Sadovsky in Nikolai Pogodin's "Aristocrats," and he came around and said, "Matthau, you say here every line wrong." Another actor might have been destroyed. I was destroyed for about twenty seconds. Then I said, "Teach me how to say every line right." One way and another, I began to learn how to talk, how to look, how to walk—how to act.

In 1946, at the Erie County Playhouse, I was in summer-stock productions of "Three Men on a Horse," in which I played Charlie, and "Ten Nights in a Barroom," in which I played Sample Swichel. I had the finest compliment of my life when I played in "Three Men on a Horse." Someone came up to me after the show and said I was the only one in the play he didn't like. "The others looked like actors," he said. "You just looked like a poolroom bum." The next summer, I played at the Orange County Playhouse in ten plays, including "My Sister Eileen," "Saint Joan," and "Arsenic and Old Lace." In those days, I did a great deal of brooding about myself. I wasn't handsome. I didn't have good clothes. I used to wonder why people would hire me when they could get college graduates and Oxford scholars. Then it became apparent that when I got up on a stage, people actually wanted to look at me. What did I have to offer? I was a big, rugged-looking guy with a big, strong voice. There was that. Also, I had a way of showing enormous ease and enormous power onstage, both of which were valuable in the theatre. The first time I really believed it was when Piscator saw me as a judge in "Volpone" and said he was impressed. I began to believe that whatever I did onstage was important to an audience. And then I began to take seriously the idea that I was going to devote my life to being an actor. When I got my first real job on Broadway, late in 1948, at a hundred dollars a week, as a candelabrum-carrier in the coronation scene and an understudy to seven old men in "Anne of the Thousand Days," I was ecstatic. I walked up to strangers and told them about it. I was even proud that the combined ages of the seven old men came to four hundred and ninety-two.

After that, I was in "The Liar," with William Eythe, playing the fourth Venetian guard. It lasted for twelve performances. In 1951, I was a foreign correspondent in "Season in the Sun" for the last eight months of the run. I then embarked on a program of getting brilliant notices for parts I played in a series of flops. I'd be called "an actor of uncanny power" and "an actor of the first rank," and my performances would be described as "sparkling" and "inventive," but the plays flopped. Whether the plays were flops or hits, I've always liked my parts. I played a New York detective in "Twilight Walk," in 1951; an art critic in "Fancy Meeting You Again," a young, unscrupulous executive in "One Bright Day," an airlines pilot in "In Any Language," and a magazine writer in "The Grey-Eyed People," in 1952; a middle-aged salesman in "A Certain Joy" and a bookstore owner in "The Ladies of the Corridor," in 1953; a Canadian atomic scientist in "The Burning Glass," in 1954; Nathan Detroit, the gambler, in the City Center production of "Guys and Dolls," a Louisiana cracker who becomes a plantation owner in "The Wisteria Trees," and a playwright in "Will Success Spoil Rock Hunter?," in 1955; the Sol Hurok character in "Once More, with Feeling," in 1958; and Potemkin in "Once There Was a Russian," in 1961.

In 1953, I made my first movie, "The Kentuckian," in which I portrayed a bad guy with a bullwhip. It was a ridiculous part, and, as with most movie acting, I had no control over the situation; I did it because I was desperately in need of money. Later, I made several movies between plays, including "Bigger Than Life" and "A Face in the Crowd." I've also done quite a bit of television acting, and I've made a television series, "Tallahassee 7000," in which I star, about the exploits of special agents in the Florida Sheriffs' Bureau. I did it for the minor convenience of making a living. In 1955, when I was playing in "Will Success Spoil Rock Hunter?," which lasted for over a year, I met my wife, Carol Grace, a beautiful and wonderful girl who had a small part in the play. We were married in 1959. I have two small children, David and Jenny, by a previous marriage.

It's on the stage that I feel comfortable, relaxed, fulfilled, delighted. I'm happy doing stage plays. Working for the screen is almost like being in the Army; you set your mind to it and you do it. On the stage, you're wide open. There are no tricks with the camera to make you look a certain way. Nobody is going to cut you out, either. The people are sitting out there, and they're going to see you full on. Nobody can fool around with your face. Nobody can fool around with your voice. You can taste and smell what the audience feels. You know if you're coming across. You know if you're being heard. You know if you're being understood. An audience deviates about a yard compared to an actor's performance, which deviates about an inch. An audience of ladies is good if you're in a hit. The critics have told them they have permission to laugh, so they start to laugh before the curtain. They come in laughing at the ushers. Theatre benefits at a comedy make the worst audiences, because people have paid forty-eight dollars for a seat and when you've paid forty-eight dollars for a seat it's hard to laugh. I love to feel I have the whole stage in the palm of my hand. It's what every actor looks for. On the stage, you have a chance to work on a part, and then to work on it some more. Sometimes it takes me six months before I find out what a line means, even if the writing is superficial. Six months after I opened in "Will Success Spoil Rock Hunter?" I stopped seeing the printed page, with all the commas and all the notations. The printed page can remain with you for months and months, until you are experienced enough and relaxed enough to forget it early in the run and make what happens seem to be happening spontaneously.

To do a play right, really, I'd like to take two years of rehearsal. You study the character by living with him. When you rehearse, what the character is saying and how he's saying it begin to work in you. You're

developing the character. Even when you're sleeping, you're developing the character. It's solidifying in your unconscious. An actor
shouldn't think on the stage. He must only do. I don't mind being in a
bad play as long as I have my chance to take the character and make
a real person out of him—a three-dimensional character. I can always
feel the audience reacting to the natural things I do onstage. Once in
England, during the war, a magician in one of our entertainments
asked for somebody in the audience to help him, and I volunteered. I
walked across the stage to him, and later one of the guys in the audience said, "You know, you walked just like a G.I." I have a tremendous
will to be heard and I have the tools to do it with. I never want to lead
the sheltered, unmingling life. I have too much fun being anonymous,
being, say, part of a large group in a cafeteria—especially since I know
I don't really have to be there. I love the chance it gives me to browse
around in people's external behavior. I can look around as much as I
like. Not that you ever imitate people as such. But you get the feel
and the smell and the taste of how they behave. I soak that up wherever I am. Then, when I'm onstage, I use it. I have my own slant on
life. I always feel alive and I'm always conscious of why people are saying things and how they are saying them. I have a tremendous emotional reaction to social injustice and stupid behavior. I'm fascinated
by the way a businessman, for example, will speak condescendingly
to an elevator operator, or the way, if I walk into the grocery wearing
shabby clothes, the clerk says to me "Whaddya want, Mac?" and if I
wear a suit and tie, he says "Yes, sir?" When you walk onstage, you
bring all of that with you, in you. You say "Good morning," and
everybody knows whether it's going to be interesting or not.

A role I have especially loved is Benjamin Beaurevers in "A Shot in
the Dark." It's a vignette, really. I don't have to take on the job of
building the plot, making the exposition, getting the audience involved in the story line. The story line is all set up for me, and all I
have to do is to sit down facing the audience for twenty minutes and
say funny lines in a funny way. I am a suave, polished, inordinately
elegant upper-class billionaire. Here is the kind of part it is. When,
sometime during our rehearsals, Harold Clurman, the director, gave
me a watch to wear, I said, "No, this man makes his *own* time, he's so
rich and so elegant." I remembered what Piscator told an actor who
was playing Orsino, Duke of Illyria, in "Twelfth Night." He lifted his

head and sniffed and said, "It smells here people." I like to work with a director on a give-and-take basis. A director says to me, "Now you have to assume a mask. This mask is on your face. Do you mind if I talk to you?" And I say, "Not at all. I'll listen to ten per cent of what you say." At one point, when Clurman said to me, "I don't like the way you walk. I want you to walk as though you were walking to music," I said, "Rock 'n' roll or Mozart?" He said, "Anything that makes you feel like an aristocrat." So I forgot music and remembered how my mother walked after she'd washed and mopped our floor and put newspapers down for us to step on; she'd go delicately from one paper to another paper, walking like an aristocrat.

When I played a detective in "Twilight Walk," I played him as a human being who just happened to be a detective. I know about detectives, because half the friends I grew up with on the lower East Side became either detectives or firemen or sanitation men—good steady jobs in Civil Service. Most actors play detectives the way they've seen other actors play detectives. I like to think I don't do that kind of imitation. I don't go to the theatre much or watch television acting. I like to watch a prizefighter or a basketball player, not another actor, whose clichés I might automatically pick up. But I like to watch great actors, like Olivier and Brando. They have no bad habits I could pick up. I got a sense of a big leap forward in 1952 when I was given the part of the cultivated, fastidious art critic in "Fancy Meeting You Again." I told Leueen MacGrath, the co-author, with George S. Kaufman, that I doubted whether I could fall in love with the classy girl I was supposed to fall in love with in the play; I wasn't well bred enough. Miss MacGrath, who played the part of the girl herself, told me off for what she called my inverted snobbism, and said that I was talking about myself and not the character I was playing. That gave me the shock I needed. When, finally, I was accepted as well bred and I kissed the girl in the play and it was believed by the audience, it opened up a whole new phase of acting for me. In fact, that's when I became an *actor*.

GERALDINE PAGE

*Convincing an audience that I am somebody else
makes me feel that I am in control of something. To
feel that you, and only you, are in control gives you
the most wonderful sense of freedom.*

I was born on November 22, 1924, in Kirksville, Missouri. I have one
brother, Donald, younger by five years, who today is a photographer
in Chicago. My father, a Boston-born osteopath, left New England to
attend an osteopathic college in Kirksville, and remained to teach
there for a while. He now lives on a small ranch in the Arizona desert
and writes books about his philosophy of life. My mother died in
1953. When I was five, my father decided to practice osteopathy in
Chicago, and moved the family there. We lived in one neighborhood
after another, and each time I'd go to a different school. When I was
nine, we moved to a small apartment on the North Side, where our
neighbors across the hall had a piano. I became absolutely obsessed
with the piano. I wanted lessons. I kept pestering for lessons, but my
family couldn't even remotely afford to let me take them. Finally, to
shut me up, they had me take drawing lessons once a week from a
neighbor, at ten cents a lesson. By the time I was in Englewood High
School, on the South Side, Papa was established in his practice, and he
rented a piano for me. I took lessons twice a week, a few blocks from
where we lived, and loved going to the lessons and walking back home
while I did my thinking—looking at the old houses on the quiet streets,

and at the wet leaves on the sidewalks. I still love walking. Every once in a while, I'll walk from Times Square to Greenwich Village, where I live.

I always wanted to be good at something, to be somebody. I used to read biographies constantly, to find out how people did it. Leonardo, Mme. Curie, Mozart. I kept going to art classes, but I became increasingly impatient with my drawing. Mother made my brother and me go to church—Englewood Methodist Church—and they had a young people's group that gave plays. The minute I got into my first play, which was called "Excuse My Dust"—I was seventeen at the time— I knew that this was what I'd been looking for. On the piano, I'd wanted to play a concerto right off and couldn't. In drawing, I had to go to lettering class and wouldn't. But in a play I could get out there onstage right away and *do* it. Right off the bat. I played the part of the girl next door—a sort of villainess, who causes all the trouble. In rehearsal, I was so sincere everybody gasped. I made a friend of mine cry by my performance. It gave me an incredible sense of power. Then we did another play, and I couldn't wait to get onstage. This time, I played a character part—somebody's mother, about forty-five years old, in "The Little Shepherd of Kingdom Come." The third part really clinched it. I played Jo in "Little Women." I was just getting out of high school, and I asked Papa if I could study at the Goodman Theatre School of Drama, in Chicago. He said I could if I could convince him I was Jo; he thought I was more the Beth type. I played the hell out of Jo, and Papa was convinced. He and I used to sit around for hours in the kitchen back home and talk, talk, talk, in what we called "kitchen sessions." When I told him I wanted to be an actress, he said, "What do you want to act for, and go around saying *other* people's words? Why don't you write your own words?" But I'd say to him, "You writers had better be careful. Actors, by an inflection, can invert your whole meaning."

I had been raised on the movies, and was addicted to them, but it never entered my head that I could be a movie actress, because I thought I wasn't good-looking enough. Besides, nice girls from Methodist families didn't drink or smoke or *become* movie actresses. Becoming an actress at all was bizarre and presumptuous, glorious and awful, all at the same time. I didn't really know there was any professional acting outside the movies until the drama director for our young people's group took us to the Goodman Theatre. The first play I saw was Pirandello's "Right You Are If You Think You Are." I was perfectly fascinated. It was so different from movies. I couldn't get over the way you could see all the people at the same time, and the way the others sat quietly while one of them talked. After getting out of high school, in 1942, I spent the summer working at Kresge's to earn money for the Goodman Theatre School. It was a wonderful job, in a store on the corner of Sixty-third and Halsted—the wildest corner in Chicago. I sold powder puffs and Kleenex, and loved it. I took the full three-year course at the Goodman School, and have never been happier. All day long, I was doing what I was actually interested in—speech and diction, body movement, history of the theatre. We acted in front of live audiences right away. We didn't just sit around and theorize. I was hungry for everything. I was insatiable. The student directors at the school found their ideal subject in me. They'd have to con most of the other first-year students into acting in one-act plays they directed, but I'd volunteer for *all* of them. I'd run from one to another. I'd be in at least five at one time.

After acting in stock at various summer theatres in the Middle West, I came to New York, in 1950. I took acting lessons with Uta Hagen, and made the rounds asking for work. I was terrible at making the rounds. One rebuff and I'd go home and cry, or go to the movies. So I knew I had to get a job some other way. That's how I happened to concentrate on Off Broadway. In 1952, I became known to the public when I played the lead in Tennessee Williams' "Summer and Smoke" at the Circle in the Square. I played the part for eight months, then went to Broadway in "Mid-Summer," by Viña Delmar. Then I made a movie, "Hondo," with John Wayne; replaced Margaret Leighton in "Separate Tables," by Terence Rattigan, on Broadway and on tour; and played in a number of television dramas. In my personal life, in the meantime, I got married to the violinist Alexander Schneider, from whom I was divorced three years later.

Acting a part can become more and more interesting with time. I played the Princess Pazmezoglu in Tennessee Williams' "Sweet Bird of Youth" for a year and a half on Broadway, and it took more work than any other part I've ever played. She kept coming out different every time I played her. I had to be objective to enjoy playing her. When I acted her objectively, I drew on my recollections of my own pain but it was *her* pain that I felt, and I was able to remember that the character lived only in the play. When I do a part, I have a sort of map of what I think it should be and how it should come out. Most of the time, the character will take over for the whole evening—with me in control, of course. Sometimes the character comes out in ways that surprise me. What's best is when the character comes out as a whole, an entity, a real person. That's hard to accomplish. You need to be really cooking to get that. Lots of times, when you're not cooking, you have to put it together. If I do something, and a bell rings somewhere in me, and it feels right, then I have a tendency to repeat what I did and to find other pieces that fit in with it. It's like a jigsaw puzzle. After the opening of a play, a lot more little pieces come in late. When I played the Princess Pazmezoglu, she would come out brassy, tough, common, and coarse, with a wonderful texture, when what I was trying to give her was a marvellous kind of dignity, the imperious quality that the director, Elia Kazan, was always talking about. I would be giving her all those other things without thinking; they just fitted her. Sometimes she would come out with more humor than other times. What it takes to pull a character together is just plain physical energy. I was just astounded the first time I realized I was actually conveying what I had intended to convey in a part. I had always had strong impressions of people and things, but they'd end there. In acting, I could *demonstrate* them. When I first did it, I amazed everybody, and I loved it. Then it got better and better. I'd be another character, but the character lived only in the play. When you take the character over and use the character, you wreck the fabric of the play, but you can be in control of the character without taking the character over. When the character uses *you*, that's when you're really cooking. You know you're in complete control, yet you get the feeling that you didn't do it. You have this beautiful feeling that you can't ruin it. You feel as though you were tagging along on an exciting journey. You don't completely understand it, and you don't have to. You're just grateful and curious.

I've had over fifteen years of acting, and one thing I've learned is not to be in a hurry. I love to study, to gather material. It just sits there inside me, and I don't use it consciously. I think I am gifted as an actress, but my range is as great as it is as a result of my having studied Method acting. Non-Method people have a tendency to "leave it to God." They say bringing a character to life on the stage either happens or doesn't happen. Method people are greedy people; they try to coax the genie out of the jar more often. Method is what *all* actors do anyway, but people who study Method do it a little more consciously and deliberately. Good acting is good acting, and it can be arrived at in different ways. People who have the ability to do what they want to do really act in the same way that a well-trained Method actor does. The old non-Method pros give consistently good performances, but they tire of their parts more easily. Method acting is good for polishing rusty corners. Often, when non-Method actors do something in a play they repeat it night after night. It's a wearing-out process, in long runs; the juice goes out of the performance. If you're trained in Method acting, you lose your fright at trying new things; you have the courage to try a new color onstage. It trains you to take accidents and weave them into the fabric of the play. I played with one brilliant actor of the old school who went to pieces one night when another actor was late making an entrance. But I loved it; I went on and on, improvising like mad. Another time, in the London production of "The Rainmaker," I accidentally knocked over a pitcher of milk. Well, I simply went around sopping up the spilled milk. I loved that, too. In "Sweet Bird of Youth," when new things happened, all the actors would respond. Instead of getting stale, we kept getting better all the time. In Method acting, you're encouraged to interact.

What's wonderful about acting on the stage is that you have the opportunity to go out there night after night and wrestle with the same problem. Even a writer doesn't have that kind of latitude and freedom. Once he gets a thing written and published, that's it. Onstage, you have unlimited freedom. When I first read a play, I can usually visualize it and see the sequence of events. In stock, whenever I couldn't figure out what a character was, I'd go into the costume room and try on different things until it started cooking in my head. Ideas just come into my mind, and I can't stop them. Then, when rehearsals start, I can begin a process of selection. After a while, when a marvellous new reading comes out—at least once in every performance—I analyze what was different about it, and decide whether it was better than the old way or whether it was fun once but I should let it go. The main thing is the ability to control your instrument, which, in the actor, is yourself. Look the way you want the character to look. Sound the way you want the character to sound. Once you've trained the instrument to do what you want, you're in control and you're free.

JOHN GIELGUD

As an actor, I have authority. In everything else, I have no authority at all.

I was born on April 14, 1904, in London, the next-to-youngest of four children of Frank Gielgud and Kate Terry-Lewis. My maternal grandmother, Kate Terry, was well known in the London theatre for her interpretation of Juliet. She retired at the age of twenty-two to get married. She was over seventy when I knew her, as a boy—a very jolly old lady who took me to the theatre. My great-aunt was Ellen Terry, who died at the age of eighty, in 1928, the year before I started playing leading Shakespearean parts with the Old Vic. When I was fifteen, I saw Ellen Terry play the Nurse in "Romeo and Juliet" at the Lyric Theatre. She was nearly blind and very unsure of her lines, but the charm of her acting saved the première from disaster. Later, I saw her play Portia in the trial scene from "The Merchant of Venice" in a theatre at the end of one of the piers at Brighton. There were a number of those old, rickety theatres at the seaside that were cheap and quite popular before the cinema. She was wheeled down in a Bath chair, but she seemed a young woman when she came onto the stage, and her white hair didn't seem to matter at all. I also heard her recite once or twice at charity benefits, and heard her read Beatrice in "Much Ado About Nothing" with an amateur group in a private home. Altogether, she was unforgettable. She had a gruff, veiled tone of voice. She had lightness and grace. When she moved, she gave the effect of dancing. She had an expansive, generous mouth and a retroussé nose, and was restless, dynamic, fidgety, and absent-minded. She always seemed to have two or three pairs of spectacles with her, and a large bag crammed with papers. Her hearing was none too good, but she would suddenly and surprisingly be shrewd and attentive. She came to see me in a special matinée of Thomas Otway's "The Orphan," in which I played Castalio, a romantic hero—I had played Romeo the year before, but she hadn't seen me—and I heard her whispering away in the box to her companion, asking questions all the time. Then I heard her say, "Now I know how he must have looked as Romeo," which almost dried me up. She once gave me a copy of "On the Art of the Theatre," written by my second cousin Gordon Craig, the theatre designer and critic, and she had scribbled it all over with remarks and advice. I also have letters from her, one with the stark instruction "READ YOUR SHAKESPEARE."

I'm the only actor in my immediate family. Both my father and my mother were too stage-struck and too frightened of acting to do it. My father was a stockbroker for fifty years. He sang and played the piano by ear, improvising most charmingly. I also play a bit by ear. My mother did not care for music, but all her children except my eldest brother, Lewis, who died in 1954, were musical. Lewis, who was ten years older than I, worked for the League of Red Cross Societies and for UNESCO, and never wanted to go into acting. My brother Val, four years older, is a theatre producer and critic. My sister, Eleanor, three years younger, is widowed, works as my secretary, and lives with me in Westminster, in an entrancing little Queen Anne house with four floors, one room on each floor. It's in the same district as my old school, Westminster, not far from the Houses of Parliament. I always liked the narrow streets there, and the old houses. Members of Parliament are supposed to have kept their mistresses there in the eighteenth century. My father used to take all of us as children, to our delight, to concerts and operas, while my mother remained at home. Both my parents, however, were very much interested in painting as well as in the theatre, and they took me as a child to plays, museums, and art exhibits. In later years, I found that looking at pictures was helpful to me in acting. When I see a picture or hear a piece of music, I see or hear in a way that appeals to my theatrical sense. It's a part, possibly, of my passion for detail. When I'm in a room, any room, I see every item of furniture, I take in every aspect of the décor, I notice the exact arrangement of dishes on a table, of food on a platter. Similarly, I miss nothing at a rehearsal. When I'm directing, I see everything; nobody gets away. Many actors never know what's going on in the rest of the play; they know only what is happening to *them*. I once discovered that a certain star didn't know who her children were in her play. When I'm on-stage, I'm terribly aware, too, of what's going on in the audience, and I see and hear what's going on back to the eighth or ninth row.

As a child, I was always told I was sensitive and delicate, and I became strong as a horse in consequence. I have terrific energy. It seems to me that I've been acting all my life. Like most children, we had a dressing-up box of costumes and hats, collected by my mother, and I can remember, while convalescing from some illness at the age of ten, draping myself in a tartan rug and marching up and down some terrace steps in our garden. This was done in secret, of course. I should have died of shame if any grownup had seen me. Today, I still get fits of wanting to dress like an undergraduate, a businessman, and a successful actor on different days—although I must say many successful actors now try to look like beatniks: shabby exhibitionists instead of smart exhibitionists. It's more democratic. As a boy, I became interested in the whole pictorial side of the theatre; I thought I wanted to design scenery. My parents wanted me to be an architect. I was terrible in mathematics at Westminster, which disqualified me for architecture, so, at the age of fifteen, I got obstinate and told my family I wanted to be an actor. They agreed to give me a period of five years to try to become one. I attended Lady Benson's school for a year on a scholarship and the Royal Academy of Dramatic Art on another scholarship.

I was very, *very* bad as a young actor. I had plenty of feeling but no idea of what to do with it. I had a beautiful voice and a dreadful walk. When I was still a student, I made my début at the Old Vic, on November 7, 1921, as the Herald in "Henry V." I had one line— "Here is the number of the slaughter'd French." I was seventeen, and was constantly giving helpful hints to the director. I was arrogant. I always wanted to be myself in the part, whatever the part was. I always looked to the outside for what to do with my feeling, instead of finding it within. As a young man, I didn't know how *not* to be myself in the part, but when I learned how, I found more of myself in the part. Mostly, my bad acting was a mannered thing. In a curious way, you're forgiven for your mannerisms when you're playing a big part but not when you're playing a small one. People seem to take an especially violent dislike to a young actor with mannerisms. I meant well, but I didn't know where to put my emphasis. I thought it was important to achieve effect, rather than truth. It's sometimes hard to know the difference in the theatre. I would wave my arms or stamp my foot without finding out why I was supposed to be doing it. I put too much energy into a part instead of making it relaxed. The first time I played Romeo, at twenty, I was a great failure. I was too self-conscious; I sang all the verse; I posed a lot, instead of finding the real animal knowledge of a young man in love. A year later, when I played the tutor in "The Cherry Orchard," I began to find the simpler approach to a part and to work from the inside out. I was not going to be beautiful as the tutor; I was going to wear spectacles and an unattractive wig, and search for the truth of the part.

After playing in "Henry V," I toured in J. B. Fagan's "The Wheel," as understudy and stage manager. Next, I was in "The Insect Play," by the Čapek brothers, and played a lovelorn butterfly, wearing a green sash, holding a tennis racket, and lying about in extravagant poses to make some sort of comment on idle, parasitic people. The play was very advanced for its time. The same year, I played an aide-de-camp to General Lee in "Robert E. Lee." In 1924, I joined J. B. Fagan's repertory company at the Oxford Playhouse, left to play Romeo for the first time, at a sort of Off Broadway theatre in London, and then returned to the repertory company. I played several parts in Chekhov—Peter Trophimoff in "The Cherry Orchard," Konstantin Treplev in "The Sea Gull," and Baron Nikolay in "The Three Sisters." I succeeded Noël Coward in parts on two different occasions—as Nicky Lancaster in "The Vortex," in 1925, and, the next year, as Lewis Dodd in "The Constant Nymph." I came to New York for the first time in 1928, when I appeared as the Grand Duke Alexander in "The Patriot." It closed after twelve performances. Those were the speakeasy days. I went round to little bars and had such a good time. In the theatre, I saw Helen Hayes in "Coquette" and Helen Morgan in "Show Boat." Then I had no more money and went home. I returned to the Old Vic in September, 1929, playing Romeo, Mark Antony in "Julius Caesar," and Antonio in "The Merchant of Venice." Nobody starred in those days. Top salary was ten pounds a week. I played Malvolio in "Twelfth Night" in 1931, and in the fall of 1934 I played Hamlet in my own production of the play. It was a great success and ran for a hundred and fifty-five performances—the second-longest run "Hamlet" had ever had in England. I played in "Romeo and Juliet" in 1935, alternating in the role of Romeo and the role of Mercutio with Laurence Olivier, in a London production that ran for a hundred and eighty-six performances—the longest run on record at that time for "Romeo and Juliet." The following year, I played Hamlet on Broadway, with a record run of a hundred and thirty-two performances. It's difficult playing Shakespeare these days. I hate playing Shakespeare without a really first-class company. There aren't more than fifty good classical actors available. The middle of a company is so hard to assemble. Today an actor is expected to achieve skill in five mediums—television, radio, the films, recordings, the stage. The dispersion has made for a shortage of good classical actors. I've varied playing classical roles with playing major ones in modern plays, and, in forty years of acting, I have played hundreds of roles. I learned some of my most important lessons about playing Shakespeare during the Second World War, when I played Hamlet for the troops in the Far East. One wanted so much to please the troops and give them relaxation. At first, I was afraid they wouldn't want to see a bald actor playing Hamlet, but then I found that they accepted the Hamlet I played. I simplified the character, and by simplifying it I think I made it true for them. Not by playing down to them. You never insult an audience by playing down to it. The simplification depended on the confidence I had in delivering the lines. The troops were a marvellous audience. I was able to lead them the way a conductor leads an orchestra. The baldness was never a problem. They recognized the authority of the part and accepted it.

In four decades, I haven't been idle in the theatre for longer than six weeks at a time, and after the first week or two I start missing the theatre terribly. I found a special kind of enjoyment, a few years ago, in doing "The Ages of Man"—the readings of Shakespeare. I found it exciting to gather and give out. I'd like to do it now as a film, if I could find the right director. It would be a nice thing to leave behind.

In Shakespeare, there's such an enormous technical amount to be learned. You're occupied for at least the first ten years in just learning the technical side of acting. So many young people today have a quick success; they go into films or television, where they can make so much more money than they can on the stage, and that's the end of it. Not that I don't admire movies. I go to them all the time—at least two or three times a week. I'm fascinated by the way they do them. I've been in a number of movies, but the only time I've ever been really happy about a part was as Cassius in "Julius Caesar."

You can't teach anybody to act your own way. If you try, you get only a poor imitation. An actor can imitate vocal tricks or special mannerisms but can't reproduce the good thing from the mind. The process of individual acting is so complicated—speaking, observing, and so many, many things, including emotion and control over the emotion, as well as your own way of selecting the most telling things out of the emotion you feel. Marie Tempest always said you ought to be able to write up your laundry bill in your head while you're acting. I find that I must fight to keep things away—thinking of what I'll have for supper, or engagements kept or forgotten. But you need to maintain balance. If you become *too* interested in what you're doing on the stage, you may dry up or fail to deliver the goods. Audiences usually think you're cleverer than you really are, but it's a mistake, I find, to have the audience aware of what they think is your cleverness. Today, the moment I feel I've got a performance I immediately start to take things away from it. I try to use less voice, less gesture, less physical effort. I try to make it more and more relaxed.

I pride myself on the fact that I can shed tears at exactly the same word at every performance. But if I allow my imagination to become too moved, I find I can't utter a syllable. I try to see each word I speak in the air. Each word has its exact value, its exact shape. The great Edith Evans has an extraordinarily personal approach to acting. She always manages to surprise you. I've directed her and acted with her, and invariably she gives me new light, new understanding. She never allows emotion to overwhelm her. She has superb control. She always finds the simplest way. She never indulges herself. She has an enormous gift of selectivity. It's very important to have ideas about a part, but you must also have flexibility. You must adapt to the company. It isn't good to act your part all on your own. We have a marvellous top line of actresses in England. I've had the great good fortune to play with actresses whose give-and-take compels you immediately to be at one with them. I had a thrilling experience with Peggy Ashcroft when we met to begin rehearsing "Much Ado About Nothing." I hadn't seen her in two years, but we were immediately in tune with each other. When it happens, it's like being married.

If you have limitations as an actor and you face them, they can help you. You have to know if you're very ugly. You have to make up your mind how you look, how tall you are. Take a good look in the glass. After a number of years, there's always the danger of falling back on what you've found effective in other parts. I caught myself doing that as a young man when I played in "The Sea Gull" a few months after playing in "The Vortex." Both parts were of rather neurotic young men. The danger—and one sees it particularly in America—is in trying to find short cuts to discovering how to do a part. Every man has his own approach and his own discipline. I suppose one occasionally might find a wonderful teacher who could help one. However, I don't understand this business of going to a psychiatrist or becoming a case in order to find help as an actor. Of all the arts, the theatre least needs psychiatry. The theatre is a kind of psychiatry of its own. An actor has to be a bit of a psychiatrist himself.

I love playing somebody in love. I hate a tragic part without any humor. Hamlet has humor. There's not much charm in Macbeth, but he does have humor. Othello does not. There's always something priggish about a man who is without humor. To play Othello, one must sustain before the audience a humorless man who has somehow to be a hero. Gaiety is a very difficult thing to do on the stage, but I love doing it. In comedy, so much depends on your partner. One comic effect leads to another comic effect. When two people are playing comedy, it's like a teacup and a saucer. In comedy, everything is always between two actors. In tragedy, it's one at a time—you're on your own. In the last act of "Hamlet," Hamlet is the only really tragic figure; the others are there to contribute to the situation. In a nervous or sad part, one gets awfully tired. I think this is particularly true of women. Women who play dominating parts become unhappy in their private lives. Women tend, more than men, to *become* the part. I've never known whether one becomes the part or the part becomes one. My own personality is so mercurial that I react strongly to a sad part. But I don't think a part has ever taken me over. When I first played Hamlet, I was self-conscious. I worried about the audience's knowing it was I. When I stopped trying to disguise myself in the part, I worried about the terrible qualities in me that the audience might not like. Then I hit on the simplifying process, and the audience accepted me. Acting is really a compromise profession, like cooking. You very, very rarely get on the stage the perfect play as you imagined it, reading it, sitting by the fire at home. You must always be prepared to make changes. So many things may go wrong, but when you add it all up you may have a marvellous pie.

There's life for an actor in the characters he plays. Being another character is more interesting than being yourself. It's a great pleasure to me. I love putting on the costume, putting on the makeup. When I did "The Ages of Man," for which I wore an ordinary dinner jacket throughout, I missed putting on the costume. I missed it very much. It's such a beautiful physical escape. I enjoy the transformation of personality. The regularity, the routine escapism of going into the dressing room at the same time every day, is very satisfying to my nature. And I particularly love the beginnings, with everyone wearing ordinary clothes. All the beginnings are tremendously exciting—thinking of the way you want to come through a door, of the way you want to move across the stage.

An actor is really no good to anything except the theatre. Actors are the most selfish people, especially in domestic life. We can be such bores. We are tediously self-examining. An actor has nobody but himself to take counsel with, because nobody else really cares what is going on inside him. Communal work troubled me as a young actor. I didn't want to rub shoulders with other people. In real life, I'm not very communal; I have a tendency to cut others off and be by myself. Now I find that in the theatre I can work communally and at the same time be private. I can give a stage performance when I'm ill and not feel it. I never notice when I'm hurt on the stage until the play is over. Onstage, it's not terribly difficult for an actor to put troubles or worries out of his mind. Even outside the theatre, if there's unhappiness around you, you're likely to be observing it rather than feeling it directly. You constantly catch yourself trying to study how people really feel emotion. You store it up for future use; you reproduce it later in other forms. If I see a bad accident, I watch the expressions on the faces of the people. The dramatic side of every emotional experience seems to be always first with the actor. You jot it down. When you see somebody dead for the first time, you can't resist making notes of the way you yourself feel. It's one of the poignant things you can remember when poignancy is called for. Almost as soon as you get a feeling, you begin to observe it. It makes you rather a monster, I think.

In the theatre, I have quite good taste; in my real life, I'm absolutely tasteless. Outside the theatre, I'm clumsy with my hands, I'm a very bad judge of character, I'm not learned. I'm always so terribly aware of how little I know. I'm sure that Laurence Olivier and Michael Redgrave are so much more learned than I am. I'm sure that Picasso must know so much and must have all the wisdom I lack. I know that I am terribly adolescent, romantic, and naïve. Most actors are adolescent, romantic, and naïve. It's alarming when an actor becomes a success. Immediately, he's quoted on things, and you find actors going into political areas and places they have no business being in. I don't need any other places myself. I find everything I love in the theatre. When I go into a theatre and get into a dressing room, it's like going into a safe place that I know, without thinking, is mine. It's like going home.

INDEX

INDEX

INDEX

ABOUT THE AUTHORS

Lillian Ross and Helen Ross, who are sisters, were both born in Syracuse, New York. Both have written for various publications, and this book is their first collaborative venture. Lillian Ross is the author of ten books, including Portrait of Hemingway, Moments with Chaplin *and* Talk Stories.